RELIGION AND THE RISE OF HISTORY

Religion and the Rise of History

*Martin Luther and the
Cultural Revolution in Germany,
1760–1810*

LEONARD S. SMITH

CASCADE *Books* • Eugene, Oregon

RELIGION AND THE RISE OF HISTORY
Martin Luther and the Cultural Revolution in Germany, 1760–1810

Copyright © 2009 Leonard S. Smith. All rights reserved. Except for brief quotations in critical publications or reviews, no part of this book may be reproduced in any manner without prior written permission from the publisher. Write: Permissions, Wipf and Stock Publishers, 199 W. 8th Ave., Suite 3, Eugene, OR 97401.

Cascade Books
A Division of Wipf and Stock Publishers
199 W. 8th Ave., Suite 3
Eugene, OR 97401

www.wipfandstock.com

ISBN 13: 978-1-55635-830-2

Cataloging-in-Publication data:

Smith, Leonard S. (Leonard Sander)

    Religion and the rise of history : Martin Luther and the cultural revolution in Germany, 1760–1810 / Leonard S. Smith.

    xvi + 290 p. ; 23 cm. —Includes bibliographical references and index.

    ISBN 13: 978-1-55635-830-2

    1. Historiography. 2. History—Religious Aspects—Christianity. 3. Luther, Martin, 1483–1546. I. Title.

D16.9 .S65 2009

Manufactured in the U.S.A.

To Sharon Faye Ronning Smith

Martin Luther on Writing

Ask a writer, preacher, or speaker whether writing and speaking is work; ask a schoolmaster whether teaching and training boys is work. The pen is light; that is true. Also there is no tool of any of the trades that is easier to get than the writer's tool, for all that is needed is goose feathers and there are enough of them everywhere. But the best part of the body (which is the head) must lay hold here and do most of the work, and the noblest of the members (which is the tongue), and the high faculty (which is speech). In other occupations it is only the fist or the foot or the back or some other such member that has to work; and while they are at it, they can sing and jest, which the writer cannot do. "Three fingers do it," they say of writers: but a man's whole body and soul work at it.

—Martin Luther, "A Sermon on Keeping Children in School," *Works of Martin Luther* (Philadelphia, 1931), 1:170. (Cf. *LW* 46:249 and *WA* 30:574)

contents

Preface · *ix*

Abbreviations · *xvi*

1 A Typology of Classical and Christian Historiography · 1

2 Martin Luther and the Foundations of a Lutheran Ethos · 55

3 Two Forerunners of the Cultural Revolution in Germany and Modern Historical Thought: Leibniz and Chladenius · 100

4 The Cultural Revolution in Germany and the Rise of a New Historical Consciousness, 1760–1810 · 126

5 From a Holy Hieroglyph to a *Wissenschaft* Alone: History as a Calling and a Profession from Ranke to Hintze · 201

Conclusion · 253

Bibliography · 263

Name Index · 287

preface

One of the characteristics of our time is the shift of social and cultural history from an emphasis on broad works of synthesis and manifestations of collective life to various forms of microhistory and the history of everyday life. Historians and history teachers, however, have always had the task of placing events within a large and meaningful framework. As a historical inquiry and synthesis, this essay is an innovative work in three main respects.

It is the first study to apply the ideal-type or model-building methodology of Otto Hintze (1861–1940) to Western historiography as a whole, or to what R. G. Collingwood called "The Idea of History," for it contains succinct and useful models for seeing, understanding, and teaching (1) the classical historiography of Greece and Rome, (2) Christian historiography from the time of St. Augustine to Voltaire, and (3) a distinctly modern type of Western historiography.

Second, it is the first work to suggest that in addition to his well-known paradoxical, *simul*, or his "at-the-same-time" way of thinking and viewing life, Martin Luther also had a deeply incarnational, dynamic, or "in-with-and-under" way. This dual vision strongly influenced Leibniz, Hamann, Herder, and Ranke and was therefore a matter of considerable significance for what Friedrich Meinecke (1862–1954) called "the rise of historicism."

Third, this essay suggests a new way of seeing, dating, and naming the formative stage of modern German thought, culture, and education. This period began in the early 1760s and culminated in 1810 with the founding of the University of Berlin, the first fully "modern" and "modernizing" university, and the Prussian and German *Gymnasium*.

Behind the title for this essay the reader will find four main questions: (1) Is the term "the Cultural Revolution" a useful designation for capturing and teaching the formative stage in the development of modern German education, thought, and culture? (2) Since a new historical consciousness—commonly called "historicism"—and the rise of a new type of Western historiography were important aspects of this Cultural Revolution, and since they arose first in Protestant Germany, was the Lutheran religious tradition especially conducive for the rise of these aspects of this revolution and of modern life? (3) Did Martin Luther have a second basic way of thinking and viewing life in addition to his well-known paradoxical *simul*, or "at-the-same-time" way? (4) If so, how have these two ways shaped a distinctively Lutheran ethos and sense of calling?

To understand the nature and rise of *modern* historical thought in the West, one must have a mental picture of Western historical thought as a whole. This inquiry is based on the conviction that such a picture can be presented most simply, clearly, and distinctly through three historical ideal types, or models that are based on a perception of time. It is also based on the view that a distinctly modern type of Western historiography and kind of historical thought came to fruition most of all in the work of Leopold von Ranke (1795–1886), the greatest and most influential of all modern professional historians. Although one of the main purposes of this essay is to suggest a new way—or at least another way—of looking at modern historiography as a whole, the main focus is, as the title indicates, the significance of religion for the rise of history.

Why, however, did the main characteristics of modern historical thought and modern professional historiography develop first in Germany and mainly by scholars who were raised and educated within the Lutheran tradition? Although many Christians since the time of St. Augustine have believed that only God knows *why* things happen, most historians can agree that it is the job of the historian to say *how* something happened and *how* something came to be. Thus one of the purposes of this inquiry is to suggest some connections between Luther's ways of thinking and viewing life and the rise of modern historical thought in Germany during the five decades from 1760 to the founding of the University of Berlin in the year 1810. There is no attempt here, however, to assert a cause-and-effect relationship between Martin Luther's ways of viewing life and either the rise of historicism or a distinctly modern type of Western historiography during that great humanistic revolution that can be called the Cultural Revolution in Germany.

The word *Historismus*, usually translated "historicism," became a word of central importance in Western historical thought primarily through the work of three great scholars at the University of Berlin during and after World War I: Ernst Troeltsch (1865–1923), Friedrich Meinecke, and Otto Hintze. Since the present inquiry is a supplement to their pioneer work on this subject, the first debt of a general nature that I want to acknowledge is to them.

This essay is also an attempt to apply the ideal-type methodology of Otto Hintze—the great pioneer historian of the twentieth century for the development of what he called "comparative constitutional history," and that others have called comparative, structural, institutional, or social history—to the study of Western historiography. Basically, however, this essay is a twentieth-century kind of historical inquiry that Meinecke called *Geistesgeschichte*, which the English-speaking world calls intellectual history or the history of ideas, and for which he was the great pioneer historian within the guild of professional historians in the twentieth century.

The fourth great early twentieth-century scholar to whom I am indebted in a general way is Max Weber. While Hintze was a great pioneer for the development of a comparative method and an ideal-type methodology for the discipline called history, Weber was the great pioneer social scientist for the development of a comparative method and an ideal-type methodology for the social sciences. In the present essay, readers will find not only a model for the study of modern Western historiography based on Hintze's ideal-type methodology, but also a further exploration of Weber's ideas of "rationalization" and "disenchantment of the world" in connection with his ideal type of a Lutheran sense of calling as contained in his brilliant, enormously stimulating, and controversial essay, *The Protestant Ethic and the Spirit of Capitalism.*

Before I acknowledge my other debts, however, I want to relate two personal experiences on which this inquiry is based and then to make a few general remarks about what one can expect or not expect to find in this essay.

The first personal experience took place when I was reading a passage from a young Leopold Ranke who was answering (in 1828) a critic of his first work, his epoch-making *Histories of the Latin and Germanic Nations from 1494 to 1514* (1824). "This passage," Ranke said, "is part of the attempt I have made to present the general directly through the particular without long digression. Here I have sought to approach no J. Müller or no ancient writer but the appearance itself, just as it emerges, only externally particularity, internally—and so I understand Leibnitz—a generality, significance, spirit . . . In and with the event I have sought to portray its course and spirit, and I have strained to ascertain its characteristic traits."[1]

When I first read this passage in 1971, the reference to the general and the particular, generality and particularity, external and internal, appearance and spirit, and especially the way he used the prepositions *in* and *with* jumped out at me; for both the passage as a whole and especially the latter two prepositions sounded very Lutheran to me. Was it possible, I asked myself, that the connected prepositions (especially for Lutherans)—"in, with, and under"—could be a key to understanding not only Ranke's way of writing history but also the Lutheran tradition as a whole? Could Ranke's way of writing history be called not only an at-the-same-time way of viewing and writing history but also an in-with-and under way? Did not Ranke always try to present the general or the universal in, with, under, and through the particular? And was not this the best way to teach students how to write history? But why did Ranke refer to Leibniz in this passage?

The answer to the latter question soon came to me (1972) when a colleague was introducing Leibniz and the *Monadology* to a select group of first-year college students in a team-taught, interdisciplinary (history, literature, philosophy, and religion) honors course called "Humanities Tutorial." As he helped those young minds picture those unique soul-like substances called monads, each programmed by God to do its thing in and through the composite body that it directed and within an organic, dynamic, pluralistic, harmonious, and God-given universe that was the best of all possible worlds, the connection suddenly became clear!

At that moment I became quite excited, for now—for the first time—I could see the origins of the German idealist tradition and the main link between Luther and Melanchthon, on the one hand, and Herder, Ranke, and the German idealist tradition through Troeltsch and Meinecke on the other. Now I could see how, at least in some respects, the Lutheran religious tradition was conducive to the rise of German historicism and to a distinctly modern type of Western historiography. Thus this passage from the young Ranke and these two experiences were the starting points of this decades-long historical inquiry.

---

1. Ranke, "Erwiderung auf Heinrich Leo's Angriff," 664–65. Unless otherwise noted, all translations from German sources are my own.

The first general remark that I want to make is that since this essay is a broad and interdisciplinary introduction to the rise of modern historical thought through the formative years of Leopold von Ranke, there is no attempt to include the vast amount of literature on each of the individuals discussed here. In my notes I have only sought to give credit to the sources that I actually used and not to all the ones that I read or that I could or should have read and used.

Second, this essay is written primarily for a general audience: students, teachers, professors, pastors, priests, or anyone interested in learning more about Martin Luther and "a Lutheran ethos" in relation to "the idea of history" and to the rise of a distinctly modern kind of historical consciousness. To aid the reader I have made extensive use of quotations from primary works, as well as from helpful secondary studies, so that he or she can be directly engaged with the thought of each of the major figures included in this essay and with the views of specialists whose research and knowledge are especially helpful.

Third, each chapter begins with a statement of the problem behind that particular part of the inquiry. Here the reader will find not only the basic questions that I am trying to answer but also some background material so that he or she does not have to be an expert in any of these subjects or to refer to other sources. At the same time this rather unusual device should help the reader decide whether my attempts to deal with these large questions are helpful, convincing, and "true" because they are based on the evidence.

Fourth, since this work as a whole is a supplement to the ways that Troeltsch, Hintze, and Meinecke defined, used, and viewed the term *Historismus*, some readers might want to start with part 3 of chapter 5, "Otto Hintze and the Demystifying of the Rankean View of History" (221-52), for it includes a sketch of their great debate over the nature of modern historical thought and the significance of this debate for the idea of history.

Since this essay is based on my entire educational experience, the list of persons I have known who contributed either directly or indirectly to this study is quite long. First, I want to express thanks and gratitude to my father, the Rev. A. Leonard Smith (1894-1960). I am indebted to him not only for the traditional kind of religious education that I received and that is portrayed in chapter 2, but also because he—more than anyone I have known—personified the Lutheran idea of "a calling."

Second, I am grateful to professors Allan Pfnister, James I. Dowie, and Fritiof Ander for awakening in me a love of intellectual and cultural history and for teaching me to see, feel, and appreciate the connection of individuals, ideas, and events in history.

Third, I am deeply indebted to Dietrich Gerhard, a student of Friedrich Meinecke at the University of Berlin, the Assistant Director of the Max-Planck-Institut für Geschichte in Göttingen, Germany, in the 1960s, and the director of my PhD dissertation (1967) at Washington University (in St. Louis, Missouri). Professor Gerhard was the best trained, most knowledgeable, and wisest professional historian I have known, and he was also my connecting link with the great historiographical traditions at Göttingen and Berlin.

Fourth, I want to honor and give thanks for another great teacher at Washington University in the early 1960s, Professor Jack Hexter. For Dr. Hexter, "doing history" was an art and a craft, and no one I have known was better at teaching history as a craft and how to write history than he. Both for my training as a graduate student and as a professor/student in his National Endowment of the Humanities Summer Seminar on "Writing History" at Yale University in 1978, I am indebted to him.

Fifth, I want to express my gratitude to Hermann Heimpel, Rudolf Vierhaus, and all the kind and helpful individuals at the Max-Planck-Institut für Geschichte in Göttingen for their gracious hospitality and assistance since the year 1962.

Sixth, I want to acknowledge my debt to those teacher/scholars and colleagues in the interdisciplinary "Core Program" (1964–1969) at Luther College in Decorah, Iowa, and "The Humanities Tutorial" (1971–1984) at California Lutheran University. Especially I am grateful to Dr. John Kuethe for his Socratic way of tutoring our students and me in the whole course of Western philosophy and for introducing me to the writings of St. Augustine, Leibniz, and Kant.

Seventh, I want to acknowledge my debt and gratitude to those kind souls who read parts or all of the manuscript for this book and who have offered helpful corrections, improvements, and suggestions: Luther S. Luedtke, Walter K. Stewart, Nathan L. Tierney, Carlyle A. Smith, Richard Cole, Dale Johnson, Peter Hanns Reill, Eric W. Gritsch, Heiko A. Oberman, Richard W. Solberg, Wolfgang Neugebauer, Robert Guy Erwin, James J. Sheehan, and Thomas A. Brady, Jr. Their kindness, however, should not be construed to mean agreement either in general or in many particulars.

Finally, and most of all, I want to thank my wife Sharon Faye Ronning Smith not only for reading the various versions of this manuscript but also for all the advice, helpful criticisms, and unflagging support that she has provided for all my academic endeavors.

abbreviations

BC	*The Book of Concord: The Confessions of the Evangelical Lutheran Church* (Translated by Arand et al., 2000).
BC-T	*The Book of Concord: The Confessions of the Evangelical Lutheran Church* (Translated by Tappert, 1959).
CSM 1	"Discourse on the Method," in *The Philosophical Writings of Descartes*, 2 vols. (Translated by Cottingham, Stoothoff, and Murdoch)
Herder, SW	Herder, Johann Gottfried. *Sämmtliche Werke*. Edited by Bernhard Suphan. 33 vols. Berlin, Weidmann, 1877–1913.
LW	*Luther's Works*
WA	*Dr. Martin Luthers Werke*. Kristische Gesamtausgabe [Schriften], Weimar: Böhlau, 1883–1993.
Werke 1	Herder, Johann Gottfried. *Frühe Schriften 1764–1772* (1985).

one

A Typology of Classical and Christian Historiography

The description of the individual psycho-physical life-unit [*Lebenseinheit*] is biography.... The progress and destiny of the human will is here apprehended in its dignity as an end in itself. The biographer should intuit people *sub specie aeterni*, as he feels himself in those moments when everything standing between him and divinity seems a superficial diversion and when he feels himself to be as close to the starry heavens as to any part of the earth. Thus biography represents the most fundamental fact clearly, fully, and in its reality.[1]

—Wilhelm Dilthey

With analogies one must compare entire stages of development and not just momentary, contemporary conditions.[2]

—Otto Hintze

History can have as its possible object everything dealing with human culture in relation to a perception of time. The concept of the individual totality is, of course, crucial to determining an object of historical study; and I would suggest that the only decisive criterion is its comprehensibility as a life-unit [*Lebenseinheit*]. The defining of objects of historical study is, in my opinion, an act of intuitive, not rational, thought. The historian's thinking here is not logical but analogical. The concept of the individual totality underlies this analogical thinking.[3]

—Otto Hintze

    1. Dilthey, *Introduction to the Human Sciences*, 85. The word *Lebenseinheit*, which was a key word both for Dilthey and for Hintze, was inserted by the author of the present study. See Dilthey, *Einleitung in die Geisteswissenschaften*, 33–34.

    2. Hintze, Review of *Acta Borussica: Behördenorganisation*, vol. 6, pts. 1 and 2, 271–72.

    3. Hintze, "Troeltsch und die Probleme des Historismus: Kritische Studien" (1927), 337. Hintze, "Troeltsch and the Problems of Historicism: Critical Studies," 384–85. Here, unfortunately, this important philosophical and methodological sentence and also Hintze's basic distinction between "possible object" and "actual objects" of history were not translated accurately. An actual object for Hintze was the subject or topic that the historian chooses to investigate.

RELIGION AND THE RISE OF HISTORY

THE PROBLEM

In 1927, Otto Hintze published an article in the *Historische Zeitschrift* called "Troeltsch and the Problems of Historicism: Critical Studies," an essay that was one of the most significant contributions to the idea of history by a professional historian during the twentieth century. Four of Hintze's contributions in this essay, apparent in the quotation cited directly above, were (1) his distinction between "actual" and "possible" objects of history, (2) his very inclusive and important statement concerning the "possible object of history," (3) his assertion that historical thinking is basically analogical, and (4) his declaration that "the concept of the individual totality underlies this analogical thinking." Since each of these ideas was conceived by the most broadly trained, "Aristotelian" (form-thinking), and "Kantian" (analytical) mind among professional historians in Germany in the first third of the twentieth century, it is strange that these ideas have not received greater attention by scholars in or outside of Germany.

If one believes, however, that each of these ideas is helpful for understanding the nature of modern historical thought, what difference could this make in one's understanding of the idea of history from the time of Herodotus? This is the first major aspect of the problem behind this chapter, and this book as a whole.

One of the ways in which Otto Hintze's third ideal type, a model of the modern Western state,[4] was the most advanced methodologically was that here he presented—as succinctly as he could—four characteristics that together composed the type.[5] One of the most useful parts of R. G.

---

4. Hintze, "Wesen und Wandlung des modernen Staats," 470–96. While Hintze's first ideal type, "Wesen und Verbreitung des Feudalismus," was published in 1929 and can be found in Hintze, *Staat und Verfassung*, 84–119, his second ideal type, "Typologie der ständischen Verfassungen des Abendlandes," was published in 1930 and can be found in Hintze, *Staat und Verfassung*, 120–39.

5. "Wesen und Wandlung des modernen Staats," 475–76. The "four different, supplementary, and reciprocal abstractions" of Hintze's ideal type of the modern state, "which formed since the Middle Ages," were "1. the sovereign power state within the realm of the European state system; 2. the relatively closed commercial state with a *bürgerlich*-capitalistic form of society and economy; 3. the liberal *Rechts*- and constitutional state with the direction toward the personal freedom of the individual; and 4. the ascending national state, encompassing all these tendencies, with the direction toward democracy."

Collingwood's *The Idea of History* is the section where he presented, as succinctly as he could, four characteristics of Christian historiography.

As a result of many years of using (1) Hintze's three ideal types to teach Western institutional development in the context of a world-civilizations course and in various courses in modern European history, and (2) his definition and view of historicism to teach the idea of history within a year-long interdisciplinary, and great-books course dealing with Western history, literature, philosophy, and religion,[6] five basic questions arose in my mind: (1) Could one apply Hintze's ideal-type methodology to the study of Western historiography? (2) Could one use his third ideal type as the chief model in this endeavor? (3) Could one use Collingwood's four characteristics of Christian historiography as one of the three main types, which together would constitute a complete typology of Western historical thought? (4) Could one develop four basic and matching characteristics to form a model of classical historiography of Greece and Rome and a model of "modern" historiography? And, most of all, (5) could the three models and the typology of Western historical thought that I developed and used for many years in my classes be useful for other teachers and for the discipline as a whole?[7] These five questions together form the second main aspect of the problem behind this chapter, and together they are a major aspect of this historical inquiry as a whole.

CLASSICAL HISTORIOGRAPHY OF GREECE AND ROME

In the opening paragraph of the essay "Wesen und Wandlung des modernen Staats" or "The Nature and Transformation of the Modern State" (1931), Otto Hintze suggested that when an historian creates a "pictorial conception" or an "intuitive [*anschauliche*] abstraction" known as an ideal type, he singles out certain basic characteristics and presents them in as pure a form as possible. These characteristics are then formed into

---

6. For Hintze's definition of *historicism*, see Hintze, *Soziologie und Geschichte*, 342; and Hintze, *Historical Essays of Otto Hintze*, 390; and chapter 5, part 3, below.

7. Basically the three models and this typology of Western historiography were completed by 1981, for at the national convention of the American Historical Association at the end of that year I delivered a paper called "Otto Hintze and a Historical Typology of Western Historiography." Since this essay was never submitted for publication, however, this session has been the only public testing of these models and this typology.

a whole that can be used to orient oneself in the confusing abundance of historical phenomena.[8]

When one looks at the development of Western historiography since the time of Herodotus, "the father of history," one can see three main stages of development, three main periods for the idea of history, and three main types of historical writing: (1) classical historiography of ancient Greece and Rome, (2) Christian historiography from the time of St. Augustine to the Enlightenment and the time and work of Voltaire, and (3) modern professional historiography since the time of the founding of the University of Berlin (1810) and the work of Barthold Georg Niebuhr (1776–1831) and Leopold von Ranke. The chief purpose behind this chapter, however, is to present a sketch of the idea of history in the West from the time of Herodotus to the time of Voltaire through two historical ideal types or models: a model of classical historiography of Greece and Rome, and a model of Christian historiography to the Enlightenment.

As an intuitive abstraction, as a historical ideal type or model, and as a stage in the development of Western historical thought, Greco-Roman historiography was

1. *epic* because wars and politics were the proper subject of this new kind of prose epic, and because Greek and Roman historians emphasized the greatness of events and heroes rather than their individuality and uniqueness;

2. *humanistic* because Herodotus created a way of seeing and presenting human events juxtaposed in time in a way that made sense, and because in contrast to the mythopoeic literature prior to Herodotus and in contrast to the theocentric historiography of the Christian epoch, Greek and Roman historians were concerned not with the actions of gods and humans but with "what men have done";

3. *rational* because the word *historia* was a Greek word that meant "research, inquiry, investigation," or "establishing the truth," and because the main concern of Greek and Roman historians was to investigate the meaning and coherence of events in terms of the purposeful action of statesmen, military leaders, and other influential men;

---

8. Hintze, "Wesen und Wandlung des modernen Staats," in Hintze, *Staat und Verfassung*, 470. "Pictorial conception" is a translation of "eine bildhafte Vorstellung."

4. *didactic* because after Thucydides, history came to be regarded as a branch of rhetoric and as an art that provided good examples to follow and bad examples to avoid; and because it was taught in schools only for the purpose of providing rhetorical examples[9] and not for the purpose of showing how things came to be.

For the ancient Greeks, Homer was the poet par excellence, and the *Iliad* and *Odyssey* were their history. The *mythopoios* or poet was literally a "mythmaker," and originally a myth was a story with no implication as to its veracity or probability. For the ancient Greeks, the poet was the historian, the philosopher, and the educator; for the poet "knew," the poet possessed wisdom (*sophia*), and the poet was the teacher.[10]

In the sixth century BCE, however, the poet's exclusive position as guardian of truth, knowledge, and wisdom was challenged by the early Greek philosophers, who sought to understand and to explain how everything in this orderly world or cosmos was derived from certain basic or eternal substances. Beside the wisdom of Homer and the poets, these *philosophers* or "lovers of wisdom" discovered a new kind of wisdom no longer dependent upon divine revelation or poetic charm. Truth was now something to be determined by rational processes of thought, for they had discovered the abstract idea of truth,[11] or what some philosophy teachers love to call "Truth with a capital T." The idea of abstract truth was a necessary preliminary to the idea of historical truth established by Herodotus and Thucydides in the fifth century BCE.[12]

When Herodotus (ca. 495–425 BCE[13]) wrote the story of the Persian invasions of Greece, he created a new kind of epic, a prose epic. Both his purpose and his language were epic, for he published this work "in

---

9. Momigliano, "Greek Historiography," 9. This article, which is an excellent introduction to and summary of Greek historiography, contains a helpful bibliography for this subject.

10. Austin, *Greek Historians*, 1–13.

11. Ibid., 16.

12. Ibid., 16–17.

13. The dates used for Herodotus and most of the historians through the eighteenth century are taken from Kelley, *Versions of History.* Kelley's dates can be compared with those in Woolf's *A Global Encyclopedia of Historical Writing* (1:408), for here the dates for Herodotus (ca. 484–420 BCE) differ considerably. For an excellent, full, and balanced account of Western historiography and historical thought through the eighteenth century, see Kelley, *Faces of History.*

the hope of preserving from decay the remembrance of what men have done," in order to prevent "the great and wonderful actions of the Greeks and Barbarians from losing their due meed of glory," and also "to put on record what were their grounds of feud."[14]

Most significantly, however, he began with the words, "These are the histories of Herodotus," which simply meant the researches or inquiries of Herodotus since that is what the word *historia* meant. The use of this word, its implications, and its connection with this first great artistic work of Greek prose[15] mark the beginning of history, for history is first and foremost a form of inquiry concerned not with what gods and humans have done, but—in the words of Herodotus—"what men have done."[16] It is interesting to note that the stem of the word *historia* was the same as for "to see," for as Charles Rowan Beye has pointed out, Herodotus deserves the title "Father of History" because he created a way of seeing and presenting human events "juxtaposed in time in a manner that makes sense."[17]

Although Herodotus and Thucydides sought to emulate Homer when they created this new kind of epic, Greek and Roman historians clearly differentiated between myth and history. Thucydides (471?–400? BCE) distrusted the accounts of poets and chroniclers because their accounts could not be tested since most of the facts, owing to the lapse of time, have been "mostly lost in the unreliable streams of mythology" (1:21).[18] He criticized earlier writers for including too many entertaining stories in their work and as too given to *mythoi* or to accepting and including oracles, omens, and other implausible and unverifiable details.[19]

---

14. Herodotus, *History of Herodotus*, 1.

15. Beye, *Ancient Greek Literature and Society*, 194. The chapter called "The Beginning of Prose" is very helpful for understanding the epic nature of Greek historiography.

16. Recently it has been suggested: "Herodotus ascribed to women a prominent role—far more prominent than that voiced by other writers of his time and culture, indeed, of any time or culture before the present generation" (Spickard et al., *World History by the World's Historians*, 75). Since it is impossible for me to verify these important but very sweeping statements, they are passed on here to readers in the manner of Herodotus.

17. Beye, *Ancient Greek Literature and Society*, 194.

18. Thucydides, *Peloponnesian War*, 47.

19. Austin, *Greek Historians*, 48–49. For a discussion of the terms *myth*, *history*, and *mythistory* in relation to Herodotus and Thucydides, see Mali, *Mythistory*, 1–5 and 18–19. In this work, however, the term *modern historiography* is used in a very different way than in the present study.

For Thucydides, a myth was a story that was improbable because it could not be supported on the basis of rational thought and critical investigation of evidence.

When Thucydides began his inquiry into the great event of his life, the Peloponnesian War, he emphasized how he had described nothing but what he had either seen himself or learned from others "by most careful and particular enquiry." He would be satisfied, he said, "if he who desires to have before his eyes a true picture of the events which have happened, and of the like events which may be expected to happen hereafter in the order of human things, shall pronounce what I have written to be useful" (1:22).

Like a reporter today, Thucydides interviewed eyewitnesses to find out what happened by asking who, what, when, where, why, and how. Like a modern professional historian, he also used documents from the city of Athens and from other cities to establish the truth and chronology of what happened.[20] Through his personal experience as a general in the war on the side of Athens and as an outside observer after he was ostracized, he was better able to visualize, to reexperience, and to reenact the war in his own mind and to present it as a single whole and as a single event in a rigorous and sovereign way. While Herodotus was concerned about the accuracy of his recording of the stories that were told to him, which he wove into his narrative with great skill, Thucydides was more concerned about the accuracy and verifiability of his account of what happened. He insisted that his work was true because it was based strictly on the evidence.

Thus with Thucydides, one can see an emphasis on evidence, on the basic procedure of the historian to interpret the evidence, and the linking of the procedure of the historian with the object of the historian: to interpret the evidence in order to present "a true picture of the events which have happened." Here we can see the historian's ideal of truth, for historians are concerned with "factual truth"[21] or with facts and events that can be established on the basis of rational and painstaking investigation of evidence existing here and now.

During the fourth century BCE, the word *historia* became the accepted name for the particular kind of inquiry and literary genre created

---

20. Austin, *Greek Historians*, 49.

21. Austin credits Thucydides with creating "a new ideal, that of factual Truth" (ibid.).

by Herodotus. In his work called *Poetics*, Aristotle used the word *history* as the accepted name for a particular kind of inquiry with its own name when he claimed that poetics was more philosophical than history since its statements were more of a universal nature while history only dealt with the particular (1451b).[22]

In the beginning section of the first book of *The Histories of Polybius*, a Greek statesman (ca. 198–117 BCE) who was taken hostage to Rome after the defeat and destruction of the kingdom of Macedonia in 168 BCE, one can see how the Greeks viewed the particular form of inquiry called *history* in the second century BCE. Again and again, Polybius pointed out, his predecessors had claimed "that the study of History is in the truest sense an education and a training for political life; and that the most instructive, or rather the only, method of learning to bear with dignity the vicissitudes of fortune is to recall the catastrophes of others."[23]

After sixteen years in Rome, Polybius returned to his homeland and wrote the story of how in a period of less than fifty-three years (220–168 BCE) "almost the whole inhabited world was conquered and brought under the dominion of Rome." To make his subject more understandable and complete, however, he decided to extend his history to include both the first war between Rome and Carthage (264–241 BCE) and also the Third Punic War, with the destruction of Carthage and Corinth in 146 BCE. This extension of his history was also an extension of the idea of history in regard to time, for his inquiry now included five generations rather than the single generation of Thucydides.[24]

The main part of this "marvelous and vast" story of how Rome became a great world empire, however, was the time from the Second Punic War to the conquest of Macedonia in 168 BCE, for "up to this time the world's history had been, so to speak, a series of disconnected transactions, as widely separated in their origin and results as in their localities. But from this time forth History becomes a connected whole."[25]

Just as Polybius believed that the Romans had created a unified world with a unified history, so also he believed that in telling this story

---

22. The most convenient place to see this "classic statement of the essential difference between history, poetry, and, if only implicitly, philosophy," is Kelley, *Visions of History*, 62.

23. Polybius, *Histories of Polybius*, 1:1.

24. See Collingwood, *Idea of History*, 34.

25. Polybius, *Histories of Polybius*, 1:3

he had created a new kind of history: "There is this analogy between the plan of my History and the marvelous spirit of the age with which I have to deal. Just as Fortune made almost all the affairs of the world incline in one direction, and forced them to converge upon one and the same point; so it is my task as an historian to put before my readers a compendious view of the part played by Fortune in bringing about the general catastrophe. It was this peculiarity which originally challenged my attention, and determined me on undertaking this work."

Combined with this, Polybius continued, was the fact that no writer of his time had "undertaken a general history. Had anyone done so my ambition in this direction would have been much diminished. But, in point of fact, I notice that by far the greater number of historians concern themselves with isolated wars and the incidents that accompany them: while as to a general and comprehensive scheme of events, their date, origin, and catastrophe, no one as far as I know has undertaken to examine it."[26]

For Polybius, this new kind of general or universal history (*historia katholike*) was superior to the kind of "episodical history" practiced by most historians, because it was better suited to achieve the main object and the chief purposes of history:

> For indeed some idea of a whole may be got from a part, but an accurate knowledge and clear comprehension cannot. Wherefore we must conclude that episodical history contributes exceedingly little to the familiar knowledge and secure grasp of universal history. While it is only by the combination and comparison of the separate parts of the whole,—by observing their likeness and their difference,—that man can attain his object: can obtain a view at once clear and complete; and thus secure both the profit and the delight of history.[27]

In this passage Polybius clearly articulated and firmly established the Hellenistic view that history should be both useful *and* delightful, but more than other Greek historians he emphasized the practical nature of history.[28] His kind of history, he said, was "pragmatic."

---

26. Ibid., 1:4.
27. Ibid.
28. Momigliano, "Greek Historiography," 15.

Like the term *historia katholike*, the term *historia pragmatike* is a basic one for the idea of history in the West. Usually modern professional historians have used the word "pragmatic" in the way Hintze did in his essay called "Troeltsch and the Problems of Historicism." For Hintze, pragmatic history was synonymous with political history. The concern of "pragmatism," he said, was "to investigate the acts of statesmen and other influential individuals," for it saw the meaning and coherence of events "primarily in terms of the purposeful actions of individuals."[29]

Most of all, however, Polybius stressed the usefulness of *his* history. It was difficult for him to believe that anyone could be "so indifferent or idle as not to care or to know by what means, and under what polity, almost the whole inhabited world was conquered," or that anyone could be "so completely absorbed in other subjects of contemplation or study, as to think any of them superior to the accurate understanding of an event for which the past affords no precedent."[30] Like most great historians, Polybius had a great story to tell, a story that was great because of its intrinsic importance for humanity.

By the year 200 BCE, the Romans had begun to write their own histories.[31] When Titus Livy (ca. 59 BCE–17 CE) conceived "the magnificent idea" of a complete history of Rome from its beginning, the Romans acquired a splendid literary account of their history as a people or nation.[32] Although both Polybius and Livy thought they were writing universal history, since to them Rome had become the civilized world, R. G. Collingwood's distinction between their kind of "oecumenical" history and the new kind of universal history developed by Christian scholars—especially during the crises of the fourth and fifth centuries—is very helpful for understanding the story of the idea of history.

While classical historiography from Herodotus through Polybius was both epic and rational, it was also deeply humanistic. The origins and meanings of the words *humanism* and *humanist* in the West are associ-

---

29. Hintze, "Troeltsch and the Problems of Historisicism," 377. (See also Hintze, *Soziologie und Geschichte*, 331).

30. Polybius, *Histories of Polybius*, 1:1.

31. See especially Momigliano, *Classical Foundations of Modern Historiography*, 88–91. Here Momigliano emphasizes the importance of Quintus Fabius Pictor, not only as the first Roman historian and for writing history in the Greek manner in the Greek language, but also for the beginning of "national history."

32. Collingwood, *Idea of History*, 36.

ated with, and derived partly from, the Ciceronian ideal of *humanitas*.[33] For Cicero (106–43 BCE), the ideal education was one that would produce the ideal orator, a man of broad culture or *humanitas*. To Cicero, *humanitas* signified all that was worthy in man.[34]

In a book called *De Oratore* (a dialogue concerning the education of an orator, and one of the most influential books in the history of Western education), Cicero sought to combine Greek culture and Roman virtue, or the best of Greek and Roman educational ideals: (1) the orator as a lover of wisdom who combined training in rhetoric with all branches of learning, *artes liberales* or *liberalis disciplina*; and (2) the orator as a practical statesman who was trained especially in history, law, and philosophy.[35] All the teachings of Cicero in *De Oratore* is contained in a sentence from another of his writings: "We are all called men, but only those of us are men who have been civilized by the studies proper to culture."[36]

For Cicero, history served a double purpose: to provide a storehouse of knowledge of rhetorical illustrations and to link us with the past.[37] "By what other voice, too, than that of the orator is history," he asked, for is it not "the evidence of time, the light of truth, the life of memory, the directness of life, the herald of antiquity, committed to immortality?"[38] History was a necessary ingredient of any kind of education for Cicero, for "to be ignorant of what happened before you were born," he insisted, "is to live the life of the child forever."[39]

Cicero also established high standards for individuals who wrote history. "For who is ignorant that it is the first law in writing history," he asked, "that the historian must not dare to tell any falsehood, and the next, that he must be bold enough to tell the whole truth?"[40]

Although Cicero emphasized that a knowledge of history was indispensable for statesmen, orators, and civilized men who shared in the

---

33. For a good introduction to the origins, context, and structure of Renaissance humanism and the significance of Cicero for its rise, see Kelley, *Renaissance Humanism*.

34. Cicero, *De Republica* i, 28, cited in Gwynn, *Roman Education*, 107.

35. See Gwynn, *Roman Education*, 100–102; and Gutek, *History of Western Educational Experience*, 55–57.

36. Cicero, *De Republica*, i, 28, cited in Gwyn, *Roman Education*, 122.

37. Gwynn, *Roman Education*, 105.

38. Cicero, *De Oratore*, 2:9, quoted in Watson, *Cicero on Oratory and Orators*, 92.

39. Cicero, *Orator*, 120, quoted in Gwynn, *Roman Education*, 105.

40. Cicero, *De Oratore*, 2:15, quoted in Watson, *Cicero on Oratory and Orators*, 99.

common culture, which Hellenistic Greeks called *paideia* and which he called *humanitas*, history was only included in ordinary education for the purpose of providing rhetorical examples; for its main function was to teach students how to be successful by teaching good examples to follow and bad examples to avoid. Thus in the Hellenistic world at the time of Cicero, history was both a branch of rhetoric and a humanistic and didactic art.

Greek and Roman writers believed that historical composition was an art that must be guided by an artist's standards.[41] They often compared history with poetry as a creative art. Quintilian (35/40–ca. 96 CE)—a famous and very influential figure in the history of Western education—expressed this view in the well-known statement: "History is akin to poetry, and may be called a poem in prose."[42]

Just as the Homeric poems were based on centuries of oral tradition and were meant to be heard, so also the stories which Herodotus collected and told were meant to be heard.[43] Thucydides, however, wrote to be read, and it is arguable that at times "he represents the first really liberated writer."[44] Although he was very skeptical of the accounts of the poets and the chroniclers, "who seek to please the ear rather than speak the truth" (1:21), his speeches—such as the famous "Funeral Oration of Pericles"—are highly effective analytical and rhetorical devices but questionable historical practice. Thucydides is one of the greatest historians of all time, however, for "Perhaps nowhere else have narrative power, rigorous analysis, and dramatic power been so effectively combined."[45]

After the time of Thucydides and the Sophists, rhetoric became the core of the educational curriculum for the Greeks and later for the Romans. The study of rhetoric—which included both speaking and writing—could be very helpful to historians for learning how to write history and to write with style, but it could be less helpful in other respects. After Thucydides and Polybius, many historians became more concerned with what was pleasing to the ear and less concerned with painstaking research. Many were content to write their interpretive works on the ba-

---

41. Gwynn, *Roman Education*, 107.

42. Quoted in Gwynn, *Roman Education*, 107. See also the short selection from Quintilian's *Institutes of Oratory* in Kelley, *Versions of History*, 79–80.

43. Beye, *Ancient Greek Literature and Society*, 199.

44. Ibid., 220.

45. Conkin and Stromberg, *Heritage and Challenge*, 12.

sis of factual material found in earlier historical works or in the work of scholars who compiled facts. This separation of research and interpretation, which Collingwood aptly called "the 'scissors-and-paste' historical method,"[46] encouraged moralizing and theorizing. Thus historians moved away from the ideal of history as research and closer to essay writing as a form of belles lettres.[47]

This was also true of the kind of literature and historical writing called *lives* by Plutarch (45/50–120/27 CE) and Suetonius (ca. 70–ca. 122) and *Biographia* by John Dryden in his introductory essay to a translation of Plutarch's *Lives* in the year 1683. For Dryden, "*Biographia*, or the lives of particular Men," was a form of history.[48] Although Plutarch did not invent biography or the biographical essay,[49] biographers often regard his *Lives* as the real beginning of this form of historical inquiry and literature.[50]

When Plutarch wrote *The Parallel Lives of Noble Grecians and Romans* (ca. 110) of the famous public leaders of Greece and Rome, he usually presented them in pairs with a Greek statesman followed by a Roman. The two lives were usually followed by a comparison in which the author attempted to show how they were alike and how they differed. Plutarch believed that outstanding men determine the course of historical events,[51] but he was more interested in understanding the essence, soul, and character of these great men than the course of events.

> It must be borne in mind that my design is not to write histories but lives. And the most glorious exploits do not always furnish us with the clearest discoveries of virtue or vice in men; sometimes a matter of less moment, an expression or a jest, informs us better of their characters and inclinations, than the most famous sieges, the greatest armaments, or the bloodiest battles whatsoever. Therefore as portrait-painters are more exact in the lines and features of the

---

46. Collingwood, *Idea of History*, 33.

47. Austin, *Greek Historians*, 65–66.

48. "The Life of Plutarch," in volume 1 of *Plutarch's Lives: In Five Volumes*, n.p.

49. For a good discussion of the development of Greek biography prior to Plutarch and also of how and when biography was regarded as a part of history, see Momigliano, *Development of Greek Biography*. For a brief discussion of the writings of Plutarch and his contemporary Suetonius, see Breisach, *Historiography: Ancient, Medieval & Modern*, 25–26, 56–57, 70–71.

50. Often he has been called the father of biography (see, for instance, Thomas T. Lewis, "Biography," in *Global Encyclopedia of Historical Writing*, 1:91–92).

51. Wardman, *Plutarch's Lives*, 3.

face, in which the character is seen, than in the other parts of the body, so I must be allowed to give more particular attention to the marks and indications of the souls of men, and while I endeavor by these to portray their lives, may be free to leave more weighty matters and great battles to be treated by others.[52]

In this famous passage, it is clear that great events and wars were the traditional and proper subject of history. It is also clear that here Plutarch distinguished between histories and lives. It is possible that when he made this statement, however, he was distinguishing not between two methods or kinds of inquiries but rather between two finished products, between an account of individuals and an account of wars or peoples.[53] It is possible that Plutarch considered his *Lives* another form within that general form of inquiry called history.[54] Whether or not Plutarch considered his work to be a new and different form of inquiry and writing or a new form of *historical* inquiry and writing, it became a very popular history and kind of history, and it can and should be regarded as a historical work.

As a historical work, Plutarch's *Lives* marks a broadening of the idea of history in several respects. First of all, it is a broadening of the subject matter of history, for history is concerned not just with wars and politics but also with individual human beings. Second, it is a broadening of the idea of history, because biography is—as Wilhelm Dilthey emphasized—a basic kind of historical thought. Third, when Plutarch chose to compare and contrast forty-six Greek and Roman statesmen, he was exercising considerable choice in selecting his objects or subjects. Like Polybius, Plutarch believed that the study of history was an education and training for political life, and his purpose in writing was political as well as moral. It did not occur to him that the historian could or should investigate the lives of individuals who were not involved in politics,[55] but his decision to focus on lives rather than great events marks an important step in the direction of freedom of choice in selecting a topic. Fourth, like a modern professional historian, Plutarch preferred to use short quotations and anecdotes to reveal the character of his subjects rather than to use speeches, in the manner of Thucydides.

---

52. Plutarch, *Lives of the Noble Grecians and Romans*, 801.
53. Wardman, *Plutarch's Lives*, 5.
54. Ibid.
55. Ibid., 246.

A Typology of Classical and Christian Historiography   15

Probably the greatest merits of classical historiography of ancient Greece and Rome were its humanism and rationalism, for the great classical historians explained what happened in terms of human reason. This emphasis on human reason, however, was both a great strength and a source of weakness.

From the time of the early Greek philosophers, much of Greek thought centered on the quest for eternal substances, unchanging forms, and eternal truths. Much of Greek thought was based on the assumption that only what is unchanging can be known. Since history was concerned with the transitory, the changing, and the particular, Aristotle and other Greek philosophers did not regard historical investigation as really philosophical or scientific.

This "substantialism," which was Collingwood's term for the tendency of the Greeks and Romans to view life in terms of unchanging substances,[56] was not helpful for writing history, for Greek and Roman historians tended to regard historical objects as eternal entities. Therefore it was difficult for them to show how things came into existence or how things came to be. Their view of change was also superficial because the ancient world had no equivalent of the concept of *Entwicklung*,[57] or a strong sense of development, and also because of their very rational view of human nature.

The classical historians believed that humans were rational beings who set rational goals. What happened in life was usually the result of individuals willing it to happen. If a man did not achieve his rational goals in life, he had missed his mark.[58] Since the Greek historians "could never assess achievement except by reference to success," as Arnaldo Momigliano pointed out, therefore "they could never teach more than prudence."[59]

Plutarch, for example, took for granted that character was to a large degree preformed by the nature one possessed at birth,[60] and so did his contemporary Tacitus (ca. 56–ca. 120).[61] Plutarch conceived of change

---

56. Collingwood, *Idea of History*, 42–45.
57. Wieland, "Entwicklung, Evolution," in Bruner et al., *Geschichtliche Grundbegriffe*, 2:202.
58. Collingwood, *Idea of History*, 46.
59. Momigliano, "Greek Historiography," 22.
60. Wardman, *Plutarch's Lives*, 132.
61. Benario, *Introduction to Tacitus*, 122.

as the development of some quality that existed from the beginning but which had not yet revealed itself in the life of the statesmen he was presenting. To some degree he was able to show change for the good, since he believed it was in the nature of humanity to ascend toward the divine. However, he could not conceive of a radical change toward the good, and he had much greater difficulty dealing with a change for the worse.[62] This Greek and Roman, this classical and Hellenistic, view of human nature[63] was not shared by Jews or by early Christians.

ST. AUGUSTINE AND THE CHRISTIAN REVOLUTION IN WESTERN HISTORIOGRAPHY

One of the most brilliant and useful aspects of Collingwood's *The Idea of History* was his analysis of Christian historiography. In his introductory sentence to a section called "Characteristics of Christian Historiography," Collingwood stated: "Any history written on Christian principles will of necessity be universal, providential, apocalyptic, and periodized."[64]

Although this is a very sharp and strong sentence, and although Collingwood did not call these four characteristics an ideal type or model, in effect he created a very useful historical model for understanding and teaching Christian historiography from the time of St. Augustine to the Enlightenment and especially to the time of Voltaire.

As an intuitive abstraction, as a historical ideal type or model, and as a stage in the development of Western historiography, Christian historiography was

1. *universal* because the Judeo-Christian tradition is based on the words, "In the beginning God created the heavens and the earth" (Gen 1:1), and because Christian historians sought to deal with the whole course of human history in time and space;

---

62. Wardman, *Plutarch's Lives*, 132–40.

63. "For Plutarch, as for all ancients, character was a fixed system of personal traits with which humans were born. Life did not change that character, it only made visible a person's traits" (Breisach, *Historiography*, 71). Breisach also points out that "the lack of a sense of overall development deprived Greek historiography of a strong sense of dynamism" (ibid., 38).

64. Collingwood, *Idea of History*, 49.

2. *providential* because events were ascribed not to the wisdom of human agents but rather to the working of providence or the hand of God in determining their course;

3. *apocalyptic* because Christians found revelation and meaning in the course of events through the life of Christ, and because they looked forward to the end of time, a last judgment, and eternal rest with God;

4. *periodized* because once this one universal course of events was divided into two main periods focusing on the life of Christ, it was natural to find lesser epoch-making events marking the beginning and end of other periods, each with its own characteristics.

Although this Christian way of viewing history was worked out at the time when the Roman Empire was becoming Christian, the origins of the Judeo-Christian tradition predate the classical civilization of Greece and Rome. The Jews were a people with a long history, and their Bible contained powerful historical narratives—such as the story of David[65]—that were written long before the *Iliad* and the *Odyssey*.

The Judeo-Christian tradition is based on a way of viewing life that is very different from that of the Greek and Roman historians. In contrast to the "substantialism" of the Greeks, the Judeo-Christian tradition is based on the first words of Genesis, "In the beginning God created the heavens and the earth." In contrast to the cyclical view of time of Polybius and many other Greeks and Romans, Jews and Christians had a rectilinear view of time. In contrast to the Greeks' optimistic view of human nature, Jews and Christians believed that humans were sinners whose intellect, will, and desires led away from God.

The Christian view of life, however, is also based on the concept of grace. As Charles Cochrane pointed out, "The doctrine of sin and grace marks, in its most acute form, the breach between Classicism and Christianity."[66] After his dramatic conversion, Paul believed that by the grace of God he was a new man. As a missionary to the "Gentiles," he proclaimed that Jesus Christ was the Son of God who through his death on the cross had canceled the unfavorable record of sins and thus had set individuals free.

---

65. Cochrane, *Christianity and Classical Culture*, 451.
66. Ibid.

But Paul also preached against "the worthless deceit of human wisdom,"[67] and the early Christian church preserved the ideal of spiritual segregation and opposition that had inspired the whole Jewish tradition.[68] For three centuries the early Christian church was involved in a great struggle with the Roman Empire and its Hellenistic culture. Roman emperors from the time of Nero regarded Christians as subversives, and the defenders of the classical tradition regarded them as enemies of culture. The rise of Christianity, the religious turning point in the life of Constantine, and the reversal of imperial policy toward Christians during his reign, however, were described and celebrated in the Christian histories of Eusebius (260?–340?).[69]

As the Roman Empire became Christian in the fourth century, the church acquired some highly educated converts and leaders who were steeped in classical culture. Just as "Western civilization" is based on a fusion of the Greco-Roman and the Judeo-Christian traditions, so also the Western view of history and Western historiography rest on a fusion that culminated at the turn of the fourth and fifth centuries. The key figures in this reconciliation of the classical and Christian traditions were the "Doctors of the Latin Church," especially St. Augustine (354–430), a man who has been called "the single most influential thinker in the Western intellectual tradition."[70] Here, however, he is seen as the author of the two most important books for establishing, understanding, and teaching a Christian view of history.

Although the *Confessions* of Augustine is a personal confession of sin, a recognition of God's truth and goodness, an offering of thanks and praise to God for his mercy and grace,[71] and a long prayer, it is also a

---

67. Col 2:8.

68. Dawson, *Making of Europe*, 26.

69. For a brief and very useful discussion of the significance of Eusebius for the development of a distinctly Christian kind of history and a way of dating events since "the Creation," see Breisach, *Historiography*, 77–84.

70. Ozment, *Age of Reform*, 3. This study is very helpful for understanding not only Western intellectual and religious thought from the time of St. Augustine to the year 1550 but also for understanding the nature and significance of Martin Luther's thought and work. See also O'Donnell, *Augustine*, and his claim that Augustine and the other "'Fathers of the Church' . . . were indeed the people who invented the belief system we call Christianity" (194).

71. Pine-Coffin, "Introduction," in *Confessions* by St. Augustine, 16. Quotations from the *Confessions* are from this translation, but they will be cited by book and paragraph

story of Augustine's intellectual and spiritual development centering on the turning point in his life, his conversion to Christianity.[72] In this unique and epoch-making "life-writing" for the Christian era of Western historiography, one can see taking place the transition to a Christian way of viewing life and history.

As a historical or time-based inquiry concerning the intellectual development of a single human mind, the *Confessions* is the story of how a well-educated[73] and sophisticated *rhetor*, or teacher of rhetoric, changed from thinking of God and the world in terms of eternal substances to thinking about God as the unchanging Creator of everything subject to change and to time.

In this story of his life, Augustine emphasized how he came to see that "the principal and almost the only cause of the error" from which he could not escape was the fact that when he tried "to think of my God, I could think of him only as bodily substance, because I could not conceive anything else" (5:10). In the same way, he also believed that evil was some kind of bodily substance and that mind was some kind of rarefied body somehow diffused in space (5:10). It was not until after his contact with St. Ambrose—another of the Latin doctors—and after reading "some books of the Platonists" (7:9) that he began to accept the words of the prologue of John; and soon it became clear to him that God made all things new and that even those things that were subject to decay were good (7:12).

Throughout the first nine books, where he told the story of his intellectual and spiritual development, he returned to this basic idea as he

---

number in the text rather than by page number in the notes. Although in the present inquiry the *Confessions* is viewed in respect to the idea of history and as a kind of historical thought and narrative, it should be understood that "the *Confessions* presents itself as prayer, a dialogue with God." (McMahon, "Book Thirteen," 218). Among the many values of this work are the references in the notes to other translations and to recent literature on this subject.

72. For a multifaceted and moving analysis of the *Confessions*, see Brown, *Augustine of Hippo*, 158–81. For Brown, the *Confessions* was both "a prolonged exploration of the nature of God, written in the form of a prayer, to 'stir up towards Him the intellect and feelings of men,'" and, at the same time, "a masterpiece of strictly intellectual history" (166–67). One of the reasons that the *Confessions* is important for all students of history is that it "gives us a fuller picture of the development of Augustine's thought than we have for anyone else in antiquity" (Cary, *Augustine's Invention of the Inner Self*, 33).

73. The great weakness of Augustine's education, as Brown points out, was the fact that he was "the only Latin philosopher in antiquity to be virtually ignorant of Greek" (Brown, *Augustine of Hippo*, 36).

wrestled with the problems of time, continuity, and stages of his life's development in relation to this God who created all things. "My infancy, he said, "is long since dead, yet I am still alive. But you, Lord, live forever and nothing in you dies, because you have existed from the very beginning of the ages, before anything that could be said to go before, and you are God and Lord of all you have created. In you are the first causes of all things not eternal, the unchangeable origins of all things that are subject to the passage of time and have no reason in themselves" (1:6).

When he finished telling the story of his life through the conversion experience, he continued to focus on the question of time as he wrestled with the problem of memory in book 10, with the concept of time in book 11, with the first verse of Genesis in book 12, and with the whole story of the creation in Genesis in book 13. Thus, while nine of the books contain a narrative of his intellectual and spiritual development, all of the books are concerned with a perception of time.

As a historical or time-based inquiry concerning the spiritual odyssey of a single human soul, the *Confessions*—a work that contains the first great *Geistesgeschichte*, or intellectual history, in Western and world history—is the story of the providence of God as seen in Augustine's life and conversion. In order to write this autobiographical inquiry, Augustine had to reenact and to reexperience in his mind his own intellectual and spiritual development. In writing this work, he attempted to explain his thought and actions both (1) from the standpoint of what he had originally thought and intended before his conversion, and (2) from the standpoint since his conversion that the major events in his life were the result of God's divine providence or the hand of God leading him in a certain direction even though he had been completely blind to this when the event took place. "You applied the spur," Augustine said, "that would drive me away from Carthage and offered me enticements that would draw me to Rome, and for your purpose you made use of men whose hearts were set upon this life of death, some acting like madmen, others promising me vain rewards. In secret you were using my own perversity and theirs to set my feet upon the right course. You know, O God, why it was that I left one city and went to the other. But you did not make the reason clear to me or to my mother" (5:8).

With this Christian view of providence, what happened in life did not have to be willed by any individual. Individual human beings acted in their own self-interest and according to their own goals, but at the same time, they were also agents of God's divine plan executing the purposes of God. The historical process was now seen as the working out of God's purposes rather than of human purposes, but humanity had been created to work God's purposes in time.

This recognition that what happens in life need not happen because someone deliberately wished it to happen, as Collingwood points out, is a necessary precondition for understanding any historical process.[74] Thus this new attitude toward human action marks a fundamental and revolutionary change in the development of the idea of history. As Charles Cochrane emphasizes, the divergence between Christianity and classicism "was in no respect more conspicuously or emphatically displayed than with regard to history; in a very real sense indeed it marked the crux of the issue between the two."[75]

In the *Confessions*, Augustine was concerned about the providence of God in his own life, but when Rome—the eternal city—was sacked by the Goths in the year 410, and Christians were blamed for this calamity, he had to think about the providence of God in relation to the history of Rome, of the Roman Empire, and of humanity as a whole. Since he had already wrestled with the questions of time, of providence, of continuity and change, and with stages of development in the microcosm of his own life, he was better prepared to take up these same problems within the macrocosm of universal or world history. As John O'Meara has pointed out, *The City of God* was the application of the *Confessions* to the history of mankind, and the inspiration of Augustine's themes was his own life.[76]

In this epoch-making work for Western civilization and historiography, Augustine discussed how "The education of the human race, represented by the people of God, has advanced, like that of an individual, through certain epochs, or as it were, ages, so that it might gradually rise from earthly to heavenly things, and from the visible to the invisible."[77] In the first ten books, Augustine wrote to defend "the City of God" against the charges and attacks of its enemies and against those who preferred their gods to "the Founder of this city." In the next twelve books and the main part of this work, he set out "to write of the rise, progress, and ap-

---

74. Collingwood, *Idea of History*, 48.
75. Cochrane, *Christianity and Classical Culture*, 456.
76. O'Meara, *Charter of Christendom*, 16.
77. Augustine, *City of God*, 319. Quotations from this work are from the Marcus Dods translation and are cited in the text by book and paragraph number (10:14).

pointed end of the two cities, one of which is God's, and the other this world's" (18:1). After discussing the origin of both cities, he discussed the ages of humanity from the first man to the flood, from the flood to Abraham, from Abraham to David, from David to the Babylonian captivity, from the Babylonian captivity "to the advent of Christ himself in the flesh," and then the city of God since the time of Christ. This was followed by an attempt to show how the earthly city also ran its course from the time of Abraham. Augustine believed that the long duration of the Roman republic and the Roman Empire was due not only to the virtues of its citizens but also to the God who "can never be believed to have left the kingdoms of men, their dominations and servitudes, outside of the laws of his providence" (5:11). Thus even the Roman Empire could be seen as a product of this divine process or as an agent in working out God's divine plan.

Thus for Augustine, as Jaroslav Pelikan summarized so well, "Not cycles, but sequence; not fate, but providence; not chaos, but order; not caprice, but pedagogy—this was, for Augustine, the meaning of the mystery of historical continuity, by means of which God was carrying out 'the education of the human race . . . through certain epochs.'"[78]

For Augustine, however, the main units of history were individual souls. Salvation depended not on the fortunes of Rome but on the grace of God. At the last judgment the citizens of these two entangled cities, the city of God and the earthly city, would be separated eternally. Until that time, God's judgment was present even though it was not apparent or could not be discerned. Thus the Christian should learn "to bear with equanimity the ills to which even good men are subject, and to hold cheap the blessings which even the wicked enjoy" (20:2). For human beings do not know "by what judgement of God this poor man is poor and that bad man rich; why he who, in our opinion, ought to suffer acutely for his abandoned life enjoys himself" (20:2). In this work St. Augustine demonstrated that Christians should try to understand the course of human history, but it was God's story, and only God really knew *why* things happened.

Although *The City of God* is a less-historical work than the *Confessions* since it is less a connected narrative account of a single human object or

---

78. Pelikan, *Mystery of Continuity*, 50. As Frederick J. Crossen also pointed out, Augustine thought "of individuals (and nations) as singular, as having a life history that may indeed exhibit typical patterns of development, but which has a comprehensive, linear, noncyclical history, a history under God's providence" ("Book Five," 86).

subject, and since it is less consistently based on a perception of time, it is the most "epoch-making" work for establishing a Christian view of history. Just as Augustine's *Confessions* can be seen as the most significant Christian inquiry and autobiographical narrative of a single human mind and soul until the time of the very different *Confessions* of Rousseau (1781), so also *The City of God* was the most influential work for the Christian view of universal or world history until the traditional Christian way of writing this kind of history was overturned by Voltaire. Although Augustine is not commonly perceived as a historian, and although in *The City of God* Augustine disqualified himself as a writer of history,[79] his two great works were of fundamental importance for the idea of history and for the development of the two poles of historical writing: the life of a single human being and world history.

As a teacher and as a bishop responsible for catechismal instruction for new church members, Augustine had already worked out a way of teaching biblical history based on six ages, before he began working on *The City of God*.[80] His six ages were based not only on landmark events taken from the biblical narrative and on the first chapter of Matthew, but also on the idea of the six days of creation and the analogy of the stages of human life from infancy (Adam to Noah), childhood (Noah to Abraham), adolescence, adulthood, and senescence to death.[81]

Although for Augustine the life of Christ was the main event in human history, it can be argued that once Augustine had divided his own life into two main stages separated by the life-changing event of his own conversion, it was natural for him to look for other ages and other epoch-making events in his own life, in teaching biblical history, and in understanding human history since the creation. More concretely, however, it is clear (1) that Augustine's six ages of humanity involved the conscious use of analogies in understanding human history in relation to a percep-

---

79. On this point, as well as on Augustine's strong criticism of philosophers because of their lack of historical understanding, see Pelikan, *Mystery of Continuity*, 35, 53. For a discussion of the significance of St. Augustine's *Confessions* for Rousseau's *Confessions* and how the word *nature* took the place of *providence* for Rousseau, see Hartle, *Modern Self in Rousseau's "Confessions."*

80. See especially Augustine's *De Catechizandis Rudibus* and Green, *Augustine on the Teaching of History*, 322–27.

81. Markus, *Saeculum*, 18. The third age was from Abraham to David, the fourth was from David to the deportation to Babylon, and the fifth from then until the birth of Christ.

tion of time, and (2) that from the beginning of the Christian epoch of Western historiography, the analogy of life stages was used in forming historical periods.

In *The City of God*, however, Augustine's six ages were not as easy to see as one would expect.[82] Around the year 615, Isidore of Seville (ca. 570–636) wrote a short chronological survey from the creation to his own day, which was based on St. Augustine's six ages. This division of history passed from Isidore of Seville to Bede (ca. 673–735), "the father of English history," and through these two men Augustine's six ages became a standard form of periodization for this Christian kind of universal or world history.

Augustine also greatly influenced the idea of history in the West when he instructed a Spanish "presbyter" known as Paulus Orosius (fl. early fifth century) to write a survey or chronicle of world history that would serve as a brief chronological supplement to *The City of God*. But in his universal chronicle, which was written in 417–418, and which was called *Seven Books of Histories against the Pagans*, Orosius emphasized "the Four Monarchies" pattern of St. Jerome (based on the prophecy in Dan 2:40) rather than Augustine's six ages.[83] Thus, in contrast to Augustine's "cosmic interpretation of history," which "redefined the relationship between the sacred and profane throughout time,"[84] the four-monarchy or the four-empire pattern of Jerome and Orosius implied that from their time to the Last Judgment, world history would be associated with the history of Rome.[85]

From the time of Augustine, Jerome, and Orosius to the seventeenth century, Christian historians used the six ages of Augustine and/or the four monarchies or empires of Jerome and Orosius in writing universal history. In these schemes, the beginnings of the last period coincided since the sixth age of the world began with the birth of Christ and the fourth monarchy began with the foundation of the Roman Empire by Caesar or

---

82. The stages of Augustine's schema come to the fore most obviously in 16:43 and 22:30.

83. Breisach, *Historiography*, 86. While the four monarchies for Daniel probably meant the Babylonians, Medes, Persians, and Macedonians, his interpreters took this term to indicate the Medes, Persians, Greeks, and Romans. See Kelley, *Versions of History*, 118.

84. Breisach, *Historiography*, 84.

85. Ibid., 86–88.

Augustus. For more than a thousand years, Christian historians within Latin Christendom believed and taught that they were living in the sixth and last age of human history, or in the fourth and last monarchy identified with Rome. From the time of St. Augustine to the time of Voltaire, Christian historians continued Augustine's pattern of two cities in their separate accounts of "sacred" history (based on the Bible) and "profane" history (based on the empires before and after Christ).

The Christian view of history worked out by Eusebius, Jerome, Augustine, Orosius, and other scholars in the fourth and fifth centuries, mark a new epoch in the development of history and a new type of historical writing. The single chronological framework for dating events "from the Lord's incarnation," which was established in the West most of all through the work of the Venerable Bede (673–735), and which was symbolized by the letters AD, became the symbol of this new Christian kind of historiography.

It was extremely important both for the whole development of this European or Western civilization and for the form of inquiry called history (1) that St. Augustine and the other "Latin Doctors" were good Ciceronians as well as good Christians, and (2) that the fusion of the classical and the Judeo-Christian traditions took place before the complete collapse of the western part of the Roman Empire. Since Augustine had written that even pagan history was a "useful discipline for the cultivated Christian,"[86] monks and clerics saved and copied the pagan histories of the Greeks and Romans as they struggled to preserve learning and to Christianize the Germanic tribes.

CHRISTIAN HISTORIOGRAPHY FROM ST. AUGUSTINE TO DESCARTES

The conversion of the Germanic tribes was a long, slow, and difficult process. With the crowning of Charlemagne—a fantastically successful Germanic warrior—as Roman emperor by the pope in the year 800, however, one can see the fusion of the classical and Christian traditions with the Germanic tradition and the beginning of a European or "Western" civilization based on these three main roots.

---

86. *On Christian Doctrine* (*De Doctrina Christiana*) 2:27; cited in Lacroix, "Early Medieval Historiography," 16.

Although Charlemagne's empire was the core of this emerging civilization, that "Old Europe"—which lasted to the Enlightenment, the Industrial Revolution, and the French Revolution—began to take shape around the year 1000.[87] In the year 962, Otto I created a powerful empire in central Europe that was later called the Holy Roman Empire. In the year 966 the King of the Poles accepted Christianity. In 975 the leader of the Magyars or Hungarians was baptized, and in the year 1000 his son was crowned by the pope. About this time the kings of Sweden and Norway became Christian.

Russia also fits into this general pattern, for in the year 988 the ruler of Kiev, Russia, accepted Christianity. In the middle of the eleventh century, however, the Latin Church and the Orthodox Church completely split, and the Latin Church went its own way. Thus Russia, which had been converted from Constantinople and not from Rome, was not a part of that Latin Christendom and that Old Europe that took shape in the eleventh century and that acquired many of its basic institutions and characteristics in the twelfth and thirteenth centuries.[88]

In the eleventh century, the Latin or Roman Church acquired a magnificent hierarchical structure from an independent and powerful papacy down to the village priest. The church became the one great institution of Latin Christendom. In the West, but not in the Byzantine Empire, development came through the church rather than through a powerful empire. The crusades, the development of canon law and Scholasticism, the revival of Roman law and the work of Aristotle, and the founding of the first universities, were major events of the twelfth century that came through the church.

As Dietrich Gerhard points out, at least from the time of Abelard (1079–1142) and his Scholastic methodology, the Aristotelian renaissance, and the first universities, one can see and trace the development of "the rational spirit of analysis and distinction [that] continually penetrates the interrelated disciplines of theology, philosophy, and law."[89] In the thirteenth century, Thomas Aquinas (ca. 1225–1274) created a new synthesis of faith and reason based more on Aristotle and Aristotelian logic, and this new synthesis, and especially his Scholastic methodology,

---

87. Gerhard, "Periodization in European History," 903. See also his excellent book called *Old Europe: A Study of Continuity, 1000–1800.*

88. See especially Gerhard, *Old Europe*, 25–56.

89. Gerhard, "Periodization in European History," 906.

partly replaced the older and more historical approach of Augustine. In contrast to the more dynamic world of Augustine, based on his trust in providence and in the God who created all things subject to change and to time, the world of Thomas Aquinas was a more static and rational one based on his trust in the rationality of God and in the harmony of faith and reason, of theology and philosophy.

Just as history was not a part of the educational curriculum of the Greek and Roman world, it was not a part of the curriculum of the cathedral schools of the eleventh century or the universities of the twelfth and thirteenth centuries. The trivium—grammar, rhetoric, and logic—was the most important part of the basic curriculum at this time, while the quadrivium—arithmetic, geometry, astronomy, and music—formed the other part of the curriculum and the rest of the seven liberal arts. After a student had received a general education in these basic studies taught by the masters of arts within the arts faculty of the new universities, he was prepared to begin professional studies within the professional faculties of theology, law, or medicine.

During the twelfth century, however, the balance within the trivium was upset as logic began driving letters from the schools. Thus in the thirteenth century, the Latin classics were not a part of the university curriculum.[90] Since history was closely associated with rhetoric and good letters, this significant educational change was not helpful for the study and writing of history.

From the time of St. Augustine to the end of the thirteenth century, monks and priests wrote the histories and recorded events within Latin Christendom. Although Bede's *Ecclesiastical History of the English Nation* can be called a great historical work, on the whole it is fair to say that in their histories, chronicles, annals, and lives of saints, monks and priests often sought to find the hand and judgment of God more than they sought through painstaking research to record the actions of human beings. Thus the abstract and one-sided rationalism and humanism of the Greeks and Romans had been replaced by an abstract and one-sided "theocentric" view of history.[91]

In the fourteenth century, however, lay "humanists" in Italy sought to return to the classical way of writing history. "Humanism began,"

---

90. Haskins, *Renaissance of the Twelfth Century*, 335.
91. Collingwood, *Idea of History*, 55.

as Donald R. Kelley emphasizes, "as an insurrection of the liberal and lowly 'arts' ... against the intellectual hegemony of 'the sciences' (theology, law, and medicine and the theoretical parts of philosophy)," for it "defined itself in separation from, and largely in reaction to, the 'clerical' and professional monopoly of learning reflected in the university from its twelfth-century inception through the Renaissance and well into the seventeenth century."[92]

Petrarch (1304–1374), "the founder and the prototype of Renaissance humanism,"[93] regarded the "modern" age since the adoption of Christianity as an age of darkness and barbarism in contrast to the "ancient," pre-Christian, and purely Roman period. Most likely the concept of the Dark Ages originated with him. In this interesting inversion of the Christian view of a pagan period of darkness followed by a Christian period of light, Petrarch substituted a cultural metaphor for a religious one[94] and set the tone for the still-Christian but more-secular view of the Italian humanists.

Instead of glorifying the virtues of saints, the Italian humanists glorified the virtues of statesmen in the manner of Plutarch, or condemned the vices of tyrants or despots in the manner of Suetonius and Tacitus. But just as the Christian theologians and philosophers of the twelfth and thirteenth centuries had revived and broadened classical philosophy, so also the Italian humanists revived and broadened the classical type of Western historiography as they sought to revive and imitate it.[95]

This is especially so in the writing of individual lives. Both Petrarch and Giovanni Boccaccio (1313–1375) glorified the heroes of ancient Rome, but Boccaccio also wrote *On Famous Women* and a *Life of Dante*, the first "real" or "lengthy" biography of a poet.[96] Although the word *biography* was not commonly used until the seventeenth century, and although the word *autobiography* was not invented until the year 1809,[97]

92. Kelley, *Renaissance Humanism*, 5.

93. Ibid., 7.

94. See Mommsen, "Petrarch's Conception of the 'Dark Ages,'" 226–42; and Ferguson, *Renaissance in Historical Thought*, 8.

95. See especially Cochrane, *Historians and Historiography in the Italian Renaissance*.

96. Fueter, *Geschichte der neueren Historiographie*, 8; and Dannenfeldt, "Italian Renaissance," 95.

97. "If biography is an ancient Greek word, though of late antiquity, autobiography

the new desire for fame that Jacob Burckhardt found in the "many-sided" men of the Italian Renaissance can be seen in the biographies and autobiographies or in the "life-writings" of the Italian humanists.[98]

It is significant for the idea of history that during the three centuries from 1500 to 1800 "the Hellenistic distinction between history and biography had been replaced by a rather uncontroversial recognition of biography as a type of history."[99] It is also significant, however, that the humanist biographers of the Italian Renaissance "continued to assume, in spite of abundant evidence to the contrary, that the character of an individual person was indelibly established at the moment of birth."[100]

Like the Greek and Roman historians, humanist historians usually identified history with a literary account of political and military events.[101] In their epic narratives, humanist historians in Italy looked for the role of "Fortune" in the manner of Polybius without rejecting or overturning the Christian view of providence.

Above all, however, the humanists sought to revive rhetoric,[102] and this included a revival of history as written by Livy, Plutarch, Polybius, and other classical historians. While the purpose of rhetoric was "to show how ethical norms could be applied to human behavior,"[103] the purpose of history was to teach by example what ought to be and the way people ought to act. In reviving rhetoric, the Italian humanists firmly established history as a form of literature.

---

is not a Greek word but a modern invention. According to the *O.E.D.* it first appeared in English in 1809 with Robert Southey" (Momigliano, *Development of Greek Biography*, 14).

98. For the expression "life-writing" and for the great broadening of this pole of Western historical writing from the Italian humanists to the time of Louis XIV, see Mayer and Woolf, *Rhetorics of Life-Writing in Early Modern Europe*. In their introduction to this collection of essays, Mayer and Woolf present ten distinct but often overlapping types of "biographical life-writing" (13) and seven types of autobiography, "the other grand category of early modern life-writing" (16). In the essay "Paolo Giovio and the Rhetoric of Individuality," T. C. Price Zimmermann shows how "the humanists saw biography as a natural outgrowth of history" (40), and how "Cicero's definition of history in the *De Oratore* (2.62–64) formed the paradigm for humanist historiography" (42).

99. Momigliano, *Development of Greek Biography*, 2.

100. Cochrane, *Historians and Historiography in the Italian Renaissance*, 415.

101. Ferguson, *Renaissance in Historical Thought*, 3.

102. Gilbert, *Machiavelli and Guicciardini*, 89.

103. Ibid.

Although some modern professional historians see "the age of the Renaissance" as the time of "the birth of modern historiography," basically the Italian humanists (1) revived and broadened the epic, humanistic, rational, and didactic type of history of the Greek and Roman historians, and (2) reestablished this kind of history alongside the traditional Christian type of universal history that Protestant teachers and writers enthusiastically embraced, and that scholars in Protestant and Catholic countries greatly broadened in the seventeenth and eighteenth centuries.

Like Polybius, Machiavelli (1469–1527) emphasized the importance of the study of history for statesmen, and also the importance of practical political experience for understanding and writing history. In his famous essay called *The Prince*, he used the concepts of *virtù* and fortune in a masterful and realistic way. When he insisted that princes must act on the basis of what is and the way men really are rather than on the basis of what ought to be and the way men should act, however, he departed both from the Christian and the humanist ways of viewing government and politics.

Because of the strong sense of realism in Machiavelli's *History of Florence*, some professional historians have seen it as "the beginning of modern historiography."[104] As Felix Gilbert points out, however, no direct path links this work with modern historiography, for there is no connection between Machiavelli's view of "the divinely inspired hero" or his cyclical view of history with modern views of the role of the individual or collective forces in history.[105] For Gilbert and other professional historians, the *History of Italy* of Francesco Guicciardini (1483–1540) did more to advance the classical kind of historiography than Machiavelli's *History of Florence*.

Like the Italian humanists, Desiderius Erasmus (1466–1536) believed that learning and the arts had declined after classical antiquity and needed to be revived. Erasmus was also convinced, however, that religion had declined since the time of the great Church Fathers and that therefore good letters *and* Christian piety needed to be revived.

---

104. Dannenfeldt, "Italian Renaissance," 101.

105. Gilbert, "Machiavelli's *Istorie Fiorentine*," 153. In this sentence, one can see the influence of Hintze's article on this subject ("The Individualist and the Collective Approach to History" [357–67] for this student of Meinecke and translator of this Hintze essay (see chapter 5, section 3, in the present study).

Erasmus and other Christian humanists strongly opposed Scholasticism, the highly theological and philosophical curriculum and methodology of the "schoolmen," for they believed that a return to the good letters of classical antiquity and to the pure Christianity of the early church could best be achieved through education and educational reform. Like his friend Sir Thomas More (1478–1535), Erasmus was ardently devoted to the literature of pagan and Christian antiquity because he found embodied in it a wisdom that could both improve individuals and renovate Christian society, both temporarily and spiritually. Thus, as Jack Hexter pointed out, *The Praise of Folly* (1511) of Erasmus and the *Utopia* (1516) of More were both creative works of literature and a significant part of the Christian humanist program of action for "social and spiritual renewal through a restoration of Gospel Christianity."[106]

This program of action by Christian humanists to reform education was well under way in northern Europe in the year 1520 when Martin Luther called upon Charles V and the nobility of the German nation to call a council to reform the Church, including the whole educational system. Christian humanists played important roles in the reorganization of the schools and universities and in the reform of education that took place both in Protestant and Catholic territories during the sixteenth century. From the Protestant Reformation through the seventeenth century, European education and the writing of history were mainly Catholic or Protestant, and history was somehow a part—but not a very important part—of the curriculum.

This did not mean, however, that strong claims for the importance of history as a discipline were not made at this time of Reformation and Catholic Reform. Jean Bodin's *Method for Easy Comprehension of History* (1566), for example, not only exemplified how the Italianate "art of history" was increasingly superseded by the French "methods of history," but also the claim that history was "above all other disciplines."[107]

Within the Catholic parts of Europe, education was more uniform than within Protestant kingdoms, territories, or cities. One reason for this, of course, was the division of Protestants into Lutheran, Reformed, Anglican, and other political and religious communities. Catholic education was also more uniform, however, because increasingly in the six-

---

106. Hexter, *More's "Utopia,"* 53.
107. Kelley, *Renaissance Humanism*, 100.

teenth and seventeenth centuries it was turned over to one Catholic order, to the Society of Jesus, or to the Jesuits.

Before Ignatius Loyola (1491–1556) founded this dynamic order of teacher-priests in 1540, he had been a Spanish soldier, he had been converted to an intensely spiritual life, and he had encountered both the Latin classics and Thomistic theology and philosophy at the University of Paris. The educational curriculum of the Jesuits was both Scholastic and humanistic, for it was based on Aristotelian logic and Thomistic theology and philosophy on the one hand, and the Latin classics and the Ciceronian view of the ideal orator on the other. The Jesuit schools and this Jesuit curriculum were of decisive importance for education in France to the present time, for French education since the sixteenth century has emphasized both logic and rhetoric,[108] both reason and style.

Jesuit education was also very successful because the Jesuits devoted great attention to educational methodology and teacher preparation. Since prospective teachers were trained by experienced teachers in the practice and methods of teaching, and since the provincials of the order were responsible for seeing that teachers acquired skills in methods of education, the colleges of the Jesuits may therefore be considered the earliest training colleges for teachers in higher schools.[109] The Jesuits really worked at developing a system of education, and their rules and methods of teaching were part of the famous *Ratio Studiorum*, or order of studies, issued by the fourth general of the order in 1599. By this time the Jesuits were the professional order of the Roman Catholic world, and by 1616 they had 372 colleges with 13,112 members in thirty-two provinces.[110]

Probably the most famous and best of these Jesuit colleges was the one at La Flèche, France. In this school that was founded by King Henry IV, and that became the custodian of his heart after he was assassinated in 1610, René Descartes (1596–1650) received the education he immortalized in a classic of French and Western education, philosophy, literature, and science called *Discourse on Method*.

Just as the first part of Augustine's *Confessions* contains a useful picture and critique of late Roman education, so also the first part of Descartes' *Discourse* contains a helpful portrait and a penetrating analysis

---

108. See Gerhard, "Development and Structure of Continental European and American Universities," 158.

109. Paulsen, *German Education Past and Present*, 83.

110. Ibid., 82.

of seventeenth-century Catholic education. Descartes had a high opinion of his Jesuit teachers, and throughout his life he was convinced that his education was the best available at that time in any European school.[111] Yet his personal and carefully worded analysis of humanist and scholastic education at its best certainly demonstrated some of its limitations.

DESCARTES' *DISCOURSE ON METHOD*, THE SCIENTIFIC REVOLUTION OF THE SEVENTEENTH CENTURY, AND THE AUTONOMY OF REASON

René Descartes is an important figure for the idea of history in the West partly because of his views in the *Discourse* concerning the strengths and weaknesses of history as a component within the educational curriculum of his day. For Descartes, history was a subject of some value because the famous deeds of men uplift the mind, because it aids in maturing one's judgment, and because "reading good books is like having a conversation with the most distinguished men of past ages."[112] Conversing with individuals from past centuries, Descartes said, was much the same as traveling; for "It is good to know something of the customs of various peoples, so that we may judge our own more soundly and not think that everything contrary to our own ways is ridiculous and irrational, as those who have seen nothing of the world ordinarily do" (CSM 1:113–14).

On the other hand, however, Descartes noted that too much travel makes one a stranger at home, and that those who are too interested in what happened in the past are often remarkably ignorant of what is happening in the present. In addition, he suggested, "fables make us imagine many events as possible when they are not. And even the most accurate histories, while not altering or exaggerating the importance of matters to make them more worthy of being read, at any rate almost always omit the baser and less notable events; as a result, the other events appear in a false light, and those who regulate their conduct by examples drawn from these works are liable to fall into the excesses of the knights errant in our tales of chivalry, and conceive plans beyond their powers" (CSM 1:114).

---

111. Pearl, *Descartes*, 22.

112. Descartes, *Discourse on the Method of rightly conducting one's reason and seeking the truth in the sciences* (Descartes, *Philosophical Writings*, 1:113). Quotations from the *Discourse* will be from this translation, and henceforth they will be cited in parentheses in the text as CSM 1, plus the page number.

Here it is evident that Descartes was looking at history from a different perspective from that of the humanists. While the humanists appreciated history mainly for its literary and moral value, Descartes found it wanting because it was too fanciful,[113] because even the most careful historians distorted the truth since they did not tell the whole truth, and because he questioned the humanist argument that history was very useful for providing examples to guide one's behavior in life.

The principal importance of Descartes' *Discourse on Method* for the idea of history, however, is its significance for what historians call "the scientific revolution of the seventeenth century." The *Discourse* was an integral part of this revolution, for as Dietrich Gerhard points out, it was Descartes "who replaced Aristotle . . . By establishing the autonomy of reason, Descartes initiated the first of the 'emancipations' that eventually became the most outstanding characteristics of the next centuries."[114]

In the *Discourse*, Descartes was also very critical of the more Scholastic side of his education and of his training in Aristotelian logic, philosophy, and methodology. His Jesuit teachers stressed logical thinking not only through the study of logic but also through the way they encouraged students to use logical arguments in the art of debate and in the methods and application of reasoned questioning.[115] Descartes was a curious youth with a strong desire to learn the truth, and this, coupled with the dialectical methodology of his Jesuit education, produced what one of his biographers has called "an obsession for certainty" and "the taste for method in all things."[116]

His passion for useful knowledge, however, led him to see a basic weakness of a system of education based on Aristotelian logic. In one devastating sentence, Descartes stated that with regard to logic, its "syllogisms and most of its other techniques are of less use for learning things than for explaining to others the things one already knows" (CSM 1:119).

Since he noted that the most outstanding minds had studied philosophy for centuries without having produced anything "which is not disputed and hence doubtful," and since the other branches of learning often borrowed their principles from philosophy, as soon as he reached

---

113. See Collingwood's interesting and helpful analysis of Descartes's statements about history (Collingwood, *Idea of History*, 59–63).

114. Gerhard, *Old Europe*, 112–13.

115. Vrooman, *René Descartes*, 42–43.

116. Ibid.

the age he was no longer under the control of his teachers, he resolved to abandon the study of letters and "to seek no other knowledge than that which he could find in myself or else in the great book of the world" (CSM 1:115).

Descartes concluded the first part of the *Discourse* and the story of his early life and education with this judgment: "But after I had spent some years pursuing these studies in the book of the world and trying to gain some experience, I resolved one day to undertake studies within myself too and to use all the powers of my mind in choosing the paths I should follow. In this I have had much more success, I think, than I would have had if I had never left my country or my books" (CSM 1:116).

At the beginning of the second part of the *Discourse*, Descartes suggests that this turning point in his life happened in Germany on a particular day (November 10, 1619), when he was caught by the onset of winter and had to spend the entire day alone in a warm room. The joy and exhilaration that Descartes felt on this day was greater than he had ever experienced. When he decided to reject the teachings and opinions he had received from his birth until he could verify them for himself, he believed that he had succeeded in solving more than a particular problem, more than the principles of a single science. What he saw at this time was the unity of all sciences, and what he thought he had discovered was a method for understanding all sciences.[117]

After he listed the four basic principles of "the method," he summarized the way he had arrived at the supreme discovery of his life: "Those long chains composed of very simple and easy reasonings, which geometers customarily use to arrive at their most difficult demonstrations, had given me occasion to suppose that all things which can fall under human knowledge are interconnected in the same way. And I thought that, provided we refrain from accepting anything as true which is not, and always keep to the order required for deducing one thing from another, there can be nothing too remote to be reached in the end or too well hidden to be discovered." (CSM 1:120).

What Descartes did not relate in the *Discourse* or in his other published works, however, was how his discovery of "the foundations of a marvelous science"[118] was connected with three dreams, and how these

117. Ibid., 55.

118. These are Descartes's own words—"mirabilis scientiae fundamenta"—for this discovery on November 10, 1619. See Vrooman, *René Descartes*, 59.

dreams were a significant part of this epoch-making day in his life and for modern Western thought. For an account of these dreams, scholars have had to rely on information provided by Descartes' first biographer, Adrien Baillet, who had access to a manuscript that Leibniz also saw but that is now lost.[119]

According to Baillet, the first two dreams were terrifying, for when Descartes awoke from the second dream, he thought he saw sparks all around his room. His third dream, however, was a complicated one that has one strong similarity with the conversion experience of St. Augustine.

In his account of his conversion experience, Augustine told how he heard a voice of a girl or boy repeating the refrain "Take it and read," and how he had interpreted this to be a divine command to open his book of Scripture: "I seized it and opened it, and in silence I read the first passage on which my eyes fell: *Not in revelling and drunkenness, not in quarrels and rivalries. Rather arm yourself with the Lord Jesus Christ; spend no more thought on nature's appetites.* I had no wish to read more and no need to do so, for in an instant, it was as though the light of confidence flooded into my heart and all the darkness of doubt dispelled."[120]

In Descartes' third dream, he was surprised to find two books in his room, a dictionary and a collection of poems called *Corpus Poetarum*. As he curiously opened the latter book, his eyes fell upon the line *Quod vitae sectabor iter?* ("What path shall I follow in life?"). A man he did not know gave him some verses that began with the words *est et non* (yes and no).

While he was still dreaming, he began to interpret the dream. The dictionary, he judged, typified all the sciences as a collective body. The *Corpus Poetarum* represented the union of philosophy and wisdom and also Descartes' view that poets often said more profound things than philosophers, and in a better way because of the divine nature of their

---

119. Baillet, *La Vie de Monsieur Des-Cartes*, 2:81–84. The summary contained in the account above is based mainly on Vrooman, *René Descartes*, 56–59. For a convenient place to see (1) Baillet's account of these dreams (in French) and a summary of each dream in English, and (2) a useful and detailed interpretation of them in relation to the *Discourse on Method*, see Cole, *Olympian Dreams and Youthful Rebellion*. Cole makes a convincing case that "the dream day" was both "an intellectual revolution" and a "vocational decision," for it was a rejection of a law career in favor of a life to be spent in "the search for truth" (61–77).

120. Augustine, *Confessions*, 8:12 (italics provided by R. S. Pine-Coffin, the editor and translator).

inspiration.[121] The "yes and no" of Pythagoras stood for truth and error in human knowledge. When he awoke from his third dream, Descartes concluded that the first two dreams were a warning from God concerning his past life, and that the third dream was a divine confirmation of his resolution to take himself as an object of study. According to Baillet, Descartes believed beyond all doubt that it was "the Spirit of Truth" that wanted to open for him, by this third dream, "the treasure of all the sciences."[122]

Through this day and night of intellectual and spiritual struggle, darkness was dispelled by "the Spirit of Truth" and by confidence in the principle of doubt. Thus Descartes found his path, his mission, and his vocation in life: to set the sciences on the right path to knowledge through his method of inquiry or through what he also called "the natural light of reason."[123] It is ironic that modern philosophy, modern rationalism, and the principle of systematic doubt were born in this intellectual and religious experience akin to the conversion of St. Augustine.

Just as Augustine's conversion experience was preceded by (1) a study of the Bible and a gradual acceptance of it as a source of truth, (2) a struggle to free his mind from a way of thinking based on eternal substances, and (3) a growing awareness of the idea of God the Creator of all things subject to change and to time, so the turning point in Descartes' life was preceded by (1) a study of mathematics and a gradual acceptance of the principles of mathematics for the discovery of true and useful knowledge, (2) a struggle to free his mind from a way of thinking based on the humanist curriculum and the Scholastic methodology of his teachers, and (3) a growing awareness that the methods of mathematics might be applied to other branches of learning.[124]

From the beginning, Descartes was first and foremost a mathematician, and throughout his life he looked at other studies, disciplines, or sciences primarily from this point of view. Of all his studies at La Flèche,

121. Vrooman, *René Descartes*, 58.

122. Maritain, *Dream of Descartes*, 15. For Maritain, it was even more extraordinary that Descartes also stated, "the genius that heightened in him the enthusiasm which had been burning in him for the past several days, *had forecast these dreams to him before he had retired to his bed*" (emphasis in original). For an English translation of the Baillet's account of this third dream, see Menn, *Descartes and Augustine*, 32–33. Menn's work certainly demonstrates the significance of St. Augustine's views of God and the soul for the development of Descartes' philosophy.

123. Pearl, *Descartes*, 19.

124. Vrooman, *René Descartes*, 54.

he was most pleased with mathematics because of "the certainty and self-evidence of its truths." At that time, however, he did not yet see "its real use" since he thought it was of service "only in the mechanical arts" (CSM 1:114). From the beginning, Descartes was looking for truth, certainty, and useful knowledge, and this he found most of all in mathematics. The problem that gradually took shape in his mind was how to arrive at the certainty of mathematics in other fields such as philosophy.[125]

Descartes was twenty-three years old at the time of this great discovery and turning point in his life, but the *Discourse* was first published in 1637 when he was forty-one or about the age of St. Augustine when he wrote the *Confessions*. Just as the *Confessions* of Augustine contains an autobiographical account of his intellectual and spiritual development focusing on his conversion, so the *Discourse on Method* of Descartes contains a "history of [his] mind" or an "intellectual biography"[126] focusing on the turning point in his life.

Although on the one hand Descartes questioned the usefulness of history for providing examples or rules for conducting one's life, on the other hand he deliberately chose to present his method, his rules, the results of his method and rules, or this work as a whole "only as a history" (*histoire*) or a story (*fable*)[127] "in which, among certain examples worthy of imitation, you will perhaps also find many others that it would be right not to follow; and so I hope it will be useful for some without being harmful to any, and that everyone will be grateful to me for my frankness" (CSM 1:112).

When Descartes applied the first principle or rule of his method to himself—"never to accept anything as true if I did not have evident knowledge of its truth: that is, carefully to avoid precipitate conclusions and preconceptions, and to include nothing more in my judgements than what presented itself to my mind so clearly and so distinctly that I had no occasion to doubt it" (CSM 1:120)—he discovered the most famous principle of modern philosophy: "But immediately I noticed that while I was trying thus to think everything false, it was necessary that I, who was thinking this, was something. And observing this truth, '*I am thinking,*

---

125. Ibid.

126. Rodis-Lewis, "Descartes' Life and the Development of His Philosophy," 39.

127. The French word *fable* is usually translated "story" since Descartes did not want to suggest that this essay was fictitious, and since he wanted it to be read with ease like a story (Vrooman, *René Descartes*, 91).

therefore I exist' was so firm and sure that all the most extravagant suppositions of the skeptics were incapable of shaking it, I decided that I could safely accept it without scruple as the first principle of the philosophy I was seeking" (CSM 1:127). From this first principle he deduced that "this 'I'—that is, the soul by which I am what I am—is entirely distinct from the body and is easier to know than the body, and would not fail to be whatever it is, even if the body did not exist" (CSM 1:127).

For Descartes, intelligent nature was distinct from corporeal nature. However, because many people never considered things higher than corporeal objects, it was difficult for them to know of the existence of God or even of the nature of their own souls. Such people, he observed, "are so accustomed never to think without picturing it—a method of thinking suitable only for material objects—that everything which is not picturable seems to them unintelligible."[128]

It is both interesting and significant, however, that when Descartes chose to present his method and his discoveries to the world, he chose to present them in the form of a "history" composed of six separate parts and pictures of his intellectual development. Like the *Confessions*, the *Discourse* is a work of art and a great piece of literature held together by autobiographical narrative. Just as in the last four books of the *Confessions* Augustine presented the results of his wrestling with the problem of memory, time, the first verse of Genesis, and the whole Genesis account of creation, so in the last four sections of the *Discourse* Descartes presented the results of his wrestling with moral rules derived from his method (part 3), proofs of God and the existence of the human soul (part 4), some problems of physics (part 5), and some prerequisites for further advances in the study of nature (part 6).

In part 6, Descartes explained why he first decided not to publish the first five parts when he completed them, why he later changed his mind, and why he wrote them in French rather than in Latin. One reason for waiting was that he thought his method was most useful for himself, for "no one can conceive something so well, and make it his own, when

---

128. Here I have departed from the translation of Cottingham, Stoothoff, and Murdoch (CSM 1:129) to follow the translation of Laurence J. Lafleur, René Descartes, *Discourse on Method*, 28. The more literal CSM translation is: "The reason for this is that they never raise their minds above things which can be perceived by the senses: they are so used to thinking of things only by imagining them (a way of thinking especially suitable to material things) that whatever is unimaginable seems to them unintelligible."

he learns it from someone else as when he discovers it himself" (CSM 1:146). One reason he changed his mind was the infinity of experiments he needed to undertake that could not be done without the help of others. Since he was writing for people "who combine good sense with application," and "who use only their natural reason in all its purity" and not for people "who give credence only to the writings of the ancients," he chose to write in the language of his country rather than in the language of his teachers (CSM 1:151).

From the time of the *Confessions* of St. Augustine to the *Discourse* of Descartes, scholars within Latin Christendom wrote their scholarly works in Latin for other scholars. Scholastics and humanists, Catholics and Protestants, wrote in Latin for an intellectual elite, especially if the particular work was a scholarly and a controversial one. Martin Luther, for example, wrote his most controversial theological works in Latin. The principle of systematic doubt would have been controversial in almost any age, but Descartes wrote the *Discourse* in an age of religious orthodoxy shortly after Galileo had been forced to recant his scientific views.

Descartes, however, was a prudent man who found in his humanist education a prudent way of dealing with this problem. By presenting his controversial ideas in the form of "a history" containing "examples of conduct" that each reader could take or leave according to his or her interest and ability, they seemed less harmful.

When he presented his ideas in the form of a simple story in the French language, he acquired a larger audience and made a major contribution to French and European literature. This autobiographical essay and this first and model *Geistesgeschichte* of modern philosophical thought, is a masterpiece of French and European literature, for it was the first scientific and philosophical work in France and in Europe that was not written in Latin, and it set the standard for scientific and philosophical writing in the French language.[129] From this time forth in France, to be scientific, philosophical, and really French, one had to be able to think and write in a clear, distinct, and "Cartesian" way.

In the classical world of Greece and Rome and in Latin Christendom to the time of Descartes, scholars had been concerned not with "science" or "the scientific method" but with the different sciences. The highest form of truth in the seventeenth century was still revealed truth, and theology

---

129. Pearl, *Descartes*, 22.

was still "the queen of the sciences." The word *science* stemmed from the Latin word meaning, "to know," and it was not restricted to any particular branch of learning.

Since the seventeenth century, however, the word *science* has often been restricted to the branches of learning and to the scheme of thought developed by Descartes and other great scholars in the West during the seventeenth century. "Modern science" is based on mathematics, and Descartes was one of the great mathematicians of the seventeenth century.[130] He derived his method from the study of mathematics, he used his method to make great discoveries in the field of mathematics, and he believed that mathematics and mathematical reasoning were the basis of "science" and the scientific method.

During the seventeenth century, Descartes and other mathematicians produced what Alfred North Whitehead has called "a scheme of thought framed by mathematicians, for the use of mathematicians."[131] As Whitehead also pointed out in his study called *Science and the Modern World* (1925), "the great characteristics of the mathematical mind is its capacity for dealing with abstractions."[132] This scheme of thought that culminated in the work of Isaac Newton was mathematical, abstract, and centered on the discovery of general rules or laws for understanding the world of nature and matter. Increasingly since the time of Descartes and Newton, the word *science* (especially in the English-speaking world) was used for this scheme of thought, and mathematics, physics, and astronomy became the model "sciences."

The *Discourse* of Descartes was an epoch-making event for the form of inquiry called philosophy, for many philosophers regard it as the beginning of "modern" philosophy.[133] Since the time of Descartes, Western

---

130. In his introduction to René Descartes's *"Discourse on Method" and "Meditations,"* translator Laurence J. Lafleur claimed that Descartes was "the father of modern philosophy, of modern mathematics, and of modern physics, optics, meteorology, and science generally" (xvii).

131. Whitehead, *Science and the Modern World*, 55

132. Ibid.

133. John Cottingham, for example, has stated: "Descartes is still rightly called the father of modern philosophy, not in the sense that our present-day belief systems lamely follow the Cartesian model, but in the richer and more interesting sense that, without Descartes' philosophy, the very shape of the problems with which we still wrestle, about knowledge and science, subjectivity and reality, matter and consciousness, would have been profoundly different" (Cottingham, "Introduction," 2–3).

philosophical thought has revolved around the Cartesian formulation of "the subject receiving experience,"[134] or the thinking and self-conscious "I" of Descartes. While the philosophical thought of the classical world took its stand on what Whitehead called "the drama of the Universe," modern philosophical thought stands on what he called "the inward drama of the Soul."[135]

Increasingly since the time of Descartes, "science" and philosophy have gone separate ways. While "natural philosophers" or "scientists" have been concerned with the world of matter, philosophers have been concerned about the world of mind. Thus in contrast to the "objective" attitude and worldview of classical and of traditional Christian philosophy, modern philosophical thought since Descartes "is tinged with subjectivism."[136]

The *Discourse* of Descartes was an epoch-making event for the form of inquiry called philosophy also because it marks the beginning of the philosophical tradition called rationalism, a tradition that is based on the idea of "natural reason" as the source of truth. Rationalists believe in the autonomy of thought, for they believe in the power of thought to discover truth by its own strength without support from "supernatural" revelation and without appeal to sense perception. Thus rationalists begin with the human mind and with a faith in natural reason or reason alone to discover truth.

Although Descartes can be seen as the central figure for the development of modern rationalism, his rationalism was much more tempered than the rationalism of the eighteenth-century *philosophes*. First of all, Descartes did not rule out divine inspiration, for he believed that his third dream was a divine confirmation of his decision to reform his own ideas and to rebuild them on foundations that were wholly his own.

Second, in the *Discourse* Descartes went out of his way to show the limits of his rationalism and to limit the first principle of his method. He recognized that people were much more influenced by custom and example than by any certain knowledge. He had no faith in the testimony of the majority since "a majority vote is worthless as a proof of truths that are at all difficult to discover," and since it is "much more likely that a

---

134. Whitehead, *Science and the Modern World*, 140.
135. Ibid., 141.
136. Ibid., 140.

single man will have discovered it than a group of people" (CSM 1:119). The world was composed of people who should not attempt to follow his example of abandoning all one's preconceived notions and starting afresh, Descartes insisted, and they were advised not to try.

Third, he went out of his way to point out that a private individual should seek neither to reform a nation by changing all its customs and destroying it to construct it anew, nor to reform the body of knowledge or the system of education. Public institutions, he argued,

> are too difficult to raise up once overthrown, or even to hold up once they begin to totter, and their fall cannot but be a hard one. Moreover, any imperfections they may possess—and their very diversity suffices to ensure that many do possess them—have doubtless been much smoothed over by custom; and custom has even prevented or imperceptibly corrected many imperfections that prudence could not so well provide against. Finally, it is almost always easier to put up with their imperfections than to change them, just as it is much better to follow the main roads that wind through mountains, which have gradually become smooth and convenient through frequent use, than to try to take a more direct route by clambering over rocks and descending to the foot of precipices.

"That is why," Descartes continued, "I cannot by any means approve of those meddlesome and restless characters who, called neither by birth nor by fortune to management of public affairs, are yet forever thinking up some new reform" (CSM 1:118).

Here Descartes sounds more like Edmund Burke than a French philosophe or a member of the National Assembly in 1789. Jesuit education at La Flèche was designed to produce faithful members of the Catholic Church and loyal subjects of the French crown, and in the case of Descartes they were successful.[137] He was an orthodox Catholic in an age of religious orthodoxy, a devoted monarchist in an age of emerging absolutism, and an admirer of the nobility when the nobles were the most powerful estate in a society based on privileged estates.

After 1650, however, "the shared core of faith, tradition, and authority" on which Western civilization was based, "was questioned in light of philosophical reason and frequently challenged or replaced by startling different concepts generated by the New Philosophy and what may still be

---

137. Vrooman, *René Descartes*, 42.

usefully termed the Scientific Revolution."[138] By the end of the seventeenth century, "the Cartesian Revolution" and "Cartesianism" had found its way into the schools of France and into the curriculum of the Sorbonne. As John Hermann Randall Jr. points out, by 1700 its practical spirit, its emphasis on method and reasoning, its aim to cultivate judgment and "to use the sciences as an instrument to perfect reason itself, it played a dominant role in fostering that passionate worship of 'reason' which was for all good Frenchmen the chief legacy of Descartes' labors."[139]

According to Randall, "The Age of Louis XIV saw the triumph of this reason in every phase of life." For Randall, the view "That there is a Divine Reason, single, universal, equal, identical for all, accessible to whomever will take the trouble to follow the right method and seek in order the clear idea it embodies, became the unifying creed of the Augustan age."[140]

UNIVERSAL HISTORY IN THE WEST FROM USSHER TO VOLTAIRE

Although Descartes called the *Discourse on Method* a history, although it was a brilliant, effective, and prudent use of the idea of history as a form of rhetoric and of teaching by example, and although many Western historians since that time have learned through experience the usefulness of the four principles of his method for doing history, it certainly was not a typical history of this age. Fortunately, Peter Hanns Reill has painted a good picture of a typical history for the century when the traditional Christian way of viewing and writing history reached its high point.

If a German scholar of the mid-seventeenth century had "been asked to compose a history of his own state," Reill suggests, "he probably would have begun his narration with the Creation, described the expulsion of Adam and Eve from Eden, recounted the stories of the Flood and the Diaspora, the history of the Chosen People, and the birth and

---

138. Israel, *Radical Enlightenment*, 3–4.

139. Randall, *From the Middle Ages*, 398.

140. Ibid., 398–99. For a succinct analysis of the significance of Descartes's *Discourse on Method* as a new method of thinking and for the rise of biblical criticism in the seventeenth century, see Scholder, *Birth of Modern Critical Theology*, 110–14. See also Scholder's discussion of the significance of the work of Jean Bodin for this subject in the chapter called "The Credibility of the Biblical Picture of the World: II. The Problem of World History," 65–87.

death of Christ." Next "he would have discussed the history of the Roman Empire or the Fourth Monarchy and then shown how his state had been founded either by a direct heir of Noah, or, if he were classically minded, by a survivor of Troy." Only then the author would chronicle the necessary battles and the changes of rule; and this "elaborate undertaking would be cramped into the confines of traditional Christian chronology, which dated the beginning of the world about four thousand years before Christ."[141]

Since even the histories of particular states were placed within the framework of universal history beginning with "the Creation," the historians of this age were very concerned about the problem of establishing a reliable biblical chronology.

One of the least understood aspects of Western historical thought, at least by many teachers and students in the United States, is the development of the modern system of dating events both forward and backward from the birth of Christ. As Adalbert Klempt pointed out, "Neither the Christians of the first centuries nor of the Middle Ages ever considered the *Christum Datum* as the center of world history." Without exception, therefore, their universal chronicles were based mainly on the conception "since the creation of the world." The expression "*ab incarnatione Domini*" was used only in a supplemental way to signify the last age of the world and therewith to provide an escatalogical orientation and to signify the second coming of Christ.[142]

The modern idea, which seems so simple and obvious today, that a way of dating events since the birth of Christ should necessarily require a way of dating events backward from the birth of Christ, was completely lacking before the last years of the fifteenth century and was commonly accepted during the eighteenth century, first in England and France and later in Germany.[143] The system of dating events backward from the birth of Christ developed out of (1) the gradual loosening of what Klempt called "the theological-eschatological interpretation of the universal-historical nexus," and (2) the need to find a fixed point unassailable to "profane-historical criticism."[144]

---

141. Reill, *German Enlightenment and the Rise of Historicism*, 75.
142. Klempt, *Die Säkularisierung der universalhistorischen Auffassung*, 82.
143. Ibid., 88.
144. Ibid., 82–83.

Historians who wrote sacred history and those who wrote profane history needed a fixed point because it was impossible for them to agree on a date for the creation of the world. Since the figures for calculating such a date were different in the various Hebrew and Greek manuscripts, it was not possible for Christian scholars to agree on one fixed year for "the Creation." Thus in the second half of the seventeenth century, scholars counted more than fifty different dates for the creation of the world. At the beginning of the eighteenth century, one scholar counted two hundred different ways of dating the creation. The highest figure for the number of years from the creation to the birth of Christ was 6,894 years and the lowest figure was 3,488.[145]

In the year 1658, a very influential history and chronology by James Ussher (1581–1656), archbishop of the Anglican Church in Ireland, was published in English[146] under a long but interesting title: *The Annals of the World. Deduced from the Origin of Time, and continued to the beginning of the Emperour Vespacians Reign, and the totall Destruction and Abolition of the Temple and Commonwealth of the Jews. Containing the Historie of the Old and New Testament, with that of the Macchabees. Also all the most Memorable Affairs of Asia and Egypt, And The Rise of the Roman Caesars, under C. Julius, and Octavianos. Collected from all History, as well Sacred, as Prophane, and Methodologically digested.*

Through a knowledge "not onely of Sacred and exotick History, but of Astronomical Calculation, and the old Hebrew Kalendar," Ussher judged that it was "indeed difficult but not impossible . . . to atain, not onely the number of years, but even, of dayes from the Creation of the World." More than that, Ussher inclined "to this opinion that from the evening ushering in the first day of the World, to that midnight which began the first day of the world, to that midnight which began the first day of the Christian aera, there were 4003 years, seventy days, and six temporarie howers; and that the true Nativity of our Savior was full four years before the beginning of the vulgar Christian aera, as is demonstrated by Herod's death."[147] Although many scholars after Ussher chose not to emphasize

---

145. Ibid., 85.

146. The Latin version of this work, *Annales Veteris Testamenti*, was first published in London in 1650, or eight years before the English translation.

147. This quotation is taken from the third page of Ussher's introductory "Epistle to the Reader." In the body of this work, Ussher discussed "The First Age of the World" to "The Seventh Age of the World," which began with the birth of Christ and of what Ussher

his calculation that the Creation occurred on a Saturday evening and the 22nd of October, for the next two centuries many Christians did accept the 4004th year before the birth of Christ as the first year of the world and followed his biblical chronology to the time of Christ.

According to the famous *Discourse on Universal History* published in 1681 by Bishop Jacques Bénigne Bossuet (1627–1704), the creation took place in the year one of the world and the year 4004 BCE, the flood in the year 1656 of the world and the year 2348 BCE, and the confusion of tongues at the Tower of Babel in the year 1757 of the world and 2247 BCE.[148]

Unlike many universal histories since the chronicle of Orosius, however, the *Discourse* of Bossuet was not a dry chronicle. It was a rather philosophical and beautifully written outline of universal history from a traditional Christian perspective. Like St. Augustine, bishop Bossuet was a highly trained and skilled orator and rhetorician, an excellent writer, a diligent bishop, and a passionate defender of the Catholic Church and the Christian faith. But his *Discourse* was published just at the time when this traditional way of viewing and writing history came under question and under attack.

As Paul Hazard convincingly demonstrates, the years from 1680 to 1715 were the time when the ideas and attitudes usually associated with the Enlightenment clearly emerged. This is the time when "Reason" became critical and aggressive, miracles came under attack, heresy came out into the open, "Moderns" rose up to battle with the "Ancients," and bishop Bossuet's *Discourse on Universal History* was attacked for its questionable chronology, and because it did not include China.[149]

At the present time, the Enlightenment is commonly identified as the hundred-year span from the Glorious Revolution in 1688 to the

---

called "our Christian epoch." While Ussher is often cited for his attempt to establish such a precise time for the creation, he is seldom cited for his calculation that the birth of Christ probably occurred in the year 4 BCE.

148. Bossuet, *Discourse on Universal History*, 9–11. In the first paragraph of this work, Bossuet refers to Moses as "the first historian, the most sublime philosopher, and the wisest of legislators" (9).

149. Hazard, *European Mind, 1680–1715*.

French Revolution in 1789,[150] from 1680 to 1789,[151] or roughly from the 1680s to the 1790s.[152] For most historians, the Enlightenment is characterized by a new faith in reason, science, progress, natural law, and the human as a rational animal. The years 1680 or 1688 are convenient and useful dates to mark the beginning of the Enlightenment, for this is the time of Isaac Newton (1642–1727) and the culmination of the scientific revolution of the seventeenth century, for the *Principia* appeared in the years 1686 and 1687. It is the time of John Locke (1632–1704), for his *Two Treatises on Government* appeared in 1689, his *Essay Concerning Human Understanding* in 1690, and his *Reasonableness of Christianity as delivered in Scriptures* in 1695.

It is also the time when a German pedagogue named Christian Keller, but better known as Cellarius, first divided history into those familiar and now almost-sacred periods—especially in the United States—called ancient, medieval, and modern history.[153] From this time, Italian history from the fourteenth century to the sixteenth century was no longer interpreted just as a revival of learning but as the beginning of an age of social progress.[154] It is also the time that the concept "Europe" began to replace the concept "Christendom."[155] Around the end of the seventeenth century, European scholars began to replace the traditional Christian view of time and space with new views and concepts.[156] This, however, was not an

---

150. Gay, *Rise of Modern Paganism*, 17. For Gay, "The Enlightenment may be summed up in two words: criticism and power" (*Rise of Modern Paganism*, xi.)

151. See the useful "Chronological Table for the German Enlightenment in the Context of Europe (1680–1789)" in Raabe and Schmidt-Biggemann, *Enlightenment in Germany*, 239–56. In his study *The Radical Enlightenment*, Jonathan I. Israel uses the term "Early Enlightenment" for the years from 1680 to 1750; but most of all he emphasizes how beginning in 1650, a "shared core of faith, tradition, and authority" was questioned everywhere in light of philosophical reason (Israel, *Radical Enlightenment*, 3), how this period of transition from 1650 to 1680 was a "Crisis of the European Mind" that "heralded the onset of the Enlightenment proper in the closing years of the century" (ibid., 14), and how the period 1680–1750 was "the more dramatic and decisive period of rethinking when the mental world of the west was revolutionized along rational and secular lines" (ibid., 20).

152. Kraminick, "Introduction," in *Portable Enlightenment Reader*, x.

153. See Ferguson, *Renaissance in Historical Thought*, 75–77.

154. Gerhard, "Periodization in European History," 902.

155. Ibid.

156. Ibid.

A Typology of Classical and Christian Historiography   49

easy task, and throughout the eighteenth century historians continued to struggle with the problem of universal history.

The most obvious limitation of the Christian universal histories through the *Discourse* of Bossuet was that although they claimed to be universal in regard to time, since they began with "the Creation," they were not universal in regard to space. During the eighteenth century, however, a large number of English scholars attempted to write a universal history that was universal both in time and space.

This history, which was the largest and most universal history to this time, was called *An Universal History from the Earliest Account of Time to the Present: Compiled from Original Authors; and Illustrated with Maps, Cuts, Notes, Chronological, and Other Tables* (1736–1765).[157] It was also a great departure from "the classical universal history from the time of its reformulation during the Reformation and Counter Reformation," for unlike the texts of Melanchthon, Johannes Sleidan, and Orazio Torsellinis, which were written primarily as instruments of information, *An Universal History* was a work of scholarly research[158] that combined critical research with history "as a narrative of historical connections."[159] In addition, it represented history as a whole in a new sense, for it marked a departure from traditional *heilgeschichtlichen* interpretations such as the four monarchies. As Helmut Zedelmaier also points out, this work (which was initiated in England in the year 1730) developed into an European research project;[160] for in addition to a German translation (the first seven volumes directed by Siegmund Jacob Baumgarten between 1744 and 1758 and the next twenty-three volumes by his student Johann Salomo Semler through the year 1766), there were also Dutch, French, and Italian translations.[161]

One of the most interesting aspects of this gigantic work, however, is the way these English scholars sought to combine sacred and profane history. Instead of accepting the biblical chronology of James Ussher,

---

157. Cited hereafter as *An Universal History*.
158. Zedelmaier, *Der Anfang der Geschichte*, 133.
159. Ibid., 134.
160. Ibid.
161. Ibid., 144, 177. As Zedelmaier also emphasizes, *An Universal History* and *Die Allgemeine Welthistorie* (the German title) made it possible for scholars to see the connections of a general history within which particular histories could orient themselves. This also meant that the connection between the whole and the part could be seen as a moving relationship that would require future revisions (ibid., 145).

which had been adopted in the margins of the reference edition of the "Authorized" or the King James version of the Bible beginning in 1701,[162] the authors of this work went to great pains in the first volume to work out a new biblical chronology wherein the creation took place in the year 4305 BCE and the flood in the year 1307 of the world, or the year 1999 before Christ. Just as in *The City of God* St. Augustine first attempted to discuss the history of the people of God from the creation before he attempted to discuss the history of the earthly city, so also the editors of this work first provided a unified account of "sacred" history beginning with the creation and then separate and "profane" accounts of the different parts of the world in "ancient" and "modern" times.

The opening lines of this fascinating work are especially interesting for understanding the whole development of the form of inquiry called history, for here one can clearly see how the Christian kind of universal history had fused with the classical-humanist tradition.

> HISTORY is, without all doubt, the most instructive and useful, as well as entertaining part of Literature; more especially, when it is not confined within the narrow Bounds of any particular Time or Place, but extends to the Transactions of all Times and Nations. Works of this Nature carry our knowledge, as *Tully* [Cicero] observes, beyond the vast and devouring Space of numberless Years, triumph over Time, and make us, though living at an immense Distance, in a manner Eye-witnesses to all the Events and Revolutions, which have occasioned astonishing Changes in the World. By these Records it is that we live, as it were, in the very Time when the World was created; we behold how it was governed in its infancy, how over-flowed and destroyed in a Deluge of Water, and again repeopled; how Kings and Kingdoms have risen, flourished, and declined, and by what Steps they brought upon themselves their final Ruin and Destruction. From these and other like Events occuring in History, every judicious Reader may form prudent and unerring Rules for the Conduct of his Life, both in a private and publick Capacity. (1:v)

It is significant that even this encyclopedic work began with the assumptions that history was the most instructive, useful, and entertaining part of literature and that through the study of history one could learn how to live a prudent and successful life. Like Bishop Bossuet, these

---

162. Muir, *Our Grand Old Bible*, 197.

Christians, rhetoricians, and humanists wanted to "instruct agreeably."[163] Humanist and Enlightenment historiography, like the classical historiography of Greece and Rome, was both pragmatic and didactic.

The eighteenth century marks the high point of history as literature written by prominent men of letters. While most eighteenth-century historians probably considered themselves humanists *and* Christians, the most famous ones probably did not.

David Hume (1711–1776), the author of a five-volume *History of England* published between 1754 and 1762, also wrote *An Enquiry Concerning Human Understanding* wherein he carefully asserted: "So that, upon the whole, we may conclude, that the *Christian Religion* not only was at first attended with miracles, but even at this day cannot be believed by any reasonable person without one."[164]

Edward Gibbon (1737–1794), author of the famous epic history called *Decline and Fall of the Roman Empire*, indicated his attitude toward "the middle ages" when he declared, "I have described the triumph of barbarism and religion."[165] Voltaire (1694–1788), the most prominent man of letters and most influential historian of them all, provided the battle cry for a whole host of anticlericals and "zealous pagans" with his cry, "*écrasez l'infâme*," or "crush the infamous one."[166]

While the first volume of the English *Universal History* illustrates how the classical type of historiography had fused with the traditional Christian type, Voltaire's *Essay on the Manners, Customs and Spirit of the Nations*—which reached its final form in the year 1769—exemplifies the conflict between these two traditions during the eighteenth century. According to Friedrich Meinecke, no Enlightenment historian had a greater impact within the whole development of historical thought.[167] For

---

163. See Ranum, editor's introduction to Bossuet's *Discourse on Universal History*, xxiv.

164. This book was first published in the year 1748 under the title *Philosophical Essays Concerning Human Understanding*. This quotation is from the famous chapter on miracles, sect. 10, pt. 2, par. 101. See also Gay, *Rise of Modern Paganism*, 404–19.

165. Cited in *Encyclopaedia Britannica*, 1954 edition, s.v. "Gibbon, Edward," which was written by J. B. Bury.

166. This is a basic theme of Peter Gay's two-volume work called *The Enlightenment: An Interpretation*. It was not until the 1760s, however, that Voltaire "mounted his great campaign to *écraser l'infâme*" (Gay, *Rise of Modern Paganism*, 385).

167. Meinecke, *Historism: The Rise of a New Historical Outlook*, 54 (Meinecke, *Die Entstehung des Historismus*, 73). Hereafter the translated volume is abbreviated as

Meinecke, the decisive motive behind all of Voltaire's historical work "was to put the whole of the world's history at the service of the Enlightenment on behalf of the human race, and to show how the Enlightenment had its roots in history."[168] Voltaire's attempt "to base a new universal cultural ideal on a fresh interpretation of universal history," Meinecke also believed, "marked the beginning of an altogether new era of the Western mind [*Geist*]."[169]

As Michael Maurer more recently suggested, Voltaire's significance can be summarized through six points: (1) the assumption from the popular philosophy of the ancient world of a fundamental constancy of human nature in all times and places; (2) the significance of history as a war against fanaticism, superstition, and the Catholic Church, which increasingly he saw as the chief enemies of the modern world of rational and enlightened human beings; (3) the goal of his historical research and narration as choosing "useful truths"; (4) history as having meaning as cultural development; (5) the question of and the problem of progress; and (6) the question of the goal of history.[170] After this passionately anticlerical historian began his *Essay* with China and then the world since Charlemagne rather than with an account of sacred and profane history since the creation, other scholars also ceased beginning their universal or world histories with the biblical account of creation and dating events from the year one.

This, however, was a gradual process. The fact that the editors of the sixty-volume second edition of *An Universal History* (1779–1784) gave up their earlier biblical chronology in order to return to the chronology of Ussher, certainly testifies to the popularity of his chronology and to the

---

"*Historism*," and the original work (1936)—which was Meinecke's third large intellectual history—is abbreviated as *Historismus*. It is important for the reader to know, however, (1) that the usual translation of the word *Historismus* is "historicism," and (2) that this is the translation that I use throughout this work except when I am referring to this English translation or quoting a passage from it.

168. Meinecke, *Historism*, 62 (*Historismus*, 82).

169. Ibid., 62 (*Historismus*, 83). Although not all scholars would agree with Meinecke's assessment of the significance of Voltaire for the idea of history in the eighteenth century, it is significant that Helmut Zedelmaier states that Meinecke's discussion of Voltaire in *Die Entstehung des Historismus* "stamped and in general formed the modern German view of Voltaire's great influence on Enlightenment historiography and early philosophy of history" (Zedelmaier, *Der Anfang der Geschichte*, 270).

170. Maurer, "Die Geschichtsphilosophie des jungen Herder," 142–45.

strength of the traditional Christian way of writing history. Ussher's dates survived the Enlightenment, for at the time of the three-hundred-year anniversary of this "Grand Old Bible" in the year 1911, some of his dates were still in the margins.[171] While some American evangelicals abandoned Ussher's year for the creation as early as the 1860s, "For some believers it remained a landmark until the late twentieth century."[172]

By the end of the eighteenth century, however, many historians had given up trying to present an account of the creation or the flood,[173] for they had no eyewitnesses or contemporary sources. They had given up trying to say anything about the end of time, because historians deal with the past and present, with what really happened and with how things came to be. What remained from the traditional Christian way of writing universal history was (1) a universal system of dating events before and after the birth of Christ, and (2) the assumption that any particular historical inquiry could be fit into a larger meaningful story called universal or world history. Thus this Christian kind of history gradually became secularized during the Enlightenment.

The eighteenth century can be seen as the second main age of transition within Western historiography. First of all, it can be seen as the late stage of the Christian period, for it marks the gradual end of a distinctly and mainly Christian type of Western historiography. By the end of the eighteenth century, the biblical account of "the beginning of history" had been "marginalized," for now historians in Germany could and did refer to the early history of humankind as "prehistory" (*Vorgeschichte*).[174]

---

171. Muir, *Our Grand Old Bible*, 197. Here Muir stated (1) that the marginal dates in the *Authorized Version* were taken from Ussher's *Annales veteris et novi Testamenti*, (2) that they were of varying value, (3) that some of them had not been materially amended since they first appeared in the 1701 edition, and (4) that "[t]here seems to be no reason now [1911] why the Authorized Version should be burdened, and even prejudiced, by what is no real part of it as such."

172. Numbers, "'The Most Important Biblical Discovery of Our Time,'" 257.

173. One of the many values of Zedelmaier's *Der Anfang der Geschichte* is its emphasis on the flood as a great natural and cultural turning point for Antoine Yves Goguet and other Enlightenment scholars just before the 1760s.

174. This is the story that Helmut Zedelmaier tells in *Der Anfang der Geschichte*, for the title of the introduction is "Die Bibel als Buch der Geschichte," and the title of the conclusion is "Das Buch der Geschichte als 'zweites' Bibel." For Zedelmaier's use of the term "marginalization," see especially pages 2, 9, 165–73, and 182–83. For the reducing of early history to prehistory, see the section called "Reduzierung der Frühgeschichte zur Vorgeschichte: August Ludwig Schlözer," 177–83, and especially the reference to Schlözer on page 298.

Second, it can be seen as an age of transition because it marks the high point of the classical type of historiography within this Christian epoch, for this was the time when the pre-Christian way of writing history gradually won out over the Christian type. Eighteenth-century historiography can also be called epic, humanistic, didactic, and—above all—rational. The great emphasis on reason with the new emphasis on progress, however, was connected with a strong tendency toward substantialism, the great weakness of classical historiography.

Third, the eighteenth century was an age of transition because during the last four decades of this century and the first decade of the nineteenth century, a new historical consciousness and a distinctly modern type of Western historiography gradually arose. Since the rise of these significant aspects of modern Western thought, education, and culture took place first in Protestant Germany and within a religious tradition that had been shaped especially by Martin Luther and Philip Melanchthon, an inquiry focusing on them and a Lutheran way of viewing life could cast additional light on the rise of history during that great intellectual and cultural revolution that took place in Germany in the years from 1760 to 1810.

two

Martin Luther and the Foundations of a Lutheran Ethos

The appeal to national character is generally a mere confession of ignorance, and in this case is untenable . . . It was the power of religious influence, not alone, but more than anything else, which created the differences of which we are conscious today.

—Max Weber[1]

"You have a different spirit," said Luther to Zwingli after the vain attempt to come to an agreement with Zwingli on the Eucharist. This difference in spirit, however, rested on a stronger rational ingredient, which distinguished the Reformed doctrine from the Lutheran as well as from the Catholic. The Reformed doctrine—"Calvinism," as it is generally called for short—tried to clear away everything magical and mythical from the religious mysteries.

—Otto Hintze[2]

THE PROBLEM

In his brilliant and provocative study *The Protestant Ethic and the Spirit of Capitalism*, published in the years 1904 and 1905, Max Weber made the striking claim that it was "the power of religious influence, not alone, but more than anything else," that created the national differences of which we are conscious today. At the present time, however, the religious origins of these national differences are not easily discernible since for centuries they have been transformed by what Weber called a process of "rationalization," and *Entzauberung*.

---

1. Weber, *Protestant Ethic*, 88–89.
2. Hintze, "Calvinism and Raison d'Etat in Seventeenth-Century Brandenburg," 98. See also the German original: Hintze, "Kalvinismus und Staatsräson in Brandenburg zu Beginn des 17. Jahrhundert," 261.

For Weber, the phrase *Entzauberung der Welt*, or the "disenchantment of the world," suggested a process of taking the magic out of life.[3] Since he believed (1) that civilizations were based on religions, (2) that originally religion was based on magic, and (3) that the basic tendency of Western civilization was the increasing tendency to rationalize all aspects of life, rationalization and disenchantment were two sides of the same coin, or the same basic tendency. Since the Reformation of the sixteenth century, however, this two-sided process has taken place in different ways within different religious traditions.

In *The Protestant Ethic and the Spirit of Capitalism*, Weber explored the relationship between Calvinism and modern capitalism. Here he did not claim that the Calvinist ethic was the cause of modern capitalism, but he did show that some Calvinist beliefs were conducive to the development of a capitalist spirit and to the rise of modern capitalism as "an historical individual" (*individuum*) or as "a complex of elements associated with historical reality which we unite into a conceptual whole from the standpoint of their cultural significance."[4]

Those religious beliefs conducive to the development of this aspect of modern life, he called rational, and those religious beliefs that were not conducive to the development of this particular aspect of modern life, he called traditional. In order to show how a particular religious ethic was instrumental for the development of modern capitalism, however, he had to create an "ideal type" (his and Otto Hintze's basic term for what Western scholars today call a model) not only of a Calvinist sense of calling but also of a Catholic and a Lutheran sense of calling as well.

For Weber, Calvinism was more rational than Catholicism and Lutheranism for the development of modern capitalism partly because it eliminated all "magical" means to salvation. For the Calvinist, he argued, the sacraments were not a means to the attainment of grace.[5] This complete elimination of salvation through the Church—which Weber believed was by no means developed to its final conclusions in Lutheranism— "was what formed the absolutely decisive difference from Catholicism." According to Weber, "That great historic process in the development of religions, the elimination of magic from the world, which had begun with

---

3. Weber, *Protestant Ethic*, 105, 221–22 n. 19.
4. Ibid., 47.
5. Ibid., 104.

the old Hebrew prophets and, in conjunction with Hellenistic scientific thought, had repudiated all magical means to salvation as superstition and sin, came here to its logical conclusion."[6]

Through this "ideal-type" or "model-building" methodology, which Weber created at this time, he was able to suggest how the rationalizing of a particular religious tradition influenced the development of one of the main characteristics of the modern Western world.

Although many scholars have participated in the debate concerning religion and the rise of capitalism that began with this book,[7] few historians, philosophers, and theologians have attempted to examine other aspects of Western thought in a similar way.[8] For example, it should be possible for scholars to show how the three great philosophical traditions of Western thought since the seventeenth century—French rationalism, English empiricism, and German idealism—are based not only on the creative minds of Descartes, Locke, and Leibniz but also on the different religious traditions in which these men were raised.

More specifically, it should be possible to show how a modern historical consciousness (commonly called historicism) and a distinctly modern type of Western historiography arose first in Protestant Germany, and to show some connections between the great religious revolution of the sixteenth century and the great intellectual and spiritual revolution that took place in Germany at the end of the eighteenth century. Is it possible that the Lutheran ethos was traditional in regard to the development of modern capitalism and at the same time rational in regard to the rise of history, both as a distinctly modern kind of historical consciousness and as a professionalized science or discipline? This is one aspect of the problem.

In his "Preliminary Remarks" to *Die Entstehung des Historismus* (1936), Friedrich Meinecke claimed that the rise of historicism was "one of the greatest intellectual [*geistige*] revolutions that has ever taken place

---

6. Ibid., 104–5.

7. See especially the collection of essays edited by Hartmut Lehmann and Guenther Roth, *Weber's "Protestant Ethic": Origins, Evidence, Contexts*.

8. Thomas Nipperdey is one historian who has attempted to use Max Weber's basic insight in a positive way and to show how Luther's religious ideas influenced the modern world, especially the whole development of modern German culture. See especially his thoughtful and very inclusive essay called "Luther und die modernen Welt," 31–43.

in Western thought."⁹ Historicism, he said, deserved to be ranked alongside the Reformation as the second great achievement of the German *Geist*,¹⁰ a word that can be translated either "spirit" or "mind."

Like Ernst Troeltsch and Otto Hintze, Meinecke associated the term *historicism* with the concepts of individuality and development (*Entwicklung*); but like his two friends, he defined this term in his own way. For Meinecke, historicism was (1) "nothing else than the application of the new life-governing principles achieved by the great German movement extending from Leibniz to the death of Goethe—to the historical world"; (2) "more than just a method of the human studies, for life and the world appeared differently when one had become accustomed to viewing things in this new way"; (3) "the substituting of a process of individualizing observation for a generalizing view of human forces in history"; and (4) based on a feeling for the individual or a sense of individuality that it created.¹¹ For Meinecke, Johann Gottfried Herder (1744–1803) was the key figure for the rise of this new historical outlook, an outlook that culminated in the work of Leopold von Ranke (1795–1886).

It is significant that in this very influential intellectual history Meinecke did not attempt to show in any detail the significance of Martin Luther for what he called the second great achievement of "the German *Geist*," and that he did not mention or discuss either the Gospel of John or the word *logos*. The main tradition on which he did focus was the significance of Neoplatonism for the rise of historicism, but were the ideas that he traced in this history also based on a distinctly Lutheran way of viewing life? This is a second aspect of the problem.

In the summer of the year 1982, a study group representing the colleges of the American Lutheran Church asked Joseph Sittler (1904–1987) the following question. "Dr. Sittler," they asked. "How is Lutheran higher education distinctive?"

First of all, Sittler suggested that teachers should train minds to see particulars and "percepts" before they teach concepts. Second, he suggested that Lutheran distinctiveness was not really a matter of doctrine. Rather, he said, it was "an ethos, an ethos that has kept alive the dialectic of the mystery of life."

9. Meinecke, *Historism*, lv.

10. Meinecke, *Historismus*, 2. Cf. *Historism*, lv.

11. Meinecke, *Historism*, lv. For Troeltsch's definition of historicism, see chapter 5, part 3, below.

Is there a Lutheran "ethos" or a disposition, character, attitude, spirit, or set of values that Lutherans share as a specific people, culture, or group that distinguishes them from other groups?[12] If so, can this ethos be seen and portrayed as a particular way of thinking and as a way of viewing life? If so, how have Lutherans maintained this ethos through the centuries? This is the third main aspect of the problem behind this chapter.

LUTHER'S TWO BASIC WAYS OF THINKING AND VIEWING LIFE

From the sixteenth century through the first half of the twentieth century, but increasingly less so since that time, one could usually distinguish a Lutheran from a non-Lutheran if he or she understood what you were talking about if you mentioned (1) that a Christian is both sinner and justified "at the same time," (2) the connected prepositions *in*, *with*, and *under*, (3) the Small Catechism, and (4) the three articles of the Creed. A knowledge of these four notions is helpful not only for understanding the development of Lutheranism but also for the development of German education, history, literature, philosophy, and theology since the sixteenth century.

To see and to understand a distinctively Lutheran ethos and a distinctively Lutheran way of viewing life, one must begin with the life, the religious experiences, and the writings of Martin Luther. "Not since Augustine," Jaroslav Pelikan rightly claimed, "had the spiritual odyssey of one man and the spiritual exigency of Western Christendom coincided as they did now."[13]

It is common knowledge that Luther's life and work were shaped by three religious experiences: (1) the vow he took in 1505 to become a monk when he was struck to the ground by a lightning bolt, (2) the awesome experience of his first Mass in 1507 when be became a priest, and, most of all, (3) the revolutionary experience associated with the idea

---

12. This question contains my understanding of the word *ethos*. It has no direct connection with the way the term is used in Elert, *Christian Ethos*, for here the word *ethos* is associated primarily with ethical conduct (see especially page 334). In Elert's larger (two-volume) and more historical work called *Morphologie des Luthertum*, however, the word *ethos* is used in a broader way. See volume 1 of Elert's *The Structure of Lutheranism*, called *The Theology and Philosophy of Lutheranism*. My use of the term *ethos*, however, was derived from a verbal statement of Joseph Sittler, and most of this essay was completed before I became familiar with Elert's work.

13. Pelikan, *Reformation of Church and Dogma*, 127.

called justification by faith, an experience that took place some time after he received his doctorate of theology (October 19, 1512), and after he began lecturing on the books of the Bible at the University of Wittenberg.

At this time Luther was a late-medieval theologian who followed the *via moderna*, or the "modern way," rather than the *via antiqua*, or the "old way." While the representatives of the *via antiqua* were followers of Thomas Aquinas and Duns Scotus, the representatives of the *via moderna* were followers of William of Occam (1300–1349).

Occam is famous in the history of philosophy for his nominalism and for the principle known as Occam's razor. While the representatives of the *via antiqua* held that universal concepts were the expressions of reality itself, since they were the higher reality behind all individuality, nominalists believed that only the individual or the particular was real, and that universals were only names or labels. Because universal concepts were conceived by the mind or based on convention, they possessed no independent reality. Thus for nominalists, universals were "models," which always required verification "by means of the sensually perceivable reality of the particular."[14] Occam's razor suggested that the simplest solution to a problem is usually the best, because it held that "entities must not be multiplied without necessity."[15]

As Heiko Oberman has emphasized in many works, nominalism is one of the most important ideas not only for understanding the Late Middle Ages, Martin Luther, and the advance of both the natural sciences and theology,[16] but also for understanding the whole course of Western intellectual history.[17] This contention certainly can be supported by look-

---

14. Oberman, *Luther: Man between God and the Devil*, 117.

15. "entia non sunt multiplicanda sine necessitate."

16. Oberman, *Luther: Man between God and the Devil*, 117. Here, Oberman asserts: "Nominalism was a major factor in the advance of both the natural sciences and theology. Subordinating speculation to experience freed physics from the confining grip of metaphysical systems that transcended experience. Once experience became experiments, modern science was born, and it was nominalism—not humanism—that paved the way."

17. See Oberman, *Dawn of the Reformation*, 58. Here Oberman states: "Yet whereas humanism shaped the early modern era, it is nominalism which determines the *Geist* and set the tone for the modern era, not withstanding the protest songs of the *via antiqua* surviving in German idealism." For a brief summary of the significance of "Luther's Ockhamist training" not only for Luther but for "mainstream Protestantism," see Ozment, *Age of Reform*, 244.

ing at the work of Max Weber, for he was one of the greatest nominalists of the twentieth century.[18]

Before Luther began his studies at the University of Erfurt (1501), two professors from the arts faculty there had expressed many times the decisive principle of the *via moderna* that "all philosophical speculation about the world must be tested by means of experience and reality-based reason, regardless of what even the most respected authorities might say." At Erfurt, Luther became a nominalist and was exposed to humanist ideas.[19]

Luther's starting point, however, and also his chief problem—both through his theological training and his own religious struggle—was how to satisfy an all-powerful, awesome, and righteous God. In the year 1545, the year before he died, Luther wrote a moving description of the spiritual and intellectual experience that was the real starting point for and the real basis of the Protestant Reformation and of a specifically Lutheran ethos. In this account he told of his strong desire to understand St. Paul and his great difficulty with the phrase, "the righteousness of God."

> At last, by the mercy of God, meditating day and night, I gave heed to the context of the words, namely, "In it the righteousness of God is revealed, as it is written: 'He who through faith is righteous shall live.'" There I began to understand that the righteousness of God is that by which the righteous lives by a gift of God, namely by faith. And this is the meaning: the righteousness of God is revealed by the gospel, namely, the passive righteousness with which merciful God justifies us by faith, as it is written, "He who through faith is righteous shall live." Here I felt that I was altogether born again and had entered paradise itself through open gates. There a totally other face of Scripture showed itself to me.[20]

Whereas he had "once hated the phrase 'the righteousness of God,'" Luther continued, "I began to love and extol it as the sweetest of words, so that this passage in Paul became the very gate of paradise for me."[21] In

---

18. For an early assessment of how Max Weber's ideal types and definitions were entirely "nominalistic," see Hintze, "Max Webers Soziologie," 140.

19. Oberman, *Luther: Man between God and the Devil*, 118.

20. Luther, *Luther's Works*, 34:337. Hereafter the American edition of *Luther's Works* is abbreviated and cited as *LW*. Cf. the translation of this passage by Alister E. McGrath, *Luther's Theology of the Cross*, 96–97.

21. McGrath, *Luther's Theology of the Cross*, 96–97 (McGrath's translation).

the next sentence of this famous statement, Luther added: "Later I read Augustine's *The Spirit and the Letter*, where contrary to hope I found that he, too, interpreted God's righteousness in a similar way, as the righteousness with too, which God clothes us when he justifies us."[22]

Although Luther scholars have not agreed when his "reformation breakthrough" took place, they do agree that the writings of St. Augustine were also of crucial importance for the development of Luther's thought prior to this breakthrough. To use the words of Heiko Oberman, Luther "had to test scholasticism by the standard of St. Augustine and then to find his way from St. Augustine to St. Paul in order to acquire the key to the Scriptures."[23]

As a result of the life-changing experience based on the idea called justification by faith alone, Luther also came to the conclusion that a person could understand a subject only if he or she was familiar with it from experience.[24] In studying the Bible, Luther once said, "You must completely despair of your own diligence and intelligence and rely solely on the infusion of Spirit." As Erich W. Gritsch pointed out after he cited this sentence, "Luther found this kind of approach to Bible study confirmed in the writings of the great church father Augustine rather than in the scholars of the Middle Ages. What Augustine had to say in his work *On the Spirit and the Letter (De spiritu et litera)*, decisively shaped Luther's early struggles with the Bible."[25]

In and through this "evangelical" experience, Luther was convinced that a Christian is at the same time a justified or righteous person and a sinner: *simul justus et peccator*. "No other phrase," Luther scholars agree, "is capable of expressing Luther's theological 'reforming discovery' as clearly and succinctly."[26] From this experience, Luther developed an "at-the-same-time" way of thinking and viewing life, a way that Martin E. Marty has called a "*simul*-vision."[27]

---

22. *LW* 34:337.

23. Oberman, *Luther: Man between God and the Devil*, 158.

24. Schwiebert, *Luther and His Times*, 288.

25. Gritsch, *Martin—God's Court Jester*, 8. For the quotation from Luther that Gritsch cites, see *LW* 48:53–54 and *WA*, Briefwechsel, 1:133.31–34, 37–39.

26. Oberman, *Reformation: Roots and Ramifications*, 61.

27. Marty, "*Simul*\A Lutheran Reclamation Project in the Humanities," 8. In this essay Marty claimed that if his interpretation was correct, "a Lutheran understanding based on the concept of *simul*-vision, will yield to no other in its high claims for human-

For this inquiry it is important to remember that Luther's theology is, as Paul Althaus pointed out in his helpful study, *The Theology of Martin Luther*, "a way of thinking."[28] Second, as Gerhard Ebeling emphasized, the formula *simul justus—simul peccator* "is the fundamental and typical characteristic of Luther's thought."[29] The clue to this, Ebeling suggested, "seems to lie in the observation that Luther's thought always contains an antithesis, tension between strongly opposed but related polarities: theology and philosophy, the letter and the Spirit, the law and the gospel, the double use of the law, person and works, faith and love, the kingdom of Christ and the kingdom of the world, man as a Christian and man in the world, freedom and bondage, God hidden and God revealed—to mention only the most important examples."[30]

Now a way of thinking and a way of perceiving or viewing life can also become a methodological principle and a style of writing. By the year 1520, Luther was a master of the use of paradox, for in the beautiful and powerful essay called "The Freedom of a Christian," he used an "at-the-same-time" way of viewing life to present a picture of what he called "the whole of Christian life in a brief form."[31] For me and for many Lutherans, this magnificent treatise is the best essay in Western literature for teaching a *simul* way of viewing life *and* for teaching paradox.

In this essay Luther explained how "the individual Christian lives in Christ through faith, in his neighbor through love."[32] Before he developed this theme, however, he presented two strong theses that "seem to contradict each other": "A Christian is a perfectly free lord of all, subject to none," and, at the same time, "a perfectly dutiful servant of all, subject to all."[33]

To explain this paradox, Luther first presented his basic "at-the-same-time" way of perceiving the nature of humankind.

---

ism and the humanities" (8).

28. Althaus, *Theology of Martin Luther*, vi.
29. Ebeling, *Luther*, 24.
30. Ibid., 25.
31. Luther, "Freedom of a Christian," in *LW* 31:343.
32. Ibid., 371.
33. Ibid., 344. For Bernhard Lohse, "This twofold thesis is the most successful and congenial statement of Paul's understanding of freedom ever achieved" (*Martin Luther*, 130).

> Man has a two-fold nature, a spiritual and a bodily one. According to the spiritual nature, which men refer to as the soul, he is called a spiritual, inner, or new man. According to the bodily nature, which men refer to as flesh, he is called carnal, outward, or old man ... Because of this diversity of nature Scriptures assert contradictory things concerning the same man, since the two men in the same flesh contradict each other, "for the desires of the flesh are against the Spirit, and the desires of the Spirit are against the flesh," according to Gal. 5[:17].[34]

For Luther, the Word of God and faith ruled in the soul or the inner man. "The inner man, who by faith is created in the image of God, is both joyful and happy because it is his one occupation to serve God joyfully and without the thought of gain, in love that is not constrained."[35] For Luther, "the outer man" should control his own body, serve his neighbor in love, live only for others rather than for himself, and live for all men on earth. "We conclude," Luther said, "that a Christian lives not in himself, but in Christ and in his neighbor. Otherwise he is not a Christian. He lives in Christ through faith, in his neighbor through love."[36]

It is difficult to overemphasize the significance of this essay for the whole development of Lutheran thought and Protestant thought in Germany since the sixteenth century, for both Lutheran thought and much of Protestant thought in Germany—as this study attempts to show—are based on Luther's "at-the-same-time" image of the inner and outer man. While on the one hand Luther constantly emphasized not only that each human being was both "spirit" and "flesh" at the same time, on the other hand he constantly insisted that each person and his or her works had to be viewed as an entirety. Both these views, as Peter Meinhold emphasized, were closely connected with Luther's basic starting place and basic idea.[37]

It is a well-known fact that Luther's main starting point, the idea known as justification through grace by faith alone, and his *simul*-vision were derived mainly from the writings of Paul and mainly from his Epistle

---

34. "Freedom of a Christian," in *LW* 31:344.
35. Ibid., 359.
36. Ibid., 371.
37. Meinhold, *Luther Heute*, 33. In his helpful little book called *Luthers Sprachphilosophie*, Meinhold shows how Luther, with his emphasis on the unity of *Geist* and *Wort*, opened a new epoch in Western philosophy of language (*Sprachphilosophie*).

to the Romans. It is also a well-known fact that Luther had a hierarchy of books within the New Testament, and that he developed what Inge Lønning,[38] Eric W. Gritsch,[39] and others have called "a canon within the canon." What Luther scholars have not agreed on, however, is what book Luther placed first within this hierarchy or canon.

At the beginning of his "Preface to the Epistle of St. Paul to the Romans," Luther claimed that "This epistle is really the chief part of the New Testament, and is truly the purest gospel."[40] In the last paragraph of this preface, Luther stated:

> In this epistle we thus find most abundantly the things that a Christian ought to know, namely, what is law, gospel, sin, punishment, grace, faith, righteousness, Christ, God, good works, love, hope, and the cross; and also how we are to conduct ourselves toward everyone, be he righteous or sinner, strong or weak, friend or foe—and even toward our own selves. Moreover this is all ably supported with Scripture and proved by St. Paul's own example and that of the prophets, so that one could not wish for anything more. Therefore it appears that he wanted in this one epistle to sum up briefly the whole Christian and evangelical doctrine, and to prepare an introduction to the entire Old Testament.[41]

Thus when one uses this preface to establish Luther's hierarchy of New Testament books or his "canon within the canon," one would conclude that for Luther the Epistle to the Romans came first.

When Luther said that a Christian "lives in Christ through faith, in his neighbor through love," however, he was expressing not only a deeply personal, Christian, and an "at-the-same-time" ethic, but also the second basic way that he thought, taught, preached and wrote.

As John Herman Randall Jr. pointed out in his two-volume work *The Career of Philosophy*, Luther was a "religious genius who used his

---

38. Lønning, *"Kanon im Kanon."* In this study, which provides a useful history of the idea of "a canon within the canon," Lønning emphasizes the significance of the letters of Paul—especially Gal 1:8—for understanding Luther's basic views on this subject.

39. Gritsch, *Martin—God's Court Jester*, 97. Here Gritsch emphasizes how Paul's Epistle to the Romans was the key book in Luther's canon, but he does point out, "Luther considered the Gospel of John and 1 Peter close companions to the Romans." Gritsch also calls attention to Luther's special love for Galatians, for he once called it "my Katie von Bora" (95).

40. "Preface to the Epistle of St. Paul to the Romans, 1546 (1522)" in *LW* 35:365.

41. Ibid.

own living experience as the touchstone by which to separate what was divine from what was mere human invention." Luther was at his best, Randall contends, "when he allows that experience freest reign, as in *The Liberty of a Christian Man*, and speaks with the authority of what he himself has felt within himself." "This appeal to inner experience, this personal mysticism," Randall also argues, "has always been the core of the Lutheran tradition, to which it has returned again and again, when its lack of independent intellectual content has entangled it too deeply with other philosophies."[42]

While Luther's first basic way of thinking and viewing life can be called a *simul* or an "at-the-same-time" way of thinking and viewing life, in and by itself it is not sufficient to capture Luther's thought as a whole, because it does not capture Luther's deeply incarnational and dynamic, mystical and holistic, individualizing and historical way of viewing life based on the power of the Word and the Spirit of God either in his life or in human history. Although for Luther the idea called justification by faith and the idea that a Christian is justified and sinner at the same time were viewed in an active and dynamic way, basically an "at-the-same-time" image is a static one that needs to be supplemented by an active and dynamic one.

Is there a term or formula that pastors and theologians, philosophers and historians, writers and teachers, could use to capture Luther's second basic way of thinking, writing, and viewing life? Is there a term that can be used to describe Luther's dynamic and deeply incarnational way of thinking and viewing life that can also be used in our modern secular world to indicate a historical way of thinking, writing, and doing history?

The best way to capture Luther's second basic way of thinking and viewing life, it is contended here, is through those connected Lutheran prepositions: *in*, *with*, and *under*. While the paradoxical richness of Luther's "at-the-same-time" or *simul* way of viewing life and the revolutionary idea of justification by faith alone were based mainly on the writings of Paul, the dialectical richness of Luther's "in-with-and-under" way of thinking, teaching, preaching, writing, and viewing life was based primarily on the Gospel of John and its great Prologue that shows how God is acting, creating, and redeeming; and how Jesus is "the Word be-

---

42. Randall, *From the Middle Ages*, 111–12. Randall also suggests, "The Reformed faith had no heritage of mysticism, like the Lutherans, and no Melanchthon to reintroduce a conflicting scholasticism" (115).

come flesh": "In the beginning was the Word, and the Word was with God, and the Word was God. He was in the beginning with God. All things came into being through him, and without him not one thing came into being. What has come into being in him was life, and the life was the light of all people. The light shines in the darkness, and the darkness did not overcome it" (John 1:1–5, NRSV).[43]

The concluding verses of this Prologue were also of basic importance for Luther's "in-with-and-under" way of viewing life; for to Luther, God was a hidden (*abscondito*) and Creator God and, at the same time, a revealed and redeemer God.[44]

> And the Word became flesh and lived among us, and we have seen his glory, the glory as of a father's only son, full of grace and truth . . . From his fullness we have all received grace upon grace. The law indeed was given through Moses; grace and truth came through Jesus Christ. No one has ever seen God. It is God the only Son, who is close to the Father's heart, who has made him known. (John 1:14, 16–18)

In this Prologue, Luther found not only the basic paradox for all Christians (Christ as the divine *logos* and the key to all human history) but also a masterful way of presenting the universal through the particular, and a masterful way of using simple prepositions to do this.

One of the best places to see the great significance of the Gospel of John for Luther's whole way of teaching, preaching, writing, and viewing life can be found in his "Preface to the New Testament."

> From all this you can now judge all the books and decide among them which are the best. John's Gospel and St. Paul's epistles, especially that to the Romans, and St. Peter's first epistle are the true kernel and marrow of all the books. They ought properly to be the foremost books . . . For in them you do not find many works and miracles of Christ described, but you do find depicted in masterly

---

43. For the significance of this Prologue not only for Luther's whole Trinitarian theology but also for his "sprachtheologisch" way of thinking, see Bayer, *Martin Luthers Theologie*, 309, 319.

44. For a brief discussion and analysis of the development and significance of Luther's understanding of the Prologue of John, see Von Loewenich, *Die Eigenart von Luthers Auslegung des Johannes-Prologes*, 8. For a large and very detailed analysis of Luther's translation of the Prologue of John and its significance not only for Luther's work as a whole but also in relation to earlier Christian scholars, see Beutel, *In dem Anfang war das Wort*.

fashion how faith in Christ overcomes sin, death, and hell, and gives life, righteousness, and salvation. This is the real nature of the gospel, as you have heard.[45]

If he would have had to do without either the works or the preaching of Christ, Luther continued,

> I would rather do without the works than without his preaching. For the works do not help me, but his words give life, as he himself says [John 6:63]. Now John writes very little about the works of Christ, but very much about his preaching, while the other evangelists write much about his works and very little about his preaching. Therefore John is the one, fine, true, and chief gospel, and is far, far to be preferred over the other three and placed high above them. So, too the epistles of St. Paul and St. Peter far surpass the other three gospels, Matthew, Mark, and Luke.[46]

"In a word," Luther summarized, "St. John's Gospel and his first epistle, St. Paul's epistles, especially Romans, Galatians, and Ephesians, and St. Peter's first epistle are the books that show you Christ and teach you all that is necessary and salvatory for you to know, even if you were never to see or hear any other book or doctrine."[47]

Now if one uses this preface to summarize Luther's hierarchy of New Testament writings, or his canon within the canon, one can certainly see why Roland Bainton claimed that for Luther the Gospel of John came first, then the Pauline epistles and First Peter, and then the other gospels.[48]

---

45. "Luther's Preface to the New Testament, 1546 (1522)" in *LW* 35:361–62.

46. Ibid.

47. Ibid. This preface and many of Luther's basic writings can also be found in a very helpful volume called *Martin Luther's Basic Theological Writings*, edited by Timothy F. Lull. See this "Preface" in Lull, 116–17. One of the best places to see the great significance of John's masterful Prologue for Luther's preaching, teaching, writing, and way of viewing life can be found in his "First Sermon" (*LW* 22:5–26), within a series of sermons on the Gospel of John in 1537 and 1538. As he preached on the main passages of this Prologue, he emphasized—as always—not only how "God was the Word," how "the Word existed from the beginning," how "All things were made through Him," and how Jesus Christ, together with the Father, "is the Creator and Preserver of all things" (22:16) but also how "No evangelist other than John was able to stress and describe this article of faith in such a masterly manner" (22:17).

48. Bainton, *Here I Stand*, 332. While "the spirit of Roman and Galatians permeated all of his [Luther's] teachings," as Fred E. Meuser has pointed out, and although Luther preached about thirty sermons on Romans, he preached many hundreds on John. ("Luther as a Preacher of the Word of God," 138). In addition, Meuser states, in 1531/32

If one looks at Luther's prefaces to the Epistle to the Romans and to the New Testament at the same time, however, one can conclude that the two highest and most indispensable books for Martin Luther and for his ways of viewing life were Paul's Epistle to the Romans and the Gospel of St. John.

One of the first results of Luther's "evangelical experience," which centered on the idea of justification by faith alone, was the way he taught his classes. When Luther began his career as a university teacher, he knew little Greek or Hebrew; but through his intensive study of the Bible and these languages, and through these years of intensive religious struggle, he became an outstanding linguist, a great Reformer, and "a Lutheran."[49] Gradually he discarded the Scholastic way of teaching and adopted a new approach, a way that E. G. Schwiebert called "the grammatical-historical method."[50]

By the year 1517, when Luther published his ninety-five theses, a metamorphosis in the faculty of Wittenberg University was well under way; for in the spring of that year Luther wrote: "Our theology and St. Augustine are progressing well, and with God's help rule at our University. Aristotle is gradually falling from his throne, and his final doom is only a matter of time. It is amazing how the lectures on the *Sentences* are disdained. Indeed no one can expect to have any students if he does not want to teach this theology, that is, lecture on the Bible or on St. Augustine or another teacher of ecclesiastical eminence."[51] Thus by the year 1517, Luther's new "biblical humanism" had won over the most influential members of the Wittenberg faculty,[52] and biblical and philological subjects—rather than philosophy—were becoming the key for theological education at Wittenberg.

The biblical humanist curriculum that Luther and his new colleague, Philip Melanchthon (1497–1560), established at Wittenberg was more conducive to the development of the form of inquiry called history than the Scholastic curriculum that they overturned. For Luther and

---

Luther "spent almost a year and a half on John 6, 7, 8. He preached more on John's Gospel in a year than on Romans in his whole life" (ibid).

49. Schwiebert, *Luther and His Times*, 289.
50. Ibid., 285.
51. "Letter from Luther to John Lang on May 18, 1517," *LW* 48:41–42.
52. Schwiebert, *Luther and His Times*, 275–302. The title of this helpful chapter is "Triumph of Biblical Humanism in the University of Wittenberg."

Melanchthon, linguistic studies and historical research were indispensable tools for understanding the Bible, for attacking medieval Scholasticism and the claims of the papacy, and for rediscovering the practices, the ideas, and the forms of the early Church. Like St. Augustine's, Luther's way of viewing life was based on the view that "The God of the Bible was the omnipotent Lord of time."[53]

One of the best early indications of Luther's new "*simul* way" of teaching, his new "in-with-and-under" way of viewing life, and his new "theology of the cross" can be seen in the following citation from his lectures on Psalms in the year 1518: "All good things are hidden *in* the Cross and *under* the Cross. Therefore they must not be sought and cannot be understood except *under* the Cross. Thus I, poor little creature, do not find anything in the Scriptures but Jesus Christ and Him crucified. For Jesus is every benefit which is attributed to the righteous men in the Scriptures, such as joy, hope, glory, strength, wisdom. But he is a crucified Christ. Therefore only such people can rejoice in Him as trust and love Him, while they despair of themselves and hate their own name."[54]

This was the message that Luther believed he had been called to teach and to preach, and these were the prepositions that Luther later used to explain that divine mystery he later called the Lord's Supper.

Although Luther developed both an "at-the-same-time" way and an "in-with-and-under" way of viewing life before the year 1520 and before he transformed the Mass into the Lord's Supper, the connected prepositions *in*, *with*, and *under* have always been associated with a Lutheran understanding of the nature and significance of this sacrament.

---

53. Gritsch, *Martin—God's Court Jester*, 98. Although Gritsch uses this statement only for Luther, this whole section called "Bible and History" (98–103) is a very useful account of how Luther's view of history was based on St. Augustine. Although "Luther expected the end of the world in his lifetime," he also attempted to construct a chronology of world history as "a succession of millennia analogous to the seven days of creation" (Gritsch, "Luther on Humor," 374). See also Lohse's statements in *Martin Luther*, where he claims "that Luther's thought of God as always active" (168), "that God never works without creating" (172), and that "Luther's style and method of thinking can best be studied on the basis of his understanding of history" (193–98). According to Oswald Bayer, "in every point" in Luther's theology, "one can feel a dynamic" (*Martin Luthers Theologie*, viii). For a full account of Luther's view of history, see Headley, *Luther's View of Church History*. For Headley, "The doctrine of the Word of God constitutes the core of Luther's theology" (19).

54. From a lecture on Psalms, 1518. Quoted by Prenter in "Luther on Word and Sacrament," 65–66. Cited in Ahlstrom, *Religious History*, 74 (italics added).

In 1519 in the essay "The Blessed Sacrament of the Holy and True Body of Christ, and the Brotherhoods," Luther emphasized not only that Christ "gave his true natural flesh *in* the bread, and his natural blood *in* the wine," but also that "he instituted not simply the one form, but two forms—his flesh *under* the bread, his blood *under* the wine."[55]

In the famous essay of the year 1520, "The Babylonian Captivity of the Church," Luther used the authority of Scripture alone to discard first four, and then five, of the seven sacraments of the Latin Church and to transform the Mass into the Lord's Supper.[56] For this and other reasons, this essay is probably the best example of the use of Occam's razor by a Christian theologian in the history of Christianity.

Luther's starting point in viewing the sacrament of baptism was the divine promise, "He who believes and is baptized will be saved" (Mark 16:16).[57] Although Luther thanked God that at least the sacrament of baptism remained "untouched and untainted by the ordinance of man,"[58] his view of this sacrament led him to criticize monastic vows and later (1521) to repudiate monasticism. His transformation of the Mass into the Lord's Supper was also a very radical change, for here he not only rejected the practice of forbidding "the giving of both kinds" to the laity, the doctrine called "Transubstantiation," and the Mass as a good work and a sacrifice; here he also parted company with what he called the "Thomistic" or "the Aristotelian Church."

At this time the doctrine called transubstantiation was supported by the Aristotelian distinction between substances and accidents. According to this view, when the priest spoke the words, "This is my body," the bread and wine retained their accidents of shape, taste, color, and the like, but they lost their substance, for which was substituted the body and blood of Jesus Christ.

---

55. *LW* 35:59–60. See also Lull, *Martin Luther's Basic Theological Writings*, 252–53 (italics added). For a good but brief account of the development of Luther's views concerning this sacrament, both before 1520 and especially of the changes in emphases between 1520 and 1529, see Althaus, *Theology of Martin Luther*, 375–403. As Althaus points out, "The conflict about the real presence gives his [Luther's] christology its final form and has dominated Lutheran theology since then. Christology and the doctrine of the Lord's Supper have mutually conditioned each other" (398).

56. Penance was the sacrament that Luther had second thoughts about in the context of this essay.

57. "Babylonian Captivity of the Church," in *LW* 36:58.

58. Ibid., 57.

In "The Babylonian Captivity of the Church," Luther explained that when he was studying Scholastic theology, he had received food for thought from an Occamist scholar (Pierre d'Ailly) who had argued

> with great acumen that to hold that real bread and wine, and not merely their accidents, are present on the altar, would be more probable and require fewer superfluous miracles—if only the church had not decreed otherwise. When I learned what church it was that had decreed this, namely the Thomistic—that is, the Aristotelian church, I at last found rest for my conscience in the above view, namely, that it is real bread and wine, in which Christ's real flesh and real blood are present in no other way and to no less a degree than the others assert them to be under their accidents.[59]

The expression "fewer superfluous miracles" is a classic example of what Weber called the increasing tendency towards rationalization in the West, but it is also a very helpful phrase for understanding the direction of Lutheran thought in Germany since the time of Luther.

In this essay Luther emphasized that the words of God should be "retained in their simplest meaning as far as possible," that laymen had never become familiar with the "fine-spun philosophy of substance and accidents," and that they "could not grasp it if it were taught to them."[60] He also objected to the doctrine called transubstantiation, because it was not based on Scripture or on a simple understanding of the words of God. "For my part," he stated, "if I cannot fathom how the bread is the body of Christ, yet I will take my reason captive to the obedience of Christ [II Cor. 10:5], and clinging simply to his words, firmly believe not only that the body of Christ is in the bread, but that the bread is the body of Christ."[61]

Since at this time the Church taught that the sacraments could not be impaired either by the unworthiness of the priest or by the indifference of the receiver, in Luther's eyes this seemed to make the sacrament too mechanical and too miraculous. For Luther, the sacrament of the altar was "a promise of the forgiveness of sins made to us by God," and he insisted that "where there is the Word of the promising God, there must be the faith of the accepting man."[62] For Luther, "the sacrament of the

---

59. Ibid., 28–29.
60. Ibid., 30–31.
61. Ibid., 34 (brackets in original).
62. Ibid., 39.

mass must be not magical but mystical, not the performance of a rite but the experience of a presence."[63]

Just as Luther insisted on the presence of Christ in the divine mystery called the Lord's Supper, so also he insisted that God was somehow present in all of his creation. It is significant that two of Luther's strongest statements concerning the omnipresence of God and God's hidden presence in all of his creation can be found in two of his books concerning the Lord's Supper.

In the year 1527, for example, Luther emphasized how the power of God "is uncircumscribed and immeasurable, beyond and above all that is or may be," and how it "must be essentially present at all places, even in the tiniest leaf."

> The reason is this: It is God who creates, effects, and preserves all things through his almighty power and right hand, as our Creed confesses. For he dispatches no officials or angels when he creates or preserves something, but all this is the work of his divine power itself. If he is to create or preserve it, however, he must be present and must make and preserve his creation both in its innermost and outermost aspects.
>
> Therefore, indeed, he himself must be present in every creature in its innermost and outermost being, on all sides, through and through, below and above, before and behind, so that nothing can be more truly present and within all creatures than God himself with his power.[64]

---

63. Bainton, *Here I Stand*, 138–39. For a brief and good statement of how for Luther "the life of faith" was a way of life," how "faith was crucial in the sacraments," how "the promise of the sacraments must be accepted by a personal act of faith," and how "the sacraments were thus intensely personal," see Hillerbrand, *Men and Ideas in the Sixteenth Century*, 75. The sacraments were intensely personal for Luther, Hillerbrand claims, "especially since they personalized the divine promise, which could be felt, touched, received. The bread and the wine in communion, the water in baptism, were visible seals of God's promise and they were personally received." (ibid.)

64. *That These Words of Christ "This is My Body,"* etc., *Still Stand Firm against the Fanatics*, in *LW* 37:57–58. See also *WA* 23:133–34. As Bernhard Lohse emphasizes in *Martin Luther's Theology*, what is unique about Luther's "speaking about God is that it is never theoretical. It is always clear that where God is concerned we have to do with the Lord of the world and history, thus with our own life" (209). For Luther, God's activity "is behind all occurrences in nature and history, as well as individual life" (213). In addition, Lohse claims that "The theme of 'hidden' and 'revealed' God threads through all of Luther's writings, from the first Psalm lectures onward" (215), and that "Respecting the doctrine of God, Luther's distinction between 'hidden' and 'revealed' is new, and for him, fundamental" (216).

Luther's "at-the-same-time" and "in-with-and-under" ways of viewing the Lord's Supper and all of God's creation can also be seen in his *Confession Concerning Christ's Supper* (1528). "We say," Luther said,

> that God is no such extended, long, broad, thick, high, deep being. He is a supernatural, inscrutable being who exists at the same time in every little seed, whole and entire, and yet also in all and above all and outside all created things. There is no need to enclose him here... for a body is much too wide for a Godhead. Nothing is so small but God is still smaller, nothing so long but God is still longer, nothing so broad but God is still broader, nothing so narrow but God is still narrower, and so on. He is an inexpressible being, above and beyond all that can be described or imagined.[65]

The view that Luther expressed in these two quotations was a basic one not only behind the *Monadology* of Leibniz, the founder of the great philosophical tradition called German idealism and also the chief forerunner for the new kind of historical consciousness called historicism, but also behind the work of Hamann and Herder and, especially through them, for that great intellectual and spiritual revolution in Germany from the 1760s through the year 1810.

While Luther's transformation of the Mass into the Lord's Supper was of crucial importance for the division of Latin Christendom into Catholic and Protestant camps, the split between Luther and Ulrich Zwingli (1484–1531) over this sacrament during the Marburg Colloquy in 1529 was a watershed in the history of Protestantism, for here Lutheran and Reformed Protestantism went separate ways. It is also one of the main events in Western intellectual history, for as Heiko Oberman points out, "the eucharistic debate between Luther and Zwingli, stands out as *the* example of the irreducible impact of intellectual history."[66]

While Zwingli and his followers insisted that the body of Christ was now in heaven at the right hand of God, Luther insisted that the body

---

65. "Confession Concerning Christ's Supper, 1528," in *LW* 37:228; *WA*, 26:339-40. For another example of how Luther used almost every conceivable preposition to express his basic religious convictions, see a statement quoted by Steven Ozment: "Where logic applied, Luther argued, one dealt with knowledge and not with faith (thesis 49). As he later put it in his inimitable way: the articles of faith are 'not against dialectical truth [Aristotelian logic], but rather outside, under, above, below, around, and beyond it' (*non quidem, contra, sed extra, intra, supra, infra, citra, ultra omnem veritatem dialecticam*)" (Ozment, *Age of Reform*, 238).

66. Oberman, *Impact of the Reformation*, 22.

of Christ was in heaven and on earth at the same time. While Zwingli insisted that spirit and flesh could not be conjoined, Luther took his stand on the words "This is my body" and would not budge from the real presence of Christ in the Lord's Supper. Better the Roman Mass, he asserted, than to understand the sacrament of the altar in memorial, symbolic, or spiritual terms. "You are of another spirit," he concluded.[67]

Although John Calvin (1509–1564) later taught a "noncorporeal presence" that was closer to the position of Luther than Zwingli was able to accept, the cleavage over the Lord's Supper—as Sydney Ahlstrom points out—"remained a basic point at issue between the Lutheran and nearly all other phases of the Protestant Reformation."[68] For many Lutherans it has always seemed that while Luther took the magic out of the sacrament of the altar, Zwingli took the mystery out. On the other hand, however, Lutheran theologians have rightly warned that no Lutheran should call the Catholic view of the sacrament of the altar "magical," because both St. Thomas and Luther believed that "Christ is the real consecrator" in the divine miracle of "the Real Presence."[69]

In the Small Catechism, which Luther published in the same year that the Colloquy of Marburg occurred, Luther defined the sacrament of the altar as "the true body and blood of our Lord Jesus Christ, *under* the bread and wine, given to us Christians to eat and drink."[70] In the Large

---

67. For a good description of this difference of spirit by one of Luther's many biographers, see Haile, *Luther*, 124–27.

68. Ahlstrom, *Religious History*, 76. For a good, recent, and thorough examination of the views not only of Zwingli and Calvin in regard to Luther's views concerning the Lord's Supper but also of the tremendous diversity of views concerning the Eucharist during the sixteenth century, see Wandel, *Eucharist in the Reformation*. For Luther, see especially Wandel's summary paragraph on page 109: "It is striking, in fact: so much of Luther's thinking on the Eucharist found acceptance. Evangelicals broadly agreed with his repudiation of the Mass as a sacrifice and a work; on this Luther and Zwingli could join hands. They also shared his centrality of the Word, both as a context for Communion and as the foundation for the liturgy." (See also the remaining points of this paragraph as well as the following sections of Wandel's chapter called "The Lutheran Eucharist.")

69. Sasse, *This Is My Body*, 44–46. Sasse also contends here, however, that St. Thomas Aquinas limited "the Real Presence." One of the most useful aspects of this study by Sasse is his presentation and discussion of the texts of the Marburg Colloquy.

70. This and the following quotations from the Small Catechism are from "Enchiridion, The Small Catechism of Dr. Martin Luther for Ordinary Pastors and Preachers," 351 (italics added), in *The Book of Concord* (1959), hereafter abbreviated BC-T. See also the more recent translations of this and other basic Lutheran texts in *The Book of Concord* (2000), hereafter abbreviated as BC.

Catechism, also published in 1529, Luther used the expression "*in* and *under* the bread and wine."[71] In the year 1577, *The Formula of Concord* also used the preposition "with"—the preposition Philip Melanchthon preferred to use—to explain what Lutherans believe concerning this sacrament.[72]

From the sixteenth century to the present, Lutheran pastors have used these three prepositions when young Lutherans have asked the obvious question, "How can the bread and wine be the body and blood of Christ at the same time?" Traditionally, Lutheran pastors have responded to this question simply by assuring them that somehow "in, with, and under" the bread and wine they will receive the body and blood of Christ and the forgiveness of their sins.

In *The Protestant Ethic and the Spirit of Capitalism*, Max Weber made two important observations about Lutheranism as an "ideal type" closely related to Luther's two basic ways of viewing life. "The highest religious experience that the Lutheran faith strives to attain, especially as it developed in the course of the seventeenth century, is the *unio mystica* with the deity. As the name itself, which is unknown to the Reformed faith in this form, suggests, it is a feeling of the actual absorption in the deity, that of a real entrance of the divine into the soul of the believer."[73]

Second, Weber also claimed that Lutheranism combines the *unio mystica* with that "deep feeling of sin-stained unworthiness which is essential to preserve the *poenitentia quotidiana* of the faithful Lutheran, thereby maintaining the humility and simplicity indispensable for the forgiveness of sins."[74]

Although Weber did not attempt to explain how Lutherans were able to inculcate these basic feelings into young Lutherans since the seventeenth century, these two statements are helpful for understanding the central significance of the Lord's Supper for Lutherans. Just as Roman

---

71. "The Large Catechism of Dr. Martin Luther," in BC-T, 447.

72. "We at times also use the formulas '*under* the bread, *with* the bread, *in* the bread'" ("Formula of Concord," in BC-T, art. 7, p. 575; cf. BC, 599). For Melanchthon's use of the preposition *with* and other similar prepositions, see Rogness, *Philip Melanchthon*, 132–35, 165. See also Gritsch, *History of Lutheranism*, 93, 97; and Wengert, "Luther and Melanchthon," 36. For one example of how Luther used the prepositions *in* and *with* together for this sacrament, see *LW* 37:325–26 and Bornkamm, *Luther in Mid-Career*, 532.

73. Weber, *Protestant Ethic*, 112.

74. Ibid., 113.

education aimed to produce worthy citizens and soldiers of Rome, so Lutheran education through the first half of the twentieth century aimed to produce true believers who were worthy partakers in the divine mystery and experience called the Lord's Supper.

THE EDUCATIONAL FOUNDATIONS OF A LUTHERAN ETHOS

To understand Lutheran education, it is helpful to remember that Martin Luther—like St. Augustine—accepted infant baptism. Since there was no religious test for membership, and since it included everyone in a territory, the Lutheran Church (in the terminology of Ernst Troeltsch) was a church and not a sect.

A second general point regarding Lutheran education is that Luther envisioned the church as a communion of true believers who regularly heard the word of God and who regularly, freely, and worthily received the sacrament of the altar. Since Luther's view of the Lord's Supper pointed in one direction and his view of baptism in another, Roland Bainton could claim that Luther "could be at once to a degree the father of the congregationalism of the Anabaptists and of the territorial church of the later Lutherans." For Bainton, the "greatness and the tragedy of Luther was that he could never relinquish the individualism of the eucharistic cup or the corporateness of the baptismal font."[75]

My response to Bainton at this point is that I would simplify this statement by leaving out the word "tragedy," for Luther's *simul* way of viewing the nature of the church was of decisive importance for the development of a distinctly Lutheran ethos. But the pressing problem, both for Luther and for Lutheran pastors to the present, was how a church could be a church in both of these respects at the same time. How could all the baptized Christians in a territory—or a congregation—be educated to be true believers who freely chose to partake in the experience called the Lord's Supper?

For Luther, the great hope for meeting this problem was to be found in the power of "the Word." When Luther preached on the sacraments, he loved to quote the statement of St. Augustine: "The Word comes to the element, and it becomes a sacrament." In one of his sermons in the year

---

75. Bainton, *Here I Stand*, 140–42.

1528, he added the significant statement, "In all his lifetime Augustine never said anything better."[76]

Although for Luther "the Word" was the dynamic essence of the sacraments, it certainly was not confined to the sacraments or to the Bible. For Luther, the gospel was "an oral preaching and a living word, a voice which resounds through the whole world and is publicly proclaimed." The Word had to be pondered. For Luther, the faith of a Christian arose not through thought, wisdom or will, but rather "through an incomprehensible and hidden operation of the Spirit . . . at the hearing of the Word."[77]

Luther certainly placed great hope in the power of the Word to transform all the baptized Christians of a territory into a community of true believers, but he also placed great hope in the power of education and in his educational booklet called the Small Catechism. This booklet is one of the most significant texts in the history of Western education because (1) it has been the chief educational document for Lutherans since the year 1529, (2) it has been the most important single writing for the development of a Lutheran-based view of life and of a distinctively Lutheran ethos,[78] and (3) "in the catechetical presentations," Luther scholars could be sure that they had "the view of Luther in its clearest

---

76. *LW* 51:189. According to Bernhard Lohse, Luther "may" have received some impulse toward "the primacy of the Word" from humanism but "more probably" owed this impulse to Augustine; but "what is decisive is that his conception of the Word was independently developed by Luther" in his first Psalms Lecture (1513-1515) (Lohse, *Martin Luther's Theology*, 52).

77. Both these quotations from Luther are cited (without reference) by Bainton, *Here I Stand*, 224. For a more recent emphasis on the significance of "hearing the Word" not only for Luther but for the Protestant Reformation as a whole, see Collinson, *Reformation: A History*. Here Collinson emphasizes how "Luther's single-minded concentration on the Word brought about real and revolutionary change" (29), how "Luther was full of something called the Word," how this was based not on "words" but rather on "the Logos of the opening words of St. John's Gospel" (33), how "[a] favorite text for Protestants was 'Faith cometh by hearing, and hearing by the word of God' (Rom 10:17)," and how "[t]he Reformation prescribed a new precedence of ear over eye" (34).

78. See Elert, *Theology and Philosophy of Lutheranism*, 8. Here Elert states, "One can say material contained in this book [Luther's Small Catechism] has been the most important factor even in the social life of Lutheran countries — and for centuries a constantly effective factor." According to Martin Brecht, "In language, understandability, and brief format," Luther's Small Catechism was "a masterpiece of religious pedagogy, one not matched in his own or in any other age" (Brecht, *Shaping and Defining the Reformation*, 277).

and most authentic form."[79] Just as Roman education and a Roman ethos were based on the Twelve Tables of Law that Roman youth were required to know, so Lutheran education through the first half of the twentieth century focused on learning, understanding, and memorizing the Small Catechism.

Luther's catechism was of basic importance not only for the Lutheran tradition and other Protestant traditions but in some respects for Catholic education as well. As Gerald Strauss emphasized in his influential study, *Luther's House of Learning: Indoctrination of the Young in the German Reformation*, Luther's catechism—which first appeared on a single sheet so that it could be mounted in a prominent place in the home—"caught on as no preceding publication of this kind had ever done."[80] "By 1530, Lutheran leaders had come to regard systematic catechization of the laity, particularly the young, as a distinguishing feature of their movement and a decisive break with the past."[81] But Strauss also shows how similar Catholic catechisms soon appeared, how religious education in Catholic Bavaria soon conformed to the pattern already established in Lutheran territories, and how "above all" these Catholic pupils "memorized the catechism."[82] As Dennis Janz points out, Luther's catechism "is often seen as the beginning of catechesis in the modern sense because of the enormous influence it had on all subsequent catechisms, both Protestant and Catholic."[83]

---

79. Prenter, *Spiritus Creator*, 259. In support of this claim, Prenter pointed out that "[t]he catechetical presentations are first of all original Luther texts. And second, they contain Luther's view in a systematic summary just as he himself wanted the congregation to get it. Because of the popular aim of the catechisms it is of course not possible to use them as an exhaustive presentation of the central validity of any individual point in his theology. But as the classic presentation of the central part in Luther's view they can always be used as a test of the validity of Luther's interpretation." Here Prenter is referring to Luther's small and large catechisms together.

80. Strauss, *Luther's House of Learning*, 124.

81. Ibid., 156.

82. Ibid., 289. For a more positive evaluation of the significance of Protestant catechisms and ordinances for sixteenth-century German society than that of Strauss and scholars who have emphasized their significance for uniformity, routine, obedience, and "the steady march of German absolutism," see Ozment, *Protestants*, 89–117, 147–48, 215–17. For a good introduction to the literature concerning "Confessionalization," see Brady, "Confessionalization," 1–20.

83. Janz, *Three Reformation Catechisms*, 14. In addition, Janz claimed, "[t]he 'Spirit of Protestantism' is grounded, perhaps, more in this document than in any other. Insofar as

Now a masterpiece of religious and educational literature such as this, however, does not just happen by itself. Good writing requires conscious effort, and Luther really worked on it. For Luther, the most important quality in writing was sincerity,[84] and the only true medium of communication "is shared experience."[85] His Latin adage could be translated, "Communication is understanding, and to understand is to communicate."[86] "Any and everything, if it is to be done well," Luther once stated, "demands the entire man."[87]

Luther was, as H. G. Haile pointed out, not only "the first in the long line of media celebrities," but also "the most prolific writer Germany has ever produced."[88] "No author," Haile also claimed, "has ever known such a large, eager readership."[89] By the year 1530, "his quill had made him the most influential man in Europe," and "none had ever attained to power by that instrument before."[90]

The one matter on which scholars of various backgrounds agree, as Erik H. Erikson summarized so well, "is Luther's immense gift for language: his receptivity for the written word; his memory of the significant phrase; and his range of verbal expression (lyrical, biblical, satirical, and vulgar) which in English is paralleled only by Shakespeare."[91]

---

this spirit has dominated the West in modern times, Luther's 'Small Catechism' must be seen to be of immense significance for the history of the West" (16–17).

84. Haile, *Luther*, 50.
85. Ibid., 52.
86. Ibid., 85.
87. Ibid., 56.
88. Ibid., 49.
89. Ibid., 64.

90. Ibid., 86. For the significance of the printing press, the great increase in the number of books on religious subjects, a growing literate audience, "the affinity between literacy, printing, and Protestantism in the early years of the Reformation," and "the urban origins of the Reformation," see not only Ozment, *Age of Reform* (especially pages 199–204), but also Ozment, *Reformation in the Cities*. In this latter work, see especially the references to the significance of Luther's and other Protestant catechisms for both the spread and the consolidation of Protestantism in the sixteenth century (pages 152–66). In this work, Ozment shows how "Protestant ideas revolutionized religious practice at local levels, simplifying religious life and enhancing secular life"; how "in its time" the Reformation was "a lay enlightenment"; and how the catechisms and the church ordinances that the Protestant Reformers wrote were a "literature of discipline" and a "literature of freedom" (165) at the same time.

91. Erikson, *Young Man Luther*, 47.

In a sermon "On Keeping Children in School," Luther expressed his views on writing in a characteristically concrete, vivid, and lively way, or in what Herder and many Luther scholars since his time have called a *lebendige* way.

> Ask a writer, preacher, or speaker whether writing and speaking is work; ask a schoolmaster whether teaching and training boys is work. The pen is light; that is true. Also there is no tool of any of the trades that is easier to get than the writer's tool, for all that is needed is goose feathers and there are enough of them everywhere. But the best part of the body (which is the head) must lay hold here and do most of the work, and the noblest of the members (which is the tongue), and the high faculty (which is speech). In other occupations it is only the fist or the foot or the back or some other such member that has to work; and while they are at it, they can sing and jest, which the writer cannot do. "Three fingers do it," they say of writers; but a man's whole body and soul work at it.[92]

One reason that the words of the Small Catechism have continued to haunt—or persistently recur—in the hearts, souls, and minds of adult Lutherans to the present time is that Luther was a great writer who put his whole body and soul into these few pages.

Since Luther had learned through his own religious struggle that a Christian should fear and love God at the same time, his explanation of the first commandment began with the words, "We should fear, love and trust in God above all things," and the nine other explanations began with the words, "We should fear and love God."[93]

One of the best examples of how Luther used simple prepositions to convey the gospel message in a *simul* way, an "in-with-and-under" way, and a very "individualizing" way can be found in his explanation of "the seven petitions" of the Lord's Prayer. In his explanation of the first petition, "Hallowed be thy name," Luther wrote: "To be sure, God's name is Holy in itself, but we pray in this petition that it may also be holy *for* [*bey* or *bei*] us."[94] For the second petition, Luther explained: "To be sure, the

---

92. Luther, *Works of Martin Luther*, 4:47. Cf. *LW* 46:249 and *WA* 30:574. For this quotation I am indebted to Jack Hexter, for this was the introductory quotation that he used for his National Endowment of Humanities summer seminar for college and university professors at Yale University in the year 1978, a seminar on writing history.

93. BC-T, 342–44.

94. *WA* 30/1:300. *Bey* is Luther's spelling, and *bei* is the modern spelling. Emphasis here and in the following quotations from the Small Catechism (BC-T) is not in original.

kingdom of God comes of itself, without our prayer, but we pray in this petition that it may also come *to* us." For the petition "Thy will be done, on earth as it is in heaven," Luther taught: "To be sure, the good and gracious will of God is done without our prayer, but we pray in this petition that it may also be done *by* [*bey* or *bei*] us."

Lutheran thought, both inside and outside Germany, was also shaped by his explanation of the sixth petition, for this is the classic expression of what can be called Luther's "unholy trinity."

> "*And lead us not into temptation.*"
>
> What does this mean?
>
> Answer: God tempts no one to sin, but we pray in this petition that God may so guard and preserve us that the devil, the world, and our flesh may not deceive us or mislead us into unbelief, despair, and other great and shameful sins, but that, although we may be so tempted, we may finally prevail and gain the victory.[95]

From the time of Luther to well into the twentieth century, these powerful words of warning were a very important component of a distinctively Lutheran ethos. One of the reasons that many Lutherans in the nineteenth and twentieth centuries were so fascinated by Goethe's *Faust* is the fact that here they could see a new, a very different, and a very influential way of looking at Luther's unholy trinity.

In his explanation of the sacrament of holy baptism, Luther used the prepositions *in*, *with*, and "*bey*" to convey the nature of this holy mystery. "Baptism," he said, "is not merely water, but it is water used according to God's command [*in Gottes Gebot gefasst*] and connected *with* God's Word." In answer to the question "How can water produce such great effects?" Luther taught: "Water, of course, does nothing by itself, but the Word of God that is *with* and *bey* the water, and the faith which relies on the Word of God *in* the water."[96]

Most of all, Luther put his whole body and soul into the part concerning the Apostles' Creed. One of the merits of his treatment of this basic creed for all Christians was the way Luther grouped all the material

---

95. BC-T, 347–48.

96. *WA* 30/31:310. Here the translation is mine rather than the ones in BC or in BC-T. In the BC translation, the answer to the question, "How can water do such things?" is translated: "Clearly the water does not do it, but the Word of God, which is with and alongside the water, and faith, which trusts this Word of God in the water" (359).

around the three saving acts of the Triune God: creation, redemption, and sanctification.[97] Another great strength of his treatment of each of "the three articles" was the individualizing way in which he established the vital relationship between "the facts confessed and the individual confessor."[98]

The conviction that every individual is answerable directly to God was the heart not only of Luther's individualism[99] but also of his individualizing way of communicating his deepest religious beliefs. Luther was the greatest individualizing writer in German history and for the whole Lutheran tradition, for these words and the other parts of the Small Catechism had a culture-forming power in Protestant Germany.

In his explanation of what Lutherans have always called the First Article, Luther taught young Christians to confess that "God has created *me* and all that exists, that he has given *me* and still sustains my body and soul, all my limbs and senses, my reason and all the faculties of my mind."[100] While this translation helped to shape the way many Lutherans in the English-speaking world view life, Lutheran thought in Germany was shaped by the words: "Ich glaube, das mich Got geschaffen hat sampt allen creaturn, mir leib unnd seel, augen, orn unnd alle gelieder, vernunfft und alle synne gegeben hat und noch erhelt."[101]

Now the word *Sinn* (*synne*) is one word that Germans since the time of Luther have sometimes used for the English word "mind," but its basic meaning and its real meaning here would be "senses." The translation of "alle Sinne" into "all the faculties of my mind" is a problematic translation, not only because it multiplies entities unnecessarily (which was something which Luther always tried to avoid), and because Luther is speaking here about the five senses, but also because that entity which Locke and the English-speaking world calls "mind" was not a separate German word or concept for Luther.

In his explanation of "The Second Article: Redemption," Luther taught young Christians to confess:

---

97. Reu, *Catechetics*, 103.
98. Ibid., 105.
99. Bainton, *Here I Stand*, 141.
100. BC-T, 345.
101. WA 30/I:292.

> I believe that Jesus Christ, true God, begotten of the Father from eternity, and also true man, born of the Virgin Mary, is my Lord, who has redeemed me, a lost and condemned creature, delivered and freed me from all sins, from death, and from the power of the devil, not with silver and gold but with his holy and precious blood and with his innocent sufferings and death, in order that I may be his, live under him in his kingdom and serve him in everlasting righteousness, innocence, and blessedness, even as he is risen from the dead and lives and reigns to all eternity. This is most certainly true.[102]

Here, Jaroslav Pelikan has claimed, "Luther penned his theologically most typical—and historically most influential—statement of christological doctrine."[103]

At the same time, however, it is also possible to agree with the statement by James L. Kittelson that "[p]erhaps the strongest statement of Luther's Evangelical theology came in his explanation to the Third Article of the Apostles' Creed."[104] Here, as always, Luther emphasized the doctrines of the grace of God in Christ and justification by faith.

> I believe that by my own reason or strength I cannot believe in Jesus Christ, my Lord or come to Him. But the Holy Spirit has called me through the Gospel, enlightened me with his gifts, and sanctified and preserved me in true faith, just as he calls, gathers, enlightens, and sanctifies the whole Christian church on earth and preserves it in union with Jesus Christ in the one true faith. In this Christian Church he daily and abundantly forgives all my sins, and the sins of all believers, and on the last day he will raise me and all the dead and will grant eternal life to me and to all who believe in Christ. This is most certainly true.[105]

Luther's explanation of this article of the Apostles' Creed is significant for the development of Protestant thought in Germany in a number of ways. First of all, this brief explanation is one of the reasons that the words *Heilige Geist*, or Holy Spirit, became one of the most beautiful expressions in the German language.[106] In Germany, Christmas, Easter, *and*

---

102. BC-T, 345 and Lull, *Martin Luther's Basic Theological Writings*, 479. Cf. BC, 354.

103. Pelikan, *Reformation of Church and Dogma*, 161.

104. Kittelson, *Luther the Reformer*, 218.

105. BC-T, 345.

106. Second only, perhaps, to the expression *Heilige Nacht* or "Holy Night."

Pentecost were celebrated in the church *and* in the culture; for Pentecost became—and still is—an important holy day and a big spring holiday in the schools and universities. Thus, in contrast to the United States—where Reformed Protestantism was the main culture-forming religious tradition,[107] and where today many college or university students do not know the term for the coming of the Holy Spirit—it is fair to say that both in the Protestant and Catholic parts of Germany, the third Person of the Trinity was and is a more important part of the culture.

Second, Luther's explanation of "The Third Article" is one of the reasons that the word *Geist* became one of the richest and most important words for German thought and culture. One indication of this is the many different meanings of this word in the *Deutsches Wörterbuch* that have been traced back to Luther.

In English, the words *spirit*, *mind*, and *soul* have very different and distinct meanings. If one has to translate the word *mind* into German, however, one has the choice of following Leibniz by using the French or German word for *soul*, to follow most Germans since the time of Herder by using the word *Geist*, or to follow the way of Kant in his *Critique of Pure Reason* by avoiding the use of this word as much as possible. It is important to know, however, (1) that the original and chief meaning of the word *Geist* is "spirit"; (2) that most German scholars since the time of Herder and Kant have never accepted Locke's image of the mind as a blank tablet or slate; (3) that especially since the time of Herder the word *Geist* means "spirit, mind, and/or soul"; and (4) that since the time of Herder, one German word—the word *Geist*—could be used to signify Luther's "inner man" in contrast to his "outer man."

Third, in and through Luther's explanation of the Third Article of what Lutherans often call the Creed, Luther taught young Christians to believe that they were called to be vessels of the Holy Spirit. In *The Protestant Ethic and the Spirit of Capitalism*, Max Weber pointed out that the "religious believer can make himself sure of his state of grace either in that he feels himself to be the vessel of the Holy Spirit or the tool of the

---

107. See especially Ahlstrom, *Religious History*, and his references to Max Weber's "Protestant ethic." For Ahlstrom, "[n]o factor in the 'Revolution of 1607–1760' was more significant to the ideals and thought of colonial Americans than the Reformed and Puritan character of their Protestantism; and no institution played a more prominent role in the molding of colonial culture than the church" (347). This excellent history is a classic example of the usefulness of the Weber thesis for understanding different national traditions within the modern Western world.

divine will. In the former case his religious life tends to mysticism and emotionalism. In the latter to ascetic action; Luther stood closer to the former type, Calvinism belonged definitely to the latter."[108]

The expression "vessel of the Holy Spirit" is very helpful for understanding Martin Luther and the Lutheran ethos. Lutherans since the time of Luther, however, would be more comfortable with the expression "servant of the Word" rather than with "vessel of the Holy Spirit."[109] While Calvinists tended to see themselves as agents of God's divine Providence, Luther and Lutherans—especially Lutheran pastors, professors, scholars, and teachers—have tended to see themselves as servants or vessels of the Word. While Calvinism is commonly seen more as an action-oriented ethos, Lutheranism has commonly been seen as a more inward-looking and contemplative ethos.

Fourth, in and through Luther's explanation of the Third Article, young Lutherans were taught to see how the Holy Spirit was an active and vital force in the microcosm of their individual lives and, at the same time, in the macrocosm of "the whole Christian church on earth." Here, as usual, Luther was teaching young Christians to see themselves within a universal framework.

Fifth, Luther's explanation of the Third Article was also of fundamental importance for the development of a Lutheran ethos because here Luther taught young Christians how to view the relationship between faith and reason. It is significant that for centuries, Lutheran youth were required to memorize Luther's words explaining the meaning of Third Article before they received their First Communion, before they chose a calling in life, before they went to the university, and before they were exposed to a world of reason and doubt. Whether it was the work of the Holy Spirit, the unforgettable words of Martin Luther, or some other cause, many of the intellectual leaders in Germany during the eighteenth

---

108. Weber, *Protestant Ethic*, 113–14.

109. In a sermon in the year 1522, for example, Luther said: "All that I have done is to further, preach and teach God's Word; otherwise I have done nothing. So it happened that while I slept or while I drank a glass of Wittenberg beer with my friend Philip [Melanchthon] and with Amsdorf, the papacy was weakened as it never was before by the action of any prince or emperor. I have done nothing . . . I let the Word do its work" ("The Second Sermon, March 10, 1522, Monday after Invocavit" [*LW* 51:77]). As William H. Lazareth writes in his "Introduction to the Christian in Society," this statement reflects the confident spirit that distinguishes Luther's ethic: "He [God] acts through me . . . I let the Word do its work!" (*LW* 44:xi).

and nineteenth centuries were preserved in the Christian faith or in what Luther called "the one true faith."

While David Hume (1711–1776), the famous eighteenth-century historian and philosopher in Great Britain, could conclude that the Christian religion "not only was at first attended with miracles, but even at this day cannot be believed by any reasonable person without one,"[110] Lutheran youth inside and outside Germany were armed with Luther's view that faith was a miracle, and that it was the work of the Holy Spirit. Just as St. Augustine taught Christians to "believe in order to understand,"[111] so Martin Luther taught Christians to behold, to perceive, and to see themselves and all components of creation in and through the eyes of faith.

Although Lutheran education through the first half of the twentieth century focused on learning, understanding, memorizing, and confessing the material in Luther's Small Catechism, by itself this was not sufficient to provide the experience on which a distinctively Lutheran ethos was instilled in young Lutherans. As part of the confirmation experience in Lutheran congregations in Germany, in the Scandinavian countries, in Estonia, in Latvia, in the United States, and in other countries, young Lutherans were examined by their pastor—often publicly before the congregation during the confirmation service—concerning their knowledge of the Ten Commandments, the Apostles' Creed, the Lord's Prayer, the two sacraments, and Luther's explanations of each of these essentials of the Christian faith before they were admitted to their First Communion.

From the sixteenth century through the first half of the twentieth century, young Lutherans usually approached "the Table of the Lord" with a sense of mystery and awe partly because of the powerful words that they had memorized or at least attempted to memorize,[112] partly because of the

---

110. This quotation is from Hume's famous chapter on miracles, section 10, part 2, paragraph 101 in *Philosophical Essays Concerning Human Understanding*.

111. Cited in Cochrane, *Christianity and Classical Culture*, 402. For further clarification of this idea and the wording and significance of this idea, see Cary, *Augustine's Invention of the Inner Self*, 40, 145, and 165, n. 40.

112. From my own experience and the testimony of many Lutheran adults and pastors, I know (1) that Lutheran pastors often rehearsed confirmands for this examination, (2) that those youth who had the most difficulty in memorizing usually got to answer the shortest and easiest questions and had a good idea of what the pastor might ask them, and (3) that the best students and the pastor's own son or daughter were much less able to guess what question or questions they would have to answer or recite. Certainly most

Lutheran emphasis on self-examination and preparation for the Lord's Supper, and partly because they were often warned by their pastor that if they took the body and blood of Christ in an unworthy way, they could be in danger of damnation.[113] Since young Lutherans were often accepted as full members of the congregation at this time, and since this sacred initiation into the most holy mystery of this community of faith usually took place at the time of puberty, Lutheran families often celebrated this event as a puberty rite whereby boys and girls were now able to dress like adults and to be treated like adults.

Although many components of the confirmation experience within Lutheranism changed between the sixteenth century and the second half of the twentieth century,[114] the one common experience of all Lutherans—

Lutheran pastors wanted all their confirmands to pass the public examination, to make certain that no one would be publicly embarrassed, and to ensure that everyone in "the confirmation class" would be admitted to "the Table of the Lord" to receive their "First Communion." This was mass education and testing in practice.

113. See BC-T, 181:5, 454:69, 483:16, 572:16, 579:57. For an understanding of the significance of the question of "worthiness," especially for the Reformed tradition after Calvin, see Wandel, *Eucharist in the Reformation*, 74, 77, 189, 190, 197, and 200–207.

114. See especially Klos, *Confirmation and First Communion*. This book included a document called "A Report for Study to the Honorable Presidents of the American Lutheran Church, Lutheran Church in America, and the Lutheran Church—Missouri Synod" that was dated December 28, 1967, and that was written by a Joint Commission on the Theology and Practice of Confirmation. In the chapter called "Spotlight on Confirmation," Klos showed how confirmation in the United States at that time was based on several assumptions: (1) "that confirmation is basically a way of preparing youth to receive their First Communion"; (2) "that confirmation provides a fitting climax to an intensive period of study based on Luther's Small Catechism"; and (3) that "confirmation is for all practical purposes a form of becoming a full member of the church" (11–14). Two of the most useful contributions of this study book were (1) a clear and simple historical account of the development of the various components of the Lutheran confirmation experience since the sixteenth century (47–75) and (2) a clear typology and chart of the religious practices associated with the different periods and traditions within this development, including "the Pietistic" and "the Rationalistic" traditions of the seventeenth and eighteenth centuries (72). In the year 1969, Fortress Press published *Confirmation and Education*, which contained ten essays focusing on the "Report," the *Study Book* by Klos, and the recommendation to Lutheran congregations in the United States to separate "First Communion" and confirmation, with "First Communion" occurring when children were in the fifth grade and confirmation when youths were in the tenth grade. For a brief and more recent account of the history of "Lutheran Confirmation Ministry," including (1) a summary of the six main "types," "Reformation emphases," "clusters of emphasis," or "Reformation interpretations" to be found in these historical studies of the 1960s; and for (2) a summary of this "ministry" from 1969 to 1999, see Lindberg, "Lutheran Confirmation Ministry in Historical Perspective," 41–84. The first of these

whether orthodox, pietist, or rationalist—was the confirmation experience based on three main elements: (1) memorizing or attempting to memorize Luther's Small Catechism, (2) being examined—often publicly before the congregation during the confirmation service— over Luther's powerful explanations of the essentials of the Christian faith, and (3) the First Communion experience whereby young Lutherans first received— in, with, and under the bread and wine—the body and blood of Christ at "the table of the Lord."

Although Luther was not very interested in the rite of confirmation itself, he was deeply concerned about the education of a child between baptism and the time he or she was admitted to the Lord's Supper. As Frank Klos also pointed out in a watershed study for American Lutherans, *Confirmation and First Communion: A Study Book* (1968), Luther emphasized especially the importance of repentance, absolution, and examination "for those who would come to Holy Communion for the first time. If this experience is to be meaningful for the child, then he has to be properly prepared. Here Luther's greatest contribution was made: He stressed the importance of catechetical education to link the two sacraments effectively."[115]

Regular participation in the Lord's Supper was of basic importance for a Lutheran ethos and a Lutheran way of viewing life, for here especially Lutherans experienced what Weber called—but not in relation to the sacrament of the altar—"a periodical discharge of the emotional sense of

---

six emphases, "Catechetical (Catechumenal or Instructional) Confirmation Driven by Catechetical Instruction," grew out of "the need for instruction and preparation of the young for the Lord's Supper," "was the earliest Lutheran practice," was "the most common form in the Lutheran Church in its first 150 years" (52–53), and is the closest one to the basic model presented in the present essay.

115. Klos, *Confirmation and First Communion*, 14. This book can be seen as a watershed study not only because (1) it was endorsed by the three largest Lutheran churches in the United States, and (2) because it was the main study book for Lutheran congregations in the United States when they voted to separate First Communion and confirmation, but also (3) because this significant change within Lutheranism as a whole can be seen as a giant step in the Americanization of Lutheranism in the United States. Psychologically it can probably be seen as the most important change—and certainly as one of the most important changes—in the history of Lutheran education. For some of Luther's key statements in regard to confirmation, see Fischer, *Christian Initiation*, 171–73. For a summary of Luther's and Melanchthon's views on confirmation, see also Turner, *Meaning and Practice of Confirmation*, 7–19 (for Luther), 23–37 (for Melanchthon).

sin."[116] But the Lord's Supper was also of basic importance because here, at the same time, Lutherans received a periodical recharge of the sense of grace so that they could go out into the world to serve their neighbor through their work, their office, or their calling.

Thus it was primarily through the confirmation and the First Communion experience (1) that young Lutherans first learned to perceive how it was possible to be a humble and repentant sinner and, at the same time, a justified Christian; (2) that in, with, and under the bread and wine they first experienced an entrance of the divine into their souls; and (3) that they first attained a sense of what Joseph Sittler once called "a dialectic of the mystery of life,"[117] a sense that was constantly reinforced through regular participation in the divine mystery called the Lord's Supper. In short, the confirmation and the First Communion experience together was the key event and the key experience within Lutheranism—both in Europe and in the United States—through the first six decades of the twentieth century in turning baptized Christians into adult Lutherans with a common ethos and way of viewing life.[118]

LUTHER, MELANCHTHON, AND THE LUTHERAN CONCEPT OF CALLING

In *The Protestant Ethic and the Spirit of Capitalism*, Max Weber emphasized that the German word *Beruf* and the English word "calling"—the English translation of this Lutheran word—were religious conceptions that suggested a task set by God.[119] These two words also suggested a

116. Weber, *Protestant Ethic*, 106.

117. The word *dialectic* is used in many different ways, but my understanding of the way Joseph Sittler used this term and phrase was closer to what I have called an "in-with-and-under" way rather than an "at-the-same-time" way, because it suggested the mystery of the process of life and therefore rested on a perception of time.

118. This model of a distinctively Lutheran type of education was dropped by most Lutheran congregations in the United States during the early 1970s with the separation of First Communion and confirmation and with the adoption of "early Communion" at the age of ten or during the fifth grade in the American school system. Just as many congregations in the United States since the early 1970s have been forced by the realities of American social life to abandon confirmation during the tenth grade and to return to the traditional age (the end of the eighth grade or just before a student enters high school), so also early Communion at the age of ten has changed; for today many Lutheran children celebrate their First Communion at age six, seven, eight, nine, or ten.

119. Weber, *Protestant Ethic*, 79.

sense of a life-task in a definite field in which to work. This moral justification of worldly activity was "one of the most important results of the Reformation,"[120] for as Weber also pointed out, "[t]he effect of the Reformation as such was only that, as compared to the Catholic attitude, the moral emphasis on and the religious sanction of, organized worldly labour in a calling was mightily increased. The way in which the concept of calling, which expressed this change, should develop further depended upon the religious evolution which now took place in the different Protestant Churches."[121]

To understand how the concept of *Beruf* developed in Germany, one must look at the life, personality, character, and work not only of Martin Luther but also of Philip Melanchthon. Together Luther and Melanchthon can be seen as the great "supplementary-antipoles" (a Hintze image,[122] and an "at-the-same-time" expression that will be used for two other polar, supplementary, and personally connected pairs of thinkers in this inquiry) at the University of Wittenberg and for the Protestant Reformation in Germany.

Just as Luther's "at-the-same-time" and his "in-with-and-under" ways of viewing life were based on his study of Scripture and on his evangelical experience (his discovery of the idea known as justification by faith), so also in and through his study of Scripture and this event he had experienced the transforming power of what he loved to call the Word. Without the firm conviction that the Holy Spirit could work even through a sinful creature such as himself, Luther could not have begun a movement for religious reform that became a revolution in the Latin or Catholic Church, in the religion and the religious structure of the West, and in Western education.

Perhaps that is why my favorite quotation in Bainton's classic study, called *Here I Stand: A Life of Martin Luther*, is a statement Luther made in the heat of battle during the Leipzig debate in 1519. At Leipzig it was the Christian theologian, university professor, and heir of a courageous prophetic tradition, and not the obedient monk, who asserted to Eck: "I

---

120. Ibid., 81.

121. Ibid., 83. Although Luther did not create the word *Beruf*, he "was the first who provided a theological basis for understanding 'calling' in the sense of secular work," and he "was also the first who overcame the assumption that monasticism or ministry was higher than other secular callings" (Lohse, *Martin Luther*, 120).

122. See n. 1 in chapter 1. See also n. 87 in chapter 5 below.

answer ... that God once spoke through the mouth of an ass. I will tell you straight what I think. I am a Christian theologian; and I am bound, not only to assert, but to defend the truth with my blood and death. I want to believe freely and be a slave to the authority of no one; whether council, university, or pope. I will confidently confess what appears to me to be true, whether it has been asserted by a Catholic or a heretic, whether it has been approved or reproved by a council."[123]

This was a statement concerning the pursuit of truth as strong as any attributed to Socrates or within the classical tradition, and it is probably no accident that the tradition called academic freedom arose primarily in Protestant Germany. As Gerhard Ebeling points out, Luther received his "certainty of vocation from the sober fact of his academic calling." "It is no exaggeration to say," Ebeling adds, "that never in the history of the university has the work of a scholar, in the study and in the lecture-room, had so direct and so extensive an influence upon the world, and changed so much."[124]

By the year 1520, it became clear that Luther's pursuit of what appeared to be true had taken him a very long way when he published the epoch-making treatise, "To the Christian Nobility of the German Nation," for here Luther urged the Holy Roman Emperor and the German princes to call a council to reform the whole church. Here he asserted that "a priest is nothing else but an officeholder," and that "there is no true, basic difference between laymen and priests, princes and bishops, between religious and secular, except for the sake of office and work, but not for the sake of status." For Luther, they were "all of the spiritual estate, all truly priests, bishops, and popes," but they did "not have the same work."

> Therefore, just as those who are now called "spiritual," that is priests, bishops, or popes, are neither different from other Christians nor superior to them, except that they are charged with the administration of the word of God and the sacraments, which is their work and office, so it is with temporal authorities. They bear the sword and rod in their hand to punish the wicked and protect the good. A cobbler, a smith, a peasant—each has the work and office of his trade, and they are all alike consecrated priests and bishops. Further, everyone must benefit so that in this way many kinds of

---

123. Bainton, *Here I Stand*, 119.
124. Ebeling, *Luther*, 17.

work may be done for the bodily and spiritual welfare of the community, just as all members of the body serve one another.[125]

For Luther, each Christian was a priest who served God through faith and his neighbor and community through his work and office.

In the treatise called "The Freedom of a Christian," Luther explained how before God all Christians were equally priests, and how as priests they were "worthy to appear before God to pray for others and to teach one another divine things."[126] Yet all Christians could not "publicly minister and teach."[127] While some Christians should serve their community as ministers and teachers, all Christians should serve their community through their work, their office, or what he later called their *Beruf*. By the year 1522, the concept of *Beruf* and Luther's full understanding of the vocation of a Christian had emerged.[128]

The Latin word *vocatio*, as Gustav Wingren points out in his book *Luther on Vocation*, could mean several things. It could refer to the proclamation of the gospel through which individuals were called to be children of God. It could mean the work a person does, such as a craftsman or a carpenter, and it could signify the action by which one rightly entered an office. While the word *Beruf* also had different meanings, Luther usually used it to mean an "outer status or occupation"; for a *Beruf* was the earthly task of a Christian.[129]

The development of Luther's concept of *Beruf* in Germany is a classic example of how the history of the modern Western world can be seen as the rationalizing and secularizing of a Christian civilization. For Luther, *Beruf* was a word he used only for Christians, for as Wingren concluded from his research: "As far as we can determine Luther does not use *Beruf* or *vocatio* in reference to the work of a non-Christian. All have station (*Stand*) and office; but *Beruf* is the Christian's earthly or spiritual work."[130]

---

125. "To the Christian Nobility of the German Nation Concerning the Reform of the Christian Estate," in *LW* 44:129–30.

126. *LW* 31:355.

127. Ibid., 356.

128. See Holl, "Die Geschichte des Wortes Beruf," 217; and Wingren, *Luther on Vocation*, ix.

129. Wingren, *Luther on Vocation*, 1.

130. Ibid., 2.

Today, however, when a professor of history in Germany says, "Teaching history is my *Beruf*," this only means that history is his or her profession; for today the word *Beruf* means "profession" or "occupation." If a professor of history wants to say, "Teaching history is my calling," he or she has to say, "Teaching history is my *Berufung*," for this is now the word that means a calling in life.[131] But this word also has an interesting secular meaning, for when an historian receives an appointment as a professor of history at a university, he or she receives a letter from a public official that certifies that he or she has been rightly "called" to this high office. Not all officials of the state (*Beamter*) receive a *Berufung* or a "call," for this term is reserved mainly for appointments of professors, higher clergy, and high judges. This custom is just one indication of the importance of professors, pastors, and jurists for the development of the professions and *der Beamtenstand* in Germany.[132]

From the time of Luther to the present, Lutheran pastors have emphasized how all ordered creation or all the institutional structures of the secular world should be seen as divinely ordained means of serving one's neighbor in one's calling or vocation. At the same time, however, Lutheran pastors since the time of Luther have encouraged their sons and young men of ability and character to prepare themselves for the calling of the "ministry of the Word."

Although Lutherans have not regarded the ministry as a special calling in the sense of a highest calling, from the beginning Lutheran pastors have taken special interest in this calling because (1) the ministry of the church was to teach the gospel and to administer the sacraments; (2) the church had the command from God to appoint ministers, and thus this office was instituted by God; and (3) only pastors were ordained by the church. In the words of the Augsburg Confession, "Our churches teach that nobody should preach publicly in the church or administer the sacraments unless he is regularly called" (article 14).

Since the time of Luther and Melanchthon, who wrote these words, Lutherans believed that the call to be a pastor came not only from the

---

131. For the history of the word *Beruf* and its relation to the word *Berufung*, see Conze, "*Beruf*," in Brunner et al., *Geschichtliche Grundbegriffe*, 1:490–507.

132. See especially Hintze's pioneer and classic studies called "Die Epochen des evangelischen Kirchenregiments in Preussen" (1906) and "Der Beamtenstand" (1911). The former essay can be found in Hintze, *Regierung und Verwaltung*, 56–96; and the latter in Hintze, *Soziologie und Geschichte*, 66–125.

church as "the assembly of all believers," but that it was also the work of the Holy Spirit. Thus from the time of Luther to the present, young Lutherans have wrestled with the problem of whether or not they were "called" by the Holy Spirit to become a pastor. This has been especially true for sons of pastors, for here the problem of a calling to preach the Word was often a strong personal and family concern.

The other calling that has been closely linked with the ministry of the Word has been the academic calling, for Lutheran pastors have always had a special interest in the professors and teachers who taught the future ministers of the Word. Many professors, historians, and writers within the Lutheran tradition were pastors' sons[133] or entered academic life first through the ministry of the Word, and/or after preparing themselves for the ministry of the Word, and/or after discovering that their real calling in life was to teach or to write rather than to preach. Since language studies have always provided the foundation for the training of Lutheran pastors and historians, from the beginning these two callings have been closely linked within the Lutheran tradition.

For "Dr. Martin Luther," a beloved title in Protestant Germany, it was a great necessity to train and to send out pastors, professors, and teachers to carry out a reform of the church. During the 1520s and 1530s, a small army of pastors and teachers were marching out of Wittenberg, and by the year 1534 they were armed with a whole arsenal of religious books containing Luther's deeply spiritual way of viewing life, including his magnificent translation of the Bible into German. As Sydney Ahlstrom pointed out in his prize-winning *A Religious History of the American People*, "Probably never in the history of the Church has any one person shown such rich theological insight in biblical interpretation, or made the Scriptures speak to people with such power and relevance."[134]

---

133. Christoph Martin Wieland, "Germany's first prolific and successful novelist," and Gotthold Ephraim Lessing, "her first and greatest critic," were both sons of Lutheran pastors (Haile, *Luther*, 340). Friedrich Gottlieb Klopstock and Johann Gottfried Herder, however, were not. According to Haile, all these men were "deeply influenced by Luther, whose language they drew upon from his Bible to inspire a new, secular age" (ibid). For a discussion of the significance of Lutheran pastors' sons for the development of German literature and German idealism, see Elert, *Morphologie des Luthertums*, 2:145–58. For a comprehensive account of the cultural significance of the Lutheran parsonage in Germany since the time of Luther, see Greiffenhagen, *Das evangelische Pfarrhaus*.

134. Ahlstrom, *Religious History*, 75. According to Bernhard Lohse, "Luther undoubtedly emphasized the authority of the biblical Word to an extent that was previously

For Hajo Holborn, a student of Meinecke who trained more than one generation of history professors in the United States, Luther's translation of the Bible was a "new interpretation of Christian faith in a new language, which only a genius could conceive." Through his translations of the New Testament (1522) and the Old Testament (1534), Luther "created a standard that became the foundation of national communication in religion, literature, politics." Luther could not have achieved this result, Holborn asserted, "if he had not succeeded in bringing the sources of Christian religion before the modern reader with the power of a creative genius."[135]

Increasingly in the twentieth century, historians became more aware of the great significance of Luther's new interpretation of Christian faith for the idea of history, for as Mark E. Blum pointed out: "Luther, in fact, is paradigmatic of German historical thought in every characteristic salient since his lifetime. His notion of a hidden authority whose purpose was within each human event, but required interpretation by the historical agent (as well as by the historical commentator) is replicated even among secular historians, and can be identified in the philosophical and social-psychological interests of contemporary German historical thinkers."[136]

The idea of history in Germany and in the West, however, was influenced also by Luther's indispensable colleague; for when the small army of students left the University of Wittenberg at the time of Luther, they were armed not only with his teachings, books, and ways of viewing life, but also with the academic outlook, the educational texts, and the educational curriculum of Philip Melanchthon. While Luther's work, teach-

---

unknown" (Lohse, *Martin Luther*, 155).

135. Holborn, *History of Modern Germany, The Reformation*, 165. For a more recent analysis of the significance of Luther's translation of the Bible for the development of the German language, see Lohse, *Martin Luther*, 112–20. See also Lohse's very useful introduction to "The History of the Interpretation of Luther" (199–237) and to the significance of Leopold von Ranke for a modern understanding of Luther and his age (217–19).

136. Blum, "German Historical Thought, 1500 to Present," in *A Global Encyclopedia of Historical Writing*, 1:359. As Blum also claims, "Luther typifies the German historical thinker in his philological precision and general interest in manifestations of language and its artifacts, his focus upon cultural change, his premise that each event is wholly singular in its character (even when it is a manifestation of an idea or principle) and his belief that history is a living dimension of contemporary thought" (ibid). See also his comments (included in *Global Encyclopedia of Historical Writing* 1:359) on Luther in relation to Leopold von Ranke's "neutral" vision embodied in the phrase, *wie es eigentlich gewesen* ("how it actually happened").

ings, and ways of viewing life became the spiritual base of Lutheranism, Melanchthon "gave it unity in creating the forms and methods of transmitting the Lutheran faith and a specifically Lutheran civilization."[137]

For the future pastors, teachers, and officials who carried the Reformation with them as they left Wittenberg, Melanchthon provided a more suitable model to emulate than "the inimitable Luther." Melanchthon's eminence and his fame as *preceptor Germaniae*, as Hajo Holborn emphasized, "rested not only on his encyclopedic scholarship and his extraordinary lucidity of presentation" but also on "a strong and distinctive character behind all his activities." It was Melanchthon "who set the personal style" for the members of the "academic groups," a term which "included not only the professors but all those directly or partly educated by them, such as ministers of the church, government officials, lawyers, or other professionals."[138] For Holborn, "Melanchthon's contribution to the creation of these characteristic social types was great, through his leadership in the reorganization of higher education in Protestant Germany, no less than through the model set by his life and thought. His influence on German social history can be called greater than that of Luther, whose personality, both earthy and prophetic, had an inimitable uniqueness."[139]

While Luther had struggled mightily to free not only his mind but the theology and church of his day from a way of thinking based on Aristotelian logic and philosophy, he had to admire how his humanist and "form-thinking" friend used this greatest of all form-thinkers "to turn the forest into a well kept garden."[140] While Luther separated religion and philosophy, Melanchthon made humanism, philosophy, rhetoric, and history the handmaidens of Protestant theology in Germany. While Luther

---

137. Holborn, *Reformation*, 199.
138. Ibid., 195.
139. Ibid.
140. Ibid., 199. Here, however, Holborn does not connect this phrase with Aristotle or with the term "form-thinker." For a good discussion in German of how Luther and Melanchthon differed, how they viewed each other, and how Luther once used the term "gardener" for Melanchthon, see Neuser, "Luther und Melanchthon, 47–61. For a good discussion in English of how Luther and Melanchthon differed and viewed each other, see Wengert, "Melanchthon and Luther/Luther and Melanchthon," 55–88.

was the great "life-viewer" of the Protestant Reformation in Germany, Melanchthon was its great "form-thinker."[141]

In his inaugural lecture at Wittenberg in 1518, Melanchthon emphasized the need to go back to the sources, the importance of linguistic studies, and also the indispensability of history for all branches of learning.[142] Through his influence, the first chair of history was established at Marburg University in Hesse around 1528. As Lewis W. Spitz points out, this put Marburg "ahead of all Roman Catholic universities including the Renaissance universities."[143]

In the year 1536, history first became a regular subject at Wittenberg when Melanchthon began to lecture on universal history.[144] In this course, Melanchthon used a chronicle that Johannes Carion—one of his students—had worked out, that Melanchthon had corrected and improved, and that he published under Carion's name in the year 1532. Melanchthon used this text in his course, translated it into Latin, and published it again (1558-1560) in a completely reworked form.[145] Although Carion's and Melanchthon's text was a rather traditional attempt to write universal history following the four-monarchies pattern of St. Jerome, it is significant that this text was used at other universities and went through eleven editions by the year 1625.[146] More than anyone else in the sixteenth century,

---

141. The terms "form-thinker" and "life-viewer" are literal translations of the words *Formdenker* and *Lebensschauer*, which were terms that Otto Hintze applied to Kant and Herder in the essay "Troeltsch und die Probleme des Historismus," 342-43. Cf. Hintze, *Historical Essays of Otto Hintze*, 390. See also the second introductory quotation for chapter 4 below and note 2 of the present chapter.

142. Dorn, "Melanchthons Antrittsrede von 1518," 141-48.

143. Spitz, "Luther's View of History,"150. This excellent essay in the collection of essays called *The Reformation: Education and History* was first published in 1989.

144. Rambeau, "Über die Geschichtswissenschaft an der Universität Wittenberg," in *450 Jahre Martin-Luther-Universität Halle Wittenberg*, 1:256.

145. Ibid., 257.

146. Ibid., 259. For a summary of this chronicle in relation to Melanchthon's basic views that a historical consciousness raises a creature to a real human being, and that a knowledge of history "is a school for life," see the chapter titled "Mensch in der Geschichte," by Heinz Scheible, in *Melanchthon: Eine Biographie*, 251-63. For a brief summary of the significance of this chronicle and also of Melanchthon's work as a whole, see Rhein, "Influence of Melanchthon on Sixteenth-Century Europe," 383-94. This collection of essays (*Lutheran Quarterly* Winter 1998) provides a good introduction to his work and to recent literature concerning his work.

Melanchthon enhanced the teaching of the traditional Christian type of universal history.

It is significant that the *perceptor Germaniae*, or teacher of Germany, more than anyone else, saw to it that history, as a mighty weapon in the battle between Roman Catholicism and Protestantism over the validity of church tradition, was given a prominent place in the new Protestant universities at Marburg an der Lahn, Königsberg, and Jena.[147]

Today Melanchthon should also be recognized as a key figure for the idea of history, both in Germany and the West as a whole, for making history a distinct academic subject and a part of the university curriculum. In addition, he was a model history teacher in Protestant Germany until the Cultural Revolution in Germany (1760–1810) when history gradually became a full-time *Beruf* (calling or profession) and a *Wissenschaft* (science or academic discipline), when a distinctly modern kind of Western historical thought—commonly called historicism—first arose, and when the educational structure that he created was completely remade.

---

147. Breisach, *Historiography*, 166. See also Breisach's account of how Melanchthon's universal chronicle was continued by his son-in-law, Charles Peucer, and how Peucer's four-volume edition of Melanchthon's chronicle led to "two entirely separate histories: one ecclesiastical, telling the story of Christ's church, and one mundane, concerned with the state as God's instrument" (ibid., 166–67).

three

Two Forerunners of the Cultural Revolution in Germany and Modern Historical Thought: Leibniz and Chladenius

> If it were possible to give a definition of "feudalism," all this debate would be unnecessary. But it is impossible to grasp the complicated circumstances of historical life, so laden with unique occurrences, in a few universal and unambiguous concepts—as is done in the natural sciences. We must rather turn to intuitive abstractions, to the creation of Ideal Types, for such types underlie our scholarly terminology. I can therefore do nothing better than, first of all, to describe the Ideal Type that underlies our concept of feudalism.
> —OTTO HINTZE (1929)[1]

THE PROBLEM

One of the problems of a claim that the present inquiry is the first attempt to apply the ideal-type methodology of Otto Hintze to "the idea of history" or to Western historiography as a whole is that each of his three ideal types has a different structure.

In the first part of the essay "Wesen und Verbreitung des Feudalismus" (1929), or "The Nature and Spread of Feudalism," Hintze first explained why historians need to create "intuitive" or *anschauliche* abstractions called ideal types. Before he could discuss whether other feudal systems could be found in the course of world history, Hintze succinctly listed, briefly described, and summarized (1) the three main traits of Western feudalism; (2) the three "transformations" associated with the appearance and nature of fully developed feudalism; (3) how these three

---

1. Hintze, "Nature of Feudalism," 23. This is an abridged version (only the first part, the part dealing with Western feudalism) of "Wesen und Verbreitung des Feudalismus," reprinted in Hintze, *Staat und Verfassung*, 84–95.

factors or functions (the military, the social-economic, and the political or governmental) went together; and (4) how feudalism developed in three major stages, stages he called early, high, and late feudalism.[2]

In the second historical ideal type or model that he published, "Typologie der ständischen Verfassungen des Abendlandes" (1930), Hintze was mainly concerned with showing how in Western Christendom one could find a main type of representative system of estates or constitutional structure, and two main subtypes: (1) "the two-chamber system" (for which England was the chief model), and (2) the *Dreikuriensystem* or the "three-curiae" system (for which France was the chief model).[3] While in this mainly "morphological" typology there was no attempt (1) to list, number, and separate out the traits of the main type or the two subtypes; or (2) to emphasize an early, high, and late stage of development as part of the ideal-type or model itself, this was not the case in the third historical ideal type or model that Hintze published.

One of the main reasons that Hintze's essay "Wesen und Wandlung des modernen Staats"(1931) or "The Nature and Transformation of the Modern State" was the most advanced methodologically was that here, before he numbered and listed the four abstractions that together constituted this ideal type,[4] he presented his fullest explanation of the nature and process of creating ideal types. For Hintze, "the modern state" was no school-like or logical kind of concept, for here one is dealing with

> a pictorial conception [*bildhafte Vorstellung*] and an intuitive [*anschauliche*] abstraction that can be called an "ideal type." Out of the material of experience, which one gains through political observation and historical study, and not without some arbitrariness, one measures and separates out characteristic traits that are then heightened to an ideal purity through an intellectual act. In itself

2. Hintze, "Nature of Feudalism," 24–30.

3. Hintze, "Typologie der ständischen Verfassungen des Abendlandes," 120–39. Although this typology was first published in 1930, most likely this was Hintze's first ideal type since on January 26, 1926, he presented a lecture with the same title to the Prussian Academy of Sciences. See Smith, "Otto Hintze's Comparative Constitutional History of the West," 71, n. 195; and reference on this page ("Akademie, II: Vf. Bd. 26: Sitzungs—Protokolle der phil.-hist. Klasse"). See also Hintze's very important essay, "Preconditions of Representative Government in the Context of World History" (1931), in *Historical Essays of Otto Hintze*, 302–53. Especially in this essay one can see how for Hintze, the three basic constitutional structures of the West—feudalism, the "Estates Constitutions," and the modern state—fit together.

4. For these four characteristics, see n. 5 for chapter 1 above.

this whole is no concrete reality and can claim no such thing. It is based, however, on historical and social reality, and it serves as a means of orientation in the confusing fullness of appearances and as a measurement standard for scholarly judgments that one can not do without.[5]

The second main reason this essay was the most advanced was because of the way this model was based on a perception of time; for here Hintze suggested that when one constructs an ideal type, a person almost automatically uses the idea of an early or formative stage of development, a full or mature stage when these characteristics become dominant, and a late stage in which these characteristics break down, decline, or are transformed by the tendencies of an age. The late stage of one type, he added, could also be seen as the early or formative stage of a new type and a new historical era.[6]

While all three ideal types in the present study are composed of four characteristic traits, only the following one attempts to employ and to emphasize the idea of early or formative stage, a full or high stage, and a late stage. Unlike all of Hintze's ideal types or models, however, there is no attempt in the present inquiry to show how the specific traits developed and spread throughout the West or to place them in the context of world history.

AN IDEAL TYPE OR MODEL OF MODERN HISTORIOGRAPHY

As an *anschauliche* or intuitive abstraction, as a heuristic device, and as a historical "ideal type" or model, modern Western historiography is

1. *professional* because history is written mainly by university professors who teach history for a living and who dominate the *Beruf*, calling, or profession called history;

2. *scientific* because historians believe—or act upon the assumption—that history is a *Wissenschaft*, a science or discipline, a method of understanding, and a mode of thought that can be taught and learned through a modern system of apprenticeship called the doctor of philosophy and the *Habilitation*,[7] or the PhD;

---

5. Hintze, "Wesen und Wandlung des modernen Staats," 470.
6. Ibid., 474–75.
7. This degree, which is higher and usually more difficult to attain than the American

3. based on the concept of *individuality* because historians use the analogy of the individual person or life-unit in forming collective individualities, and because they are trained to look for the individual, the distinctive, and the unique in whatever human object or subject they study;

4. based on the concept of *Entwicklung* or *development* because these are the words historians use in constructing a meaningful, connected narrative based on a perception of time and on the analogy of the life-process of a single human being.

The early or formative stage for this distinctly modern type of Western historiography was the years from the 1760s to the founding of the University of Berlin in the year 1810, the full or mature stage was from Niebuhr and Ranke to Hintze and Meinecke, and the late stage was the years since 1933 (1) when the German universities were discredited and damaged by Hitler and the catastrophe called World War II, and (2) when the center for the study of history in the West moved from Germany to the United States and also to France. The main focus here, however, is with the formative stage of this model, with what Meinecke called "the rise of historicism," and with the rise of those basic concepts and ideas of the modern Western world—*Beruf, Wissenschaft, Individualität*, and *Entwicklung*—during an age that can be called the cultural revolution in Germany.

LEIBNIZ SETS THE STAGE

The chief forerunner for the rise of historicism, of the cultural revolution in Germany, and of the critical-historical tradition within Lutheranism was a universal scholar named Gottfried Wilhelm Leibniz (1646–1716). Just as French thought and culture were decisively influenced by the

---

PhD, qualifies a person to lecture at a German university. While the *Habilitation* became the chief qualification for entrance into the historical profession in Germany during the nineteenth century, by the end of the nineteenth century the American PhD was becoming the entrance degree for professional historians in the United States. For the development of the *Habilitation* and the rapid increase in the number of *Privatdozenten* in Germany during the nineteenth century, see McClelland, *State, Society, and University*, 166–71. For a good description of "the institutionalizing of the new spirit of *Wissenschaft*" and how this new kind of "apprenticeship" developed in the German universities during the nineteenth century, see McClelland, *State, Society, and University*, 171–81.

thought and work of René Descartes, and just as English and American thought and culture were decisively influenced by the thought and work of John Locke, so German thought and culture were decisively influenced by the thought and work of Leibniz.

As Peter Reill points out in *The German Enlightenment and the Rise of Historicism* (1975), the questions that the *Aufklärers* sought to answer were posed by Leibnizian philosophy; for the "interaction between western ideas and Leibnizian assumptions gave the philosophy of the *Aufklärung* [the Enlightenment] its own unique character, a philosophy that directed German thinkers to evolve a method of social analysis founded on history."[8]

Like Descartes, Leibniz was one of the great minds of "the scientific revolution" of the seventeenth century. Like his contemporary John Locke, he was one of the great minds of the formative years of the Enlightenment. The great influence of this universal mind and scholar, however, came primarily in Germany and especially during the years of "the cultural revolution" in Germany, or during the years from the 1760s to 1810. By this time, German scholars could really see the depth and breadth of his thought for themselves, rather than through the eyes of the philosopher Christian von Wolff (1679-1754) and his followers; for only one of Leibniz's major works—his famous and widely read *Essais de Theodicée*—was published during his life. Although Leibniz was a historian who was ahead of his age in regard to method, "the real contribution he made to the growth of modern historical thought stemmed from his philosophy . . . upon the generation of Herder."[9]

In *The Idea of History*, R. G. Collingwood emphasized how Leibniz "applied the new methods of historical research to the history of philosophy with momentous results," and how he "can even be called the founder of that study." In addition, Collingwood claimed, "We owe to

---

8. Reill, *German Enlightenment*, 7.

9. Holborn, *History of Modern Germany, 1648-1840*, 154. Although this statement does not take into consideration the influence of Leibniz on Chladenius and other German scholars in the 1740s and 1750s for the development of modern historical thought, it is still substantially correct. For a more comprehensive statement concerning "the significance of Leibniz for historiography," see the essay with this title by Lewis W. Spitz in the *Journal of the History of Ideas* (1952) 333-48. For the significance of Leibniz as an early "Programmatiker und Praktiker quellenkritischer historisher Forschung," and also for literature focusing on Leibniz as a historian, see Zedelmaier, *Der Anfang der Geschichte*, 52.

him the conception of philosophy as a continuous historical tradition in which new progress comes about not by propounding completely new and revolutionary ideas but by preserving and developing what he calls *philosophia perennis*, the permanent and unchanging truths which have always been known."[10]

Leibniz's work was also of fundamental importance for the idea of history and for the cultural revolution in Germany for six additional reasons. In and through his work, (1) he brought West European thought, the scientific revolution, and the Enlightenment to Germany;[11] (2) he established and decisively shaped the first society or academy "der Wissenschaften" (of the sciences) in Germany; (3) he established and shaped the German understanding of *Wissenschaft*, or science; (4) he created a new *simul*, dynamic, and spiritual way of viewing the universe (God's acting in, with, and through soul-like substances called monads) that "haunted the minds" of many of those Protestant scholars who created, or at least helped to create, those powerful movements called German idealism, romanticism, nationalism, and historicism;[12] (5) he provided a critique of the rationalism of Descartes and of the empiricism of Locke that was of basic importance for Herder and Kant and therefore for the whole direction of German thought, education, and culture; and (6) he carefully prepared Protestant theology "for harmony with science and its implications."[13] In these respects, Leibniz set the stage for the cultural revolution in Germany and for the critical-historical tradition within Lutheranism.

Gottfried Wilhelm Leibniz was the son of a professor of moral philosophy at Leipzig who died in 1652 and left his young and brilliant son a good library and a love of historical study. The title and subject of his bachelor's dissertation in 1663 was significant both for his life and for the idea of history, for *De Principio Individui* ("On the Principle of the Individual") "was inspired partly by Lutheran nominalism . . . and em-

10. Collingwood, *Idea of History*, 62–63.

11. For Holborn, "Leibniz was not only the father of German Enlightenment but also the progenitor of German idealism, particularly as represented by Herder, Hegel, and Schelling" (Holborn, *History of Modern Germany, 1648–1840*, 162).

12. The phrase "haunted the mind" is borrowed from Reill, *The German Enlightenment and the Rise of Historicism*: "Still the image of the monad haunted them [the Aufklärers]: the impetus to investigate a given unity as though it contained logical, epistemological, and aesthetic categories that were harmoniously conjoined formed a starting point for most of their endeavors" (Reill, *German Enlightenment*, 7).

13. Randall, *From the German Enlightenment*, 53.

phasized the existential value of the individual, who is not to be explained either by matter alone or by form alone but rather by his whole being (*entitate tota*). This notion was the first germ of the future 'monad.'"[14]

After Leibniz invented a calculating machine that was exhibited to the Royal Society in London and to the Academy of Paris, he was elected to the London Society (1673) and to the French Academy (1700). In the latter year he founded the *Societät der Wissenschaften* or Society of Sciences in Berlin and became its first president. In addition, he made plans for societies or academies of sciences in Dresden, Vienna, and St. Petersburg. In contrast to the Royal Society in England, however, the academies of sciences that Leibniz envisaged included the study of nature and the liberal arts at the same time.[15]

Just as Leibniz was responsible for the establishment and the inclusive scope of the Society or Academy of Sciences in Berlin, which became the model academy in Germany, so also he was most responsible for the creation of the modern German conception of *Wissenschaft*, or science.[16] Whereas Descartes and many natural philosophers in France and Great Britain tended to equate reason and science with mathematics, Leibniz did not believe that an extension of the mathematical method was sufficient to embrace all valid truth. Especially it was not sufficient to embrace cognition of the individual besides the general.[17] In his theory of knowledge, Leibniz distinguished between truths of *reason*, which were universal laws or facts that could be ascertained through conceptual analysis and analytical reason, and truths of fact, which dealt with the contingent arrangements of this world that were ascertained through experience.[18] While on the one hand Leibniz believed in the ultimate unity of reason, science, and the scientific mind, on the other hand he believed that there were different kinds of truths, or different paths for pursuing truth.

This epistemological distinction was of fundamental importance for the creation of the modern German conception of science. Whereas in the English-speaking world *science* came to be restricted mainly to the study of nature, in Germany any scholarly pursuit was called a *Wissenschaft*

---

14. Sorley, "Leibniz, Gottfried Wilhelm," 884-88.
15. Holborn, *History of Modern Germany, 1648-1840*, 155.
16. Ibid.
17. Ibid.
18. See Rescher, *Leibniz*, 118.

or science, "provided it proceeded on the basis of a method appropriate to the particular subject."[19] Therefore, in Germany it was much easier for scholars to formulate the idea that the Greek and Roman art and the branch of rhetoric or literature called history, or *Historie*, as it was called in Germany through the first half of the eighteenth century, could become a science.

Leibniz also helped to shape the cultural revolution in Germany and the direction of German thought in and through a ninety-paragraph essay known as "The Principles of Philosophy" or "The Monadology," which was first published in 1720. For Leibniz, a monad was a simple substance without parts that enters into composites (§ 1).[20] Since monads had no parts, "neither extension, nor shape nor divisibility were possible," for they were "the veritable atoms of nature and, in brief, the elements of all things" (§ 2). Each monad was unique (§ 9), but like all created beings, monads were subject to continual change (§ 10).

For Leibniz, "the ultimate reason of things must be in a necessary substance in which the diversity of changes is only eminent, as in its source," and "[t]his is what we call God" (§ 38). "Thus God alone is the primitive unity or the first [*originaire*] simple substance; all created or derivative monads are products, and are generated, so to speak, by continual fulgurations of the divinity from moment to moment, limited by the receptivity of the creature, to which it is essential to be limited" (§ 47).

To Leibniz, all of life was connected, and each monad was a "living mirror of the universe" (§ 56). Although the points of view of all monads differed, these different perspectives were perspectives of a single universe that had been legislated by God. Thus, "each created monad represents the whole universe" (§ 62).

Even more distinctly, Leibniz believed, each monad "represents the body which is particularly affected by it, and whose entelechy it constitutes. And just as this body expresses the whole universe through the interconnection of all matter in the plenum, the soul also represents the

---

19. Holborn, *History of Modern Germany, 1648–1840*, 155.

20. The translation cited here is from Leibniz: *Philosophical Essays*, edited and translated by Roger Ariew and Daniel Garber (1989). This translation is also available in Leibniz, *Discourse on Metaphysics and Other Essays*, edited and translated by Daniel Garber and Roger Ariew (1991). References to *The Monadology* will be indicated in the text by paragraph number.

whole universe by representing this body, which belongs to it in a particular way" (§ 62).

For Leibniz, the body and its monad, entelechy, or soul together "constitutes what may be called a living *being*, and together with a soul constitutes what may be called an *animal*" (§ 63).[21] Thus "each organized body of a living being is a kind of divine machine or natural automaton, which infinitely surpasses all artificial automata" (§ 64). Even in the smallest portion of matter, Leibniz claimed, "there is a world of creatures, of living beings, of animals, of entelechies, and of souls" (§ 66). For Leibniz, not only the soul was indestructible, "but so is the animal itself, even though its mechanism often perishes in part, and casts off or puts on organic coverings" (§ 77).

These principles, he said, "have given me a way of naturally explaining the union, or rather the conformity of the soul and the organic body. The soul follows its own laws and the body also follows its own; and they agree in virtue of the harmony pre-established between all substances, since they are all representations of a single universe" (§ 78). To Leibniz, "les Esprits" were "reasonable souls" (§ 82) who were created in the image of God, who were "capable of entering into a kind of society with God" (§ 84), and who composed that assemblage of spirits called "the City of God" (§ 86).

It is significant for the direction of German thought (1) that Leibniz associated the term *Esprits* with "reasonable souls," (2) that this term was translated into German as *die Geister*, and (3) that in Germany the word *Geist* became a *simul* word that signified both a spiritual *and* rational soul, both a spirit and mind created in the image of God. For Leibniz, souls that were capable of reflection and could grasp what one called *Moy, Substance, Ame, Esprit* (*Ich, Substanz, Seele, Geist*), or "immaterial things and truths," were called *Esprits, Geister,* or "spirits."[22] It is also significant that in some English translations of the *Monadology*, the term *les Esprits* is translated "minds," for just as the term *mind* has been the basic concept of English philosophical thought since the time of Locke, so the word

---

21. The common German translation of "un vivant" is "Lebewesen." The latter word is very similar to the word "Lebenseinheit," a key term for Dilthey and Hintze.

22. For a convenient side-by-side comparison of the French texts and standard German translations of Leibniz's two great essays from the year 1714, see Leibniz, *Vernunftprinzipien der Natur und der Gnade, Monadologie*. For these particular terms see especially pages 10-11.

Geist has been the key concept of German philosophical thought since the time of Herder and the early writings of Hegel.

From the time it was published to the present, *The Monadology* has usually seemed strange and fanciful to French rationalists and to English and American empiricists. To many Lutherans, however, here Leibniz presented a way of viewing life that was very appealing.

Why has this essay had a powerful influence especially for Lutherans? Why, especially, did the young Leopold Ranke defend his way of doing history (a way that Troeltsch, Hintze, and Meinecke called historicism) with a statement of his understanding of Leibniz?

In his account of the rise of historicism, Meinecke showed how Shaftesbury, Leibniz, Arnold, and Vico were important "forerunners" for this new historical outlook. Although Meinecke's main emphasis was on the significance of Neoplatonism for the rise of historicism, he also acknowledged the significance of German Lutheranism and Pietism for "the main line" of development, a line that "leads from pietism through the 'Sturm und Drang' [Storm and Stress] movement to historism".[23]

Although Meinecke did not have much to say about the significance of Luther's thought for Leibniz or for each of the main figures in this study, he did point out that "Shaftesbury, Leibniz and Arnold all lived and thought in an atmosphere of spiritual independence from worldly authority, and faithful dependence on the Almighty. This, in the ultimate analysis, was the secret of their preparation for the coming of historicism."[24] This is also a key and crucial point for the rise of historicism in Germany, as one can see especially in the work of Herder and his mentor, Hamann.

One of the reasons that the work of Leibniz has had such a strong influence for Lutherans, of course, was that he was reared and educated within that religious tradition. Leibniz's Lutheran upbringing, as Hajo Holborn points out, "shone through many of his philosophical beliefs. In the construction of his monadology, with its refusal to admit the influence of monads on each other, Luther's insistence upon the absolute dependence of the individual soul on God assumed new expression."[25]

---

23. Meinecke, *Historism*, 35.
24. Ibid., 37.
25. Holborn, *History of Modern Germany 1648–1840*, 158.

On the other hand, however, Holborn also emphasized how Leibniz changed the central experience of Lutheran religion. While the starting point for Luther was recognizing his sinfulness and his constant need for forgiveness, for Leibniz "sinfulness was nothing but a relative debility. An angry God Leibniz could not see. Both as the architect of this world and the guarantor of the order of the universe, God appeared to Leibniz as an eternally friendly father."[26] "Luther would have condemned the whole character of this religiosity," Holborn argued, "which identified soul and reason."[27]

Although it can be argued that Leibniz, like Luther, was very concerned with showing the God-given unity of soul and body, of the inner man and the outer man, and identified soul and reason with the inner man, was Holborn right in his main contention that "Leibniz represented a new form of religion"?[28]

First of all, as Nicholas Rescher pointed out, "more than any other modern philosopher" Leibniz "took seriously the idea of a *creation* of the universe, giving it a centrally important place in his system. Like the theories of the medievalists for whom he had such great respect, his system put God as the *author of creation* at the focal position in metaphysics."[29]

Second, there is no doubt that Leibniz was an ecumenical Christian, for as Friedrich Meinecke pointed out,

> Leibniz is a good example of the truth that both the loosening up of dogmatic and ecclesiastical thought after the end of the Wars of Religion, and the development of the natural sciences in the later part of the seventeenth century, were prerequisites for the rise of historism. This eirenic thinker and mediator between the different confessions saw the one Christian truth, which he still accepted as such with dogmatic conviction, nevertheless existing as a matter of actual fact in different individual forms, which could not simply be condemned. The natural light of reason, far from being in contradiction to faith, confirmed him in the belief that the fundamental truths of Christianity were essentially at one with it. His dearest and deepest wish was to use the aid of reason to bring the confessional varieties of belief to this oneness: the "spirit who

26. Ibid.
27. Ibid., 159.
28. Ibid., 158–59.
29. Rescher, *Leibniz*, 13 (emphasis in original).

loves unity in diversity" is one of the most characteristic phrases in his *Nouveaux Essais*.[30]

That is why Leibniz, like many ecumenically minded Lutherans in the second half of the twentieth century, was temperamentally close to Melanchthon and especially to his formulation of basic Christian beliefs in the Augsburg Confession.[31]

Third, as Werner Elert pointed out, "Leibniz lived on the optimism of the Lutheran belief in God," and from an historical point of view he belongs to a picture of historical Lutheranism as a "supraindividual phenomenon in the history of thought."[32] For Luther and for Leibniz, God's creation was *Das Reich der Gnade*, or a realm of grace.[33] For Luther and for Leibniz, God was transcendent and immanent, omniscient and omnipresent at the same time. For Luther and for Leibniz, the Gospel of John was a basic source for their ways of viewing life.[34]

Unlike Luther's, however, Leibniz's *simul* way of viewing life was based on the concepts and *The Principles of Nature and Grace*, which was the title of one of his latest works,[35] rather than on the concepts of sin and grace.[36] This shift of emphasis within historical Lutheranism, which was accompanied by a shift away from the letters of Paul and toward the Gospel of John, had great significance both for the later Herder and for the intellectual and cultural revolution in Germany from 1760 to 1810.[37]

Undoubtedly, Leibniz can be seen as a major figure for the rationalization of a specifically Lutheran civilization. On the other hand, if

---

30. Meinecke, *Historism*, 16.

31. See Hildebrandt, *Leibniz und das Reich der Gnade*, 71.

32. Elert, *Structure of Lutheranism*, 475. See also Steven Ozment's significant and recent statement (first published in 2004) about the nature of Lutheranism: "Lutheran faith was, above all, reassurance that God was true to his Word and might confidently be trusted." Steven Ozment, *A Mighty Fortress: A New History of the German People*, 185. As one might expect from the title of this interesting and well-written work, here one can see the significance of Martin Luther for the history of the German people as a whole.

33. See especially Hildebrandt, *Leibniz und das Reich der Gnade*

34. For Leibniz, see Hildebrandt, *Leibniz und das Reich der Gnade*, 265–66.

35. "Principes de la Nature et de la Grace fondés en Raison," which has been translated into English as "Principles of Nature and Grace, Based on Reason," in Leibniz, *Philosophical Essays*, 206–13.

36. See Hildebrandt, *Leibniz und des Reich der Gnade*, 257, 275–77.

37. Ibid., 265. Here Hildebrandt emphasizes how "the idea of the *Johannes-Kirche*" was cultivated by Schwenkfelt, Lessing, Herder, and Schelling.

Lutheran distinctiveness is defined as an ethos, a Christian ethos (1) that "has kept alive the dialectic of the mystery of life," and (2) that is based on an "at-the-same-time" way and by an "in-with-and-under" way of viewing life, then Leibniz can be seen not as offering a new form of religion but rather as a major figure within that historical individuality and religious tradition called Lutheranism.

For some scholars, Leibniz's thought and work can be characterized as a mighty effort to stem "den Beginn der Entseelung des europäischen Geistes, [the beginning of taking the soul out of the European spirit]"[38] and the disenchantment of a Christian civilization that seemed to be threatened not only by atheism and a mechanistic view of the universe but also by Cartesian rationalism and Lockean empiricism. Certainly Leibniz would not have disagreed with this interpretation, for a central motive for Leibniz was "the construction of a philosophic system he regarded as capable of meeting all the rational exigencies of the world view of contemporary science on the one hand and Christian doctrine on the other."[39]

One of the aspects of Leibniz's upbringing that helped to shape his philosophy was the Lutheran view of the Lord's Supper. As Daniel C. Fouke pointed out, "As part of his general defense of Christianity and his efforts at ecclesiastical reunion, the Eucharist remained a philosophical concern for Leibniz from the 1660's to the end of his life." "Each stage of his philosophical development and every modification of his system," Fouke claims,

> was accompanied by an explanation of the Eucharist and a demonstration that his system is compatible with Transubstantiation. These explanations and demonstrations aimed simultaneously at defending the rationality of belief in the mysteries of the faith, at providing a neutral philosophical analysis of the metaphysical meaning of the Eucharist, and at showing the superiority of his own philosophy over that of the Cartesians who had suffered censure because of the unorthodoxy of their own explanations of Transubstantiation.[40]

38. Hildebrandt emphasizes not only that Leibniz was thoroughly familiar with Luther's disagreement with Erasmus over "The Bondage of the Will," that "[h]e saw in the mechanistic worldview, as based especially on Hobbes, not just an attack on Christian dogma but the beginning of *der Entseelung* [taking the soul out] of the European spirit" (ibid., 66).

39. Rescher, *Leibniz*, 38.

40. Fouke, "Metaphysics and the Eucharist in the Early Leibniz," 145–46.

"As a Lutheran," Fouke also pointed out, "Leibniz knew his own church held to a real presence of Christ in the Eucharist and was convinced that this was the intended meaning of Christ's own pronouncements."[41] What Fouke emphasizes in this study, however, is that while Leibniz's early metaphysical analysis of the meaning of the real presence convinced him that it was indistinguishable from transubstantiation, "as Leibniz became increasingly concerned with mathematical physics and as his metaphysical views took on a life of their own, his explanations of Transubstantiation became less and less important in the development of his own metaphysical views, and were reduced to an obligatory parameter within which he exposited his system in order to show compatibility between his own philosophy and Roman Catholic orthodoxy."[42]

In the year 1709, when Leibniz was asked by a Catholic scholar (Des Bosses) how the doctrine of the real presence of Christ's body in the Eucharist could be defended on Leibniz's principles, he replied that as a Lutheran he was personally committed neither to transubstantiation nor to consubstantiation, for all that he was prepared to accept was that Christ's body was "present" in the sense "that it is perceived (by God and the blessed) at the time that it is received."[43] Certainly one of the reasons that the *Monadology* has had a strong appeal to many Lutherans is that if one accepts the real presence of Christ in the Lord's Supper, it is easier to accept the views of Luther and Leibniz that God is somehow present and active also in every part of his creation.

In the metaphysics of the late period of his life, Leibniz held "that the only true unities are soul-like forms and that any multitude presupposes these for its existence."[44] Until the end of his life, as Donald Rutherford also pointed out, "Leibniz defends the view that no monad ever exists completely detached from an organic body."[45] For Leibniz, as Ernst Cassirer stated in his early work concerning Leibniz's system (1902), "the relation between form and material, soul and body, resulted in a condi-

---

41. Ibid., 146.
42. Ibid.
43. Rutherford, "Metaphysics: The Late Period," 159.
44. Ibid., 129.
45. Ibid., 136.

tion of strictest correlation: both can only be set forth in and with each other."[46]

As Cassirer pointed out in *Die Philosophie der Aufklärung* (1932), for Leibniz "the individual no longer functions merely as a special case, as an example; it now expresses something essential in itself and valuable through itself."[47] Although for Leibniz the concept of individuality had to be linked with the concept of universality, the central thought of Leibniz's philosophy was to be found "neither in the concept of individuality nor in that of universality," for these concepts were "explicable only in mutual relationship." They not only reflected on each other, but in this reflection they begat "the fundamental concept of harmony which constitutes the beginning and the end of the system." "'In our own being,'" says Leibniz in his essay *Of the True Mystical Theology*, "'is contained a germ, a footprint, a symbol of the divine nature and its true image.' This means that only the highest development of all individual energies—not their leveling, equalization, and extinction—leads to the truth of being, to the highest harmony, and to the most intensive fullness of reality. This fundamental conception calls for a new intellectual orientation because not only has a transformation in individual results taken place, but the ideal center of gravity of all philosophy has shifted."[48]

The growth of German thought, as Cassirer also pointed out, "is guided by the influence of Leibniz." The main trend of his thought, however, "gained recognition very slowly, fighting for every inch of the ground; but its penetration is, nevertheless, deep and effective."[49]

One of the main reasons that Leibniz's philosophy gained ground especially in Protestant Germany was that it was a deeply spiritual and dynamic way of viewing life that was compatible with St. Augustine's and Luther's ways of viewing life. Just as St. Augustine saw God as the unchanging Creator of all things subject to change and to time, and just as Luther saw the triune God as the Word become flesh and as the active but hidden force above, behind, and in all of his creation, so Leibniz saw God as the unchanging substance and legislator of a connected, harmonious, organic, and dynamic universe composed of active but hidden soul-like

---

46. Cassirer, *Leibniz' System*, 407–8. This is an excellent study for showing the connection between the philosophies of Leibniz and Kant.

47. Cassirer, *Philosophy of the Enlightenment*, 32.

48. Ibid., 33.

49. Ibid., 80–81.

substances called monads. For Herder and for Ranke, each of these three ways of viewing life was an important component of a new and deeply historical way of viewing life, which Troeltsch, Hintze, and Meinecke called historicism.

Leibniz also influenced the direction of German thought and culture through his critique of Locke's famous work, *An Essay on Human Understanding*. In the long philosophical dialogue called *New Essays on Human Understanding*, which was first published in 1765, Leibniz rejected both the blank page and the empiricism of Locke, and the rationalism and dualism of Descartes.

In the preface to this work, Leibniz wrote:

> Our disagreements concern points of some importance. There is the question whether the soul in itself is completely blank like a writing tablet on which nothing has as yet been written—a *tabula rasa*—as Aristotle and the author of the *Essay* maintain, and whether everything which is inscribed there comes solely from the senses and experience; or whether the soul inherently contains the sources of various notions and doctrines, which external objects merely rouse up on suitable occasions, as I believe and as do Plato and even the Schoolmen and all those who understand in this sense the passage of St. Paul where he states that God's law is written in our hearts (*Romans*, 2:15).[50]

In this preface, Leibniz also raised the question whether all truths depend on experience, that is, on induction and instances, or if some of them had some other foundation: "For if some events can be foreseen before any test had been made of them, it is obvious that we contribute something from our side. Although the senses are necessary for all our actual knowledge, they are not sufficient to provide it all, since they never give us anything but instances, that is particular or singular truths. But however many instances confirm a general truth, they are not sufficient to establish universal necessity; for it does not follow that what has happened will always happen in the same way."[51]

These questions, which Leibniz discussed in several hundred pages of dialogue, clearly reflect "a quite different conception of knowledge and science from that of British empiricism. Knowledge is not for him the passive effect of experience, describing and reproducing it in a copy, but

---

50. Leibniz, *New Essays on Human Understanding*, "Preface," 48.
51. Ibid., 49.

an active organization and interpretation of existence—a conception that has remained characteristic of the German tradition."[52]

German scholars since the late eighteenth century, as John Herman Randall Jr. also emphasized, could agree with Locke that truths of reason had to be firmly grounded in experience. But few "who had been bred in the tradition of Leibniz . . . could ever accept the observational and descriptive theory of science built up by the British and the French. Though founded on an experience of facts, knowledge for them had still to be a matter of the reasons why, reasons that could not be reduced to a mere succession of sensations. The subject matter of their critical analysis might, indeed must, be furnished by sense; but that analysis was futile if it stopped with sensations and reached no rational explanation."[53]

The questions that Leibniz raised in the preface to his *New Essays on Human Understanding* were the same ones that Immanuel Kant raised after he had read this work, and after David Hume had demonstrated how experience could only provide instances or singular truths. The way Kant answered these questions in his *Critique of Pure Reason* in the year 1781 was as significant for the development of German thought, education, and culture as Locke's *Essay on Human Understanding* has been for the English-speaking world. It is significant, however, "that Kant regarded himself as justifying the conception of Leibniz against that of the British, by a more critical method."[54]

CHLADENIUS AND THE IDEA OF A HISTORICAL SCIENCE (*GESCHICHTSWISSENSCHAFT*)

In the preamble to his *Prolegomena to Any Future Metaphysics* (1783), Immanuel Kant stated:

---

52. Randall, *From the German Enlightenment*, 48. See also page 42, where Randall claims that the dialogue form of the *New Essays* "accentuates the opposition between the two sets of underlying assumptions about knowledge, the presuppositions that were to be sharpened but not fundamentally questioned in the tradition of British empiricism, and those of Leibniz embedded deeply in the classical German philosophy. These differences in intellectual attitude and premises illustrated in Leibniz on the one side and Newton and Locke on the other have persisted in the two national traditions to this day, determining how common problems shall be faced and how new developments shall be interpreted."

53. Ibid., 76–77.

54. Ibid., 49.

If it becomes desirable to organize any knowledge as science, it will be necessary first to demonstrate accurately those peculiar features which no other science has in common with it, constituting its peculiarity; otherwise the boundaries of all sciences become confused, and none of them can be treated thoroughly according to its nature.

The peculiar characteristic of a science may consist of a simple difference of object, or of the sources of knowledge, or of the kind of knowledge, or perhaps of all three conjointly. On these, therefore, depends the idea of a possible science and its territory.[55]

In 1752, thirty-one years before Kant made this significant statement and thirteen years before Leibniz's *New Essays on Human Understanding* was first published, Johann Martin Chladenii or Chladenius (1710–1759)—"Doctor of Holy Scripture, Professor of Rhetoric and Poetry, and also Pastor of the University Church of Erlangen"—published a book called *Allgemeine Geschichtswissenschaft, worinnen der Grund zu einen neuen Einsicht in allen Arten der Gelahrheit gelegt wird*.[56] A very literal translation of this title into English is, "General Science of History, Containing the Basis for a New Insight into all Arts of Learning." It is both interesting and significant that (1) the first sophisticated "hermeneutics" for a *Geschichtswissenschaft* in Germany, and (2) the first serious discussion of the object, sources, and kind of knowledge of this "new science" were written by a Lutheran pastor and theologian; for from the time of Luther and Melanchthon through the first half of the eighteenth century, history was primarily a handmaiden for theology, the queen of the sciences and the most highly professionalized academic discipline in Protestant Germany. As John Herman Randall Jr. pointed out, "The chief intellectual concern in Germany remained religion and theology."[57]

In the preface, Chladenius provided a number of reasons that led him to write this book. First of all, he suggested, it was a result of divine providence that had led him to teach a great variety of subjects at the universities of Wittenberg and Leipzig before he came to Erlangen. Since so much of his work as a teacher of rhetoric, the Bible, "church antiqui-

---

55. Kant, *Prolegomena to Any Future Metaphysics*, 13.

56. This book was published in Leipzig. Since there were no page numbers in the preface, none are provided here. Page references for the rest of this book are indicated in the text within parentheses or brackets.

57. Randall, *From the German Enlightenment*, 52.

ties," and systematic theology involved the study of historical texts, since a great part of holy doctrine was based on the art of "historical cognition" (*Erkenntnis*) and since there was a real need to bring clarity to the "individual concepts" of history, he decided to undertake the new and difficult task of writing a philosophical and systematic "hermeneutics" for interpreting historical texts.

In the preface, Chladenius also explained how the major question he had to face in writing this study was whether it should be written mainly for the use of religious instruction or for other kinds of instruction as well. The chief motivation for choosing the first path would be to explain and defend revealed truth. In the end, however, he decided to present a "General Science of History" because this would be more useful, because all truths could be divided into general truths and historical truths, and because such a study would also provide good service to theology.

The key word that Chladenius used throughout this work was *eine Begebenheit*, a word that can be translated as an "event" or "occurrence," but which he used in a more inclusive way. For Chladenius, *eine Begebenheit* was first of all "a change in the world, in its reality, which can be observed"(2). It was a thing or object one could see and grasp as a single entity in relation to both space and time. If a row of similar changes followed directly after the other, together they could be seen as *eine Begebenheit*. Thus for Chladenius, a history (*eine Geschichte*) was "a connected row of *Begebenheiten*" (4).

For Chladenius, a "historical sentence" was a sentence or judgment about *eine Begebenheit* (3). The sentences, in which a history was expressed, were called a narrative. Thus history and narratives belonged together (8), and thus history always required both a narrator and an observer (14).

For Chladenius, "the science of historical cognition" was a part of *der Vernunftlehre*, or the theory of knowledge; but from the time of Aristotle to the time he was writing, Chladenius claimed that the theory of knowledge was based almost entirely on general truths, on logic, and on cognition in general. It is interesting that the first of two times when Leibniz was mentioned in this book, it was in reference to the need for a science of historical cognition, and especially for greater attention to the concept of probability (*des Wahrscheinlichen* [26–27]).

Another basic concept for Chladenius was the word *Anschauen*, which meant, "to look upon," "to view," or "to contemplate." For

Chladenius, *Anschauen* was more than a glance, for it was a many-sided and uninterrupted view of an object (31). The place from which one's eyes viewed an object he called the *Sehepunckt*, or the viewing or vantage point. The viewing point of an observer was influenced by the distance from an object, by the side of the object the viewer could see, and by the material between the viewer and the object (37). This idea, that history was based on a way of perceiving called an *anschauende Erkenntnis* became one of the most important ideas for German historical thought in the late eighteenth century and for the whole historiographical tradition in Germany.[58]

For Chladenius, there were two main kinds of *Begebenheiten* that the observer perceived from a vantage point: 1) bodies or physical entities, which usually could be seen or touched; and 2) "moral beings or things," which were changes in the human soul, especially of the will (59). Since human beings consisted of both bodies and souls, a *Sehepunckt*, or viewing point, also involved both the external and the internal condition (*Zustand*) of the observer (100). Although Chladenius believed that this distinction was of basic importance for almost all historical cognition, he believed that it was used and applied only by Leibniz, and only here and there in his metaphysics and psychology (100–101).[59]

In all histories, however, the observer only had a particular outlook and insight, and this had obvious consequences for the narrative of the historian (114–15). The narration of an event was never completely the same as the event itself, for a narrative was always based on the picture that had formed in the soul of the observer (116). Since historians could not avoid using words that reflected the observer's sensations and feelings, Chladenius insisted that a narrative was a representation of an event (119). A narrative could also never be the same as what it portrayed, because it necessarily involved a transformation (115) and abbreviation (268) of what happened, and because there were many hidden aspects and "unresearchable" secrets in what Chladenius called the *Begebenheiten* of the human soul (265–66). Since a history was defined by Chladenius as a row of *Begebenheiten* that fit together, historical cognition was therefore

---

58. According to Reill, "The idea of direct understanding, called by the eighteenth-century Germans *anschauende Erkenntnis*, dominated the epistemology of the latter half of the eighteenth century" (*German Enlightenment*, 98).

59. The *Theodicée* was the only work by Leibniz that was cited by Chladenius either in the text or in his list of works cited.

a row of intuitive judgments (*Anschauungsurtheilen*) based on reports, narratives, documents, and statements that spread from one soul to another (275).[60]

Much of the language and many of the ideas that Chladenius discussed in this book can also be found in his earlier work, *Einleitung zur richtigen Auslegung vernünfftiger Reden und Schriften*[61] or *Introduction to the Right Interpretation of More Rational Speeches and Writings* (1742). Here, however, *Historie* was still regarded as one of the "schöne Wissenschaften," "belles lettres," or the fine arts such as poetry, eloquence, antiquities, and rhetoric.[62] Because "the art of writing histories" (*Historien*) rested on the ability to make rejuvenated pictures ("verjüngte Bildern zu machen"), Chladenius said, it required exact contemplation.[63] Especially in this earlier work, one can see how the idea of a *Sehe-Punckt* (1742) or *Sehepunckt* (1752) was derived from Leibniz.[64]

It is very significant for the idea of history, however, (1) that the terms *Geschichtswissenschaft* and *Begebenheit* were new in 1752, and (2) that now the word *Geschichte*—rather than *Historie* or *Historien*—had become the dominant term. It is significant, as Reinhart Koselleck pointed out, (1) that the word *Geschichte* as a "collective-singular" term—in contrast to the plural words *Geschichten* and *Historien*—appeared in Germany between the years 1750 and 1770, and (2) that interest in *Geschichte* as a unity marked its beginning as an object and theme of philosophy, rather than of rhetoric, as it had been since the time of Aristotle.[65] It is also significant for the whole idea of history in the West that in Germany *die Geschichte*

---

60. For a good summary and analysis of how Chladenius described the transformation of a *Geschichte* in the sense of what really happened into a historical narrative, see Ermarth, "Hermeneutics and History," 193–221. In respect to this transformation, Ermarth states: "Chladenius' observations here are to my knowledge the first instance of systematically developed critical self-consciousness concerning the history of history itself. For this alone, he deserves an esteemed place in the 'channel' of modern historical thought. Here he could be called a genuine explorer" (ibid., 213).

61. Chladenius, *Einleitung*.

62. Ibid. 105 and 234.

63. Ibid., 215.

64. Ibid., 188.

65. See especially Koselleck, "Geschichte V. Die Herausbildung, 647–91. Koselleck's account of the development of "des modernen Geschichtsbegriffs" is of fundamental importance for understanding the development of historical thought in Germany from the 1750s to the year 1810.

was "a new reality concept" and "a new reflection concept" at the same time, and that during the last third of the eighteenth century it replaced the word *Historie*.⁶⁶

Although much of the language of the *Allgemeine Geschichtswissenschaft* is not that of our age, some of its ideas are quite modern. The idea that every history is written from a particular viewing point and from a particular point of view, from the position of the outer person and from the condition of the soul of the inner person, is quite consistent with Luther's theology and with the philosophy of Leibniz, but it is also of fundamental importance for modern historical thought.

One of the basic ideas of modern historical thought, as Koselleck also pointed out, was the clear distinction that Chladenius made between a particular history (*die Geschichte*) and how it was viewed and presented by the historian. As Chladenius noted in his earlier work, customarily people believed that the history (*die Geschichte*) and the presentation of the history were one and the same. To construct a history and to make historical judgments, Claudenius insisted, the historian had to understand this distinction: "The history [*die Geschichte*] is one thing, the presentation of it is different and manifold"(195). From the concept of the *Sehe-Punckt*, Chladenius said, it follows that persons who saw the same thing from different viewing points had to have different conceptions of it (189).⁶⁷

In his *Allgemeine Geschichtswissenschaft*, Chladenius also emphasized the difference between nonpartisan (*unparteyischen*) and partisan narratives that, contrary to knowledge and conscience, deliberately distorted and obscured. A nonpartisan narrative, he said, could not mean to narrate an event without all perspectives (*Sehepunkten*), for that was not possible. At the same time, however, a partisan narrative could not mean to narrate a matter (*Sache*) and history (*Geschichte*) only according to "his perspective," for this would mean that all narratives were partisan (151–52).

"With this declaration, that perspective judgment and partisanship were not identical," Reinhard Koseleck declared, Chladenius established a theoretical framework "which still today is unsurpassed."⁶⁸ With the

---

66. Ibid., 653.

67. Ibid., 696–97. Each of these sentences was quoted and emphasized by Koselleck.

68. Ibid., 697.

understanding that the criteria for forming judgments and historical presentation could not be reduced to mere partisanship, Koselleck also suggests, then Herder's idea that each age, each nation, and each individuality possessed its own justification was possible.[69]

One of the ideas that one can see first in Chladenius and later in the work of Hamann and Herder was the idea in the *Allgemeine Geschichtswissenschaft* that the concept *Geschichte* included not only past and present but also future things, since it included the idea of revelation (15). Thus Chladenius could assert, "Then *die Geschichte* in and for itself has no end" (147).[70] A narrative of a particular history, however, did have to have an end, because it could not be considered a history if it had no connection with the general concept under which it could be grasped as an "*individuum*."[71]

Although the *Allgemeine Geschichtswissenschaft* of Chladenius was an insightful attempt to establish a philosophical foundation and a theory of knowledge for this new science, historians have had some difficulty in dealing with this book and in showing direct connections between his writings and the development of history as an academic science or discipline in Germany.[72] One of the first difficulties historians have had in dealing with Chladenius is the fact that his *Allgemeine Geschichtswissenschaft* was such a rare book even in Germany.[73] Second, it is difficult to know how much the main concept that Chladenius used throughout this book, *eine Begebenheit*, directly influenced other writers.[74] Nevertheless, histo-

69. Ibid., 697.
70. Ibid., 651–52.
71. Ibid.
72. See Reill, *German Enlightenment*, 112.

73. In the early 1980s, for example, this book was not available at the University of Göttingen, and there I was told that the two places where it was available were Munich and Prague. Thus I had to go to Munich to see it. In 1985, however, it was reprinted.

74. It was also an important term for Sigmund Jacob Baumgarten, an important contemporary of Chladenius, and also for many later Enlightenment scholars (see Zedelmaier, *Der Anfang der Geschichte*, 139–40, 176, and especially 196). In 1796, for example, Friedrich Meier wrote: "*Geschichte ist die Darstellung von Begebenheiten.* [*History* is the presentation of occurrences.]" See Horst and Fleischer, *Elemente der Aufklärungshistorik*, 369. It was also a useful term at the beginning of the twentieth century for Ernst Bernheim in his important work called *Lehrbuch der historischen Methode und Geschichtsphilosophie*. Bernheim was one of the first historians to recognize the significance of Chladenius for what Collingwood later called "the idea of history." For a useful introduction to the literature dealing with Chladenius to the year 1978, see Friedrich,

rians needed a word and concept like this to capture individual objects and subjects as a whole, and to trace their development in time.

As Hintze most clearly pointed out, a historian has to be able to see his or her object and subject as a connected whole, both as a life-unit and as a life-process, in order to write its history.[75] Although Chladenius occasionally used the word "individual" or "individuality"(either in Latin or in German) to mean a particular concept, object, or subject, it was not a basic concept for him or an interchangeable word for *eine Begebenheit*.

The other basic word and concept for modern historical thought, the word *Entwicklung* ("development"), does not appear in this book. Although for Chladenius, *eine Begebenheit* was a changing historical object and subject, the word *Veränderung* is not the same as the basic concept of the nineteenth century in Germany and the West: the word *Entwicklung* and the concept of development.

Another basic word and concept of German thought since the 1760s, the word *Geist* or *spirit* seldom appears in this pioneer study.[76] Here the basic concepts of the formative period for modern German thought and culture, the concepts *nature* and *Geist* are not yet basic terms.

One of the ways in which Chladenius was an important forerunner for the period of cultural change in Germany from the 1760s through the first decade of the nineteenth century, was that his work pointed "to the direction which the thought of the Aufklärung would travel."[77] More than anyone else in Germany, however, Chladenius also deserves to be recognized today as the father of (1) the idea of a *Geschichtswissenschaft*,[78] (2)

Sprache und Geschichte, 31–41.

75. See Hintze, "Troeltsch and the Problems of Historicism," 381–91; see also Hintze, *Soziologie und Geschichte*, 334–43, the third introductory quotation to chapter 1 above, and my translation of Hintze's definition of historicism below, in chapter 5, part 3.

76. The main exception to this is the first paragraph of the first chapter where Chladenius uses the expression "der unendliche Geist."

77. Reill, *German Enlightenment*, 112. Reill does a good job not only of resurrecting many of the ideas of Chladenius (105–12), but also of tracing the significance of the idea of an *anschauende Erkenntnis* for Johann Christoph Gatterer (112–18), for the German Enlightenment, and for the rise of historicism.

78. In his helpful essay for understanding the progress and limits of "The Institutionalization of History in 18th-Century Germany," Konrad H. Jarausch stated that one indication of the gradual emancipation of history from the status of an auxiliary discipline for the higher faculties of theology and law was "the appearance of the term *Geschichtswissenschaft* in the Göttingen lecture announcements around 1770" (41). Three aspects indicating "the partial institutionalization" (47) of history at this time, however, were (1)

a hermeneutics for this "new science,"[79] and (3) the ideas that a distinctly historical way of understanding life is based both on an *anschauende Erkenntnis* ("intuitive perception") and a particular perspective. For this orthodox Lutheran theologian, who never composed a history, the *Allgemeine Geschichtswissenschaft* was an important result of and an important part of his interdisciplinary calling.

In the first half of the eighteenth century, historical study in Germany lagged behind that of France and England, and within Germany it was mainly an auxiliary discipline for the theology and law faculties. As Konrad Jarausch has pointed out, however, it was the connection of history with these higher faculties "which endowed history with sufficient prestige to turn it into a *Wissenschaft*—in contrast to its onetime peers eloquence and poetry."[80] Thus during the second half of the eighteenth century, historical research, which prior to this time had been mainly a domain of the jurists and theologians, was established within the field of history within the German universities.[81]

This change can be seen especially at the University of Göttingen in the 1760s, when a society for completing a translation of *An Universal History* was founded, and when this project was transferred from the hands of the theologian Semler (after volume 30 in 1766) to the hands of

---

that "the stranglehold on secondary teaching in the Latin schools left the historians in the philosophical faculty without a profession to train for," (2) that "the professorship was not yet a profession either" (31), and (3) that "history had not yet firmly established itself as a legitimate discipline with its own critical method, subject matter, etc." (46).

79. For the significance of the *Allgemeine Geschichtswissenschaft* of Chladenius for the whole development of the "critical-historical" study of source materials and its various categories, see Muhlack, *Geschichtswissenschaft im Humanismus und in der Aufklärung*, 383–84. See also his very helpful discussion of the significance of this work for the whole development of "the theory of historical cognition" on pages 76 through 85. In this very thorough and helpful book, Muhlack emphasizes how humanistic and Enlightenment historiography was pragmatic and didactic. In contrast to the view of the present study, however, Muhlack's view of historicism is based on that of Croce rather than the views of Hintze and Meinecke.

80. Jarausch, "Institutionalization of History in 18th-Century Germany," 36. In this essay, which deals with the institutionalization of history in Germany both in Protestant and the Catholic universities, Jarausch emphasizes that during the Enlightenment "history was not a discipline with firm boundaries but rather an emerging disciplinary complex in several faculties" (ibid.), and that "the interaction of scholarship within the disciplinary complex of theology, law and history led to a marked sophistication of historical methods" (ibid., 37).

81. Zedelmaier, *Der Anfang der Geschichte*, 178.

the Göttingen historian Johann Christoph Gatterer.[82] With this new director, this translation effort became a project of "des königlich-kurfürstlichen Institutes der historischen Wissenschaften," a project that continued into the nineteenth century, and that was not dependent on its English model.[83]

During the five decades from 1760 to 1810, a new type of Western historiography gradually arose in Germany. At this time history gradually moved in the direction of a full-time *Beruf*—both as a calling and as a profession—*and* a *Wissenschaft* primarily at the University of Göttingen and primarily through the work of "the Göttingen historians": Johann Christoph Gatterer (1727–1799), August Ludwig Schlözer (1735–1809), Ludwig Timotheus Spittler (1752–1810), and Arnold Hermann Ludwig Heeren (1760–1842). As Herbert Butterfield stated many years ago, it was this university "which prepared the way for what was to be the Scientific Revolution in historical study";[84] for here one could see "a broadly based movement and a continuous development," and it was here that historical scholarship came closest to "the system established by the nineteenth century school."[85] Whereas Butterfield admitted that "the dynamic ideas which helped to transform historical study may have risen outside the universities," in Göttingen "they were critically considered and carefully combined so as to form a system of historical scholarship." "Whether we envisage the attitude adopted to this kind of scholarship, or the treatment of universal history, or the revision of national and regional studies, the school of Göttingen seems to bring us to the very brink of the modern world. In the case of some of these things, the very next step is Niebuhr, or Ranke, or the Monumenta Germaniae Historica."[86]

---

82. Ibid., 177–78.
83. Ibid., 178.
84. Butterfield, *Man on his Past*, 42. The title of the chapter on the Göttingen historians is called "The Rise of the German Historical School."
85. Ibid., 60–61.
86. Ibid., 61. Although Butterfield emphasized how the development of this system of historical scholarship was a gradual process, he also called it "an intellectual revolution." For the significance of the University of Göttingen for the beginnings of history as a modern historical science, see Rudolf Vierhaus, "Die Universität Göttingen," 1–29. Here Vierhaus asserts that first in Göttingen, history became an "independent" and "institutionally established *Wissenschaft*" (13).

four

The Cultural Revolution in Germany and the Rise of a New Historical Consciousness, 1760–1810

> Spirit [*Geist*] is the nature of Lutheranism, just as it is the nature of Christianity, free conviction, testing, and self-determination. Without this spirit of freedom, everything is or becomes like a corpse [*Leichnam*]. The rights that Luther had, we all have; may we also exercise them, firm and great like him
>
> —Johann Gottfried Herder[1]

> Historism was able to win acceptance because the long-dominant idea that rationality originated in the individual consciousness was superseded by the powerful idea of an all-embracing life that is beyond the grasp of the individual's rational powers and that includes the rational person within itself. The opposition of "life-viewers" [*Lebensschauern*] and "form-thinkers" [*Formdenkern*] is not a phenomenon of our time alone. It was clearly present in Herder's later view of Kant; and in a variety of forms and combinations, it has remained with us to the present day.
>
> —Otto Hintze[2]

The Problem

One of the basic frustrations of American teachers of German education, history, language, literature, philosophy, and religion is that there is no adequate interdisciplinary period term to capture and portray that great and formative age for the development of modern German thought, culture, and education: the last four decades of the eighteenth century and

---

1. Herder, *Sämmtliche Werke*, 19:52. Hereafter this work is cited as Herder, SW.

2. Hintze, "Troeltsch und die Probleme des Historismus," 342. Cf., Hintze, "Troeltsch and the Problems of Historicism," 395.

the first decade of the nineteenth. During these five decades, a cultural or humanistic revolution took place in Germany that—together with the other revolutionary movements of the seventeenth and eighteenth centuries—shaped the Western world in the nineteenth century. What it lacks, however, is a name.

In the year 1959, when R. R. Palmer published the first volume of a two-volume work called *The Age of the Democratic Revolution*, he showed how the American and French revolutions could be seen as the two chief events in this age from 1760 to 1800, an age that he created. In a chapter of the second volume (1964), Palmer used the title "Germany: The Revolution of the Mind" to show how by the end of the eighteenth century, some German writers believed that Kant's philosophy was an intellectual revolution that was in some ways comparable to the political revolution in France. Palmer also emphasized, however, that there was no revolution in Germany before 1800, for the great changes there came in the following decade when "The Revolution from Above" affected "a territorial and legal transformation that wiped out many aspects of the Old Regime."[3]

Is the idea of seeing the 1760s as the beginning of a "Revolution of the Mind" a useful period term for understanding and teaching an age that included both Hamann and Kant, both Herder and Goethe, both Schelling and Hegel, both Fichte and Schleiermacher, both the culmination of the *Aufklärung*—or the German Enlightenment—*and* the rise of historicism and of those powerful intellectual forces of the nineteenth century known as German idealism, romanticism, and nationalism? If this age is extended to the year 1810 so that it includes "The Revolution from Above," Hegel's *Phänomenologie des Geistes* (1807), the first part of Goethe's *Faust* (1808), and the breakthrough of a distinctly modern system of education with the founding of the University of Berlin (1810) and the Prussian and German *Gymnasium*, it could be a very useful period term not only for historians, philosophers, and theologians but also for teachers of education, literature, and the social sciences.[4] Then it

---

3. Palmer, *Struggle*, 426–27.

4. For a good interdisciplinary discussion of the 1760s as a good beginning time for what has often been called "The German Movement," see Dann, "Herder und die Deutsche Bewegung," 308–40. For Dann, the best year to mark the beginning of a new stage for German culture and society is the year 1765, when a new generation announced itself (324–25).

would be possible to show students how the modern Western world was shaped not only by the scientific revolution of the seventeenth century, by the Enlightenment (especially in France, Great Britain, and the United States—as it is in most history texts in the United States), by the American and French revolutions, and by the Industrial Revolution in Great Britain, but also by a sixth revolution.

But what should this revolution be called? The term "Revolution of the Mind" is not adequate, for it was both an intellectual *and* a spiritual revolution. The term "Revolution of the *Geist*" is better because this word means both "mind" and "spirit" and because this is the time when this word became a key concept for modern German thought and culture. The two chief problems with this term, however, are (1) that it, too, does not do full justice to this formative period for modern German thought, culture, and education; and (2) that it would be a very difficult one for teachers in the English-speaking world to use. Since period terms are models that have to be judged by their usefulness, is the term "the cultural revolution" the best interdisciplinary term to see, capture, and use to portray this time and place? This is the first aspect of the problem behind this chapter.

In a helpful, little-known, and almost unavailable address that Sydney Ahlstrom gave to a group of Lutheran educators in the year 1974, he suggested that when one considers the Lutheran tradition in an educational context, it could be seen "as flowing in three major currents which have remained more or less distinct even though they have constantly influenced each other during the long course of post-reformation history": (1) the scholastic, which is also called the orthodoxist, (2) the pietistic, and (3) "the Critical."[5]

The first of these currents, which arose in the sixteenth century and flourished in the seventeenth, was based on an enormous confidence in "the infallibility and total sufficiency of the received biblical text" and also on "a wholehearted adoption of Aristotelian metaphysics."[6] For Ahlstrom, the "Pietistic current" that centered in Protestant Germany during the seventeenth and eighteenth centuries, was a "vast and humanly essential form of evangelical religiosity" and "a necessary result of the Reformation." This current placed a strong emphasis not only on the inner life of the Christian soul but also on doing good works. Because of its emphasis

---

5. Ahlstrom, "What's Lutheran about Higher Education—A Critique," 8.
6. Ibid., 9.

Cultural Revolution in Germany and a New Historical Consciousness 129

on the subjective dimension of religion, it was constantly engaged in a struggle with "Christian rationalism, both Orthodox and Enlightened." In addition, Ahlstrom claimed, "this current provided important spiritual grounds for a romantic understanding of religion."[7]

What Ahlstrom had to say about the "critical tradition," however, is most helpful and significant for this inquiry; for here he suggested how the work and time of Kant was significant not only for the Lutheran tradition but also for the modern Western world. When "one speaks of the rise of Protestantism," Ahlstrom stated, one confronts what he called "the 'critical tradition' in Lutheranism and therewith the scholarly and philosophical activities which dominated the 19th century."[8] For Ahlstrom, Immanuel Kant (1724–1804) was probably "the leading exemplar" of this third tradition, for his work was "at once the turning point in modern philosophy and a crucial bridge between Enlightened and Romantic views of reality." In other ways, Kant could also be seen "as carrying-out certain aspects of the program of Luther himself, bearing out, as it were, the philosophical implications of the Reformation."[9]

For Ahlstrom, the first and most important thing about "the critical tradition" was that "it came to terms with modern science and no longer viewed the search for knowledge of the natural world as an enemy of religion." "Equally important," he believed, "and for many more troublesome, it began a serious investigation of the whole historical world." For Ahlstrom, the nineteenth century had to be seen as "the age of historical renaissance," and at this time "critical scholarship" became involved "in the whole field of religion, the history of scriptures, of ancient civilizations, of churches and their divergent doctrines, and finally the history of world religions."[10]

Now these statements contain only an outline of what Ahlstrom said in this brief address, but they provide a good starting point for a brief sketch of the rise of a new kind of historical consciousness in relation to this third current or tradition within Lutheranism and to this Cultural Revolution in Germany. Would it not be more helpful, however, to call

---

7. Ibid., 10–11.
8. Ibid., 11.
9. Ibid.
10. Ibid.

this third main current "the critical-historical tradition"? This is the second main aspect of the problem behind this chapter.

In his book *The German Enlightenment and the Rise of Historicism* (1975), Peter Hanns Reill provided a helpful supplement to Friedrich Meinecke's pioneer work called *Die Entstehung des Historismus* (1936). One of the ways that Reill's book was a helpful supplement is that, as the title suggests, it showed how the German Enlightenment and the rise of historicism went hand in hand.

It was also a helpful supplement because Reill avoided the major figures of eighteenth-century Germany in order to show how the Enlightenment and historicism were advanced by university-trained academics, lawyers, and Protestant clergymen who had been activated by Pietism, and who "sought to resolve the contradictions between Pietism, orthodoxy, and rationalism through the use of history supported by critical reflection and philosophical inquiry." Their goal, Reill claims, "was to rescue religion, not destroy it, through a transformation of its meaning and function."[11] All the elements that defined the *Aufklärung* and differentiated it from "the Franco-British Enlightenment," Reill emphasized, "found expression in the Aufklärung's historical consciousness";[12] for the "Aufklärers' religious convictions led them to espouse an idea of history that postulated an interaction between spirit and nature." For them "the freedom of spirit attested to the existence of God," and spirit and genius were "inexplicable qualities that defied logical analysis." While to them, spirit was conceived "as an independent force, it did not exist outside history"; for each "historical form contained a spiritual element and an element ascribable to material and historical factors."[13]

According to Reill, the large majority of the *Aufklärers* first planned to study theology, changed their minds while attending the university, but remained professing Christians.[14] "The Aufklärers, he said, "no longer felt compelled to speculate about the origins and the final meanings of things"; for they "accepted the miracle of creation and the impossibility

---

11. Reill, *German Enlightenment*, 6.
12. Ibid., 8.
13. Ibid.
14. Ibid., 77.

of defining God," and "they were convinced that an investigation of God's creations was in itself a hymn of praise to Him."¹⁵

A third way Reill's work can be regarded as a helpful supplement to Meinecke's pioneer study was the way he tied the rise of historicism to the political and social structure in Germany, to the universities, and to the work of the Göttingen historians. For Reill, the *Aufklärung* could be characterized as "an intellectual movement formed by the conjunction of three elements: the legacy of Leibnizian philosophy, the *Ständestaat* tradition, and the Protestant religious tradition generated by the appearance of pietism." As Reill also pointed out, this movement "was bourgeois in spirit, critical of absolutism, opposed to attitudes associated with the court, but not revolutionary in nature." While its "intellectual center was the university and its leading proponents were drawn from the professional classes," the "most important single center was the newly founded university of Göttingen "[1737].¹⁶

Just as Reill's book was a useful supplement to Meinecke's pioneer study on the rise of historicism, so today there is a need to supplement Meinecke's and Reill's studies through another look at some of the major figures for the rise of modern German thought in relation to the rise of modern historical thought.¹⁷ This is a third aspect of the problem behind this chapter.

For many reasons, the three aspects of the problem behind this chapter are discussed in relation to the thought and work mainly of just three of the great scholars of this formative age for modern German thought and culture: Johann Georg Hamann, Johann Gottfried Herder, and Immanuel Kant. The chief purpose behind this chapter is to suggest how a distinctly modern kind of historical consciousness arose out of a "Revolution of the *Geist*," as it has been called in Germany,¹⁸ or what in

---

15. Ibid., 33.

16. Ibid., 7–8.

17. This, of course, has been done by Reill and many other scholars since 1975. In the essay "Science and the Science of History in the Spätaufklärung," for example, Reill showed how a basic change in "the explanatory model" of the nature of science in the second half of the eighteenth century influenced Herder's later work. In *Aufklärung und Geschichte*, 430–51.

18. In the year 1968, Jürgen Gebhardt edited a book of essays called *Revolution des Geistes; Politisches Denken in Deutschland 1770–1830: Goethe, Kant, Fichte, Hegel, Humboldt*. In the introductory essay, "Zur Physiognomie einer Epoche," Gebhardt emphasized that the period from 1770 to 1830 was the time when German philosophy,

the English-speaking world can best be called a "Cultural Revolution." It was especially during these five decades that the word *Geist*—which came to signify not only the "spirit" *and* "mind" of an individual but also the spirit of an age, a nation, or even of the world as a whole—became a word of central importance for German thought, education, and culture. The fact that this spiritual and intellectual revolution in Germany can be expressed by a religious word in German, and either by a secular or a religious word in English, is just one indication of how these two languages have gone in different directions since the time of Hamann, Herder, Kant, Goethe, and Hegel and of the significance of "the linguistic turn" that took place in Germany in the late eighteenth century.[19]

One of the basic reasons that the term "Cultural Revolution" is the best one for this period of German intellectual and cultural history is that the five decades from 1760 to 1810 constitute the time when the word *Kultur* became a basic historical concept of German and Western thought and literature, when it attained its modern meaning, and when it was applied—as it is now—to a nation as a whole.[20]

A second main purpose behind this chapter is to suggest how the rise of German historicism was closely associated with what Otto Hintze called "the powerful idea of an all-embracing life that is beyond the grasp of the individual's rational powers and that includes the rational person within itself."[21] From the time of Hamann and Herder through the death of Ranke in 1886, many German historians believed that God was present in nature and in human history, that the study of history was a calling,

---

education (*Bildung*), and literature were created (7), a time that is often called "The Goethe Age."

19. For the use of the expression "linguistic turn" for Germany in the late eighteenth century, see Kelley, "Mythistory in the Age of Ranke," 7–8. See also Kelley's statement that the goal of romantic hermeneutics "was—by moving from words to meaning, from *Wort* to *Geist* and perhaps to *Zeit-* and *Volksgeist*—to understand an author as he would have wished to be understood" (ibid., 8).

20. The history of the word *Kultur* as a basic historical concept in relation to the word *civilization* has been documented very well by Jörg Fisch, "Zivilisation, Kultur," in *Geschichtliche Grundbegriffe*, 7:679–774. See especially 705–16 where Fisch shows how the term *Kultur* was broadened, popularized, and historicized beginning in the 1760s; how it was broadened from the individual to the collective (both to peoples and humanity); how it was broadened and historicized especially by Herder; and how by the year 1801, it had attained its fully modern meaning.

21. See the second introductory quotation to this chapter.

and that the history of humankind could not be comprehended by reason alone.

A third main purpose of this chapter is to investigate and clarify how Herder was the great "life-viewer" and Kant the great "form-thinker" of this age, for their differences were of fundamental importance for Friedrich Meinecke and Otto Hintze, the great life-viewer and the great form-thinker of German and Western historical thought in the first third of the twentieth century. In the process of this investigation, however, I came to see that it was Hamann and Kant, more than Herder and Kant, who could best be seen as the great "supplementary antipoles"[22] of this spiritual, intellectual, and cultural revolution in Germany from 1760 through the educational changes that took place in Prussia in the year 1810.

JOHANN GEORG HAMANN'S "AT-THE-SAME-TIME" AND "IN-WITH-AND-UNDER" THEOLOGY OF LANGUAGE

In an insightful essay concerning "Luther and the Modern World," Thomas Nipperdey suggested that the modernizing potential of Lutheranism was actualized in a "second phase of Protestantism," a phase that coincided with the rise of the modern world since the late eighteenth century. Like Max Weber, Nipperdey believed that "the disenchantment of the world and the rationalization of our conduct of life ... did not take place against religion but rather the reverse, through religion." This hypothesis, he suggested, could be substantiated by looking at Luther, for Luther "established themes of life, a grasping toward the world, social-moral norms, and behavioral patterns which in all forms of his church remained virulent." For Nipperdey, Luther's "intensification of religion is one of the most important roots of the modern world, of the modern type of human being."[23]

For Nipperdey, Luther was not "the father of the modern world," but he created something that Nipperdey and the sociologist Eisenstadt called a "modernizing potential" or a "mentality" that strongly favored "the rise and establishment of the modern world since the late eighteenth century when other modernizing factors—economic, political, and in-

---

22. A "supplementary antipole" is an image from a letter (August 30, 1921) by Otto Hintze to Friedrich Meinecke (see also n. 87 in chapter 5 below).

23. Nipperdey, "Luther and die modernen Welt," 35.

stitutional—appeared and as the pre-modern elements of the world and also the old Protestantism became weaker." In this "second phase of Protestantism," Nipperdey claimed, "the Lutheran modernizing potential became actual."[24]

In this helpful essay, Nipperdey summarized how the modernizing potential of Lutheranism was actualized under six main points, just two of which can be mentioned here. First of all, the modern world is individualistic, and here Nipperdey emphasized how Luther's personalistic faith contributed to an "inner freedom" that not only helped to make the individual independent but also contributed to the development of that phenomenon that "we Germans" call Lutheran *Innerlichkeit*, or inward looking. According to Nipperdey, the theme of life for Luther and Lutheran Christians was "God and soul, not God and the world as with the Calvinists"; and he also thought that the secular German ideal of *Bildung*, or education as "self-cultivation" and "self-realization," followed from this Lutheran *Innerlichkeit*.[25]

Second, Nipperdey held that "the modern world is a world of reflection and of knowledge," and here he emphasized the unique relationship between "university and *Wissenschaft*" within the Lutheran tradition. Luther was a teacher of Holy Scripture, and the pulpit and the rostrum were his places of work. "It was professors, rather than pope or council," Nipperdey argued, "who determined the right doctrines, to which the princes also were subject," and this remained an inheritance of the Lutheran church. "It is a pastor church," Nipperdey claimed, and in Germany the pastors were "university-educated theologians" and scholars. More intensively than anywhere else, he argued, "the other university pupils, the jurists and the officials especially, were taught and formed in the shadow of theology." Thus for Nipperdey, "All intellectual modernization since the early Enlightenment and all free scholarly reflection took place in theology and not next to it or against it."[26] "Our world," he also maintained, "is a world of schools, *Wissenschaft*, reflection, the word," and "it comes to a considerable degree out of Lutheran roots.[27]

24. Ibid.
25. Ibid., 36–37.
26. Ibid. 37–38.
27. Ibid., 39. The other four characteristics of our modern world that Nipperdey emphasized and discussed in relation to the modernizing potential of Luther were (3) that "the modern world is a world of work, accomplishment, discipline, and efficiency";

As John Herman Randall Jr. emphasized in his thorough and impressive account of German philosophy from the German Enlightenment to the age of Darwin, the appeal to religious experience in Germany was very different than what happened in France and England. In Germany, he argues, religion "was thrown back on a deeper and more immediate experience, and found there an inward certainty of emotion and insight that reason could only take as a basic datum."[28] Unlike the evangelical revival of the Wesleys, however, the German appeal to religious experience "enlisted the foremost thinkers, and far from opposing the creation of a new German culture, it became its central drive." According to Randall, all "those new values of individualism, self-reliance, and humanistic moral idealism which the enlightenment had tried to support by 'reason' and failed, were incorporated into its program." Thus in Germany, "a far more thoroughgoing reconstruction of the religious tradition than the apostles of natural religion had dreamed of, and a far more successful modernism" appeared. For Randal, the appeal to religious experience in Germany was much "more sensitive and understanding of the values it was trying to combine, both old and new alike." Even more than that, he claims, it "managed to organize the German tradition" and "laid down the main outlines which Western culture was to follow for the next hundred years."[29]

Although Göttingen was the chief intellectual center not only for the rise of history as a profession (*Beruf*), as an academic discipline (*Wissenschaft*), and as a system of scholarship but also for the reform of education in Germany during the last four decades of the eighteenth century,[30] the city called Königsberg in East Prussia (now Kaliningrad,

---

(4) that "the modern world is—other than the old one—a dynamic world, a world of constant change and movement, of growth, of innovations, of unrest and naturally also of instability'"; (5) that "the modern world is a secular, profane world that is no longer under the guardianship of belief and church, and modern history is the history of secularization"; (6) that "the modern world is a world of the casualties of modernization, of new constraints and bondages, of new wounds and new misfortunes; it is a world of uncertainty and instability, of dangers and of destructive tendencies." See also the following essay by Nipperdey ("Probleme des Modernisierung in Deutschland" [especially pages 46 and 47] in the same volume.) See also Nipperdey's essay, "Luther und die Bildung des Deutschen," in *Luther und die Folgen*, 13–27.

28. Randall, *From the German Enlightenment*, 92.

29. Ibid. In this volume, one can see how the word *Geist* became and remained the key word for German philosophy.

30. For the significance of the University of Göttingen not only for the whole educa-

Russia) is a good place to begin the story of this cultural revolution. It is a good place (1) because it was the city of Johann Georg Hamann and Immanuel Kant, the great "supplementary antipoles" of this spiritual and intellectual revolution, and (2) because it was here that Johann Gottfried Herder received the training that made it possible for him to become the chief figure for the rise of a new historical consciousness that Troeltsch, Hintze, and Meinecke called historicism and that—as they agreed—was based on the concepts of individuality and development.

More than anyone else in Germany in the year 1760, Johann Georg Hamann (1730–1783) personifies the beginning of a great religious, intellectual, and cultural revolution in which religion was the driving force, and that was opposed to the dominance of French thought, culture, and language and to the anti-Christian views of Voltaire.

As Joseph Nadler claimed in the year 1949, Hamann "was the best authority and the most determined opponent of the French *Geist* in Germany."[31] This opposition, however, was based on religious rather than nationalistic grounds.[32] As W. M. Alexander suggested, "Hamann was one of the first Christian thinkers to recognize that he lived—as did the early Church Fathers—in a non-Christian world."[33] As much as anyone, Alexander also stated, Hamann could claim the title "the first modern Christian thinker."[34]

As Isaiah Berlin pointed out in *The Magus of the North: J. G. Hamann and the Origins of Modern Irrationalism* (1993), Hamann was "the first out-and-out opponent" of the French Enlightenment of his time; for his attacks upon it were "more uncompromising, and in some respects sharp-

---

tional system but also for the development of the "New Humanism" in Germany at the end of the eighteenth century, see Friederich Paulsen, *Geschichte des gelehrten Unterrichts auf den deutschen Schulen*, 2:9–46. One of the main points that Paulsen makes about "this second Renaissance" (7) is the significance of the revival of the study of Greek culture, language, and literature for the rise of the "New Humanism" in Germany.

31. Nadler, *Johann Georg Hamann*, 19.

32. Ibid. While Nadler uses the broader expression "aus weltanschaulichen Gründen," Hamann's worldview was based on his strong religious convictions. For a good introduction to the literature on Hamann to the year 1956, see Gründer, *Hamann-Forschung*. Since, as Gründer pointed out, it is almost impossible to read Hamann without commentaries (15), in this section I have made ample use of translations and commentaries by experts.

33. Alexander, *Johann Georg Hamann*, 14.

34. Ibid.

er and more revealing of its shortcomings, than those of later critics."[35] For Berlin, this "profoundly sincere, serious, and original" man was also "the founder of a polemical anti-rationalist tradition which in the course of time has done much, for good and (mostly) ill, to shape the thought and art and feeling of the West."[36]

While these two statements certainly call attention to the importance of Hamann's thought and work for the modern Western world, many Hamann scholars would have serious reservations about the term "polemical anti-rationalist tradition" and would not judge his influence as mostly harmful.

Like his great contemporary, Immanuel Kant, Hamann was born, educated, and worked—but not as a university professor—in Königsberg. Unlike his very rational and very Prussian friend, however, Hamann was a passionate and deeply religious man whose way of viewing life was based on a dramatic religious experience.

Like many of the scholars of the *Aufklärung* and the Cultural Revolution in Germany, Hamann came from a religious family and considered the possibility of becoming a Lutheran pastor. While he was a student at the University of Königsberg (1746–1752), he was a student of theology first before he switched to law. During this time, however, an inclination developed in him—to use his own words—for "antiquities and criticism, and thence for belles lettres, poetry, novels, philology, the French writers with their poetic gift of description and depiction, of pleasing the imagination, and so on."[37]

In March 1758, when he was a poor and very despondent young man in London, he immersed himself in the Bible and underwent a life-changing religious experience. Directly afterwards he wrote an account of his early life that focused on this event, and that he called "Thoughts About My Life." It was written for himself or his father and brother, he said. In these thoughts "I have spoken with God and myself" (*Sämtliche Werke* 2:42). As Isaiah Berlin pointed out, Hamann "had been converted to the religion of his childhood, to Lutheran Protestantism"; and, most

---

35. Berlin, *Magus of the North*, xv.
36. Ibid.
37. Hamann, *Sämmtliche Werke*, 2:21. Here I have used the translation of Ronald Gregor Smith, *J. G. Hamann 1730–1788: A Study in Christian Existence with Selections from his Writings*, 140. Hereafter references in the text (in parentheses) will be to Nadler's edition of Hamann's works, and references to translations will be in the notes.

significantly, it was "his application of this new light, which burned for him until the end of his days, that gives him historical importance."[38]

According to Frederick C. Beiser, the application of this new light is what also made Hamann a significant figure in the history of philosophy. "If we were to summarize Hamann's significance in the history of philosophy," Beiser states, "we would have to stress his role in the revival of Luther."[39] Hamann's mission was "to defend the spirit of Luther when the *Aufklärung* threatened to destroy it," and he "never made any disguise of his great debt to Luther" or of his efforts to see "a restoration of his master's doctrines."[40] For Beiser, some of the many Lutheran themes that reappeared in Hamann's writings were "the authority of the Bible, the importance of a personal relationship with God, the denial of freedom of the will, the superrationality of faith, and the necessity of grace."[41]

For Beiser, however, it was especially important to note "the manner in which Hamann kept Luther's spirit alive," for he defended Luther "by exploiting the latest ideas of modern philosophy, especially the skepticism of Hume." Using modern weapons," Beiser claims, Hamann "made Lutheranism seem not antiquated and superstitious but modern and irrefutable."[42]

Before his religious experience in London, however, Hamann only knew Luther through the *Small Catechism* and the catechismal instruction of his youth.[43] Today scholars believe this little book, which Hamann memorized at this time,[44] must have made a strong and lasting impression on him, for all of his life he spoke of it only in terms of highest respect. In London, scholars believe, Luther's message of the inexpressible, unmerited, and justifying love of God broke into Hamann's heart.[45] Later

---

38. Berlin, *Magus of the North*, 14.
39. Beiser, *Fate of Reason*, 17.
40. Ibid.
41. Ibid.
42. Ibid.
43. Baudler, *Im Worte Sehen*, 305.
44. Bayer, *Zeitgenosse im Widerspruch*, 55.
45. Baudler, *Im Worte Sehen*, 305–6. For a both interesting and important statement about the Lutheran emphasis on memorization for the development of German education and culture, see Holl, *Cultural Significance of the Reformation*, 112. "What orthodoxy gave youth with its emphasis on memorization, meditation, and comparison of Bible passages was a mental discipline of the first order. Without this education the great and universal progress that Germany made during the Enlightenment would have been

in his life, he said that he admitted to "no other orthodoxy than our small Lutheran Catechism" (3:173).

From the time of this turning point in his life, Hamann's faith, life, and thought focused on the Holy Scripture, on the Word become flesh, and—to use the language of Luther's Small Catechism—on the God who "has created me," on the Savior who "has redeemed me," and on the Holy Spirit who "has called me through the Gospel." For the rest of his life, Hamann's life was based on the conviction, "I believe that by my own reason or strength I cannot believe in Jesus Christ my Lord or come to him" (BC-T 344–45). For Luther and for Hamann, faith was a gift, a miracle, and the work of the Holy Spirit.

This did not mean, however, that Hamann was not concerned with questions of human reason. As James C. O'Flaherty points out, there was no subject with which Hamann was "more concerned throughout his entire career subsequent to the London conversion than the question of the powers and limitations of human reason."[46] It is ironic, as O'Flaherty also points out, "that a thinker whose primary concern was to underscore the importance of faith should actually have addressed himself more frequently to the question of the nature of reason, and in so doing have become the counterpart of his companion and adversary, Immanuel Kant, a thinker who had deliberately ruled out faith in order to deal with the problem of reason."[47]

For O'Flaherty, it was also interesting to note that "long before Kant turned his attention to the question of cognition, Hamann had been wrestling in his own way with the problem of the nature and limits of reason." The fact that "these two great thinkers came to radically different conclusions," O'Flaherty emphasizes, "should not obscure the fact that they were largely concerned with the same problem."[48]

While he was still in London, Hamann recorded more of his thoughts in an essay called "Fragments." In this collection of thoughts he wrote, "Nature and history are therefore the two great commentaries on the divine Word, and this Word is the only key to unlock a knowledge of both."[49]

---

unthinkable" (ibid). See also Holl's claim that "Of the specific intellectual disciplines, apart from theology, history stood closest to the Reformation" (ibid., 117).

46. O'Flaherty, *Johann Georg Hamann*, 82.
47. Ibid.
48. Ibid.
49. Smith, *J. G. Hamann*, 166 (*Werke*, 1:302).

As one of his biographers stated, Hamann was "thoroughly penetrated by the Logos."[50] In the words of another Hamann scholar, "Everything was for Hamann a sign or symbol of the divine."[51]

Hamann really became known as a writer through an essay called "Sokratische Denkwürdigkeiten," or "Socratic Memorabilia," which was published in the last month of the year 1759. One of the reasons that this essay was significant for the Cultural Revolution in Germany was its timing. At this time when the Enlightenment was at a zenith, and when Socrates was the most admired philosopher, Hamann presented a version of Socrates that was in direct contrast to the portrait of this age.[52]

A second reason for the essay's significance was Hamann's use of the word *genius* and his emphasis on the idea that the genius was free from abstract rules.

> What for a Homer replaces ignorance of the rules of art which an Aristotle devised after him, and what for a Shakespeare replaces the ignorance or transgression of those critical laws? Genius is the unanimous answer. Indeed, Socrates could very well afford to be ignorant; he had a tutelary genius, on whose science he could rely, which he loved and feared as his god, whose peace was more important to him than all the reason of the Egyptians and Greeks, whose voice he believed, and by means of whose wind . . . the empty understanding of a Socrates can become fruitful as well as the womb of a virgin.[53]

Although the main thrust of this Socratic essay was not primarily on human genius but rather on divine action in this world accomplished through inspired individuals, it was "a misinterpretation regarding this point which caused him to become a fountainhead of the *Genie* cult in the eighteenth century."[54]

Third, the *Socratic Memorabilia* was of great significance for this Cultural Revolution because "it constituted the spark which ignited the fires of *Sturm und Drang*" (Storm and Stress). "It is surely one of the ironies of cultural history," as O'Flaherty also observed, "that Johann Georg Hamann, the fervent champion of religious faith in an age of unbelief,

---

50. Nadler, *Johann Georg Hamann*, 218.
51. Smith, *J. G. Hamann*, 64.
52. O'Flaherty, *Hamann's Socratic Memorabilia*, 5–7.
53. Ibid., 171 (*Werke*, 2:75).
54. O'Flaherty, *Johann Georg Hamann*, 55–56.

should have become the high priest of a literary movement characterized by the cult of unbridled emotion.[55]

It is difficult to exaggerate, as Frederick Beiser claims, the many respects in which Hamann influenced the *Sturm und Drang*: "The metaphysical significance of art, the importance of the artist's personal vision, the irreducibility of cultural differences, the value of folk poetry, the social and historical dimension of rationality, and the significance of language for thought—all these themes were prevalent in, or characteristic of, the *Sturm und Drang*. But they were first adumbrated by Hamann, and then elaborated and promulgated by Herder, Goethe, and Jacobi.[56]

A fourth way that the *Socratic Memorabilia* was significant for this spiritual and intellectual revolution was that here "Hamann introduces— some in quite embryonic form—almost all the major motifs of his later works: pedagogy, history, myth, faith and reason, genius and inspiration, the imitation of nature, and the philosophy of language."[57]

A fifth way that the *Socratic Memorabilia* was significant for this revolution in the humanities was that here Hamann demonstrated to his friend Kant (one of the two persons who attempted to mitigate the strong religious passions of the new Hamann, who tried to lead him in a more rational path of thought and life, and to whom this essay was dedicated, but not by name) that he was going to go his own way. "I am surprised," Hamann said, "that no one has yet undertaken to do as much for history as Bacon has accomplished for physics. Bolingbroke gives his pupil the advice to study ancient history in general as heathen mythology and as a poetic lexicon. But perhaps all history is more mythology than this philosopher thinks, and is, like nature, a book that is sealed, a hidden witness, a riddle which cannot be solved unless we plow with another heifer than our reason."[58] From this time Hamann's way was a crusade against the worship of reason, against abstract systems of thought, and against the deistic and moralistic religion of this age of reason.

---

55. O'Flaherty, *Hamann's Socratic Memorabilia*, 127–28. Although the age commonly known as the Enlightenment is often portrayed as an age of unbelief, and although Hamann certainly thought that he was living in an age of growing unbelief, it is the argument of this essay that the Cultural Revolution in Germany was a spiritual, intellectual, and cultural revolution in which religion was a driving force.

56. Beiser, *Fate of Reason*, 16.

57. O'Flaherty, *Johann Georg Hamann*, 61.

58. O'Flaherty, *Hamann's Socratic Memorabilia*, 151 (*Werke*, 2:65).

It is certainly interesting, as Frederick Beiser points out, not only that this "seminal work in the history of philosophy" was "the first influential attack upon the *Aufklärung's* principle of the sovereignty of reason," but also that Hamann's work was conceived as a response to Immanuel Kant himself.[59] The general thesis of "this seminal work" is that faith transcends the province of reason, for it is neither demonstrable nor refutable by it.[60] Thus for Hamann, faith is neither rational nor irrational since reason cannot either prove or disprove it.[61] And thus while Kant believed that "it is reason that gives our life significance, Hamann believes it is faith."[62]

In the year 1762, Hamann's "Aesthetica in Nuce" was published in a collection of essays titled *Crusades of the Philologist*. While the purpose of the *Socratic Memorabilia* had been "to relate classical culture to Christianity," the purpose of the "Aesthetica in Nuce" was to relate Middle Eastern culture to Christianity.[63] Its significance for this cultural revolution, however, was very great, for as Frederick Beiser claims, (1) "it became the bible for the aesthetics of the *Sturm und Drang*," (2) it became "the holy writ for the epistemology of the *Romantiker*," (3) in it the "Romantic apotheosis of art, intuition, and genius also finds its origins," and (4) "it is still of the first importance for post-Kantian philosophy."[64]

In this essay, Hamann proclaimed, "Poetry is the mother-tongue of the human race, as the garden is older than the field, painting than writing, song than declamation, barter than commerce" (2:197). "Speech," he said, "is translation—from the language of angels into a language of men, that is, thoughts into words, things into names, images into signs" (2:199). "The opinions of philosophers," he wrote, "are readings of nature, and the dogmas of the theologians readings of Scripture." "The author [God]," Hamann continued, "is the best interpreter of his words; he may speak through creatures—through events—or through blood and fire and vapor of smoke, of which the language of the sanctuary consists." For Hamann, "The book of creation contains examples of universal concepts which God desired to reveal to the creature through the creature;

---

59. Beiser, *Fate of Reason*, 19.
60. Ibid., 28.
61. Ibid., 29.
62. Ibid., 31.
63. O'Flaherty, *Johann Georg Hamann*, 64.
64. Beiser, *Fate of Reason*, 33–34.

the books of the covenant contain examples of secret articles which God desired to reveal to man through man. The unity of the author [*Urheber*] is reflected in the very dialect of his works; in all of them a note of immeasurable height and depth!"[65] Here, as throughout his work from the time of his conversion experience, Hamann demonstrated what O'Flattery called "the basic epistemological role of faith."[66]

Toward the end of this essay Hamann wrote: "After God had spoken exhaustively through nature and the Scriptures, through creatures and seers, through poets and prophets, he spoke to us in the evening of days through his Son—yesterday and today! until the promise of his future—no longer in the form of a servant [*Knechtsgestalt*] should be fulfilled.[67]

Like Martin Luther, Hamann combined an "at-the-same-time" and paradoxical way of thinking and writing with a deeply incarnational way based on the Gospel of John and the divine *Logos*. For Hamann, as James O'Flaherty asserts, "God is the One in whom all opposites coincide, and it is this principle of the *coincidentia oppositorum* which, embodied in the Logos and manifested above all in the 'form of a servant,' in which Christ appeared [*Knechtsgestalt Christi*], succeeds in reconciling opposites within the human psyche. Only when such a reconciliation has taken place may one speak as a whole human being, in acceptance of, and in no way ashamed of, his full humanity."[68]

In *Die Entstehung des Historismus*, Friedrich Meinecke emphasized how "Möser, Herder, and Goethe were the three greatest and most effective among the first pioneers of the new sense of history in the eighteenth century."[69] Since Meinecke believed that the main line of development of historicism in Germany was from Leibniz and Pietism through Storm and Stress to historicism, and since he emphasized the importance of Hamann both for Herder and for Goethe, today Hamann deserves to be seen as a major figure for this aspect of the spiritual, intellectual, and cultural revolution in Germany from 1760 to 1810.

In his account of Herder's early years, Meinecke briefly summarized the significance of Johann Georg Hamann for Herder's religious and in-

---

65. O'Flaherty, *Johann Georg Hamann*, 66 (*Werke*, 2:203–4).
66. Ibid., 53. See also Hempelmann, "*Gott ein Schriftsteller!*"
67. O'Flaherty, *Johann Georg Hamann*, 67 (*Werke*, 2:13).
68. Ibid., 43.
69. Meinecke, *Historism*, 295.

tellectual development. In Hamann, Meinecke states, "Herder was confronted with the disturbing figure of an original and independent thinker of great psychological and spiritual force."[70] For Meinecke, the close contact between Hamann's and Herder's thought could not be explained simply by the teacher-student relationship, for to him "the common features in these two men's outlook" went back "to a common source, namely Platonism—using that word in the widest sense."[71]

Although Meinecke was right when he claimed that Hamann (1) was "an original and independent thinker of great psychological and spiritual force," (2) had "a new and powerful sense of the God-given unity of body and soul," and (3) began to survey the world of history with a new fund of vitality, today many Hamann scholars would not use the word *irrationalism* to describe his thought,[72] and they would not agree that the common features in Herder's and Hamann's outlook had a common source in Platonism.[73] What Hamann and Herder shared most of all was a love of language and literature, of history, of the Bible, of the poetry and language of the Old Testament, of the Psalms, of the Gospel of John, of the Gospel message of the Word become flesh, and of Luther's masterful use of language and music in translating and proclaiming this evangelical message.

For Herder, Hamann was "a Christian Socrates." Today this man, who liked to be called "the Magus of the North," can be seen not only as the Christian Socrates for Herder, but also as the Christian and Lutheran Socrates and prophet of and for this Cultural Revolution in Germany.

In his account of the significance of Goethe for the rise of historicism, Meinecke provided a tribute to Hamann that is very helpful for understanding his significance for this age. "There is a fundamental feature in Goethe's historical thought which makes it superior to all his succes-

---

70. Ibid., 301.

71. Ibid.

72. Isaiah Berlin, however, would be an exception to this statement. See his essay "The Magus of the North," 64–71, and the letters from James C. O'Flaherty and Berlin over this issue in this journal, 68. Berlin's article was drawn from his book called *The Magus of the North: J. G. Hamann and the Origins of Modern Irrationalism*.

73. Platonism and Neoplatonism were of basic importance for Herder but less important for Hamann. In addition to Meinecke's discussion of the significance of Neoplatonism for Herder and what Meinecke called the "Deutsche Bewegung," see also Gerhard Kaiser's chapter called "Neuplatonismus, Mystik und organische Staatslehre," in *Pietismus und Patriotismus im literarischen Deutschland*, especially 143–52.

sors without exception—a clarification and refinement of Hamann's basic idea. Goethe maintained that he could glimpse behind all higher actions of historical man a supremely natural and beneficent power at work, and so could view even the round of everyday life as something hallowed by its primal form."[74]

In his fine tribute to Hamann, Goethe credited him with the principle "Everything that we undertake to perform, whether by deed, by word, or otherwise, must arise from all our powers united together; everything in isolation is worthless."[75]

One of the aspects of Hamann's thought which has been dealt with extensively since the time of Meinecke is the importance of Luther's writings and way of viewing life both for Hamann and for his age. When Hamann returned to Königsberg in January 1759, he immersed himself in the writings of Martin Luther. Through his own religious experience and through his intensive study of Luther's writings, Hamann became the best Luther expert of his day.[76] It is significant that three of the greatest figures for the rise of German literature in the early years of this Cultural Revolution—Lessing, Hamann, and Herder—were the outstanding Luther experts of their day.

As Michael Embach has noted, "Hamann, in his unprecedented audacity, confronted, placed in question, and deepened the autonomous humanism of his time with his biblical, reformational, and incarnational faith."[77] The rediscovery of "Luther's word-power," as Embach also states, formed a part of the newly awakened historical consciousness of this age.[78] Of these three Luther scholars, experts on Luther agree, Hamann understood and interpreted Luther the best,[79] identified with Luther's teachings the most, and was closer to him—both religiously and psychologically—than any person during this age. From the time of his con-

---

74. Meinecke, *Historism*, 448.

75. Goethe, *Aus meinem Leben: Dichtung und Warhrheit*, 514 (from book 12). Cited and translated by Marcia Bunge in Bunge, "Introduction," 6.

76. Bornkamm, *Luther im Spiegel*, 22.

77. Embach, *Lutherbild Johann Gottfried Herders*, 187.

78. Ibid., 47.

79. Bernhard Lohse, for example, said that Hamann's interpretation of Luther "was far superior to that of all his contemporaries" (*Martin Luther*, 213).

version experience, he sought "to rediscover Luther," and his approach was—as he claimed—"to Lutherize."[80]

For Hamann, as Fritz Blanke puts it, Luther was a "proclaimer of the miraculous incarnation in its supernatural fullness, preacher of a justifying faith, and warrior against reason."[81] For Hamann, Luther was "a prophet" in the biblical sense of an expositor of the word of God.[82] For Blanke, Hamann was one of very few Protestant and German theologians since the time of Luther "who in a similar deep way felt that Luther was a spokesman of God."[83]

As Peter Meinhold claims, "Hamann's Theology of Language" was based on his congenial feeling for Luther's understanding of language and of the relation between Spirit and Word. Luther's understanding of this relationship, Meinhold states, "was based on the idea of Augustine that the Spirit is hidden in letters and that only through the mediation of the Word, which was formed by single letters, can it be reached." It was from this starting point, Meinhold believes, that "Luther developed the idea that the living, spoken and written word provides the cover [die Hülle abgibt], under and in which the Spirit is really present."[84]

"Proceeding from this thought that the word represents the concretizing of the spirit," Meinhold continued, Luther—in his conflict with the *Schwärmer* (enthusiasts) and their separation of spirit and letter—took his stand on the view "that the outer cover could be seen as the clothes and embodiment, under and in which the Spirit was really present." From this starting point and from the close connection between *Word* and *Geist*, Meinhold claims, Hamann built his theology of language.[85]

In the passage from Meinhold and from this starting point, it is possible to see one of the main roots not only of the idealist tradition in Germany and of Thomas Carlyle's attempt to explain this "clothes" image to the English-speaking world in that great, difficult, and delight-

---

80. Hamman, *Briefwechsel*, 1:307. See also Knoll, "Herder als Promotor Hamanns, 217, in *Herder Today: Contributions from the International Herder Conference Nov. 5–8, 1987, Stanford, California*. Hereafter this work is cited *Herder Today*.

81. Blanke, "Hamann und Luther," 47.

82. Bornkamm, *Luther im Spiegel*, 18.

83. Blanke, "Hamann und Luther," 47. The only one who came close to him in this respect, Blanke believed, was Zinzendorff.

84. Meinhold, "Hamanns Theologie der Sprache," 54.

85. Ibid.

fully humorous novel called *Sartor Resartus*; it is also possible to see how Hamann's "philosophy" or "theology of language," and his deeply incarnational thought can be called an "at-the-same-time" way and an "in-with-and-under" way of thinking and of viewing life. For Hamann, the origin of language was divine and human at the same time. "Because God spoke humanly," he said, "the human being could also understand Him."[86]

In an essay called "J. G. Hamann as Theologian," Fritz Blanke emphasizes that one governing principle for Hamann was "das Geistleibliche."[87] According to Blanke, Hamann was convinced that "everything spiritual had to take on a sensuous form (through sight or hearing), which meant a body, before it could be grasped by human beings. *Body* is used here in the widest sense as "word," "language," "history," and "nature." The Spirit could enter all of these earthly formations. He always enters one of these when he wishes to allow entrance to us humans. We never have the Spirit directly but always in concrete historical form."[88]

The second basic principle that governed Hamann's thought, Blanke emphasizes, was "the unity of creation."[89] Hamann developed this idea in opposition to the natural-law concept of the Enlightenment that began with what the individual possessed from nature rather than with the rights nature had over the individual. "The *Aufklärer* (and not only they, but basically all modern European philosophy)," Blanke said, began with the rational consciousness of the individual. To Hamann, this was an idolatry of the *Ich*, or the "I"; for God had created nature and spirit together, and all cognition was a recognition of what was already

---

86. Bayer, *Zeitgenosse im Widerspruch*, 122. Here Bayer succinctly points out (1) that Hamann took his stand on "dem göttlichen und *zugleich* menschlichen Ursprung der Sprache," and (2) that "Weil Gott menschlich redet, kann der Mensch ihn auch verstehen."

87. Blanke, "J. G. Hamann als Theologe," in *Hamann-Studien*, 11. For the significance of Hamann's new view of "des Menschen als leib-seelischer Ganzheit," "der natürlich-sinnlichen Seite des Menschen," and "nature and the Bible as corresponding revelations of God" not only for Herder but also for this age as a whole, see Kaiser, *Pietismus und Patriotismus*, 27–31. According to Kaiser, Herder's lifework as a whole was built on Hamann's view of "the personal revelation of God in nature and language [Schrift]," although for Herder the revelational character of creation was seen "more under an historical aspect" (28). For Herder, Kaiser claims, "Revelation took place through history and nature" (ibid).

88. Blanke, "Hamann als Theologie," in *Hamann-Studien*, 11–12.

89. "Schöpfungszusammenhangs" (ibid., 15).

there.⁹⁰ Therefore Hamann's way of viewing life was based not only on a *Geistleiblichkeitsanschauung*, or a "spirit-body view," but also on a "unity-of-creation" view. It is significant that Blanke thought Hamann's view of the relationship between nature and spirit was directly related both to Luther's view of the Lord's Supper and to his explanation of the first article of the Creed in the Small Catechism.⁹¹

For Oswald Bayer, "the chief moment" in Hamann's understanding of history and human reason was his understanding of "God the Holy Spirit, the *spiritus creator*." This was always associated with a particular understanding of "word and text [*Schrift*], sound and letter." Bayer emphasizes that the disagreement between Lessing and Hamann concerning an understanding of the word *Geist* was an argument concerning the relationship of word and *Geist*. Like Luther, but unlike Lessing and most of the intellectual leaders of the German Enlightenment, Hamann believed that the Spirit comes directly "through the corporeal, oral, public, and external word."⁹²

In his very useful book about Luther as mirrored in German intellectual history (*Luther im Spiegel der deutschen Geistesgeschichte*), Heinrich Bornkamm argues that Hamann developed a philosophy of language "as something *Realgeistige* (as Ranke later said) and dynamic, like the presence of something transcendental in the individual (like the body and blood of Christ in the elements of the Lord's Supper). What he said on this subject is saturated through and through with the words of Luther's Bible and Luther's thought. Here Hamann sought nothing less than to perceive God's incarnation in Jesus Christ, in the cross, in the Bible, in the word of speech as the basis of all natural and historical reality."⁹³

In a book with the interesting title *Im Worte Sehen: Das Sprachdenken Johann Georg Hamanns* (*In Word Seeing: the Linguistic Thought of . . . Hamann*), Georg Baudler emphasized how Hamann's whole way of thinking was based on his conversion experience in London and the powerful words of Luther's Small Catechism, which he had learned as a youth and which he really came to understand first in London out of his own experience.

---

90. Ibid., 15-16.
91. Ibid., 16.
92. Bayer, *Zeitgenosse im Widerspruch*, 174-75.
93. Bornkamm, *Luther im Spiegel*, 22.

Cultural Revolution in Germany and a New Historical Consciousness 149

> The human cannot through his or her "own reason or strength" come to Christ, but only through the power of the Word, through the command [*Anspruch*] of God, as He grants directly to humans in the sacraments. "The water by itself does nothing," Hamann had learned in the section concerning baptism, "but the Word of God, which is with and by [*bei*] the water, and the faith which relies on the Word of God in the water."[94]

The section concerning the Lord's Supper was also crucial for Hamann, for here he found the words: "Eating and drinking, of course, do nothing, but the words: Given and shed for you for the remission of sins." According to Baudler,

> These sentences penetrated the central core of Hamann's thought not just because in London he had experienced in himself the reality of the speaking Word of God; but just as significant, at least, was the effect of the other component of these sentences of the *Catechism* on Hamann: The word of God is really and truly "with," "*bei*," and "in" the water, as well as *bei* the bread and wine. In Hamann's London understanding, water, bread, and wine were not just profane symbols for a sacral process, but just the reverse as sacral symbols acting for the given reality as a whole, with which the human continuously corresponds and communicates.[95]

Throughout his life and work, Hamann demonstrated not only what Hintze called "the powerful idea of an all-embracing life that is higher than the individual's rational powers and that includes the rational person within itself,"[96] but also what Isaiah Berlin called a view "that all things and events were a great hieroglyphic script that needed only a key, which God's words alone provided, to reveal the nature and the fate of man and his relationship to the world and to God."[97] For Berlin, the key and twice-cited passage from Hamann's writings that best captured his "dark and mystical" way of viewing both language and life was,

> Every phenomenon of nature was a name—the sign, the symbol, the promise of a fresh and secret and ineffable but all the more intimate chosen union, communication and communion of divine energies and ideas. All that man in these beginnings heard

---

94. Baudler, *Im Worte Sehen*, 306.
95. Ibid.
96. See the second opening quotation of this chapter.
97. Berlin, *Magus of the North*, 22.

with his ears, saw with his eyes, contemplated or touched with his hands, all this was the living word. For God was the Word. With the Word in his mouth and in his heart, the origin of language was as natural, as near and as easy as a child's play.[98]

Perhaps the best testimony in English to Hamann's deeply incarnational or his "in-with-and-under" way of viewing life can be found in the opening paragraph of Isaiah Berlin's preface to *The Magus of the North*. Here Berlin emphasized how the phrase "God-intoxicated man" fits Hamann "far better than the wildly romanticized Spinoza of the eighteenth-century German critics," for to Hamann everything was created by God, served his "unscrutable purposes," and "speaks to us, his creatures, made in his image." Thus for Hamann, everything was revelation and a miracle, and causality was illusory. Not only stones and rocks and Holy Writ "speak the Lord"; for in addition to this, "the whole of history, facts, events, all that human beings are, think, feel, do—and not only human beings: nature, fauna and flora, earth and sky, mountains and streams, and all natural events—speak to us directly; are the form and substance of language in which God implants knowledge in us."[99]

For Berlin, Hamann was "a genuine nominalist" in whom "the union of mysticism and empiricism as against rationalism here emerges in full strength for perhaps the first time."[100] "As a defender of the concrete, the particular, the intuitive, the personal, and the unsystematic . . . he [Hamann] has no equal."[101]

98. Ibid., 80, 118.

99. Ibid., xiv.

100. Ibid., 45.

101. Ibid., 91–92. The full sentence, quoted in the text only in part, represents both the strength and the weakness of Berlin's interpretation of Hamann. "As a defender of the concrete, the particular, the intuitive, the personal, and the unsystematic—this is the tendency which, for such cultural historians as Troeltsch and Meinecke, distinguishes, indeed divides, the Germans from the rational, generalising, scientific West—he [Hamann] has no equal." The part of this quotation that was excluded in the text above (the part between the dashes in this note) is a weakness of Berlin's book, for it is a classic example (1) of a widely held view or tendency known as Germany's *Sonderweg* ("special way"), and (2) of how many scholars have used Troeltsch and Meinecke to emphasize and to judge Germany's "peculiar" or "abnormal" path of development. This is much easier to do if one does not emphasize the significance of the Kantian side of German thought, education, and culture and the Hintze side of German historical thought and his understanding of the term *historicism*. The purpose of the present essay is not to judge Germany's path but rather to help to understand it more fully by relating it to

While Hamann's life and work can be seen as the beginning of a revolt or a counterrevolution against the dominance of French language, thought, and culture in Germany and to the anti-Christian views of Voltaire, it can also be seen as the beginning of a great spiritual, intellectual, and cultural revolution. Both through his own writings, letters, and personality and through his significance for the life and work of Herder, Goethe, and Hegel, Hamann's "at-the-same-time" and "in-with-and-under" theology of language and way of viewing life had incalculable significance for the Cultural Revolution in Germany and for the whole direction of German and Western thought.

In his study called *The Fate of Reason*, Frederick Beiser claims that although it is not as well known, "Hamann's critique of reason was just as influential as Kant's"; for "its criticism of the purism of reason proved to be especially important for post-Kantian thought." Herder, Schlegel, and Hegel "all accepted Hamann's advice to see reason in its embodiment, in its specific social and historical context." In addition, Beiser claims, "the emphasis upon the social and historical dimension of reason, which is so important for post-Kantian thought, can trace its origins back to Hamann."[102]

According to Isaiah Berlin, "It is doubtful whether without Hamann's revolt—or at any rate something similar—the worlds of Herder, Friedrich Schlegel, Tieck, Schiller, and indeed Goethe too, would have come into being."[103] For Berlin, Hamann was "the first standard-bearer of a revolt" or a counterrevolution, not only in Germany but in Europe, and perhaps its "most original figure."[104]

The culmination of this Cultural Revolution in the fields of language and literature came in the year 1808 with the publication of part one of Goethe's *Faust*. Here one can find the classic portrayal in German and Western literature of a highly educated and modern human being

---

a particular religious tradition that originated and centered in Germany, but that has influenced the thought and culture of some other nations even more.

102. Beiser, *Fate of Reason*, 18.

103. Berlin, "Magus of the North," 105. Similarly strong statements can also be found in other Hamann scholars. According to Oswald Bayer, "The work of Herder and Goethe, of 'Sturm und Drang,' and the Romantics is inconceivable without Hamann" (Bayer, "Johann Georg Hamann," in *Die Aufklärung*, edited by Martin Greschat, 347). This volume (volume 8) in Gestalten der Kirchengeschichte, edited Martin Greschat, also has helpful essays on Semler, Kant, and Herder.

104. Berlin, "Magus of the North," 106.

wrestling with "the devil, the world, and our flesh" *and* with the basic Johannine and Christian paradox, "In the beginning was the Word."

As Jaroslav Pelikan claimed in the last volume of *The Christian Tradition: A History of the Development of Doctrine*: "Just as the *City of God* of Augustine was the premier literary statement of the central themes in the patristic 'triumph of theology,' and as the *Divine Comedy* of Dante Alighieri was the most celebrated poetic embodiment of the medieval understanding of 'nature and grace,' so the classic dramatization both of the positive and the negative relations between 'Christian doctrine and modern culture' . . . was almost certainly the verse drama *Faust*, by Johann Wolfgang von Goethe."[105]

JOHANN GOTTFRIED HERDER'S CULTURAL, SPIRITUAL, AND HISTORIZING REVOLUTION

As Frederick H. Burkhardt claimed, the closing years of the eighteenth century in Germany "saw the beginning of a period of intellectual and literary activity which has rarely been equaled in the history of the human mind." It is no exaggeration to say, Burkhardt also contended, that Johann Gottfried Herder (1744–1803) "enriched more different fields of knowledge than any man of his time. Literature, education, philosophy, history, theology, philology, jurisprudence and biblical criticism all received fruitful and lasting contributions from his pen."[106]

While Kant was the great "form-thinker" of this intellectual revolution or this "revolution of the mind" in Germany, Herder was its great "life-viewer," the person who most embodies the idea of a "cultural revolution," and the central figure for the rise of the new historical outlook or consciousness called historicism. Herder most embodies the idea of a cultural revolution in Germany not only because he more than anyone else was "the founding father" of a national concept of culture based on the idea of the singularity of a people (*Volk*) with a common language

---

105. Pelikan, *Christian Doctrine and Modern Culture*, 1. As Pelikan also stated: "For during the century or so that followed Goethe's death, the relation between tradition and doubt articulated in his *Faust* became a spiritual and intellectual presupposition for Christian thinkers of widely varying outlooks" (ibid., 2).

106. Burkhardt, "Introduction," 3. For an account of the significance of Herder and Kant for eighteenth-century anthropology and for a very inclusive introduction to the literature on this subject, see Zammito, *Kant, Herder, and the Birth of Anthropology*.

and culture, but also because of "his turn from the high culture of the educated and the elite to the culture of the simple and pre-intellectualized people."[107] While Kant best represents that eighteenth-century mode of thought that Friedrich Paulsen called "*saeculum philosophicum*," Herder was the leader of "that great revolution in the humanistic sciences," and for that mode of thought that Paulsen called "*saeculum historicum*."[108]

Especially in the work of Herder, one can see what Ahlstrom called a serious investigation of "the whole historical world" and the beginning of that "age of historical renaissance" that involved "critical scholarship in the whole field of religion, the history of scriptures, of ancient civilization, of churches and their divergent doctrines, and finally the history of world religions." Especially with Herder, one can see how history became a spiritual calling or *Beruf* before it became a full-time profession or *Beruf*.[109]

From the time of Luther to the middle decades of the eighteenth century, the word *Beruf* was mainly a theological word that was used—as it was for Luther—for the personal task and duty of a Christian. Thus it was clearly distinguished from the Latin *Professio*. By the eighteenth century, however, the word *profession* had become a German word, and it was applied especially to the realms of science (*Wissenschaft*), handwork, and art.[110]

During the second half of the eighteenth century, however, the word *Beruf* gradually took on the meaning of "profession" and gradually took the place of this word. At the same time, however, the old meaning of the word *Beruf* was maintained in theology by the word *Berufung*.[111] Thus at the same time that history was gradually moving in the direction of a full-time *Beruf* or profession at the University of Göttingen, it was also moving in the direction of a full-time office with more status and prestige, because

---

107. "Das neue bei Herder ist zum zweiten die Wendung weg von der hohen Kultur der Gebildeten, der Eliten, hin zu der Kultur des einfachen, vor-intellektuellen Volkes." Thomas Nipperdey, "Auf der Suche nach der Identität," 116. One of the great values of this essay are the seven basic elements of a "national conception of culture," which he discusses within a European—rather than just a German—framework.

108. Paulsen, *Immanuel Kant: His Life and Doctrine*, 396–97.

109. Particularly since the 1970s, a great deal of research and writing has been done on the subject of "the professionalization" and "institutionalization" of history in Germany during the second half of the eighteenth century. See especially Jarausch, "Institutionalization of History in 18th-Century Germany," 27–48.

110. See Conze, "*Beruf*," in *Geschichtliche Grundbegriffe*, 1:498–99.

111. Ibid., 499–503.

the holder of this office was an official of the state. Certainly one of the reasons for the increasing status and prestige of history during the five decades of the "Revolution of the *Geist*" or the "Cultural Revolution" in Germany was its close connection with the professional faculties of theology and law. Although the separation of the words *Beruf* and *Berufung* took place during the last decades of the eighteenth century, it is helpful to remember that throughout the nineteenth century and into the twentieth, the term *Beruf* never completely lost its original meaning of an "inner calling" rather than just an external profession or occupation.[112]

In his masterful account of the development of Herder's historical thought in *Die Entstehung des Historismus*, Friedrich Meinecke claimed that "the three chief spiritual forces of a general nature to which Herder was indebted were the Enlightenment, pietism, and Platonism."[113] Later in this chapter, Meinecke stated that a fourth chief mental influence centered on the great personality of Shakespeare.[114]

While Meinecke was not wrong in showing the significance of these forces or influences for Herder's life and work, it is surprising (1) that he did not discuss in any detail the great influence of the thought, writings, and work of Martin Luther for Herder's work and/or for the rise of historicism;[115] (2) that he did not discuss the significance of the Gospel

---

112. Ibid., 506–7. For a good discussion of how the humanistic concept of natural talent, the traditional Lutheran view of calling (*Beruf*), the pietist ideal of conversion, and the new secular ethic of vocation (*Beruf*) fused during the eighteenth century, see La Vopa, *Grace, Talent, and Merit*. For the general reader, the epilogue (386–98) would be especially helpful.

113. Meinecke, *Historism*, 298–99. Two pioneer studies that emphasize the significance of Pietism for the development of German patriotism as an aspect of modern German culture are (1) Koppel S. Pinson's *Pietism as a Factor in the Rise of German Nationalism* (1934) and (2) Gerhard Kaiser's *Pietismus und Patriotismus in literarischen Deutschland* (1961; 2nd edition, 1973). See also Hartmut Lehmann's evaluation of—and supplement to—these works in the essay "Pietism and Nationalism," 233–47. In contrast to Pinson and Kaiser, however, the present study emphasizes how Hamann's, Herder's, and Ranke's religious views and ways of viewing life were based directly on their intensive study of Luther's writings rather than on the pietists as intermediaries between Luther and each of them.

114. Meinecke, *Historism*, 303.

115. For an important and useful study of the significance of Martin Luther's use of language (especially on the significance of his use of the words and ideas of "nation" and "Word"—not only for many German scholars during the years from 1770 to 1850 but also for Coleridge and for European thought as a whole), see Perkins, *Nation and Word*. For the significance of Luther for this subject, see especially chapter 2 in Perkins, called

of John or of the word *logos* for Hamann or Herder, or for their age as a whole;[116] and (3) that he did not focus very much on one of the main words and concepts for Herder throughout his life, for this "Revolution of the *Geist*," and for Meinecke's own kind of history (*Geistesgeschichte*): the word *Geist*.[117]

For Meinecke, historicism represented "a liberating of precisely the deepest moving forces of history, the human mind and soul, that had been held captive by a judgement that confined itself to general terms." "Man, it was maintained, . . . had remained basically the same in all periods of which we have any knowledge. This opinion was right enough at heart, but did not grasp the profound changes and the variety of forms undergone by the spiritual and intellectual life of individual men and human communities, in spite of the existence of a permanent foundation of basic human qualities."[118]

Although Meinecke certainly recognized that Herder's way of viewing life was based on a distinctly Christian view of history, he did not attempt to show how Herder's new kind of historical thought and new kind of universal history were closely connected with his calling as a Lutheran pastor and educator. This omission is rather surprising, because Herder was the greatest Luther scholar in Germany after the death of his mentor Hamann, because Meinecke believed that "the core of historicism" was "an individualizing way of viewing life," and because Luther was—as Hamann and Herder recognized, but not in these words—the greatest

---

"Reformation: Luther and the Bond of Nation and Word," 32–50.

116. For the significance and influence of the Gospel of John and the *logos* for Lessing, Hamann, Herder, and later for the romantics and idealists in Germany, see especially chapter 6, "Nation and Logos: The Influence of the Fourth Gospel," in Perkins, *Nation and Word*, 99–110. "Through the influence of such as Herder and Klopstock," Perkins claims, "the 'Word' became the carrier of the German spirit, a dynamic weapon in the battle to assert German identity" (Perkins, *Nation and Word*, 26).

117. In *Die Entstehung des Historismus*, however, Meinecke did show the significance of the word *esprit* for Voltaire (especially 101–5; *Historism*, 77–81) and Montesquieu (especially, 150–55; *Historism*, 118–22). For Meinecke, however, the main point here was that "[t]his survey should have sufficiently indicated Montesquieu's attitude towards the two basic ideas of the future historism—the idea of individuality, and the idea of development" (*Historism*, 122, *Historismus*, 155). See also how Gerhard Kaiser also emphasizes the basic significance of these two concepts for the rise of historicism, and supplements this work by Meinecke in the chapter "Pietismus und Geschichte" in *Pietismus und Patriotismus*, 160–79.

118. Meinecke, *Historism*, lv–lvi (*Historismus*, 2–3).

individualizing writer in German history and within the religious tradition called Lutheranism.

In his study called *Geschichte der neueren Historiographie*, Eduard Fueter emphasized how Herder's historical thought was influenced by his theological education, and how it was "entirely theologically oriented."[119] In and through his life and work, Herder created a new "at-the-same-time" and a new "in-with-and-under" philosophy of history based on the concepts of individuality and development, and that Troeltsch, Hintze, and Meinecke called historicism. Today Herder's kind of historicism can be defined as the sympathetic understanding of all individuals, peoples (*Völker*), nations, languages, religions, cultures, and ages within the context of one theocentric, humanistic, and *kulturgeschichtlich* universal history.[120]

Today Herder is best known not only for his contributions to the philosophy of history, German literature, and the philosophy of language,[121] but also "on the fact that he is the father of the related notions" of historicism, the *Volksgeist*, and *nationalism*,[122] a word that he coined.[123] What students of history should also know, however, is that more than anyone to this time, he was "the historian of the human soul,"[124] of the human *Geist* or spirit, of peoples and nations, and of education and culture or of what he called *Bildung* and *Humanität*. Thus his work marks a broadening of the scope, the matter, and the idea of history far beyond Voltaire or any of his predecessors.

119. Fueter, *Geschichte der neueren Historiographie*, 408-9.

120. For Herder's *kulturgeschichtlich* kind of world history, see Förster, "Johann Gottfried Herder: Weltgeschichte und Humanität," 363-87.

121. Bunge, "Introduction," 1. *Against Pure Reason* (in which Bunge's introduction appears) is a good introduction to the nature and significance of Herder's life and work, for it contains a good introduction, many useful selections and translations from his writings as a whole, and also a bibliography of writings by and on Herder, in both English and German. For a good and more recent bibliography of the writings on Herder, see Bultmann, *Die biblische Urgeschichte in der Aufklärung*.

122. Berlin, *Vico and Herder*, 145.

123. Holborn, *History of Modern Germany: 1648-1840*, 327. In her study *Nation and Word, 1770-1850*, Mary Anne Perkins states: "No study of European nationalism can ignore the fact that in the period in question, the influence of German thought on concepts of 'Nation' and 'Word' is paramount" (6). She also asserts that "German thought and literature, more than any other in this period, contributed to the *idea* of nationhood philosophically, historically, and culturally" (8).

124. Holborn, *1648-1840*, 327.

To understand the life and work of Johann Gustav Herder, it is helpful first of all to know that he was a deeply religious man who believed that the world came from God and was on the way to God.[125] From his early days, Herder's faith was based on the conviction "that a living human being could only be born out of a living God."[126] To use his own words, "Our entire existence in time and eternity depends on God. We came out of his hand, we wander in his hand, and sooner or later we shall return to his hand."[127]

Herder was born and raised in a town called Mohrungen in East Prussia (now Morag, Poland) where both of his parents were devout Christians and strong pietists. Outwardly, one of his biographers claims, the young Herder was a quiet, dutiful, and industrious student who read voraciously and who received solid training in Latin and Greek; inwardly this sensitive schoolboy gave his heart and feelings to two worlds, to nature and to history.[128]

In the year 1762, Herder became a student at the University of Königsberg where he first enrolled as a student of medicine but quickly changed to theology. In Königsberg, Herder was strongly influenced by the supplementary "antipoles" of this Revolution of the *Geist*, by Immanuel Kant and Johann Georg Hamann.

The Kant who fascinated Herder was the author of *The General History of Nature and the Theory of the Heavens* (1755), who lectured on astronomy and physical geography, who spoke about the laws of nature, and who had not yet developed his "critical philosophy." Herder enthusiastically attended all of Kant's lectures, he often met with him privately to discuss philosophy and poetry, and through "his best teacher" he was won over to the cause of the *Aufklärung*.[129]

At the same time, however, Herder was also won over by Hamann, the first great critic of the *Aufklärung*, the father of *Sturm und Drang*, and

---

125. Dobbek, *J. G. Herders Weltbild*, 10.
126. Ibid., 21.
127. Herder, "Abschiedspredigt" in Riga on 17 May 1769, in Herder SW 31:133.
128. Dobbek, *Johann Gottfried Herder*, 35.
129. Beiser, *Enlightenment, Revolution, and Romanticism*, 192. In this chapter, "The Political Theory of F. G. Herder," Beiser emphasizes not only that almost every aspect of Kant's *Allgemeine Naturgeschichte und Theorie des Himmels* "had a lasting effect on Herder," but also that "It was indeed this work that laid the foundations for Herder's later historicism" (193).

Luther's greatest champion for this entire age. "In large part," as Frederick Beiser claims, Herder resolved this conflict "by a compromise, by granting valid points to both sides."[130]

As a young theology student in Königsberg in the year 1762, Herder was particularly fortunate to have Hamann as a teacher, friend, and mentor. Hamann was the best possible person to defend the rights of faith and feeling against the skepticism and rationalism of the young Kant. More than Kant, and more than any other person, Hamann's influence on Herder was "more lasting, deeper, and more personal."[131] For Hamann and Herder, religion was an original human phenomenon, and only faith and direct feeling of the divine—rather than knowledge—leads to God.[132]

One of the ways in which Hamann was a very helpful mentor was in directing Herder's voracious reading. It was significant for Hamann, Kant, Herder, and for this Cultural Revolution as a whole that in the years 1761-1762 Rousseau's *Social Contract*, *Nouvelle Héloïse*, and *Émile* appeared, and that Rousseau reached the height of his fame.[133] It is also significant, as Hajo Holborn suggests, that while the first of these books had a great impact in France, the ones containing his views on education had the greatest impact in Germany; for there "it was Rousseau's educational program that kindled a flame, whereas his political ideas, though exercising a certain influence in Kant and Fichte, failed to set a fire."[134]

Especially through Hamann's tutoring, Herder learned to read English, and during his years of study at Königsberg (1762-1764), Shakespeare, Bacon, Hume, and Shaftesbury—as well as Montesquieu and Rousseau—became important ingredients of his worldview. Like Ha-

---

130. Ibid.

131. Haym, *Herder nach seinem Leben und seinen Werken* (1880) 1:53. While there is no doubt that the personal relationship between Herder and Hamann was closer, stronger, deeper, and longer-lasting than Herder's relationship with Kant, Beiser makes a strong case that Herder remained true to the teachings and naturalism of the precritical Kant and to the *Aufklärung*. For Beiser the relationship between Herder and Hamann is summarized in these words: "If we were to describe in a word how Herder adopted and assimilated Hamann's thought, then we would have to say that he secularized it. In other words, he explained it in naturalistic terms and justified it in the light of reason" (Beiser, *Enlightenment, Revolution, and Romanticism*, 195).

132. For Herder, see Dobbek, *J. G. Herders Weltbild*, 27.

133. Holborn, *History of Modern Germany, 1648-1840*, 324.

134. Ibid., 324-25.

Cultural Revolution in Germany and a New Historical Consciousness   159

mann, Herder loved the Bible, and later he claimed that it was his love for the Bible alone that led him to theology.[135]

Although Herder did not have much to say about his formal theological training at the University of Königsberg, his life and work were based on the traditional training for a Lutheran pastor. Like many of the great humanists of his day, Herder was trained in rhetoric, the other liberal arts, Latin, and Greek. Unlike many of the great humanists of his day, however, he was also (1) a biblical scholar who was trained in Hebrew, New Testament Greek, and biblical exegesis; (2) a classical scholar who was equally at home in studying the classical texts of Greece and Rome and, at the same time, all the basic texts of the Judeo-Christian tradition; and (3) a Lutheran pastor, theologian, teacher, and administrator who was trained to be a public speaker and an educator. As Ernst Benz pointed out, separating Herder's literary work from his theological work forecloses a real understanding of him; for "from the beginning" religion and its manifestation awakened in him the deepest perceptions and occupied him the most.[136]

Like Luther, and like most Lutheran pastors, Herder believed that he was called by the Holy Spirit and by the church to preach the gospel and to be a servant of the Word. During the years from 1764 to 1769, when Herder became a successful and respected preacher and educator in Riga, he wrote down—but did not publish—his idea, ideal, and picture of "Der Redner Gottes," or "the speaker of God" in an essay with that title.

The speaker of God that Herder depicted was not the kind of orator to be found among the poets, Ciceronians, actors, philosophers, and statesmen. He was not an artist who used rhetorical devices to captivate his audience. Instead he was a man whose speech carried some weight for

---

135. Dobbek, *J. G. Herders Weltbild*, 11.

136. Benz, "Johann Gottfried Herder," in Heimpel et al., *Die Grossen Deutschen*, 2:217. See also Sheehan, *German History, 1770–1866*, 201, for here he emphasizes how Herder saw his "scholarly activities as an extension of his calling as a preacher." Any reader interested in the development of "Eighteenth-Century Culture" in Germany should consult Sheehan's chapter with this title. Here Sheehan emphasizes how a new kind of culture emerged in central Europe in the course of the eighteenth century (152), how this new kind of culture can be called a "literary culture" (152–53), how "[b]y the 1770s, Germans had begun to achieve a vernacular literary tradition comparable to that of the French and English" (161), how many of the *Aufklärer* "usually accepted the significance of religion for culture and society," and how "their goal was a spiritual realm in which faith and reason might coexist, each strengthening and strengthened by the other" (175).

a person because he was the one who had baptized him; who prepared him for the Lord's Supper; who spoke with his parents, their children, and friends when they were sick; and who stood by them at their deathbed. In short, he was the important person who was present at all the basic changes in a person's life.[137]

For Herder, the orator of God was a *Seelsorger*—a pastor or spiritual advisor—whose words went to the soul, who spoke with "the tone of the soul," and whose words brought his hearers to devotion and to feel the presence of God. A sermon, he said, should be a unity or whole wherein "the idea of the picture" was morality, the composition was "a situation of humanity and life," and "the color of the picture was religion."[138] For Herder, a sermon should be a "breakthrough of grace" that "shows me my sphere, my world, calling and my heart!"[139] From the beginning, this young pastor sought to preach, speak, and write from the heart in a free and individualizing way.

According to Rudolf Haym, Herder's chief and most thorough biographer, Herder was more successful in reaching his life goals as a preacher than in any other area of his life and work.[140] During his years in the cosmopolitan city of Riga, when he became a Free Mason, the rationalistic and moralistic tendencies of the Age of the Enlightenment are apparent in his sermons and writings. During the years from 1771 to 1776, however, when he was a court preacher in Bückeburg, his sermons focused more deeply on the inner religious life and on the traditional faith that his rural listeners had learned in the *Catechism*. After the year 1776, when through the influence of his friend Goethe he was appointed General Superintendent of the Clergy in the small but famous duchy of Weimar, his sermons—according to Haym—reveal both of these tendencies at the same time.[141]

From the beginning of his ministry to the end of his life, however, Herder tried to be—and was for his listeners—an orator of God and a *Seelsorger* who tried simply "to clarify and to follow the gentle, soft stream of the words of Christ and to draw something from each step, as much as

---

137. Herder, SW 32:4.
138. Ibid., 32:7–8.
139. Ibid., 32:10–11.
140. Haym, *Herder* 2:340.
141. Ibid., 2:340–41.

my hand can grasp, that can stimulate and strengthen me and my listeners at this moment."[142] For Haym, Herder was a man who was "filled with the spirit of Christianity," and he claimed that Herder's contributions to homiletics were on the same level as his contributions to aesthetics.[143]

Like Luther and Hamann, Herder was a great biblical scholar for whom the Holy Bible was his alpha and omega. The Bible was the first book that Herder discovered, and throughout his life the language of the Old Testament and of Luther were his models for *lebendige* language—for language that was full of life. Just as Herder remembered how Luther was educated through the Psalms of David, so his taste was formed on the Old Testament.[144]

For Herder, the poetry of the Old Testament held a special place, for it signified what real poetry is. Here, instead of symbolizing and allegorizing, he found experiences presented in forms and colors that filled the heart and thought of those who were singing and listening.[145] Here he found poetry that was created for a purpose: to incite, thank, praise, warn, or strengthen. Because this poetry had a particular function in the life of a *Volk*, it had to be understood in connection with the situation out of which it grew.[146]

Hebrew poetry also held a special place for Herder because it was *göttlich*, or divine. It was no accident that whenever he was dealing with the history of poetry, he began with the poetry of the Israelites, for to him it was an "altar of the one God of truth and virtue" and the *Urbild* or original model for genuine poetry.[147]

When Herder approached the Bible, he approached it in several ways at the same time. First of all, as Wilhelm Dobbek points out, the Bible was to be read in a human way since it was human through, and through. Herder always sought the divine in the human and the human in the di-

142. Herder, "Antrittspredigt" in Weimar (1776) SW 31:436.

143. Haym, *Herder*, 2:342.

144. Cillien, *Johann Gottfried Herder*, 55. For Hamann's significance in helping Herder develop this taste, see Bayer, *Zeitgenosse im Widerspruch*, 170. Here Bayer claims "that there is no doubt that Hamann's understanding of history and time, which through Herder's mediatorship and transformation produced [*mit hervorbrachte*] the historical consciousness of the nineteenth and twentieth centuries, stemmed chiefly and decisively from his [Hamann's] close connection with the Bible."

145. Cillien, *Johann Gottfried Herder*, 55.

146. Ibid.

147. Ibid., 56.

vine.¹⁴⁸ Second, he sought to understand the Bible out of the particular circumstance and, at the same time, out of the spiritual and intellectual thought of the peoples in that part of the world which today is called the Middle East. Third, Herder interpreted the Bible in a historical way. Fourth, he also viewed and studied the Bible as poetry.¹⁴⁹

Today it is commonly recognized that Herder was (1) "one of Germany's most significant literary critics," (2) "an initiator in the field of comparative literature," and (3) "among the founders of literary-historical criticism."¹⁵⁰ It is also commonly recognized today that he inspired a new interest in Hebrew language and ancient Hebrew literature and that he also made significant contributions to New Testament studies as well. Because of the way he "enriched New Testament studies by discussing contradictions in the gospels, the written Hebrew and oral traditions informing them, and their diverse historical contexts," today he is recognized "as a founder of historical, redaction, and form criticism of the Bible.¹⁵¹

For Herder, books of the Bible were treated as pieces of history. At the same time, however, the Bible was never just a historical text, and books of the Bible were never just pieces of history. To this Lutheran pastor, the Bible was "a special kind of book which contained the revelation of God and which was the historic evidence of His great housekeeping. Through history, through experience, and through leadership of a people—as a model for the whole human race—God speaks to us also in the Old Testament."¹⁵²

As a special kind of book, Herder believed that it should be read in a special kind of way. Especially when he was speaking as a pastor, he gave free rein to this special love. "Nature, like sweetness and love, is everywhere only one. When your heart inspires you with the words of

---

148. Dobbek, *J. G. Herders Weltbild*, 36.

149. Ibid., 36–37.

150. Bunge, "Introduction," 2–3.

151. Bunge, "Human Language of the Divine," 311. See also her essay "Johann Gottfried Herder's Auslegung des Neuen Testaments," 249–62. Here Bunge argues that while for Herder *Einfühlung* was the "invitation" to discover the multiple sides of a text, he used a combination of philological, literary, historical, and linguistic means to understand a text, that he recognized the limits of human understanding in this endeavor, and that above all he sought to apply a text to life (ibid., 259).

152. Haym, *Herder nach seinem Leben und seinen Werken*, 2:87.

Cultural Revolution in Germany and a New Historical Consciousness 163

this book to pray, to speak, to observe, to love, then you can do this in an unhindered way like Isaiah, Christ, and John."[153]

For Herder, the most striking biblical expression of the unity of Christ with the Father—which was the basic concept of the New Testament revelation to him—was the Johannine formulation of Christ as the eternal, personal Word in God.[154] Like Luther, Leibniz, and his mentor Hamann, Herder's dynamic way of viewing life was based on the Gospel of John. For Herder, this book was "ein Evangelium des Geistes."[155]

Herder's special way of reading the Bible was directly related to the way he read, studied, and wrote history. According to Meinecke, the young Herder could be carping and petty in his criticisms, but at the same time he read "for direct sympathetic insight into the life of the past," for "the soul's sake, as the Christian seeking salvation might read his Bible," and "in the compulsive spirit of a man who intends to extract from history the last ounce of meaning it can offer to a seeker after God." "No one before him," Meinecke added, "had read history in this spirit."[156]

No one before him viewed and wrote history in this spirit either. For Herder, history was above all an access road to God.[157] The way to read a text or to comprehend the world was through direct experience and out of the power of one's feelings. His way was always *Einfühlung* (a word which he invented[158]), to feel his way into a text or an event, to grasp and to understand it, and then to give expression to it in words. Herder also used the term *Mitgefühl*—a word that also meant acquiring insight through empathy or sympathetic understanding—for his way of reading texts, of viewing life, and of writing history. The goal of this deeply Christian soul and the tolerant human being was not to judge but to understand, for he understood very well that nothing gets in the way of understanding more than judging.

Like Rousseau, Herder felt that he and his feelings were unique. But while Rousseau's *Confessions* (1781) was based on the idea that when

---

153. Ibid. (cited by Haym with no reference).
154. Ibid., 1:634.
155. Ibid., 2:545.
156. Meinecke, *Historism*, 304,
157. Dobbek, *J. G. Herders Weltbild*, 28.
158. Meinecke, *Historism*, 297.

Nature created him she broke the mold, the young Herder expressed similar feelings in verse form in an earlier and a very different way.

> Was ich bin, Geist!—so bin ich Gott—
>
> O Gott, was gabst du mir!—all deine Welt
>
> Schaff ich dir in mir nach.[159]
>
> [What I am, Spirit!—so am I God—
>
> O God, what you gave me!— all your world
>
> I re-create for you within me.]

Certainly one of the main sources for Herder's love for the individual, the particular, and the unique was what Dobbek called "his consciousness of his own worth,"[160] or what Herder regarded as the God-given, creative, and unique nature, power, and capacity of his own soul. As Dobbek also points out, "Herder's *Humanitätsidee* is entirely an expression of his rich personality."[161] And just as Herder himself was constantly developing, "so also the concept of development was the core of his philosophy of history."[162]

Just as Augustine's attitude toward Rome in the *City of God* was both theological and historical,[163] so also all of Herder's work was both theological and historical at the same time.

From the time of his earliest writings, Herder believed that no human being had exactly the same feelings as another.[164] "The inner sanctuary of our soul," he said, "is and remains inexpressible, not demonstrable, and unexplainable."[165] For Herder every individual soul is created in the image of God and has something to offer to humanity. From the time of his earliest writings, Herder's task was "to collect the spirit of each people in its soul" ("den Geist jedes Volkes in seiner Seele zu sammeln").[166]

---

159. Cited in Benz, "Johann Gottfried Herder," in *Die Grossen Deutschen*, 2:212.
160. Dobbek, *J. G. Herders Weltbild*, 79.
161. Ibid., 105.
162. Ibid., 139.
163. Ibid., 101.
164. Herder, SW 32:23.
165. Cited by Dobbek from a letter to Friedrich H. Jacobi in 1792 (*Herders Briefe: Ausgewählte*, Introduction and comment by Wilhelm Dobbek, 349), in *J. G. Herder's Weltbild*, 80.
166. Cited in Dobbek, *Johann Gottfried Herder*, 96.

The most revolutionary element in Herder's thought for this Cultural Revolution, for the great intellectual tradition called German idealism, and for modern historical thought was the idea that just as every individual "soul" is unique,[167] so also every language, people, nation, age, and human *Gestalt* (form), or cultural individuality, has its own unique *Geist*, or spirit.

Although Herder emphasized both the diversity and uniqueness of human beings, nations, religions, and cultures, he also believed "that all human beings are one because they are made in God's image."[168] For Herder, humanity was the highest and greatest historical individuality, and he was most interested in the education of the human *Geist*, or spirit. While Kant focused on the question what is reason, and Hamann focused more on the question what is language, Herder focused on the question, "What is humanity?"[169]

One of the keys for understanding Herder, this "Cultural Revolution" in Germany, and modern German thought and culture is Herder's formula: "Geist in der Gestalt, Seele im Körper," or "Spirit in the form, soul in the body."[170] Just as every individual should strive to develop his or her "soul" to its God-given capacity, so each people or nation should strive to develop its language, poetry, music, literature, thought, culture, and its *Geist* to its God-given capacity. This is certainly one of the basic ideas not only for the rise of the "New Humanism" and of the new *Humanitätsidee* during this great and formative age for modern German literature, philosophy, thought, education, and culture, but also for the rise of the most powerful force of the modern world: an idea that Herder called "nationalism," which was based on his idea known as the *Volksgeist*.[171] "More clearly than any other writer," Isaiah Berlin claims, Herder "conceived and cast light upon the crucially important social function of 'belonging'—on

---

167. Meinecke points out (1) that Herder used the term *soul* "in the sense Hamann used the term, as inseparably bound up with the sensual nature of man," and (2) that this "all-around awareness of human nature as a psychosomatic whole is one of the most important elements of the new historical thought" (*Historism*, 313).

168. Bunge, "Introduction," 15.

169. Kelley, *Fortunes of History*, 8.

170. Cited in Dobbek, *J. G. Herders Weltbild*, 89. See also Herder, SW 22:323.

171. Herder, however, did not coin this word. Its first known use was by Hegel in the year 1793 (Wieland, "Entwicklung, Evolution," in *Geschichtliche Grundbegriffe*, 2:215).

what it is to belong to a group, a culture, a movement, a form of life. It was a most original achievement."[172]

For Herder, the spirit of change was the core of history,[173] and from the beginning he was very aware of how the artistic taste of a nation changed in the course of time. In or around the year 1764, for example, he discussed the significance of the study of various religions for unlocking "the spirit of a nation,"[174] and in the year 1767 he used the expression "der Geist eines Zeitalters," or the spirit of an age.[175] Can any greater harm be inflicted on a nation, he asked, than to be robbed of "its national character, the uniqueness of its *Geist*, and its language?"[176] Thus from the time of his earliest writings, Herder was aware that every age had its own spirit or *Zeitgeist*, another basic word for modern historical thought, which he coined.[177]

By the year 1769, Herder was contemplating a "universal history of the world's formation," which would be a "magnum opus of the human species, on the human spirit, the culture of this earth, of all regions, ages, peoples, forces, fusions, and laws."[178] In this passage from Herder's "Journal

---

172. Berlin, *Vico and Herder*, 194.

173. Herder, *Frühe Schriften 1764–1772*, 158. This volume (cited hereafter as Herder, *Werke* 1) is the most convenient place to trace the development of Herder's language in his early, published writings.

174. Herder, *Against Pure Reason*, 78 (Herder, SW 32:146). Herder, however, was not the only famous person at this time who emphasized the word *Geist* or who spoke of a "*Nationalgeist*." The latter term was introduced by Justus Möser in the year 1761, and in 1765 he published a widely discussed pamphlet called *Von dem deutschen Nationalgeist* in which he sought to invigorate the German national spirit. See Kaiser, *Pietismus und Patriotismus*, 16 and 34; and also Sheehan, *German History, 1770–1866*, 198. For the significance of Montesquieu and his use of the word *esprit*—which at first was not translated into German—for the development of the word *Geist* in Germany, see Vierhaus, "Die Universität Göttingen und die Anfänge der modernen Geschichtswissenschaft im 18. Jahrhundert," in *Geschichtswissenschaft in Göttingen*, 21.

175. Herder, *Werke* 1:330.

176. Ibid., 376. In this regard it is helpful to recognize not only that Herder was "at home in seven languages and literatures," but also that like Lessing, he "devoted himself to building the foundation for a new national culture, which he also saw as a social as well as a spiritual enterprise" (Sheehan, *German History, 1770–1866*, 165).

177. Dobbek, *J. G. Herders Weltbild*, 152.

178. Herder, *On World History*, 34. The phrase "Universal history of the world's formation" is a translation of "Universal-geschichte der Bildung der Welt." For the significance of this phrase, see Bollacher, *Johann Gottfried Herder: Geschichte und Kultur*, especially the article by Yoichiro Shimada, "Individualgeschichte und Universalgeschichte bei Herder:

of My Travels," one can see how Herder provided a kind of outline for a new kind of universal history, cultural history, and intuitive approach.

On the one hand, Herder's intuitive approach required that he trust his feelings and believe in inspiration.[179] On the other hand, however, Dobbek and other scholars claim that Herder was never a mystic or an irrationalist, because what he felt and wrote had to be controlled by rational proof and reason.[180]

Like Luther, Herder believed that he was also called to be a teacher, for he was a teacher "by origin, inclination, inner calling, and external commission."[181] In Königsberg he was a tutor at a pietistic boarding school. During his five years in Riga, he was a tutor at the cathedral school. In September 1770, he met a young law student named Johann Wolfgang Goethe in Strasbourg and brought him into contact with Homer, Pindar, Shakespeare, folk poetry, the history of language, a literary movement known as Storm and Stress, and with the concepts of individuality and development.

For Meinecke, "the new and revolutionary idea," which Herder imparted to Goethe, "was that the individual was inimitable."[182] This idea—which Goethe (and Meinecke) immortalized in the expression *Individuum est ineffabile*, and which Meinecke used as the introductory quotation for his study of the rise of historicism[183]—was also the heart and soul of Meinecke's way of viewing life and way of writing *Geistesgeschichte*.

As Meinecke emphasized, the Bückeburg period of Herder's life was of crucial significance for the development of his philosophy of history based on the concepts of individuality and development, a philosophy that to Meinecke overcame the Enlightenment philosophy of history. In his very influential work called *Auch eine Philosophie der Geschichte zur Bildung der Menschheit*, or *Yet Another Philosophy of History of the*

Geschichtlichkeit als konstruktives Prinzip des *Reisejournals*," 39–49. Here Shimada shows how the *Reisejournal* can be seen as "a preparatory work" for Herder's *Auch ein Philosophie der Geschichte zur Bildung der Menschheit* and the *Ideen zur Philosophie der Geschichte der Menschheit*.

179. Dobbek, *J. G. Herders Weltbild*, 19.
180. Ibid.
181. Ibid., 196.
182. Meinecke, *Historism*, 309.
183. "Have I not already written to you, '*Individuum est ineffabile*', from which I derive a whole world? (Goethe to Lavater, 1780)" (Meinecke, *Historism*, vi).

Education of Humanity (1774),[184] Herder challenged the philosophy of history of his age, particularly as it was manifest in France.

> The universal, philosophical, philanthropic tone of our century readily applies "our own ideal" of virtue and happiness to each distant nation, to each remote period in history. But can one such single ideal be the sole standard for judging, condemning, or praising the customs of other nations or periods? Is not the good scattered throughout the earth? Since one form of humanity and one region cannot encompass the good, it has been distributed in a thousand forms, continually changing shape like an eternal Proteus throughout all continents and centuries. Further, as this Proteus changes and continues to change, humankind always remains only humankind, even if it does not strive for greater virtue or individual happiness. Nevertheless, a *plan in this continual striving* is evident. My great theme![185]

After Herder claimed, "The latest fad of recent philosophy (especially in France) is doubt!" he expressed one of the basic ideas of this Cultural Revolution: "Do you see the growing tree? Those striving human beings? Human beings must pass through different periods of life! All periods are obviously in *progress*! All strive together in *continuity*! Between each period are apparent *resting places, revolutions, changes*! Nevertheless, each period has in itself the *center* of its own happiness."[186] Here one can see the birth of a new historical consciousness and the heart of historicism as a way of viewing life: the Rankean idea that "every epoch is immediate to God."[187]

In this book, *Yet Another Philosophy of History of the Education of Humanity*, Herder "effected a smooth combination of organic development from below and divine guidance from above, leading from one stage to another."[188] In its religious aspect, as Meinecke also said, "it proclaimed that God revealed Himself today and always, and that there is no such

---

184. See the beautifully translated selection from this work in Herder, *Against Pure Reason*, 38–48.

185. Ibid., 44 (emphasis in original).

186. Ibid., 45.

187. Ranke, "Epochs of Modern History," 159. For a good introduction to and translation of this famous quotation and this part of a lecture from the year 1854, see Ranke, "Epochs of Modern History," in Ranke, *The Secret of World History: Selected Writings on the Art and Science of History*, 156–64.

188. Meinecke, *Historism*, 323.

thing as an age without God." It was Herder's "increasing trust in God during these years," Meinecke believed, that "enabled him to carry over his aesthetic feeling to historical phenomena which before then and subsequently were out of his reach." Thus it became possible for him "to weave connecting threads of a teleological kind between all these elements and so develop an all-round sense of universal history."[189] "Never before," Meinecke claimed, "had the great subject of humanity and its historical character been treated at one and the same time with such vital depths and penetration and such cosmic depth."[190]

From the beginning of his work at Bückeburg, Herder was first, foremost, and "doubtless with his whole person a clergyman."[191] From this time to the end of his life, however, he was also an administrator in charge of schools and education for the principality where he lived. For him, this task was no less important than his work as a preacher.[192] Although he was seldom given the means to carry out his educational reforms, Herder was convinced that his "double calling" as clergyman and educator coincided for the highest of all tasks—the education of mankind and the advancement of *Glückseligkeit*, or happiness.[193]

As Herder's biographers agree, Herder possessed a deeply pedagogical nature, and all of his work had an educational purpose. His revival of the concept and the ideal of *humanitas* or *Humanität* greatly influenced Western thought and education; for he was the first one in German intellectual history "to open up *die Idee der Humanität* in its entire depth and all its riches, thereby making possible its further and later development by Goethe and Wilhelm von Humboldt."[194] For Herder, the "education of mankind for humanity [*Humanität*]" was the great theme of his life.[195] For humankind, he believed, history was the scene for all development.[196]

Herder's view of history was inseparable from the basic Christian view of world history as *Heilsgeschichte*, or salvation history.[197] His whole

189. Ibid., 322.
190. Ibid., 360.
191. Cillien, *Johann Gottfried Herder*, 27.
192. Ibid.
193. Ibid., 27–28.
194. Dobbek, *J. G. Herders Weltbild*, 203.
195. Cillien, *Johann Gottfried Herder*, 13.
196. Dobbek, *J. G. Herders Weltbild*, 108.
197. Benz, "Johann Gottfried Herder," in *Die Grossen Deutschen*, 2:218.

view of history was based on a theology of history, which he adopted above all from Luther, whereby God was the Lord of history who guided the fate of all peoples and individual humans toward a great and common final goal. As Ernst Benz also claims, Herder's other basic view, that "the transcendent is not abstract but is there only in concrete embodiment," had "good Lutheran origins."[198]

Herder's historical interpretation, with all of his striving to be close to reality, was—as Dobbek emphasized—always religious. "A sacrament of the earth and this world [*Diesseits*]," he called it one time. 'Religion, the great work of the household of God through centuries and peoples, take me, so that I may teach you many times, which perhaps is my duty on earth' ... 'Spirit of God over (at first, "under") the nations! Spirit of the laws, customs, and arts, as they follow each other, develop, and drive the other away,' was to be his program in Bückeburg."[199] In these words one can clearly see not only how for Herder history was a calling, but also how his work—like the work of Luther—marks a great shift toward "this world" within a firmly Christian worldview.

In his study of Herder's picture of Luther (*Das Lutherbild Johann Gottfried Herders*), Michael Embach showed how the Protestant Reformation was a model of historical development for Herder. Embach also emphasized "the emancipatory aspect" of Luther's language for Herder's understanding of the development of the German national language, and how Herder believed that Luther had taught "an entire nation to think and to feel."[200] Especially during his Bückeburg period, when he first became deeply involved in the study of Luther's writings, Herder first gained a

---

198. Ibid., 218–19. For the significance of Herder's new historical consciousness, his emphasis on the concepts of individuality and development, his sense for the historical that he carried into theological problems, and his heritage from Luther for the beginnings of historical theology, see Scholder, "Herder und die Anfänge der historischen Theologie," 425–40. For the rise of modern critical theology prior to Herder and the rise of historicism in the late eighteenth century, see Scholder, *Birth of Modern Critical Theology*. While for Scholder the age of rational criticism was "the first stage in the development of historical-critical theology," with the rise of historicism and the young Herder's insight that "human beings and their world are in principle historical," it was possible for Ferdinand Christian Bauer to achieve "a synthesis between rational criticism and historical understanding" and thus become "the founder of historical-critical theology in the modern sense" (ibid., 142–44).

199. Dobbek, *J. G. Herders Weltbild*, 143.

200. Embach, *Das Lutherbild Johann Gottfried Herders*, 48–49.

deep understanding of the Middle Ages and of Luther's theology.[201] This, Embach claimed, was a change that can hardly be overemphasized for the whole further development of German *Geistesgeschichte*.[202] It was during this period that Herder best came to appreciate the power of Luther's hymns and diligently worked to preserve them in their original form.

It was also at this stage in Herder's life, Embach emphasizes, that the rise and development of the Reformation became for him the general model for all world-historical changes.[203] At this time, Herder developed a way of viewing history based on both organic and revolutionary ways of perceiving life, for he was able to develop a picture of the Reformation as an organic development out of the Middle Ages and, at the same time, as a revolution. Here two of his basic images—evolutionary growth (*verborgenes Wachstum*) and revolutionary change (*gewaltsamer Durchbruch*)[204]—were combined to describe this model revolution for Herder, and for understanding the course of human history. Thus the Protestant Reformation became Herder's Revolution of the Spirit, or *Geist*.

It is significant for the whole idea of history in the West not only that Herder had a special love for the word *Entwicklung* ("development") and made it a basic term for the study of world history, but also that he was the one who introduced those paired concepts "Revolution-Evolution."[205] For Herder, historical development was a continuation of the development of nature, for both were different aspects of a unified development and God-created cosmos.[206]

201. Ibid., 74. See also Meinecke's statement that "Herder's greatest contribution to a sympathetic reassessment of the individual spirit of an epoch, boldly challenging all accepted opinions, was in respect to the Middle Ages" (*Historism*, 337).

202. Embach, *Die Lutherbild Johann Gottfried Herders*, 88.

203. Ibid., 162–63, 168.

204. Ibid., 169.

205. Wieland, "Entwicklung, Evolution" in *Geschichtliche Grundbegriffe*, 2:204–7. Wieland also emphasizes how the word *Entwicklung* appeared first in Germany in the last third of the eighteenth century, that the ancient world had no such comparable concept, that Old European society had no need of such a concept, and that it appeared first in a historical-political sense with Möser and Herder (ibid., 202–3).

206. Ibid., 205. See also Rudolf Stadelmann's analysis of the three aspects of the *Entwicklungsbegriffe* for Herder—the causal, the teleological, and the organic—in *Der historische Sinn bei Herder*, 68–87. Here Stadelmann claims that while Schelling raised *die Organismusidee* to a world principle, and while Hegel applied it to the state, without doubt it was Herder who mastered this idea for the realm of history (ibid., 80).

During the Weimar period of Herder's life, as Embach emphasizes, the "national-patriotic component of Herder's picture of Luther," and a more "cultural-historical" and humanistic perspective became dominant. It was at this time (1794) that Herder published the introductory quotation to this chapter, "*Geist* is the nature of Lutheranism."

It is more accurate to say, however, that *Geist* was the nature of Herder's understanding of Lutheranism *and* a key to understanding his way of viewing history. Although body, soul, and spirit were always a given unity for him,[207] as they were for Hamann, and although all of Hamann's and Herder's work was based on the concepts "Word" and "Spirit," Hamann's emphasis was more on the Word while Herder's emphasis was more on the Spirit.

Throughout his life and work, Herder was especially indebted to Luther, Leibniz, and Hamann. First, he was indebted to these men for the basic feeling of his life, the unity of all creation.[208] Like Luther, Leibniz, and Hamann, Herder firmly believed that God "has created me and all creatures." Both in Luther and in Leibniz, Herder could find the idea of the macrocosm and the microcosm, the universal and the particular, the divine and the human at the same time.

Now, as Dobbek suggests, "analogy as method, to grasp the divine through the human and the reverse, was thereby possible."[209] Analogy as method, as Hintze most simply and clearly pointed out, is the key to historicism; for to him historicism was a method based on the concepts of individuality and development, which were based on the two analogies that Herder constantly used, of a life-unit and a life-process.

Second, Herder was indebted to Luther and Leibniz for one of the key ideas of his life: the idea and concept of individuality. Although most scholars agree that Herder adopted this mainly from Leibniz, it was derived also partly from Luther. As Heinrich Bornkamm has pointed out, Hamann awakened in Herder "a deep sense of the divine in the individuality in general and particularly in Luther's mentality and preaching, a mentality and preaching that were born out of the Word of God."[210]

---

207. Dobbek, *Herders Weltbild*, 89.
208. Ibid., 67. The reference here is only to Leibniz.
209. Ibid.
210. Bornkamm, *Luther im Spiegel*, 24.

More than anyone before, Herder recognized Luther's genius with words and language, and Luther as a "genius of the deed."[211] Through his love for music, *Volk* music, and poetry, Herder could hear the *Volkslied*, or folksong (a word which Herder first used[212]), in Luther's hymns.[213] Although Herder did not let the world know that he wanted to be the Luther for his day or a "second Luther," it was no secret in his family.[214]

Third, Herder was deeply indebted to Luther and to Leibniz for his dynamic way of viewing life. For Herder, "a genius of the deed" like Luther was a piece of the historical world, and the Reformation was therefore a model of revolutionary change.[215] In Leibniz's *Monadology*, Herder could see a universal, harmonious, organic, and connected development or process of life, which could be adapted to the Christian idea of universal history. If monads could affect and influence each other, as Herder believed,[216] then these living units of Leibniz could become real historical individualities—each with its own unique *Geist* that reflected the universe—within one universal and meaningful development called world history.

Like Luther, Leibniz, Hamann, and Ranke, Herder developed a way of presenting the general or the universal in, with, and under the particular in a new and unique way. For example, Herder believed not only that human beings learned to think and speak at the same time, but also that they possessed a way of thinking "in, with and through" which a language was formed.[217] Unlike Luther, Hamann, and Ranke, however, Herder combined an "in-with-and-under" way and an "individualizing" way of thinking, writing, and viewing life with "a generalizing" way since he constantly sought to discover general laws of nature and history.

---

211. Ibid.

212. Viëtor, *Goethe*, 18–19.

213. Ibid.

214. See Haym, *Herder und seinem Leben und seinen Werken*, 1:582–83, 708.

215. Bornkamm, *Luther im Spiegel*, 24–25.

216. Kaiser, *Pietismus und Patriotismus*, 145.

217. See especially Dobbek, *J. G. Herders Weltbild*, 103. Here Dobbek cites a revealing sentence for Herder's way of thinking, a statement from his *Fragmenten* (Herder, SW 2:25) "Was muss es der Denkart für Form geben, dass sie sich in, mit und durch die eine Sprache bildet." (What kind of thinking is necessary to be formed in, with, and through a language.)

In his very helpful essay called "Herders Stellung zu Luther," or "Herder's Relation to Luther," Heinz Bluhm emphasizes that throughout his life Herder dealt with Luther from four basic standpoints: (1) personality and character, (2) artistic and linguistic, (3) theological-religious, and (4) the cultural significance of Luther and the Protestant Reformation.[218]

Although Herder—like Lessing—was certainly aware of the Mephistophelian (*die mephistophelische*) vein in Luther's personality, unlike Lessing's, Herder's statements about Luther's personality and character were always full of praise.[219] For Herder, "our Luther" was a powerful, noble, and "heart-quickening" personality, "a true prophet and preacher of our fatherland," and the "responsible, moral leader of the German people."[220]

Throughout his life, Herder was inspired and enchanted by Luther's powerful use of language. From the beginning he believed that his age had nothing to equal Luther's magnificent literary achievement: the translation of the Bible into German. For Herder, Luther's Bible was a high point in the history of the German language, and Luther was the one who awoke and unleashed a sleeping giant: the German language (Herder, SW 1:372).

According to Bluhm, "Luther's language in general and his Bible in particular" were the wellspring not only for Herder but also for "the Germans of Herder's time."[221] One of Herder's greatest achievements for this Cultural Revolution in Germany was to call the young Goethe's attention to the sound, the "lebendige" gait and action of Luther's life, songs, and writings.[222] For Herder, Luther was and remained "the great master of our language" (15:47). Through Luther, Herder said, the people (*das Volk*) "received the Bible, at least the *Catechism*, in their hands" (Herder, SW 17:87).

While Herder never changed his early views of Luther's character and personality or on his masterful use of language, Bluhm and other

---

218. Bluhm, "Herders Stellung Zu Luther," 179. Bluhm treats each of these four standpoints in a separate part of his essay.

219. Ibid., 180.

220. Ibid., 182–83, 187.

221. Ibid., 184.

222. The words that Bluhm quotes here from Herder are also full of life: "'sein [Luther's] Leben, Lieder und Schriften wie ganz sind sie Klang, lebendiger Gang, Handlung!'" (ibid., 185 [Herder, SW 7:318]).

scholars have shown that Herder's relation to Luther's basic religious and theological views did change. During the Riga years, Bluhm and other scholars agree, Herder was not deeply interested in the basic theological ideas of Luther but became greatly interested in Luther's theology during the years he was a pastor in Bückeburg. Especially at this time Herder penetrated deeply into the basic theological convictions of Luther, he accepted Luther's theology of the fallen sinner and God's mercy without reservation, and he defended Luther's basic conviction concerning "The Bondage of the Will."[223] During the late years of his Weimar period, however, Herder turned away from Luther's views concerning the bondage of the will and accepted the more humanistic views of Erasmus and Goethe concerning the freedom of the will.

For Bluhm, this decision by Herder had "epoch-making significance" for German intellectual history,[224] for it signified a victory of Weimar over Wittenberg by a man who lived in both worlds, but who helped the more modern view to win out. It is significant that while Luther and Hamann were very earthy men with a deep sense of their sinful natures, this man, whom Hamann liked to call his Plato, moved away from the Pauline, Augustinian, and Lutheran emphasis on sin and grace, and closer to Leibniz—to his *Theodicy* and to his emphasis on nature and grace.

Although Herder moved away from the theology of Luther toward the end of his life, this did not entail a movement away from Luther or from an appreciation of the cultural significance of Luther's work and of the Reformation. For Herder, Luther was one of the greatest Reformers in world history. For him, Luther personified the principle "that was the basis for all healthy religion, happiness, and truth: the freedom of conscience."[225] During Herder's Weimar period, it was this Luther, the warrior for freedom and humanity, who came more into the foreground. While Hamann had shown great understanding of Luther the theologian, and while Lessing had a sympathetic understanding of many aspects of Luther as a "hero of the spirit," Herder had the greatest understanding and appreciation of Luther as an artist and of his whole personality.[226]

223. Bluhm, "Herders Stellung Zu Luther," 191–93.
224. Ibid., 196.
225. Ibid., 197.
226. Ibid., 200.

Most of all, however, Herder shared the conviction of Luther and Hamann that God acted through human beings, and that somehow God was present in all of his creation and in all human history. Because Herder saw God in all aspects of nature and of human history, and because he—more than anyone else—made Benedict Spinoza a respectable philosopher for Christians in Germany to read and to study,[227] he has often been called a pantheist. To Hajo Holborn, for example, Herder "represented a more or less qualified pantheism, although as a theologian he wished to retain some semblance of theism."[228]

The question of pantheism is both a very important and a very controversial one not only for understanding Herder but also for understanding many of the great scholars within the Lutheran tradition since the time of Herder. In his helpful account of the historical and philosophical significance of the "Pantheism Controversy," which began in the summer of 1783 between F. H. Jacobi and Moses Mendelsohn, Frederick Beiser suggests some reasons pantheism was especially attractive to many radicals within the Lutheran tradition.

The early freethinkers in Germany, Beiser asserts, eagerly embraced Luther's idea of an immediate relationship to God. But thanks to Spinoza, they no longer saw the Bible as an infallible guarantee of that relationship. From Spinoza they had learned that the Bible, like other human documents, was a product of history and culture. Since the Bible, then, could not guarantee an immediate relationship to God and was not a sure means of access to him, the early radicals concluded that the answer was to be found in "our own immediate experience, our direct awareness of God within ourselves," in reflecting upon oneself, and "to listen to God within us."[229]

According to Beiser, the appeal of pantheism "ultimately lay deep in Lutheranism itself." Thus it was no accident that "most of the later Spinozists had Lutheran backgrounds, that they did not accept the au-

---

227. For a good account and analysis of how Herder defended Spinoza from the charges of atheism and fatalism, and how he changed "Spinozism" and made it an appealing doctrine for the post-Kantian generation in Germany, see Beiser, *Fate of Reason*, 158–64. For Beiser, Herder's "synthesis of Leibniz and Spinoza—a pantheistic vitalism or a vitalistic pantheism—remains the central achievement of Herder's *Gott, Einige Gespräche*." It was Herder's "vitalistic pantheism," Beiser claims, that "became the inspiration for Schelling's and Hegel's *Naturphilosophie*" (ibid., 163).

228. Holborn, *History of Modern Germany, 1648–1840*, 327.

229. Beiser, *Fate of Reason*, 51–52.

thority of the Bible," that "they insisted on the need for an immediate experience of God," and that pantheism "was thus the secret credo of the heterodox Lutheran."[230]

Part of the appeal of Spinoza's pantheism at the end of the eighteenth century, Beiser also claims, "was its religious attitude toward the world, an attitude that was still consistent with, if not the result of, modern science." Spinoza's pantheism seemed to be "a viable middle path between a discredited theism and deism, on the one hand, and a ruthless materialism and atheism on the other."[231]

According to Beiser, two conditions had to be fulfilled in order for the "pantheistic tendency latent within Lutheranism to realize itself": (1) the authority of the Bible had to be discredited, "which was satisfied by the growth of biblical criticism," and (2) "Luther's ideals had to be maintained, . . . which was fulfilled through the pietistic movement."[232]

In order to understand the rise of Spinozism in late eighteenth-century Germany, Beiser asserts, it is important to note that there was "a single Spinozist tradition running from the late seventeenth century into the late eighteenth century," and that it "was constantly under the inspiration of Luther." For Beiser, the one characteristic feature of "*Goethezeit* pantheism" that betrays Luther's persistent influence "is the insistence of almost all later Spinozists upon the importance of having an experience of God, of standing in communion with nature as a whole." According to Besier, "We find this expressed time and again in Goethe, Schelling, Schleiermacher, Novalis, Hölderlin, and Herder." It was this "mystical strand of *Goethezeit* pantheism," Beiser also insists, "that distinguishes it from the rationalism of orthodox Spinozism."[233]

"Yet what is the feature of *Goethezeit* pantheism," Beiser asks, "other than a reassertion of Luther's ideal of an immediate relationship to God?" In addition, Beiser claims, "What was true of Spinozism in the late seventeenth century did not cease to be true of it in the late eighteenth: it was Lutheranism without the Bible."[234]

---

230. Ibid., 52.
231. Ibid., 60.
232. Ibid.
233. Ibid., 60–61.
234. Ibid., 61.

If late eighteenth-century Spinozism meant Lutheranism without the Bible, however, then Herder certainly cannot be called a Spinozist.[235] But can he be called a pantheist?

Many Herder scholars would not call Herder a pantheist. First of all, pantheism is usually identified with a doctrine or view that involves a denial of God's personality, and that tends to identify God and nature or to identify the Deity with the various forces and workings of nature. One reason that few Christians, now or at the time of Herder, would call themselves pantheists is that the key doctrine and test for Christians since the Council of Nicaea in 325 is the dogma of the Trinity. Thus for most Christians, pantheism and Christianity are two different beliefs.

Second, many Herder scholars would not agree with Holborn's statement that Herder's basic position was "more or less a qualified pantheism," for they know how hard Herder struggled at Weimar against the tendency of Kant and many professors within the German universities at that time to educate Lutheran pastors who emphasized only the first article of the Apostles' Creed and not the second and third articles as well.[236] Many Herder scholars believe that to the end of his life, he remained a strong theist, a good Christian, a "true believer," and a conscientious Lutheran pastor, *Seelsorger*, and servant of the Word.[237]

Herder, however, has often been called a panentheist, a word which was invented in Germany by a German philosopher, Carl Christian Friedrich Krause (1781–1832), and which has been applied to many German scholars—including Leibniz, Schleiermacher, and Ranke—within the German idealist tradition. *Panentheism* is both an "at-the-same-time" word and an "in-with-and-under" word, for it means that everything is *in* God. It is a word that has been used especially for Protestant scholars

---

235. Beiser states that Herder was by no means a strict Spinozist, that he refused to call himself one, that he freely combined Spinoza's pantheism and naturalism with the pantheism and naturalism of other philosophers, and that he thus created his own eclectic mixture (ibid, 162).

236. Ursula Cillien, for example, states: "There can be no doubt that Herder never wanted to be a pantheist and also that in his thinking, his feeling and in his belief he never was" (*Johann Gottfried Herder*, 71). Cillien also points out that for Herder, Luther's explanation of the second article of the creed was "the most beautiful and clearest commentary" on the life of Jesus (ibid., 65).

237. For a helpful account and appreciation of Herder's work as a Christian preacher, pastor, theologian, and writer, see Herbert von Hintzenstern, "Johann Gustav Herder," in Greschat, *Die Aufklärung*, 363–81.

in Germany who believed that everything is in God and in his hand, for God was both transcendent and immanent, both in heaven and on earth, both in all of his creation and in human history.[238]

Certainly Luther's ideal of an immediate relationship to God, a pietistic education, and the rise of modern science and biblical criticism help one to understand what Beiser called the "mystical strand of *Goethezeit* pantheism."[239] Taken together, however, they do not fully explain (1) why Lutherans more than other Protestants were attracted to pantheism, (2) why so many scholars within the German idealist tradition continued to regard themselves as true believers, and (3) why so many scholars within the Lutheran tradition *and* the German idealist tradition have been called panentheists. Here it is helpful to understand not only Luther's "in-with-and-under" way of viewing life but also the rise of the third main tradition within Lutheranism: the critical-historical tradition.

Today it is commonly recognized (1) that before the second half of the eighteenth century, German philology was not on a par with the French, Dutch, or English; (2) that this changed especially through the work of Johann Joachim Winkelmann (1717–1768) and Christian Gottlob Heyne (1729–1812);[240] (3) that Siegmund Jacob Baumgarten (1706–1757) was one of the most important pathfinders (*Wegbereiter*) for "the breakthrough *die historische Bibelkritik* in Germany,"[241] (4) that

---

238. Recently this term has been linked by theologians with the term *sacramentalism*, with Martin Luther, and with what I have called Luther's "in-with-and-under" way of viewing life. The best example I have seen of this can be found in Larry L. Rasmussen's very Lutheran way of defining the terms *sacramentalism* and *panentheism*: "Sometimes called 'panentheism,' sacramentalism recognizes and celebrates the divine in, with, and under all nature, ourselves included. The creaturely is not identified *as* God, however. (This is pantheism, not pan*en*theism.) Nature and the world are thus not of themselves divine and are not worshiped. Rather, the infinite is a dimension of the finite; the transcendent is immanent; the sacred is the ordinary in another, numinous light—without any one of these terms exhausting the other. Sacraments themselves are symbols and signs that participate in the very Reality to which they point, but they are not themselves worshiped. To identify something earthly as holy and sacred is not to say it *is* God. Rather, it is *of* God. God is present in its presence" (Rasmussen, *Earth Community, Earth Ethics*, 239). For Rasmussen's use of the term *panentheism* even for Luther, see especially 272–94. It is certainly conceivable that Herder was the first great forerunner of Rasmussen's "evolutionary sacramentalist cosmology" (247), and that Herder's work should be examined from this perspective.

239. Beiser, *Fate of Reason*, 61.

240. Muhlack, "Historie und Philologie," 54.

241. Schloemann, "Wegbereiter wider Willen," 149.

180 RELIGION AND THE RISE OF HISTORY

Johann Salamo Semler (1725-1791) and Johann David Michaelis (1717-1791) are generally considered to be the founding fathers of *die kritischen Bibelwissenschaft*, or of the historical-critical method of studying the biblical books;[242] and (5) that it was primarily followers of Luther in Germany who developed "higher criticism" of the Bible.[243] While Winckelmann's masterpiece *Geschichte der Kunst der Alterthums* (*History of Ancient Art*) appeared in 1764 and was soon recognized as a permanent contribution to European literature, Heyne was the first to attempt a scientific study of Greek mythology. Here especially it is helpful to look at the significance of Herder's work for the rise of the third main tradition within Lutheranism: the critical-historical tradition.

After Christian Gottlob Heyne became a professor at the University of Göttingen (1763), he was closely identified with the professionalization of philology, with the historical-critical method, and with the Göttingen historians: Gatterer, Schlözer, Spittler, and Heeren (a Heyne student). Through these and other university professors in Germany from the 1760s to 1810, the historical-critical method became the basic principle of all historical writing,[244] including the field called church history.[245] It is

242. Löwenbrück, "Johann David Michaelis' Verdienst und die philologisch-historische Bibelkritik," 157. This collection, called *Historische Kritik und biblischer Kanon in der deutschen Aufklärung*, also has a piece by Gottfried Hornig, "Hermeneutik und Bibelkritik bei Johann Salamo Semler," 219-36. In this essay, Hornig points not only to the basic significance of Luther's and Melanchthon's distinction between "Worte Gottes" and "Heiliger Schrift" for Semler (227-32), but also that he viewed the "Grundgedanken der paulinischen und johanneischen Christologie und Heilserkenntnis" (the basic thoughts of Pauline and Johannine Christology and perception of salvation) as decisive (231). For the significance of Semler for the beginnings of a "New-Testament *Wissenschaft*" in the eighteenth century, see Merk, "Anfänge neutestamentlicher Wissenschaft im 18. Jahrhundert," 37-59. See also Sheehan, *Enlightenment Bible*, especially his account of the significance of Herder and the Luther Bible (168-76) for the development of "The Cultural Bible" or a Bible that was embedded in the matrix of "culture" by the 1780s (220).

243. For example, see Marius, *Martin Luther: The Christian between God and Death*, 359, 483.

244. See Muhlack, "Historie und Philologie," in *Aufklärung und Geschichte*, 69-74.

245. See especially Stroup, "Protestant Church Historians in the German Enlightenment," 169-91. In this essay, Stroup illustrates how the transcendent view of God gave way to a panentheistic "something" that was immanent within the historical process, how the Göttingen church historians prepared the way for a "melting down" of *historia sacra* into world history, and how by "the end of the Enlightenment sacred and profane history were so intertwined that it was hard to disentangle them" (ibid., 170-72). To see how Herder's historical view of religion contributed to the development of several disci-

significant, however, that the rise of philology and history as independent sciences or disciplines in Germany was closely associated with the "New Humanism" and with the rise of historicism, and therefore with the new outlook associated most of all with Herder.[246]

For Herder, history was a mode of thought, a method of understanding, *and* a calling. In his famous work called *Reflections on the Philosophy of the History of Mankind*, one can see a new kind of philosophy of history and a new kind of universal history. It was a new kind of universal history because it was theocentric, humanistic, and *kulturgeschichtlich* at the same time. For Herder, as Dobbek pointed out, "Everything in the world lives from God, and God lives in everything. This 'everything' [*Alles*] is always human. For Herder, the real task of human existence was to fathom the divine in the human and thereby give human life a divine sense and a divine task."[247]

Herder called this *Humanität*.[248] His *Reflections on the Philosophy of the History of Mankind* was based on the development of this *Humanität* in and through nations and peoples and out of their special conditions and circumstances through the various stages of their development and through the various stages of human history.[249]

In order to create this new kind of history, Herder constantly used polar concepts and analogies, including analogies of the stages of life. Most of all, however, he used the concept of individuality, which was based on the analogy of a life-unit or a single human being; and the concept of development, which was based on the analogy of a life-process. For Herder the "collective individuality," a term that he used, "was a culture conceived as a constant flow of thought, feeling, action, and expression."[250] Herder's great strength was his ability to feel, see, connect, and present living units or collective individualities—peoples, nations, societies, religions, cultures, and civilizations—that are the building blocks for any attempt to write world history. For Friedrich Meinecke, Herder's "greatest strength

---

plines in the area of religious studies, see Marcia Bunge's essay "Herder's Historical View of Religion and the Study of Religion in the Nineteenth Century and Today," 232–44.

246. See Muhlack, "Historie und Philologie," 50 and 74–75.
247. Dobbek, *J. G. Herders Weltbild*, 32.
248. Ibid.
249. Ibid.
250. Berlin, *Vico and Herder*, 200.

was his ability to think in terms of whole peoples and the spirit that inspired them."[251]

In his introduction to *Reflections on the Philosophy of the History of Mankind*, Frank E. Manuel claims: "Herder broke the bounds of what could be included in history with an impetuosity that makes previous enlargements of the historical vision puny."[252] Herder made "all moments of time in all cultures worthy of respect," and Manuel calls this "a Christianization of the historic process as well as a democratization to a degree that had never been achieved before."[253] In addition, Manuel states, Herder was the kind of historian "who sees the particular as impregnated with the universal, but still seeks the particular in all its uniqueness."[254]

Like Herder's *Yet Another Philosophy of History*, his *Reflections on the Philosophy of the History of Mankind* can be called an "at-the-same-time" and an "in-with-and-under" philosophy of history and world history. For Friedrich Meinecke, "the great idea" of the earlier work, which was so important for historicism, and which can still be seen in the later work, was "the idea that as in the Kingdom of God in general [*wie im Reiche Gottes überhaupt*], so also in history, everything is simultaneously both means and end."[255] In the same way as for his mentor Hamann, for Herder the idea called *coincidentia oppositorum* was central to his thought.[256]

While for Augustine the realm of God was "the city of God," and while in the English-speaking world this realm is called the kingdom of God, in German the realm of God was and is *das Reich Gottes*. Thus in his explanation of "the second petition" of the Lord's prayer in the Small Catechism, "Dein reich komme," Luther taught young Germans to recite: "The kingdom of God [*Gottes reich*] comes of itself, without our prayer, but we pray in this petition that it may also come to us" (BC-T 346).

It is difficult for individuals at the beginning of the twenty-first century to understand the power of the images of *das Reich Gottes* and *der Geist Gottes* for Herder and for this Revolution of the *Geist* in Germany; for as August Wilhelm von Schlegel (1767-1845) once said,

---

251. Meinecke, *Historism*, 355.
252. Manuel, "Editor's Introduction," xv.
253. Ibid., xvii.
254. Ibid., xi. For Manuel, this statement also applied to Vico.
255. Meinecke, *Historism*, 363.
256. For Herder, see Dobbek, *J. G. Herders Weltbild*, 70-78.

Cultural Revolution in Germany and a New Historical Consciousness 183

"The revolutionary wish to realize *das Reich Gottes* is the elastic point of progressive education [*Bildung*] and the beginning of modern history." For Jürgen Gebhardt, this statement by Schlegel expressed the program of the German "Revolution des Geistes" and also the "geistig-historische Kontext" of its genesis.[257]

Like his teacher Friedrich Meinecke, Hajo Holborn believed that the trend toward a new concept of humanity, "which had gathered momentum from Shaftesbury to Rousseau and Winckelman, found its consummation in Herder." For Herder, truth was a product "of the whole creative power of the individual, and it was expressed in language, myth, religion, and poetry rather than reflection." Consequently for Herder, there was "not a single truth or norm," for no "single religion, age, or nation possesses the whole content of humanity, which runs through history in thousands of forms and in continuous change."[258]

As in the *Theodicy* and other writings of Leibniz, however, Herder's justification of the ways of God to humanity was based (1) on the concepts of nature and grace, (2) on the conviction that this was the best of all possible worlds, and (3) on the view that the world was "an organization of immaterial units of force [*Krafteinheiten*]."[259] In his answer to Voltaire's *Candide* and *Essay on the Customs and Mores of Nations*, Herder said: "All the works of God have their stability in themselves, and in their beautiful consistency: for they all repose, within their determinate limits, on the equilibrium of contending powers, by their intrinsic energy, which reduces these to order. Guided by this clue, I wander through the labyrinth of history, and every where perceive divine harmonious order: for what can any where occur, does occur; what can operate, operates. But reason and justice alone endure: madness and folly destroy the Earth and themselves."[260]

---

257. Gebhardt, "Zur Physiognomie einer Epoche," 13. The quotation from Schlegel that Gebhardt cites comes from a journal called *Athanaeum*, composed and edited by piece called "Fragments" (*Athanaeum* [1798] 1:2, 236). A 1970 photographic printing exists of the original *Athenaeum* publication.

258. Holborn, *History of Modern Germany, 1648–1840*, 325–26.

259. Kaiser, *Pietismus und Patriotismus*, 144–45. Here especially Kaiser notes how Herder plays down Leibniz's idea of preestablished harmony and vastly strengthens his notion of God's immanence and of the world as organism based on individual organisms.

260. Herder, *Reflections on the Philosophy of the History of Mankind*, 116–17.

As H. Stuart Hughes emphasized in *Consciousness and Society: The Reorientation of European Social Thought 1890–1930*, "[i]n the period from about 1770 to 1840, German philosophers and writers had been the schoolmasters of Europe."[261] As Hughes also emphasized, "the enormous merit of German social thought was that it dwelt *in the historical world*."[262] As Donald L. Kelley has more recently emphasized, "Herder, then, emphasized concrete, historical experience, and so established the conceptual grounds for historical studies."[263]

Since the time of Herder, the rise of historicism, and the rise of the critical-historical tradition within Lutheranism, it can also be said that the enormous merit of the Lutheran tradition—at least in Germany—was that it dwelt in the historical world.

IMMANUEL KANT'S AT-THE-SAME-TIME PHILOSOPHY

Like Hamann and Herder, Immanuel Kant was a major figure in what William Carr has called the "German cultural revival" and that "cultural renaissance which blossomed in Germany after the Seven Years' War"; for between "1770 and 1830 the genius of the German people poured forth in philosophy, drama, poetry, and music." "The names of Goethe, Schiller, Lessing, Kant, and Mozart," Carr claims, "made the German-speaking world the cradle of Europe for half a century, ending the long dominance of French cultural values."[264]

---

261. Hughes, *Consciousness and Society*, 184.

262. Ibid., 293 (emphasis in original).

263. Kelley, *Fortunes of History*, 8. For an excellent summary and analysis of the significance of Herder for the idea of history and especially for the development of "cultural history," see Kelley, *Faces of History*, 244–49. In this section called "Cultural History," Kelley emphasizes how "Lutheran spirituality gave German *Geist* a very different force than French *esprit* or even English *spirit*" (244), and also the significance of the shift in terminology in Herder's *Yet Another Philosophy of History* in 1774 to his *Ideas for the Philosophy of History of Mankind*; for the latter represented "Not *Geist* but *Kultur*" (247). For Kelley, Herder's "*History of Humanity* (1775) presented a manifesto of cultural history" (249). See also Liebel-Weckowicz, "Herder, J. G," in *Encyclopedia of Historians and Historical Writing*, 1:527–28. Here it is asserted that Herder "laid the foundation for the modern approach to the history of mankind," and also that the scope of his arguments [in his *Reflections*] "makes it possible to consider Herder the first modern cultural historian."

264. Carr, *Origins of the Wars of German Unification*, 16.

Cultural Revolution in Germany and a New Historical Consciousness 185

Immanuel Kant was born in Königsberg in the year 1724 and began lecturing at the University of Königsberg in the year 1755. In the year 1781, he published a book still regarded as a revolution in the field of philosophy, the famous *Critique of Pure Reason*. In this study Kant agreed with the British empiricists, and with Leibniz, that all our knowledge begins *with* experience. Like Leibniz, however, Kant believed that not all knowledge arises *out* of experience. While the empiricists believed that all our knowledge must conform to the objects that it experiences, Kant—like Leibniz—believed that human understanding brings something to the objects that it experiences. Unlike Leibniz, however, Kant was able to work out an "at-the-same-time" epistemology, or theory of knowledge, in a clear and convincing way.

First of all, Kant's *Critique of Pure Reason* is based on the distinction between what he called "pure" and "empirical" knowledge."

> THERE CAN BE NO DOUBT that all our knowledge begins with experience. For how should our faculty of knowledge be awakened into action did not objects affecting our senses partly of themselves produce representations, compare these representations and, by combining or separating them, work up the raw materials of the sensible impressions into that knowledge of objects which is entitled experience? In the order of time, therefore, we have no knowledge antecedent to experience, and with experience all our knowledge begins.
>
> But though all our knowledge begins with experience, it does not follow that it all arises out of experience.[265]

In this epoch-making book for modern philosophy and modern German thought, Kant showed how humans possess two basic forms of *innere Anschauung*—or forms of intuition or perception—which precede experience. Therefore they were "a priori" and "pure" forms of knowledge. These two basic forms were time and space. It is both interesting and significant that Kant used the words "inner forms of *Anschauung*" for the two most basic ways a human being arranges the manifold impressions received through the senses, for they were like lenses for perceiving and organizing what we experience through our senses.

While the British empiricists from Locke to Hume agreed that "the mind" functions in a passive role whereby it must conform to the given object, Kant came to believe that this was a passive and dualistic view

---

265. Kant, *Immanuel Kant's Critique of Pure Reason*, 41 (emphasis in original).

of cognition.[266] His new hypothesis was that what the British called "the mind" is active. Instead of beginning with the object as something already given, to which "the mind" must conform, Kant reverses the order and conceives of the object as in some respects constituted by the a priori contributions of the knower. This is known as Kant's "Copernican Revolution." The effect of this "revolution in epistemology" was "to turn the self from a passive receiver of sensations into an active participant in the process of knowing."[267] Instead of a sensational epistemology, Kant created what scholars have called "his idealistic epistemology."[268] More recently, Kant's "Copernican Revolution" has been portrayed as one aspect of a "cluster of factors that, together, could be called the Epistemological Revolution."[269]

In addition to these basic inner forms of *Anschauung*, Kant also tried to show how human beings possess "categories" of thought, such as quantity and quality, that deal more specifically with the way they unify or synthesize experience. Although the word *Geist* or "mind" is not a basic word in this work, philosophy teachers in the United States often emphasize that for Kant "the mind" is not *tabula rasa*, a white paper, or a blank page; it is organizing or formative capacity.

Although these inner forms of *Anschauung* and these categories of thought made it possible for individuals to organize sensations into ordered experience, Kant also believed that human knowledge was limited by the manner in which our faculties of perception and thinking organize the raw data of experience. The world that we can experience through our senses Kant called "phenomenal" reality, and the nonsensuous world or purely intelligible world he called "noumenal" reality. For Kant, scientific knowledge was limited to the phenomenal world of objects that we can experience through the senses, to the world of time and space. Although God and the soul stood outside of this world, they were very important in his philosophy.

In his book *Immanuel Kant: His Life and Doctrine* (1899), Friedrich Paulsen—a philosopher at the University of Berlin and one of the great scholars in the field called history of education—explained in a nontech-

---

266. Livingston, *Modern Christian Thought*, 64.
267. Mazlish, *Riddle of History*, 113.
268. Ibid., 114.
269. Ziolkowski, *Clio the Romantic Muse*, 9–10.

nical way Kant's critical and "at-the-same-time" philosophy: "In its final form, his thought approached the boundaries of mysticism," for man has "a double life, a temporal life of sense as a member of nature, and a transcendent, timeless life as a member of the intelligible world."[270] While mathematics was a form of knowledge dealing with the sensible world, metaphysics was a form of knowledge dealing with the intelligible world. Through the complete separation of these two worlds, Paulsen explained, validity in its own domain was secured also for metaphysics. This meant that metaphysics was secured against the demands that its objects should be represented as perceptible objects in time and space, for "God and the soul stand entirely outside of space and time."[271]

Another basic feature of Kant's "at-the-same-time" philosophy was the way he put limits on human reason. According to Kant, our human consciousness can never know an object as a "thing-in-itself," or what it was like when it was not being perceived. Thus for Kant, knowledge was a cooperative affair between the knower and the thing known, but we can never know another thing as it is in itself.

Although both Hamann and Herder rejected Kant's critical philosophy and wrote critiques of it that have received much attention by scholars in recent years,[272] Kant's *Critique of Pure Reason* was one of the greatest achievements of this intellectual and cultural revolution in Germany. In and with Kant's critical philosophy, German scholars were armed with a sophisticated theory of knowledge that began with the outside objects of perception of the empiricists and, at the same time, with the consciousness of the "thinking I" of the rationalists.

For Meinecke, "the development of the critical method" depended on "a full breakthrough of the sense of individuality" and also on the theory of knowledge offered by Kant's philosophy; for until then the critical method could not be given "an inner assurance that would protect it against the arbitrary imaginations of pragmatism."[273] Meinecke also believed that Kant's philosophy prepared the way for a full recognition of the complicated process by which the subjectivity of the researching *Geist*

---

270. Paulsen, *Immanuel Kant: His Life and Doctrine*, 65.

271. Ibid., 90.

272. For a good account in English of the genesis, contents, and consequences of Hamann's "Metakritik," which was completed in 1784 but not published until 1800, see Beiser, *Fate of Reason*, 37–43.

273. Meinecke, *Historism*, 24.

"is quite as often a source of power as it is a hindrance in the acquisition of knowledge."[274]

While here Meinecke summarizes the significance of Kant's achievement for the rise of a modern historical consciousness, Paulsen summarizes the significance of Kant's achievement for many Christians in and outside Germany during and since this formative period for modern German thought and culture. For Paulsen, there was "no doubt that the great influence which Kant exercised upon his age was due just to the fact that he appeared as a deliverer from an unendurable suspense." While science seemed "to demand the renunciation of the old faith," on the other hand Pietism "had increased the sincerity and earnestness of religion, and given it a new and firm root in the affections of the German people." For Paulsen, Kant's philosophy offered a way out of this dilemma, for it "showed a way to be at once a candid thinker and an honest man of faith." For this, Paulsen claimed, "thousands of hearts have thanked him with passionate devotion."[275]

For Paulsen, this was similar to what the Reformation had brought in Germany. Just as Luther had revolted against the confusion of religion and science in Scholastic philosophy and had sought to make faith independent of knowledge, and conscience free from external authority, Kant had banished religion from the field of science, and science from the sphere of religion, thus affording freedom and independence to both. "At the same time," Paulsen claims, Kant "placed morality on a Protestant basis, not works, but the disposition of the heart."[276]

On the other hand, however, Kant was too much a man of the Enlightenment and too Prussian just to trust the disposition of the human heart. Ethics, he insisted, had to be based on reason as the governor of our will, on a sense of duty, and on law. His famous Categorical Imperative ("Act only on that maxim whereby thou canst at the same time will that it should become a universal law") is a classic example of Kant's "at-the-same-time" philosophy.

As Hajo Holborn has pointed out, Kant's philosophical ethics "showed its origin in the old Lutheran ethics, which his pietistic mother and early teachers had planted deeply into his heart." While Kant's criti-

---

274. Ibid., 64.
275. Paulsen, *Immanuel Kant: His Life and Doctrine*, 6–7.
276. Ibid.

cism "of the shallow utilitarian ethics of the eighteenth century bore a genuinely Lutheran stamp," in his "philosophy of religion, particularly in his assumption of a 'radical evil' in man, similar Lutheran traits became noticeable."[277] Is Holborn right, however, in asserting that "Kant did not think of himself as a real Christian"?[278]

In his study called *Kant on History and Religion* (1973), Michel Despland claims not only that "Kant believed himself to be a Christian,"[279] but also that "the core of Kant's philosophy of history" was "an affirmation of divine purpose in history, a divine purpose fully consonant with the rational purposes which men, as free beings who set ends for themselves, strive after."[280]

Although scholars have disagreed on whether or not and to what degree Kant considered himself to be "a real Christian," there is little doubt that his critical philosophy was a turning point for Christian theologians and for the science or discipline called theology. As Jaroslav Pelikan stated in one of his earliest works, one can find Lutheran influences in Kant's epistemology, in his view of time and space, in his moral philosophy, in his notion of the calling, and in his view of radical evil. Lutheran theology, he said, can be grateful to Kant "for freeing it from the onerous responsibility of proving by means of reason that which is known by faith."[281]

According to James C. Livingston, Kant's importance for modern theology "lies in the fact that he both extended Hume's critique of traditional natural theology *and* laid the theoretical groundwork for an entirely new approach to theology." In the Preface to *The Critique of Pure Reason*, when Kant said that he had "found it necessary to deny knowledge in order to make room for *faith*," this sounds "exactly like Hume in its denial of any relationship between religion and matters of empirical knowledge." But for Livingston, this is as far as the similarity goes, for it is important to note that "Kant is contrasting *faith* with empirical *knowledge*, not faith and reason." Religious faith and knowledge were not "radically opposed

---

277. Holborn, *History of Modern Germany, 1648–1840*, 337.

278. Ibid.

279. Despland, *Kant on History and Religion*, 246.

280. Ibid., 53.

281. Pelikan, *From Luther to Kierkegaard*, 92. See also his interesting analysis of "The Primacy of 'Geist'" in German philosophy after Kant or in the philosophy of Fichte, Schelling, and Hegel. Here Pelikan was very critical of their kind of "spiritualism" whereby it is difficult to see the Christian view of the incarnation.

in Kant as in Hume," for they were "two quite different, though equally necessary aspects of reason." For Livingston, "Kant's pivotal role lies in the fact that he freed theology from the corrosion of classical empiricism while maintaining the rationality of religious belief."[282] This "fact" is exactly what Leibniz, Kant's great forerunner, and the great forerunner of this intellectual and cultural revolution in Germany, had sought to accomplish in his *New Essays on Human Understanding*.

Today it is commonly recognized that Kant's *Critique of Pure Reason* in the year 1781 ushered in the Kantian "Copernican Revolution" in philosophy *and* theology. As Livingston pointed out, Kant sought to steer "a middle path between skepticism and dogmatism. He denies any knowledge of the attributes of God in himself and yet finds a legitimate function in the idea of a God of perfect intelligence, goodness, and justice 'for us,' that is, in the interests of our knowledge of nature and its laws."[283]

As Livingston also points out, whereas traditionally morals were grounded in theology, "Kant reverses this order and attempts to demonstrate that the fundamental beliefs of religion are in need of the support of moral reason."

> Thus Kant can say that "it is reason, by means of its moral principles, that can first produce the concept of God." This is Kant's "Copernican Revolution" in theology! Here Kant reveals his kinship with, and his dependence upon Rousseau. Kant, like Rousseau, rejects speculative theology based on metaphysical proofs. For him the only way to knowledge of God is through the moral conscience, the only genuine theology is ethical theology... Religion is, for Kant, "trust in the promise of the moral law."[284]

Like Luther, Livingston could have said, Kant rejected speculative theology based on metaphysical truths. For Luther and for Kant, religion was a matter of trust in "the promise," a promise "for us."

"As a man of the German Enlightenment," as Allen W. Wood points out in an essay in *The Cambridge Companion to Kant* (1992), "Kant regarded the concerns of science and morality as *of course* also religious

---

282. Livingston, *Modern Christian Thought*, 63 (emphasis in original).
283. Ibid., 68.
284. Ibid., 69.

concerns."²⁸⁵ The arguments of "this deeply religious thinker"²⁸⁶ did not show that there is a God and a future life, but only that belief in this would be very desirable for a moral agent to have. In this respect, Kant's moral arguments were rather like Pascal's wager, which tried to show not that Christianity was true, "but that Christian belief would be advantageous to have."²⁸⁷ On the other hand, however, Wood also asserts: "No thinker ever placed greater emphasis on reason's boundaries than Kant; at the same time, none has ever been bolder in asserting its unqualified title to govern our lives."²⁸⁸

When Kant was buried by the cathedral in Königsberg, his *simul*-vision and his *simul* philosophy were captured in the words from his *Critique of Practical Reason* (1788) that were placed on the *Stoa Kantiana* above his grave: "The starry heavens above me, and the moral law in me." "Two things," Kant said, "fill the mind [*das Gemüt*] with ever new and increasing admiration and awe, the more often and more continuously one reflects upon them: *the starry heavens above me and the moral law in me*."²⁸⁹

It is significant that while Kant's epoch-making *Critique of Pure Reason* began with two carefully chosen prepositions, the conclusion to his *Critique of Practical Reason* also began with two carefully selected prepositions. Unlike Luther, Kant was not a great writer; but like Luther, he knew how to use carefully chosen prepositions to express his "at-the-same-time" way of thinking and viewing life.

It is also significant (1) that Kant used the word *Gemüt* in this famous sentence, (2) that this word has usually been translated as "mind" when it

285. Wood, "Rational Theology, Moral Faith, and Religion," 414.
286. Ibid.
287. Ibid., 404.
288. Ibid., 414. For the significance of Lessing, Herder, and Kant for the development of a new attitude toward theology, see the concluding sentences by Leonard Krieger in an essay called "The Philosophical Bases of German Historicism: The Eighteenth Century" in *Aufklärung und Geschichte*, 263: "If the rise of the new aesthetics sanctified particularity, the new attitude toward theology, created rather than reflected by Lessing, Kant and Herder, sanctified universality. The temporal schemes of these philosophers show that the idea of development, which affords the connection with any individuality, came as much from the idea of a divine connection among all events as from the idea of individuality writ large."
289. Kant, *Kritik der praktischen Vernunft*, 174. Usually in this passage the word *in* is translated "within."

is translated into English, (3) that this word can be translated as "mind," "spirit," "heart," "soul," "nature," or "feeling," and (4) that here Kant used an "at-the-same-time" word that really suggests the inner person and not mind alone.

Before Kant's death in the year 1804, writers in Germany already associated his philosophy with a great revolution that was comparable to the French Revolution. As R. R. Palmer pointed out, Germans took pride in excelling in philosophy and in the realm of thought. "No other people," Palmer asserts, "showed such a passion for metaphysics or such concern for the absolute and the unconditional," and in Germany the doctrine of Kant "was of importance at the more commonplace level of the history of ideas." As Palmer also points out, "There was a feeling with Kant a great intellectual revolution had been affected in Germany, commensurate in magnitude to the merely external revolution of the French. As an obscure journalist named Geich wrote in 1798: 'Our nation has produced a revolution no less glorious, no less rich in consequences than the one from which has come the government of the [French] Republic. This revolution is in the country of the mind.'"[290]

Although Kant's "Copernican Revolution" can be called "a revolution of the mind" or "a revolution of the *Geist*," the latter word was not a basic word for him either in his *Critique of Pure Reason* or for his work as a whole. In his study *Geist und Revolution: Studien zu Kant, Hegel und Marx*, Helmut König sought to confront "die idealistische Revolution des Geistes" with the Marxian theory of revolution.[291] Although König believed that the philosophy of Kant could be called "eine Revolution des Geistes" because of its great significance in the history of thought,[292] in a note to this statement he also pointed out that with Kant the concept *Geist* hardly played a role: "When it appears in his writings, usually it is used as a disparaging designation of the pneumatological *Geister* concept of rational psychology. First in the 'Critique of Judgment' does he approach a positive use of '*Geist*' in the singular and thereby launched its development into the central concept of German idealism."[293]

---

290. Palmer, *Struggle*, 430–31. Most likely the word "mind" here would be a translation of the German word *Geist*.

291. König, *Geist und Revolution*, 7.

292. Ibid., 26.

293. Ibid., 177. In this note, König suggested that readers should compare this statement with the article "*Geist*" in the *Historisches Wörterbuch der Philosophie*, 182ff.

Cultural Revolution in Germany and a New Historical Consciousness 193

Like Luther's revolution in the sixteenth century, Kant's revolution was a revolution of the "inner man" or person. In many respects Kant can be understood as "a secularized disciple of Luther,"[294] for his work can be understood "as a secular form of Lutheran *Innerlichkeit*."[295]

In an essay called "The Revolutionizing of Consciousness: A German Utopia?" Rudolf Vierhaus discussed the consciousness of a "revolution in the human spirit [*Geist*],"[296] an "intellectual revolution," or a "revolution of the mind and spirit" at the end of the eighteenth century and the beginning of the nineteenth as "the Revolution of Consciousness." This revolution of the mind and spirit, Vierhaus also asserts, "was not merely claimed as a German equivalent of the political revolution in France, a substitute for a realignment which was long overdue, and as an outstanding achievement; it was also seen as a revolution that was more important in the long term because by transforming the consciousness of men it laid the basis for their better action."[297]

Since the time of Herder and Kant, the word *Geist* has been the chief word for German thought and culture to express the spirit, mind, and soul of the inner human being *and*, at the same time, the spirit of a people, nation, or age. Especially through the work of Georg Wilhelm Friedrich Hegel (1770–1831), however, this word also came to signify the "spirit" that moves world history. Since for Hegel "man is spirit," Hegel believed that "faith in the power of spirit is the first condition of philosophizing."[298] In Hegel's speculative system, "man realizes himself as *Geist*—in the double sense of mind and soul—when philosophy persuades him of both his religious nature (or potential), and his religious destiny."[299]

Indeed, this article is very helpful in showing how the rise of the word *Geist* became the "ruling fundamental concept" within German idealism. (ibid, 182). Even in Kant's *Critique of Judgment*, however, the word *Geist* is seldom used. When it is used, it could best be translated "spirit" rather than "mind."

294. Eiben, *Von Luther zu Kant*, 6.

295. Ibid., 160.

296. Vierhaus, "Revolutionizing of Consciousness: A German Utopia?" 561. It is significant that this particular phrase was written in the year 1788 and that Vierhaus uses this quotation at the beginning of his essay.

297. Ibid., 573. As Vierhaus also points out, "The 'revolution of the spirit', however, or revolutionizing of consciousness, remained limited to the narrow stratum of the educated" (ibid., 574).

298. Dickey, "Hegel on Religion and Philosophy," 307–8.

299. Ibid., 308.

The culminating point of this "Cultural Revolution" or this "Revolution of Consciousness" in the field of philosophy came in the year 1807 with the publication of Hegel's "greatest work" and "probably one of the ten most profound works in all philosophy," his *Phänomenologie des Geistes*.[300] Although Hegel's greatest influence on his contemporaries came during the years from 1818 to 1831 when he was a professor at the University of Berlin, it is fair to say that with the appearance of this book in the year 1807, "Hegel's intellectual development was, in all essentials, complete."[301]

One of the most significant contributions of the *Phänomenologie* to this Cultural Revolution was Hegel's critique of the religious thought of the Enlightenment, on the one hand, and his defense of traditional Christian faith on the other. In this discussion it is obvious that Hegel believed that he was standing outside and beyond the stage in the development of Western thought called the Enlightenment, and that he regarded his philosophy a synthesis of Enlightenment and faith. For J. N. Findlay, Hegel was "a great Christian theologian" whose "philosophy is essentially a philosophy of redemption."[302]

One of the reasons that this work—which in 1977 was translated into English as *Phenomenology of Spirit* instead of *Phenomenology of Mind*—is significant for the whole development of German and Western philosophy is that Hegel, more than anyone else, was the philosopher who "historized" philosophy.

In his study called *Enlightenment, Revolution, and Romanticism: The Genesis of Modern German Political Thought*, Frederick C. Beiser showed how during the 1790s the most potent threat to the *Aufklärung* came from the rise of historicism.[303] In this particular work, Beiser does not focus either on Hegel or on his *Phänomenologie des Geistes*; but in *The Cambridge Companion to Hegel*, which he edited, he does focus on "Hegel's Historical Revolution." In an excellent chapter called "Hegel's Historicism," Beiser states: "History cannot be consigned to a corner of Hegel's system, relegated to a few paragraphs near the end of the *Encyclopedia* or confined to his *Lectures on the Philosophy of History*. For as many scholars have long

300. Rauch, *Hegel and the Human Spirit*, 10.
301. Harris, "Hegel's Intellectual Development to 1807," 42.
302. Findlay, "Foreword," xxvii.
303. See Beiser's useful summary of the main characteristics of historicism, in *Enlightenment, Revolution, and Romanticism*, 5-6.

since recognized, history is central to Hegel's conception of philosophy. One of the most striking and characteristic features of Hegel's thought is that it *historizes* philosophy, explaining its purpose, principles, and problems in historical terms." For Beiser, "Hegel's historicism amounted to nothing less than a revolution in the history of philosophy," for it implied "that philosophy is possible only if it is historical, only if the philosopher is aware of the origins, context, and development of doctrines."[304]

One of the most important aspects of Hegel's *Phänomenologie des Geistes* for this age and for this revolution in the humanities was his strong belief and statement that "now is the time" to raise philosophy to the status of a science: "To show that now is the time for philosophy to be raised to the status of a Science would therefore be the only true justification of any effort that has this aim, for to do so would demonstrate the necessity of the aim, would indeed at the same time be the accomplishing of it."[305] By the year 1810, Hegel's desire to raise philosophy to the status of a science had become a goal for many German educators and patriots.

Now the story of the development of a German national consciousness and identity from Friedrich Carl von Moser's invention of the term "German national spirit" (1765),[306] and Herder's creation of the idea known as the *Volksgeist* to the end of the Holy Roman Empire and the collapse of Prussia (1806), to Fichte's "Addresses to the German nation (1807–1808) and to "the anti-Napoleonic movement" has been told many times.[307] What I want to emphasize, however, is why the year 1810 is a useful date to mark the culmination of the Cultural Revolution in Germany.

In his *Encounters with Nationalism*, Ernst Gellner claimed that "by far the most important investment or possession of modern man" is access to

---

304. Beiser, "Hegel's Historicism," 270. In one of the notes (298 n. 3) for this excellent and very readable essay, Beiser states: "The definitive study of the origins of historicism is Friedrich Meinecke's *Die Entstehung des Historismus* (Munich, 1959). Unfortunately, Meinecke does not discuss Hegel."

305. Hegel, *Phenomenology of Spirit*, 3–4.

306. Moser, *Von dem deutschen Nationalgeist* (1765).

307. For a good account of these events, see Dann, *Nation und Nationalismus in Deutschland*, 45–60. At the beginning of the nineteenth century, Dann claims, the German cultural society and nation reached a high point of scholarly and cultural productivity (53). For a good account of these events within the context of European history since the Middle Ages, see Schulze, *States, Nations, and Nationalism*.

a "shared High Culture" or to a school-transmitted culture.[308] During the years from 1760 to 1810, "the German nation" certainly acquired a great common culture, but it was not until 1810 that it first acquired a modern school system to transmit that culture to a large number of individuals.

The institutional culmination of this intellectual and cultural revolution came from March 1809 to June 1810 when Wilhelm von Humboldt, as chief of the department of education for the Prussian state, "created the institutional forms of Prussian and German education which were to last until 1933."[309] In the field of higher education, Wilhelm von Humboldt, Johann Gottfried Fichte, Friedrich Schleiermacher, and the other great founders of the University of Berlin[310] sought to raise philosophy to the dignity of a *Wissenschaft*. Thus the traditional arts or philosophy faculty was replaced by a new kind of philosophy faculty,[311] the study of the liberal arts was transferred to the *Gymnasium*, or to the new kind of secondary school that replaced Melanchthon's "Latin schools";[312] and the Western university now became a center for research, for the discovery of new

---

308. Gellner, *Encounters with Nationalism*, 46. As Thomas A. Brady Jr. has asserted, "The high culture of modern Germany initially was disproportionately Protestant culture, except in art and music" (*Protestant Reformation in German History*, 32). Here Brady emphasizes how "the political legacy of the Reformation era, which added religious 'two-ness' to the late medieval heritage of 'many-ness,'" (31) influenced the whole course of German history to the present.

309. Holborn, *History of Modern Germany, 1648–1840*, 474.

310. Although Humboldt was no longer in office in the fall of 1810 when the University of Berlin opened, he worked to see "that leading scholars such as Fichte, Schleiermacher, Wolf, Böckh, Niebuhr (as reading Academy member) Savigny, Eichhorn, Hufeland, and others were called to and connected with the young University of Berlin" (Neugebauer, "Das Bildungswesen in Preussen seit der Mitte des 17. Jahrhunderts," 2:678). Although Neugebauer rightly emphasizes that it was not until the "Pre-March period" or the time before the Revolution of 1848 that Prussia as a whole acquired a statewide, state-supervised *system* of education, the collection of these great scholars at the University of Berlin in 1810 supports the idea of seeing this year as a culminating point of a cultural revolution in Germany and, at the same time, the beginning of a modern kind of education in Germany.

311. Although some of the arts faculties in Germany were called philosophy faculties during the eighteenth century, in Berlin the central importance of the philosophy faculty within the university as a whole was new and revolutionary.

312. Holborn, *History of Modern Germany: 1648–1840*, 475. In this excellent section called "The *Gymnasium*," Holborn emphasized that this institution "was the true love of the reformers" (ibid.), and that "there is no question that the *Gymnasium* made the new German culture, as it had come into being during the half century prior to 1815, the common property of a large class of Germans" (ibid., 476–77).

knowledge, and for the training of doctors of philosophy who were both lovers of wisdom and highly trained specialists at the same time.

As Thomas Nipperdey has pointed out, the basic educational ideas and ideals of the "new humanistic" movement "were not a monopoly of Prussian scholars or institutions—Göttingen, Jena, Leipzig, later Würzburg and Heidelberg played a role in the history of reform—, but they came together in Prussia: the founding of the University of Berlin is its classic realization."[313] As Nipperdey also claims, it was well-educated Prussian officials, rather than professors, who established the foundations for "a new bureaucracy, a new *Wissenschaft*, and a new university," and who made the year 1810 a turning point by creating "the modern and the modernizing university."[314] With this change the state became a "Kulturstaat" responsible for culture, and the Prussian military and bureaucratic state also became a state of "Wissenschaft und Bildung." Here the new "Wissenschaftsidee, Wissenschaft als Selbstzweck, Wissenschaft als Forschung"—or the new idea of science (and/or scholarship), science for its own sake, science as research—was realized.[315] At first, the University of Berlin was a university of philosophers and philologists, for it centered on *Kultur* rather than nature. In the 1830s, however, the modern natural sciences also became powerful.[316]

It is difficult to overemphasize the significance of the new type of German university both for Germany and for the West as a whole, for as Nipperdey also claimed: "The great changes, crises and conflicts which determined the *geistige* history of the German people—the philosophical and historical reshaping of Christianity, the transformation of the world picture through the historical and the natural sciences, the belief in progress and the doubt in progress, the unfolding of the concept of the nation, the discovery of society, the cultural struggles, the political controversies, and the coming to grips with Marxism—, these were all centered in university discussions."[317]

For Nipperdey, the modern university—for which the University of Berlin was the prototype—was a part of Prussia, heir of reform, and

---

313. Nipperdey, "Preussen und die Universität," 142.
314. Ibid., 144.
315. Ibid., 146.
316. Ibid., 148.
317. Ibid.

an "incarnation *des Geistes*" that strongly influenced the national movement, the idea of Prussia as "a state of *Geist* and freedom," and a belief in Prussia's "deutschen Beruf."[318]

Since the time of the founding of the University of Berlin and the Prussian and German *Gymnasium*, *Kultur* served as an important focal point of German national consciousness. By *Kultur*, as Charles E. McClelland has stated, "German intellectuals meant essentially the spiritual and intellectual *cultura animi* of Renaissance humanism, a set of skills and values designed to produce the best possible human being."[319] "*Kultur* was the ethical goal of the state and its servants, including the educational establishment. Individual *Bildung* was the means; *Wissenschaft*, the method; educational and scientific institutions, the structure; and the educational establishment of *Gymanisien* and universities provided the personnel for the achievement of ever-higher levels of *Kultur*."[320] *Kultur*, *Bildung*, and *Wissenschaft*—these were the terms that symbolized not only the high sense of mission and obligation of the academic establishment in Germany from 1810 to 1933 but also its great accomplishments in many fields of endeavor.

Certainly one of Germany's greatest accomplishments was the leading role it played in the development of a new kind of historical consciousness and a new type of Western historiography. In several respects the year 1810 can also be seen as the culminating year for the rise or formative stage for a distinctly modern type of Western historiography, *and* at the same time as the beginning year for the mature, the full, or the high stage of this type. Although history was gradually becoming a professionalized academic discipline at the University of Göttingen dur-

---

318. Ibid., 153. See also Nipperdey's excellent account of the educational reforms in Prussia in the year 1810 in his classic study, *Deutsche Geschichte 1800-1866*, 57–65. When the Prussian state established state examinations for *Gymnasium* teachers in the year 1810, it founded a new profession and career with its own standards (ibid., 62). For a thorough discussion of the rise of many of the basic characteristics of the modern research university at Göttingen in the late eighteenth century and especially of how in 1810 the University of Berlin became the chief model for many of the basic characteristics of the modern research university (especially the Doctor of Philosophy and the dissertation), see Clark, *Academic Charisma*.

319. McClelland, "Wise Man's Burden," 45.

320. Ibid., 50. See also McClelland's discussion of the term *Wissenschaft* and how this "almost untranslatable word" implied "the systematic pursuit of knowledge" (ibid., 49).

Cultural Revolution in Germany and a New Historical Consciousness 199

ing the previous five decades, the year 1810 was of crucial significance for the emergence of a new kind of Western historiography.

It was a watershed year first of all because at this time Berthold Georg Niebuhr (1776-1831)—"the first commanding figure in modern historiography, the scholar who raised history from a subordinate place to the dignity of an independent science,"[321]—was made court historiographer for the Prussian monarchy and began his famous lecture on Roman history. Although Niebuhr was neither a professional historian nor one of the newly called professors at the University of Berlin,[322] these lectures and his two-volume *History of Rome* (1811-1812) mark a new stage and age in the development of the critical-historical method and the discipline called history.[323]

The year 1810 can also be seen as a useful date to mark the beginning of a distinctly modern type of Western historiography because (1) at the University of Berlin history was entrusted to a specialist in the subject and method of history who taught *only* history, the professor of history;[324] (2) by this time "historicism," the critical-historical method, and the critical-historical tradition within Lutheranism were firmly established at this model university for the modern Western world; and (3)

---

321. Gooch, *History and Historians in the Nineteenth Century* (1958), 14.

322. For the beginning, rise, and the whole development of "der moderne Geschichtswissenschaft" at the University of Berlin, see volume 82 in the series of publications by the Historische Kommission zu Berlin: *Geschichtswissenschaft in Berlin im 19. und 20. Jahrhundert*. For the significance of the year 1810 for this whole development, see the essay by Reimer Hansen called "Die wissenschaftsgeschichtlichen Zusammenhänge der Entstehung und der Anfänge der modernen Geschichtswissenschaft," especially pages 15-16.

323. For Heinrich Ritter von Srbik, these lectures were in fact "the birth certificate of modern historiography" (*Geist und Geschichte* 1:217). For a good and recent account of the nature and significance of these lectures, see Ziolkowski, *Clio the Romantic Muse: Historizing the Faculties in Germany*, 26-32.

324. Gilbert, "Professionalization of History in the Nineteenth Century," 325. For information about Friedrich Rühs, the first professor of history at the University of Berlin, see Zedelmaier, *Der Anfang der Geschichte*, 178 and 296-98. It is significant not only that Rühs wrote several parts of the last volumes of the *Fortsetzung der Algemeinen Welthistorie* between 1803 and 1814, and that he was named historiographer of the Prussian state in 1817, but also that he wrote a 274-page manual on historical methodology called *Entwurf einer Propädeutik des historischen Studiums* that was published in 1811, and that was reprinted, published, and introduced by Hans Schleier and Dirk Fleisher. It is also interesting that Zedelmaier basically ends his story about "The Beginning of History" with Rühs and his manual on historical methodology.

at this time Berlin became a center for the "historizing" of the faculties in Germany.[325]

Most of all, however, Berlin soon became the university of Leopold von Ranke, the man who more than anyone before or since personified not only the new kind of professional and scientific history of the nineteenth century, but also the new kind of historical consciousness which Troeltsch, Hintze, and Meinecke called "historicism." Especially with Ranke, Berlin became and remained the chief center in the West for a distinctly modern type of Western historiography to the year 1933. At Berlin, the professor of history was expected to be a philosopher—or a lover of wisdom—and, at the same time, a highly-trained researcher, publishing scholar, and scholar/teacher who taught philosophy in, with, and under the profession (*Beruf*) and the academic discipline (*Wissenschaft*) called history.

---

325. For the "historizing" of the study of philosophy especially by Hegel, of theology especially through Schleiermacher, of law especially through Savigny, and also for the study of medicine around the year 1810, see Ziolkowski, *Clio the Romantic Muse*. As Ziolkowski points out, "The sense of history had the effect of temporalizing every facet of human thought, within the faculties and without" (181). For the historicizing of Protestant theology, especially in Prussia from the turbulent period from 1789 to 1815 to the early 1920s, see Howard, *Protestant Theology and the Making of the Modern German University*. For Howard, it was during the years from 1789 to 1815 that (1) "the ailing premodern institution most conspicuously began its metamorphosis into the secularized research university that we recognize today"; also (2), "it was most notably in post-revolutionary Prussia, beginning with the dramatic founding of the University of Berlin in 1810, that *the modern university* first appeared on the historical stage" (4, emphasis in original).

five

From a Holy Hieroglyph to a *Wissenschaft* Alone: History as a Calling and a Profession from Ranke to Hintze

In all history God dwells, lives, is to be found. Every deed testifies to Him; every action preaches His name, but above all, I think, the great interactions of history. He stands there like a holy hieroglyph, perceived only in its outline and preserved lest it be lost from the sight of future centuries.

Boldly then! Let things happen as they may; only for our part, let us try to unveil this holy hieroglyph. And so shall we serve God; so are we also priests, also teachers.

—Leopold Ranke (1820)[1]

I should prefer to conceive of historicism as nothing more than another mode of thought, another set of methodological categories.

—Otto Hintze (1927)[2]

THE PROBLEM

In most academic disciplines in the United States today, the chief founder of a modern science or profession is known to almost all students in that particular field and also to many well-educated persons in related fields of knowledge. Why is it, however, that so many history students and well-educated individuals in the United States have never heard of Leopold von Ranke, the scholar who—more than anyone else—established history as a professionalized academic discipline, and who most personifies the nineteenth-century ideal of history as an art and a science?

---

1. Ranke, "To His Brother Heinrich at the End of March 1820," in *Secret of World History*, 241. See also Ranke, *Sämmtliche Werke*, 53/54:88.

2. Hintze, "Troeltsch and the Problems of Historicism," 373.

If this is true in regard to Ranke, the historian who wrote more great histories than any historian ever, is it surprising that so many history students and well-educated persons in this country have never heard of Otto Hintze, a historian who is best known today for his articles and essays?

Certainly the great catastrophes of the twentieth century called World War I, Nazi Germany, World War II, and the Holocaust have much to do with this, for these events were accompanied by great intellectual changes. One of these was the migration of intellectuals out of central Europe to the United States beginning in the 1930s, a change that H. Stuart Hughes has called "The Sea Change."[3] Second, at this time when the German universities were discredited and greatly weakened by the Nazis and World War II, leadership within the field of history shifted from Germany to the United States and also to France. Third, much of the writing on German history and historiography in the United States since 1933 has emphasized Germany's *Sonderweg*, or its special, deviant, or peculiar path.

Two of the dangers behind a work that focuses mainly on the significance of one country and one religious tradition for the rise of history are that it might be seen either as a new kind of "special path" or as an example of Lutheran "triumphalism." By focusing first on Ranke, probably the most Lutheran and certainly the most influential of all professional historians during the nineteenth century, and then on Hintze, the twentieth-century historian who completely rationalized, secularized, and "demystified" Ranke's religious way of viewing history, I hope that I have avoided these two dangers and have followed a Rankean way of doing history, that is, with a sympathetic understanding.

The second major problem behind this chapter is how, at the same time, to tell the story of the origins of the most significant argument of the twentieth century concerning the nature of modern historical thought, a debate that began with Ernst Troeltsch, Friedrich Meinecke, and Otto Hintze in Berlin about the nature of historicism. One of the reasons that Hintze's definition of historicism is significant for the idea of history and for a story focusing on religion and rise of history is that it offers a completely rationalized, secularized, and demystified alternative to Meinecke's later, "Neo-Idealist," and quasi-religious definition.

---

3. Hughes, *Sea Change*.

RELIGION AND HISTORY FOR THE YOUNG LEOPOLD RANKE

> The gigantic historiographical work of Leopold von Ranke grew out of the ground of a Lutheran kind of spirit [*Geistesart*] and religiosity.
>
> —*Carl Hinrichs (1950)*[4]

> Reading Ranke is like being in church.
>
> —*Dietrich Gerhard (1961)*[5]

> Science in its modern connotation is characterized by the collective prosecution of a singular method, and it is in this sense that Ranke initiated the modern science of history.
>
> —*Leonard Krieger (1977)*[6]

The best and most significant example in Western historiography of how history became a calling before it became a profession, and of how history was transformed from a calling into a profession is the life and work of Leopold von Ranke (1795–1886). Here this story is summarized through the publication of his first history in the year 1824, his appointment as an associate professor at the University of Berlin in the following year, and his response to the main criticism of this book in 1828.

Leopold Ranke was born in 1795 in a town in Electoral Saxony, a territorial state that became a part of Prussia in 1815. Except for his father, the Ranke family was a dynasty of Lutheran pastors. Although Leopold's father was a lawyer, he had begun his studies in the field of theology, he was a devoutly religious man, and he sometimes regretted that he had not become a pastor.[7] Although the father was not ill disposed towards the enlightened currents of the late eighteenth century,[8] it is fair to say that Lutheran piety was the dominant spirit of the Ranke home.[9] As

---

4. Hinrichs, "Rankes Lutherfragment von 1817 und der Ursprung seiner Universalhistorischen Anschauung," 299.

5. A classroom response to a question at Washington University (St. Louis) in 1961.

6. Krieger, *Ranke: The Meaning of History*, 4.

7. Ranke, "Dictat von October 1863," *Sämmtliche Werke*, 53/54:6.

8. Ibid.

9. Kupisch, *Die Hieroglyphe Gottes*, 10. While this is the general consensus by most historians dealing with the young Ranke, for a detailed and somewhat revisionary account of the "orthodox" nature of his family and home, see Henz, *Leopold Ranke: Leben*,

Theodore H. Von Laue has pointed out, "The earliest and most persistent of all the formative influences in Ranke's life was the protestant version of Christian religion."[10]

Ranke received his basic education first in an elementary school in his hometown and then in two boarding schools for the best students in his principality. The curriculum of the secondary school at Pforta, where Ranke completed five years of study, was still based on Melanchthon's curriculum and his combination of Protestantism and humanism, for its educational goal was to prepare young men for a calling in a God-given and rational social structure.[11] Melanchthon's humanistic curriculum and the study of classical languages provided a solid religious, humanistic, and philological foundation for Ranke's life and work. At Pforta his notes also show an immersion in modern German literature, or in the writings of Lessing, Schiller, and—above all—of Herder.[12]

To this secondary-school student, however, "theology was still the greatest of all sciences."[13] In his intensive reading of the Bible, the books that he read the most were "the Gospels more than the Epistles, the Psalms more than the prophets, and chiefly the historical books of the Old Testament."[14]

From 1814 to 1817, when Ranke was a student at the University of Leipzig, theology and the classics were the center of his interests. Here he continued his biblical studies, especially of Galatians, the other letters of Paul, and the Psalms. It gave him great pleasure, he said, to translate the Psalms from the Hebrew in a way that was rhythmical and as close to the original text as possible.[15]

At the same time, however, he resisted what he called the "moderate rationalism" of the theology that was dominant at Leipzig. While he could

---

Denken, Wort, 1795–1814, 65–121.

10. Von Laue, *Leopold Ranke: The Formative Years*, 11. Leopold Ranke became Leopold *von* Ranke in 1865 when he was ennobled by King Wilhelm I of Prussia. He had been appointed royal historiographer by King Friedrich Wilhelm IV of Prussia in 1841.

11. Vierhaus, *Ranke und die soziale Welt*, 11.

12. Krieger, *Ranke: The Meaning of History*, 40. For the influence of Herder's work for the young Ranke and how their "panentheism" differed, see Henz, *Leopold Ranke*, 193–204 and 220–28.

13. Ranke, "Dictat vom October 1863," in *Sämmtliche Werke*, 53/54:16.

14. Ibid., 21.

15. Ibid., 29.

bear the practical aspects of this rationalism, he was strongly opposed to its theoretical convictions. All his feelings, he said, were opposed to the rationalism that surrounded him. To him it was "unsatisfying, superficial, and stale;" for as he also concluded, "I believed unconditionally."[16]

The core of Ranke's course of studies at Pforta and at the University of Leipzig, however, was the classics. At this time "critical philology was particularly cultivated in Germany," and the classics and philology were the liveliest subjects in the academic curriculum.[17] As Von Laue also points out, "Ranke had mastered the essentials of the historical method long before he became a historian."[18]

For his doctoral dissertation (1817), Ranke chose a great prose work in the field of classical literature: the history of Thucydides. Since this dissertation has vanished, historians have not been able to study this aspect of his work at Leipzig. In his autobiographical dictations, however, Ranke briefly reported that he read Thucydides with great care, that he excerpted his political teachings, that he bowed before this powerful and great mind (*Geist*), and that he did not seek to translate his work.[19]

Historians have, however, been able to examine the nature and significance of Ranke's strong interest in and research of the life and work of Martin Luther. At the time of the Luther Jubilee in 1817, or the three-hundredth anniversary of the publication of Luther's Ninety-five Theses, Ranke made an intensive study of Luther in order to write a biography based on a study of authentic documents. To use his own words, "I seized upon Luther, at first only to learn his German and to master the fundamentals of the modern German written language. But at the same time I was deeply stirred by the greatness of his content and his historical role. In the year 1817 I actually made an attempt to narrate Luther's history in his own language. You can understand that I was also engaged deep in my soul with theological problems for I had never abandoned theological studies."[20]

---

16. Ibid.
17. Von Laue, *Leopold Ranke: The Formative Years*, 12–13.
18. Ibid., 21.
19. Ranke, "Dictat vom October 1863," in *Sämmtliche Werke*, 53/54:30.
20. Ranke, "Autobiographical Dictation (November 1885)," in *Secret of World History*, 37–38 (*Sämmtliche Werke*, 53/54:49). In addition to *The Secret of World History: Selected Writings on the Art and Science of History* (a useful selection and translation of some of Ranke's key writings), see also Ranke, *Theory and Practice of History*.

In the year 1926 "Das Luther-Fragment von 1817" first became available to scholars,[21] and in the year 1973 a new and more complete edition was published under the title "Fragment über Luther. 1817."[22] Most of the material in the "Luther Fragment" consists of notes based on an intensive study not only of Luther's writings but also of other original sources related to the Protestant Reformation in Germany. Thus two of the things to note about Ranke's first attempt to write history are (1) that his fundamental approach was to base his work only on original sources and on "nothing but the sources,"[23] and (2) that while Luther was his original starting point, increasingly this project grew into a history of the Protestant Reformation in Germany, a history in which Luther was the center point.[24]

In his introductory comments to this "Luther Fragment," Ranke emphasized how with Luther one does not need to separate his life and teachings, for "he lived in his teachings and his teachings lived in him."[25] In this statement, Fulvio Tessitore asserts, one can see the basic methodological and hermeneutical thesis of this endeavor; for Ranke believed that Luther was one of the few heroes (Christian or non-Christian) in which "word and deed" (*Wort und Tat*) have been expressed.[26]

In and through this fragment and his diaries, notebooks, and letters from this time, historians have been able to show how much of Ranke's way of viewing life was shaped by or at this time. From this time one can see how his life and work were based on an "at-the-same-time" way of viewing life that emphasized the individual, or the particular, and the general, or the universal, at the same time.

According to Rudolf Vierhaus, from the time of the "Luther Fragment" one can see how all of Ranke's work was based on the philosophical idea

21. Ranke, "Das Luther-Fragment von 1817," 311–99.

22. Ranke, "Fragment über Luther," 329–466.

23. Fuchs, "Vorwort," 36.

24. Ibid., 35.

25. Ranke, "Fragment über Luther," 341. In this paragraph Ranke also emphasizes that in Luther only one spirit speaks "out of him," as "we hear in the controversies over the Lord's Supper or indulgences, but internally living and always new." The task, he said, was "to grasp and make clear this basic principle and to find and present it in his whole life. That is what we call character. Constant enthusiasm [*Begeisterung*], unbroken holding to the eternal."

26. Tessitore, "Ranke's 'Lutherfragment' und die Idee der Universalgeschichte," 26. See also Ranke, "Fragment über Luther," 398.

that "every particular is an unmistakable, necessary, and fully authorized appearance of a universality, a divine idea."[27] For Ranke, the idea of the "entirety" (*Ganzes*) or the "general" (*Allgemeine*) was always the correlate to the particular. Although Ranke's research was always based on understanding and presenting the particular, it was also based on the idea that everything "is general and individual spiritual life."[28]

According to Carl Hinrichs, the chief problem for this "Lutheran Christian with an active religiosity" was and remained how to connect the singular and the particular with the general, the universal, and the absolute.[29] The first main source and help that Ranke found in solving this problem was Luther, especially Luther's interpretation of Psalm 101 and his commentary on Paul's letter to the Galatians.[30] Here, above all, Ranke found the ideas of God's efficacious power in history and the hiddenness of God in history. For Ranke, Luther himself was one of those great men (*Wunderleuten*) whom God awakened, taught, and ruled.[31] In Luther and his affect on his age, Ranke could see how the world was given "a new skin," and how in such epoch-making men the individual merged into the general.[32] In the "Luther Fragment," Hinrichs concluded, one can find the seed (*Keim*) of Ranke's "universal-historical view."[33]

As James M. Powell more recently stated, Ranke's "Luther Fragment of 1817 reflected a religiosity which saw in history the hidden expression of the will of God," and throughout his life "he saw a divine meaning and purpose in history."[34]

27. Vierhaus, *Ranke und die soziale Welt*, 17.

28. Ibid., 18. The reference Vierhaus gives for this quotation is to Ranke's *Englische Geschichte Vornemlich Im 17. Jahrhundert*, volume 1 (14) Vorrede S. ix.

29. Hinrichs, *Ranke und die Geschichtstheologie der Goethezeit*, 106.

30. Ibid., 108–9.

31. Ibid., 109.

32. Ibid., 111. While for Hinrichs, Luther was the first great influence for the development of Ranke's worldview, Fichte was the second, Goethe the third, and Neoplatonism the fourth (ibid., 108). While to Ranke, Barthold Niebuhr symbolized the empirical side of the historian's work and the study of the particular, Fichte and Goethe were sources for the Platonic and the Neoplatonic elements that helped to form Ranke's unique kind of panentheism (ibid., 117–18).

33. Ibid., 124. For an earlier and briefer account of the significance of Luther and other influences on the young Ranke, see Hinrichs, "Rankes Lutherfragment von 1817," 299–321.

34. Powell, "Introduction," xiv.

In his fascinating study called *Die Hieroglyphe Gottes*, which traces the relationship of religion and history for the great German historians from Ranke to Meinecke, Karl Kupisch briefly indicates the significance of Ranke's "Luther Fragment" for understanding him at this time, and also for his life and work as a whole. On the one hand, these fragments show how Ranke was fascinated by Fichte, by Schlegel, and by Goethe's genius. On the other hand, however, they also show how "the panentheistic character of German idealism" was joined with the Protestant inheritance.[35]

While Kupisch emphasizes that Ranke never gave up the "panentheistic idea" that one can see in these fragments, he also insists that this idea was always connected with the conviction that Jesus Christ was God in human form. Throughout his life Ranke acknowledged that he was an evangelical Christian, but as Kupisch also states, "an idealistic thread ran through this faith."[36]

In the "Luther Fragment," Kupisch claims, one can feel where Ranke was headed with his often stammering but "almost hymn-like aphorisms"; for he wanted "to make Luther's biblical witness to the revelation fruitful for himself through an outline of a historical theology (*Geschichtstheologie*) that he could see." For the young Ranke, as Kupisch also claims, humanity and history were not in contradiction with God's actions, for history "is a continuous medium of God's revelation."[37]

When Kupisch emphasized "the panentheistic" nature of Ranke's way of viewing life and writing history, he—like Hinrichs and many other scholars—was confirming the view of Ranke that Friedrich Meinecke laid down in his "Supplement" to his *Die Entstehung des Historismus*. Here Meinecke had emphasized that in Ranke there is no question of pantheism, but one can "catch glimpses of a quite positive panentheism." For Ranke, God was above the world that was made by him, that was inspired by his spirit, and that was therefore "related to God, yet at the same time earthly and imperfect." For Meinecke, "[t]his clear separation between the creator and his creation, which was an echo of his Lutheranism, made it possible for him to allow his need for critical and empirical truth very free play over against the practical world of matter and spirit."[38]

35. Kupisch, *Hieroglyphe Gottes*, 12.
36. Ibid.
37. Ibid.
38. Meinecke, "Supplement: Leopold von Ranke," 506. This supplement was a "[m]emorial address given on 23 January 1936 in the Preussische Akademie der

When Elisabeth Schweitzer edited Ranke's "Luther-Fragment" in the year 1926, she also provided an interesting account of its origins.[39] The decision to study Luther (December 1816), she claims, was a central point in Ranke's intellectual life; for it marked "a breakthrough" from the passivity of the learner to the activity of the independent and creative scholar. Next to Luther, she claims, it was Fichte and Barthold Niebuhr who inspired him at the time of this intellectual and spiritual breakthrough.[40]

In his very interesting and helpful analysis of the significance of Ranke's intensive study of Luther, Leonard Krieger contends that it was also a kind of conversion experience, a kind that he calls "an intra-Lutheran conversion."[41] "Overtly," Krieger explains, Ranke's religious conversion "was a sudden breakthrough into an immediate sense and total absorption of Luther's original spirituality." For Krieger, this experience "jelled what had been fragmented into a new awareness of coherence that meant the arrival at a new stage on life's way,"[42] for what the young Ranke needed "was precisely the coherence in his view of life that his formal studies failed to provide." According to Krieger, the notebooks that Ranke kept at Leipzig not only served him as "a kind of personal diary of the mind and as an outlet for spontaneous writing projects" but also showed "an inner struggle for which his sudden insight into Luther provided a settlement and his abortive biography of Luther a resumption on another plane."[43] Thus for Krieger, the real meaning of Ranke's conversion "lay in his flashing realization that the reformer's marvelous achievement of communicating his personal internal vision to all of Europe was the model synthesis of spirit and appearance." It was this "active spirit of Luther's spirituality," Krieger emphasizes, "that had such a shattering impact on the young Ranke."[44]

While Krieger argues that Ranke's "first conversion" was a conversion to or through Luther and his intense spirituality, the second basic conver-

---

Wissenschaften." (ibid.)

39. Schweitzer, "Die Entstehungsgeschichte des Fragments," in *Deutsche Geschichte im Zeitalter der Reformation*, 6:378–88.

40. Ibid., 382–83.

41. Krieger, *Ranke: The Meaning of History*, 49.

42. Ibid., 47.

43. Ibid., 53–54.

44. Ibid., 57.

sion of his life was "a conversion to history."⁴⁵ This second conversion took place during the years from 1818 to 1825 when he was a teacher of classics at the Friedrichs *Gymnasium* in Frankfurt on Oder, a city within the Kingdom of Prussia. This conversion to history was aided by the facts that during these years the teaching of history was becoming increasingly important at this school, and that part of Ranke's responsibilities was to teach ancient history.⁴⁶ As Ranke stated, "I had now become completely an historian, which was occasioned by my teaching office. But from the very beginning I combined historical studies with original research and made them my own."⁴⁷

It was also aided by the fact that now, for the first time, he had direct access to a library with a large collection of historical works. Here he began a systematic study of the ancient historians and later histories of the ancient world, such as Niebuhr's *Roman History*, and also the historical works of the postclassical period. In this library he could read books "from all the centuries," and later in life he thought this reading made him more independent from the conflicts of the day.⁴⁸

At this time he was fascinated by the writings of Walter Scott, but he could not forgive him for including material in his work that was completely nonhistorical. In comparing Scott's work with the books and material from the past that he found in this library, he became more convinced that "the historical remnants themselves were more beautiful and in any case more interesting than romantic fiction." Therefore he decided that in his work he would avoid the fictitious and keep strictly to the facts.⁴⁹

The conversion to history, however, was directly related to Ranke's strong religious convictions and the increasing realization that to study and write history could be a calling. While he was a teacher at this *Gymnasium*, one can clearly see not only how his life and work were based on a distinctly Lutheran ethos and sense of calling, but also how his calling to understand the course of world history came to center on the

---

45. Ibid.

46. One of the first courses that Ranke taught at Frankfurt was "The Universal History (*Universalgeschichte*) of the ancient World to the End of the Western Empire," a course which he soon narrowed to the histories of Greece and Rome (ibid., 369).

47. Ranke, "Autobiographical Dictation (November 1885)," 37 (*Sämmtliche Werke*, 53/54:60).

48. Ibid., 38 (*Sämmtliche Werke*, 53/54:61).

49. Ibid.

study of modern European history. All these aspects of his life and work can be seen in a letter that he wrote to his brother Heinrich at the end of March in the year 1820.

First of all he wanted to inform his brother of his new project.

> Now comes my vacation, and there awaits for me a capital piece of work. I want to learn something about the life of the nations in the fifteenth century, of the renewed germination of all the seeds sown by antiquity—as if the old blooms had been blighted, and the long planted seed sprouted high. I still know nothing about it. But at least I foresee that these strivings, formations, desires were a thing not only of the literate nobility but in a certain form of the people. I know this from the Reformation. Even though the Gospel was revealed by God's grace originally to Luther, the success of the message was based on completely different grounds. Only dry wood quickly catches the flame.[50]

After Ranke had pointed out how he also hoped to learn about "the way in which empire and papacy died and gave forth a new breath of a new life," he linked his new calling with the way he had been taught to view the sacred nature of the Lord's Supper:

> Fichte, I think, once said that his love of the living past, of its idea, this inner drive to acquaintance with antiquity in its depth, leads to God. I cannot forget the saying: "Who takes the Lord's body and does not believe does it to his judgement." But is it not thus: that those who only shallowly and superficially grasp the past sinfully also do it to their own judgement? Their sorrow deepens; their life becomes more shallow; their thinking, more congealed. What once occurred in Italy now happens to so many, as if the indwelling spirit revenges itself for being mocked.[51]

In the next two paragraphs, which were cited at the beginning of this chapter, the priestly nature of his new calling was captured in one of the most striking metaphors of Western historiography: "to try to unveil this holy hieroglyph."[52] Thus by the year 1820, as Carl Hinrichs pointed out, Ranke had found the idea of his life, his true profession, and his calling—

50. Ranke, "To His Brother Heinrich at the End of March 1820," in *Secret of World History*, 240–41; see also Ranke, *Sämmtliche Werke*, 53/54: 88; and Ranke, *Das Briefwerk*, 17–18.

51. Ranke, "To His Brother Heinrich at the End of March 1820," in *Secret of World History*, 241.

52. Ibid. Wines titles this important letter "The Holy Hieroglyph."

to decipher the "tale of world history" ("der Mär der Weltgeschichte").[53] For Ranke, revelation and development were intertwined, for somehow humanity and its history were the incarnation of God.[54] For the rest of his life, as Alfred Dove pointed out in the year 1888, "Ranke unshakenly held fast to a religious view of the nature and worth of his discipline [*Wissenschaft*]."[55] And by the year 1820 he had also discovered where he would begin to decipher this tale, and where his historical research would always center—in the Latin and Germanic nations from the late fifteenth through the eighteenth century.

In the year 1824 the first results of his new calling were published in a book entitled *Histories of the Latin and Germanic Nations from 1494-1514*. In the preface to this famous work, he wrote a phrase that soon became the slogan for the new kind of professional and scientific historiography which he—more than anyone else—personified, and that still remains the most famous one in modern historical literature: "To history has been assigned the office of judging the past, of instructing the present for the benefit of future ages. To such high offices this work does not aspire: It wants only to show what actually happened [*wie es eigentlich gewesen*]."[56]

Thus to Ranke, as Felix Gilbert emphasized, the study of the past had "a much greater aim than the teaching of morals or instruction in the conduct of politics," for there was "a priestly dignity in the historian's task to show 'wie es eigentlich gewesen.'"[57] One reason that this phrase soon

---

53. Hinrichs, "Leopold von Ranke," 3:300. Ranke first used the expression "the tale of world history" in a letter to his brother Heinrich on November 24, 1826. See Ranke, *Sämmtliche Werke*, 53/54:162 or Ranke, *Das Briefwerk*, 102.

54. Hinrichs, "Leopold von Ranke," 3:297.

55. Dove, "Ranke's Leben im Umriss," 156. This essay was first published in volume 27 of the *Allgemeine Deutschen Biographie* (1888).

56. Ranke, "Preface" to *Histories of the Latin and Germanic Nations from 1494-1514*, 57 (*Sämmtliche Werke*, 33:v-viii).

57. Gilbert, *History: Politics or Culture?* 45. Gilbert closes the chapter called "Ranke and the Meaning of History" and his excellent discussion of the significance of this phrase with these points. In the preceding chapter, "Ranke's View of the Task of Historical Scholarship," Gilbert shows how Ranke's work was based on the concept of history as an autonomous discipline, and how he claimed "a place for history in the university structure that it had never previously held" (20). See also Donald R. Kelley's interpretation of Ranke's famous statement "To show how things really happened"; for Ranke's understanding of *Geschichtswissenschaft* "was not the hope of transcending a 'human point of view,' of surveying human behavior *sub specie aeternitatis*; on the contrary he sur-

became a basic one for modern Western historiography was because it marked a clear departure from the didactic characteristic of Western historiography since the time of the Greek and Roman historians, and from the view that a chief function of history was to teach success by providing good examples to follow and bad examples to avoid.

Important as this phrase has been for the discipline called history, however, it was not Ranke's main concern in the preface. Most of all, he was concerned about the basic historical individuality that he created at this time.[58] The first point of view behind this book, he said, was that "I regard the Latin and Germanic nations as a unity." This notion differed from three analogous concepts: (1) "the concept of a universal Christendom," (2) "the concept of Europe," and (3) "the most analogous concept, that of a Latin Christianity." His object or subject, however, was not so broad, for "Slavic, Lettic, and Magyar tribes which are a part of the latter have a peculiar and particular nature," and were therefore not included in his book. "By focusing on what is foreign to this unity only where necessary, in passing and as something peripheral," he explained, "the author will keep close to the racially kindred nations either of Germanic or Germanic-Latin descent, whose history is the core of all modern history."[59]

In the following paragraph, the man whom Fritz Stern rightly calls "the father as well as the master of modern historical scholarship,"[60] told his readers: "In the introduction I shall try to show—primarily in the narrative of foreign undertakings—how these nations developed in unity and common enterprise. This is one aspect of the point of view on which this book is based; the other emerges directly from the contents themselves. The book deals only with a small part of the history of these nations, a

---

rendered the roles of superhuman judge and prophet, which historiographical rhetoric had so long preserved" (Kelley, *Fortunes of History*, 135).

58. According to Carl Hinrichs, one of three ways in which this was an "epoch-making" work was that in its introduction the conception "of the unity of the Latin and Germanic nations and their common development" appeared for the first time (Hinrichs, "Leopold von Ranke," 3:301).

59. Ranke, "Preface," 55–56. Although Ranke never limited his historical interest to this "core," and although it was never so sharply differentiated in his later works as it was in this book, it was always the center of Ranke's interest and research. See Schulin, *Die weltgeschichtliche Erfassung des Orients*, 159–60.

60. Ranke, "Preface," 54.

part which might well be considered as the beginning of modern history. But it is only histories, not history."[61]

For the historian, Ranke insisted, there were two main requirements: "The strict presentation of the facts, contingent and unattractive though they may be, is undoubtedly the supreme law. After this, it seems to me, comes the exposition of the unity and progress of events."[62]

In each of the three paragraphs quoted above, one can see how from the beginning, Ranke's thought and work were based on the two concepts that Troeltsch, Hintze, and Meinecke identified as the basic ones of modern or "specifically historical thought": the concepts of individuality and development.[63] In the introduction, Ranke was able to portray "the unity of the Latin and Germanic nations and their common development" in a masterful fashion, but this was not true of the book as a whole. Thus both in the first and last paragraphs of this preface, he indicated that this book was not as perfect as he had originally thought.

The way he expressed this in the last paragraph is both important and famous, for it clearly reveals the connection between his sense of calling and what he once called "the holy hieroglyph." "A sublime ideal does exist: the event in its human intelligibility, its unity, and its diversity; this should be within one's reach. I know to what extent I have fallen short of my aim. One tries, one strives, but in the end, it is not attained. Let none be disheartened by this! The most important thing is always what we deal with, as Jakobi says, humanity as it is, explicable or inexplicable: the life of the individual, of generations, and of nations, and at times, the hand of God above them."[64]

While the merits of this book were sufficiently impressive for him to receive an appointment as an associate professor at the University of Berlin, it was severely criticized by Heinrich Leo, a slightly younger historian (b. 1799) who moved from the University of Berlin to Halle in 1828. In the spring of that year, Ranke's "Reply to Heinrich Leo's Attack" was published in the *Hallischen Literaturzeitung*.[65]

61. Ibid., 56.
62. Ibid., 57.
63. See especially Hintze, "Troeltsch and the Problems of Historicism,"381.
64. Ranke, "Preface," 56–57. For a discussion of the significance of Luther's view of a hidden God for Ranke, see Schulze, "Der Einfluss lutherischen Geistes auf Rankes und Droysens Deutung der Geschichte," 108–42, especially 119–27.
65. See Ranke, "Erwiderung auf Heinrich Leo's Angriff," 659–66.

The first part of Ranke's three-part reply consists of several detailed pages in which he defended his research and use of sources. The third part of this article, where Ranke rejected the charge of "a lack of philosophical education and thoughtfulness," has received more attention from later professional historians; for here Ranke sought to defend probably the strongest, the most revealing, and the most controversial religious statement in this book.

"Each time at the decisive moment," Ranke had said, "something enters which we call chance [*Zufall*] or fate but which is God's finger." In the second edition of his work, this statement was left out;⁶⁶ but in his reply to Leo, he sought to explain what he meant by it. While in the ancient world everything had been credited to fate or the direct intervention of the gods at the decisive moment, materialists credited everything to accident. The path that he had taken, Ranke explained, was a middle position between these two extremes.⁶⁷

Certainly for Ranke, historians agree, this expression was more than just a middle way between two extremes. As Friedrich Meinecke stated in his "Supplement" to *Die Entstehung des Historismus*, Ranke

> held fast to the basic conceptions of Christian philosophy, the providence of God and His guidance in the whole drama of human history. This did indeed provide a way out of some difficult problems. He did not, however, altogether overcome them, but rather (in true Rankean manner) toned them down by resisting the temptation to trace the finger of God in each movement of history—as much from a sense of reverence for the divine mysteries, as from a feeling of critical responsibility. Now and again, in the great moments of history, Ranke thought he could discern the hand of God at work, but this was faith rather than knowledge.⁶⁸

---

66. To see how the older Ranke dropped, changed, or toned down statements in later editions of his early work, see especially Friedrich Baethgen, "Zur geistigen Entwicklungsgeschichte Rankes in seiner Frühzeit," 337–53.

67. Ranke, "Erwiderung auf Heinrich Leo's Angriff," in *Sämmtliche Werke*, 53/54:665.

68. Meinecke, *Historism*, 506–7. In his letters, however, Ranke did not hide his belief in providence, the hand of God, or the finger of God when he thankfully looked back at his own life. See Fuchs, "Einleitung" to Leopold von Ranke, in *Das Briefwerk*, xvi–xvii. Both as an old man and as a young man, Ranke believed that he "was born to study history" (Letter to Heinrich Ranke, February 18, 1824, in *Das Briefwerk*, 53).

In the second and most important part of his reply to Leo, Ranke sought to answer complaints about his presentation. The surprising thing about this section, however, is how little attention historians have paid to the following sentences in the last paragraph:[69] "This passage is part of the attempt I have made to present the general directly through the particular without long digression. Here I have sought to approach no J. Müller or no ancient writer but rather the appearance itself, just as it emerges, only externally particularity, internally—and so I understand Leibnitz—a generality, significance, spirit . . . In and with the event I have sought to present its course and spirit, and I have strained to ascertain its characteristic traits."[70] This lack of attention is surprising, because in these three sentences one can see Ranke's basic way of viewing history, his basic methodology, and two main roots of his worldview and methodology.

First of all, in each of these three sentences one can see how Ranke's methodology was based on an "at-the-same-time" way of viewing life. As many experts on Ranke have recognized, from the time of the "Luther Fragment" Ranke always sought to present the particular and the general at the same time. But Ranke's *simul* way of thinking, writing, and doing history went far beyond these opposites; for in his view of history—which to him was both a science and an art[71]—"opposition" (*Gegensatz* or *Widerstreit*) and "mutual interaction" (*Wechselwirkung*) are persistent themes.[72]

69. In Krieger's *Ranke: The Meaning of History*, for example, the name of neither Leo nor Leibniz appears. For an account of the nature and significance of the controversy between Leo and Ranke, see Baur, 112–23. This book contains a useful list of publications dealing with Ranke, but it too does not focus on the significance of the last paragraph of this section.

70. Ranke, "Erwiderung auf Heinrich Leo's Angriff," 664–65.

71. For a very useful discussion of this Rankean view, see Vierhaus, "Historiography between Science and Art," 61–69.

72. Pelikan, "Leopold von Ranke as Historian of the Reformation," 91. For Ranke's constant emphasis on "the world historical importance of the great powers," on "the links between the external and the internal," and on how conflict "must be the salient point of description" to portray the multiperson drama tending "to equilibrium or to a new constellation of forces," see Schulin, "Universal History and National History," 70–81. For Ranke's "at-the-same-time" way of writing history, see Schulze, "Der Einfluss lutherischen Geistes auf Rankes und Droysens Deutung der Geschichte,"108–41. For Ranke's role as a historian of the Reformation within the whole context of Reformation historiography since the time of Luther and Melanchthon, see Dickens and Tonkin, *Reformation in Historical Thought*. For Dickens and Tonkin, Ranke was not only (1) "the best-equipped and most productive historian" of the nineteenth century (150), and (2)

Second, these three sentences reveal Ranke's roots in the Lutheran and German idealist traditions; for just as the Lutheran tradition is based on Luther's distinction between the inner man and the outer man, so the German idealistic tradition was based on the distinction between outward appearance and internal spirit. Both in the Lutheran and in the German idealist traditions it was assumed that God was the root of all human and natural phenomena, for as Theodore H. Von Laue pointed out, "the fundamental assumption of contemporary idealism that God's thoughts are at the root of all human (as well as natural) phenomena was common to the age."[73] The particular significance of Ranke's statement concerning his basic way of viewing outward appearance and internal spirit, however, is to its source; for here he claimed that it was based on his understanding of Leibniz. Here, especially, one can see how Leibniz was a link between Luther and Ranke.

Third, in these sentences one can see how Ranke's "at-the-same-time" way of viewing life and methodology were inseparably linked with an "in-with-and-under" way of viewing life and methodology. His way, he said, was "to present the general directly through the particular." "In and with the event," he sought not only "to present its course and development" but also "to ascertain its characteristic traits."

When Ranke used the prepositions *in* and *with* to proclaim his basic methodology, he did not link this important statement with a religious way of thinking or viewing life; for in the next sentence he suggested that a poetic and artistic expression such as this should also be allowed in the field of history.

Historians know, however, that at the time of the "Luther Fragment" (1817), Ranke was a firm believer in the Lord's Supper; for in a letter that Heinrich Ranke later wrote (1819 or 1820) to his older brother, he emphasized how much Leopold's personal statement of faith concerning this sacrament had meant to him.[74]

---

the historian who more than anyone else made the University of Berlin the best history school in Europe (168), but also (3) an historian who "acquired a range of specialties scarcely rivaled by any historian before or since" (ibid.).

73. Von Laue, *Leopold Ranke: The Formative Years*, 15.

74. See Oncken, *Aus Rankes Frühzeit*, 3–4. For the significance of the Lutheran view of the Lord's Supper for Ranke's way of thinking and viewing life, see Donald R. Kelley's thought-provoking statement: "Ranke's sense of the spirit could also be expressed in the view that God was truly in our consciousness. In a sense historical consciousness was an analogue of Lutheran consubstantiation, in which human substance brought the subject

Historians also know that eight years later (February 1825), when Leopold informed Heinrich about the opportunities for research that he would soon have at the University of Berlin, the younger Ranke ("devoutly and sacrificially, like a priest at the altar"[75]) affirmed: "I seek the truth with all my strength. I am certain of the omnipresence of God and believe that one can certainly grasp it with hands. At the present I am in the mood to swear a thousand times that I will live my whole life in fear of God and in history . . . All of my efforts shall contribute to the recognition of the living God, the God of our nation and the world."[76] Thus, like Luther and Leibniz, Ranke believed in the omnipresence of God.

What is new about this vow, however, is that here a young scholar swore that he would attempt to grasp the omnipresence of God in, with, and through a calling called history. The amazing thing about this vow is how successful he was in establishing this calling as a profession, a science, and an autonomous academic discipline.

In part this success was due to the fact that from the beginning he had developed a method for doing history that really worked. In his very helpful book called *Ranke: The Meaning of History*, Leonard Krieger suggests how Ranke initiated the modern science of history: "Science in its modern connotation," he said, "is characterized by the collective prosecution of a singular method, and it is in this sense that Ranke initiated the modern science of history."[77] "The four Rankean principles which have constituted the canon of scientific history," Krieger claims, "are the objectivity of historical truth, the priority of facts over concepts, the equivalent uniqueness of all historical events, and the centrality of politics—and each of them Ranke immortalized in a memorable formulation."[78]

---

into contact with the spirit, and in this sense, with the divine" (Kelley, *Fortunes of History*, 134).

75. Oncken, "*Aus Rankes Frühzeit*, 6.

76. Ranke, Letter to Heinrich Ranke on February 17, 1825, in Ranke, *Sämmtliche Werke*, 53/54:139; and in *Das Briefwerk*, 73-74.

77. Krieger, *Ranke: The Meaning of History*, 4.

78. Ibid. In addition to these four scientific principles, Krieger also discusses Ranke's "unscientific counterpoint," or the "four principles of philosophical or theological history which may be placed in explicit counterpoint to his four principles of scientific history" (ibid., 10-20). Just as Krieger demonstrates here his own at-the-same-time methodology, throughout the book he also demonstrates the relationship between the general and the particular in each stage of Ranke's life and career.

In addition to these principles, one can see three basic methodological principles that Ranke used to write history. First of all, his method, as Otto Hintze most simply and clearly explained, was to use the concepts of individuality and development as methodological concepts. This is the way Hintze defined the nature of historicism, and this is the way historians do history; for first they have to see and grasp a human object or subject as an historical individuality before they can trace its development in time.

Second, as Ranke revealed in his reply to Leo, his method was always to look for the particular and the general, the external and the internal *at the same time*. From the beginning this was a basic methodological principle for him.

Third, as Ranke also revealed in his reply to Leo, his basic method was to present the general "directly through the particular," or "in and with the particular event." This was the essence of what Meinecke called Ranke's "individualizing" way of viewing life. Although this way of viewing life grew out of a particular religious and philosophical tradition, today it can be regarded simply as a methodological principle.

To make a true historian, Ranke once said, two qualities are needed. The first "is a participation and joy in the particular in and for itself." Second, he said, "it is essential that the historian also have an eye for the universal."[79] Thus Ranke's kind of historicism has been called "the sympathetic acceptance of every individual event and personality in the frame of universal history."[80] But how did Ranke do this? How could he write so many excellent histories that were both particular and universal at the same time? Perhaps the best way to answer these two questions is by saying that Ranke developed a way of writing history in which he sought to present the general or the universal in, with, under, and through the particular.

After Ranke had written several great works of historical research and narrative (including his *History of the Popes during the Last Four Centuries* [1834-1836], his *History of the Reformation in Germany* [1839-1847], his *History of Prussia* [1847-1848], his *History of France in the Sixteenth and Seventeenth Centuries* [1852-1861]), he made one of his most famous, quoted, and revealing statements about his calling as a professional his-

---

79. Ranke, *Secret of World History*, 102-3 (Ranke, *Weltgeschichte* 9, part 2:vii–xi).
80. Von Laue, *Leopold Ranke: The Formative Years*, 4.

torian. In his *History of England in the Seventeenth Century* (1859–1868), Ranke said that he had tried "to extinguish my own self, as it were, to let the things speak and the mighty forces appear which have arisen in the course of the centuries."[81]

One of the most interesting and significant interpretations of this statement was made by Otto Hintze in an almost-unknown book review in the year 1906.[82] Unlike during the time of Ranke, Hintze said, the writing of his own day was a child of epistemological criticism, which had made the historian more aware of the subjective nature of the picture that he presented, and of the fact that the cognitive intellect formed the material of reality according to his own categories. But how far, he asked, could this subjective action go and still claim the name of historical scholarship? This was the point where the teachings of historical methodology were important. In this respect, Hintze said, Ranke's statement about his wanting to extinguish his own self in considering the object of his study was perhaps the best epistemological statement that Ranke made.[83] The image that Hintze used to defend this famous statement was to explain that the historian is really "a translator" and not a "copyist."[84]

This Rankean statement, however, can also be seen within the context of the Lutheran tradition. From the time of Luther, Lutheran pastors have been trained to see themselves as servants or vessels of the Word. Just as Luther believed that God could speak through even a Christian theologian and university professor, and just as the young Ranke vowed to serve God through his callings to be an historian and a university professor, so also a much-older Ranke suggested that he wished merely to be a vessel of the great events and "mighty forces which have arisen in the course of centuries." Just as the Rankean dynasty of pastors (and Leopold's brother Heinrich) had been ordained to serve God as servants and vessels of the Word, so this "ordained historian"[85] earnestly sought to allow the story of

---

81. See Krieger, *Ranke: The Meaning of History*, 5, for this is his translation of this famous statement (*Sämmtliche Werke*, 15:103).

82. Hintze, Review of *Die Probleme der Geschichtsphilosophie: Eine erkenntnistheoretische Studie* (2nd edition, 1905) by Georg Simmel, 809–14.

83. Ibid., 810.

84. Ibid. For a summary in English of this important review, see Smith, "Otto Hintze's Comparative Constitutional History of the West," 460–68.

85. This appropriate term for Ranke's sense of calling is used by Krieger, *Ranke: The Meaning of History*, 26.

human actions and events to speak directly to us in, with, and through his histories. Never before and never since has the priestly nature of history as a calling been demonstrated and articulated so well and for so many years as it was in the life and work of Leopold von Ranke.[86]

OTTO HINTZE AND THE DEMYSTIFYING OF THE RANKEAN VIEW OF HISTORY

> The profound and warm-hearted little work of art, which you gave me for my birthday, really touched my heart . . . It encouraged me to thank you personally not only for this meaningful card, but for everything you have been to me in a friendship which has filled more than half of my life . . . I myself have—by and large within a common foundation—always found in you something of a supplementary antipole [*ergänzenden Gegenpol*].
>
> —*A letter from Hintze to Meinecke (August 30, 1921)*[87]

> Hintze's further development, as we hoped, made him one of the great ones in the discipline [*Wissenschaft*]. To be sure, he was only known in the circle of experts, like a very high mountain range—which one first notices from the vantage of a high pass.
>
> —*Friedrich Meinecke (1941)*[88]

In 1947 when Felix Gilbert presented a bibliographical survey of wartime German historiography in the *American Historical Review*, he wrote: "There is no doubt that with the perspective which only the passage of

---

86. In addition to Ranke's writings that appear in the fifty-four volumes of his *Collected Works*, his oeuvre also includes a nine-volume work on world history. During the last years of his life, when he was half blind, Ranke worked through two secretaries to produce this work on world history. For a summary of this work and its relation to the "Luther Fragment" of 1817, see Hinrichs, *Ranke und die Geschichtstheologie der Goethezeit*, 161–254.

87. This beautiful letter of friendship in the German Staatsarchiv Stiftung Preussischer Kulturbesitz Berlin-Dahlem, Nachlass Meinecke, Rep. 92, Nr. 15, can also be found as an appendix in Smith, "Otto Hintze's Comparative Constitutional History of the West," 606–7. Since there is still no academic biography of Hintze, this dissertation—which is available from UMI Dissertation Services in Ann Arbor, Michigan—is still the most complete source of information (especially the first chapter) on Hintze's life and work. See also appendix 4 in that dissertation, a list of the lectures and seminars that Hintze gave during his career at the University of Berlin from 1896 to 1920 (610–17).

88. *Friedrich Meinecke Werke*, 8:95.

time provides, Hintze emerges as the most important figure in German historical scholarship of the twentieth century."[89] In 1947 this was a prophetic but audacious statement, for at that time Hintze's work had been almost forgotten even in Germany. It was also an audacious statement because it was made by a student of Friedrich Meinecke (1862–1954), the most famous and influential German historian of the twentieth century, seven years before his teacher's death.

It was no accident however, that such a statement would come from a Meinecke student, that the first inclusive essay in English about the significance of Otto Hinzte's work was written by another Meinecke student,[90] and that these two Meinecke students—Felix Gilbert and Dietrich Gerhard—were the honored guests and chief speakers at the first international conference focusing on Hintze's work.[91] It was no accident, because Meinecke was Hintze's closest friend, and because Meinecke always called his students' attention to Hintze's work.[92]

Otto Hintze (1861–1940) was a professional historian whose entire professional career (1896–1920) was at the University of Berlin. When Gustav Schmoller recommended Hintze in 1895 for the *Habilitation*, or the right to teach at this university, he stated that Hintze "possesses the most embracing historical, literary, juristic, and *staatswissenschaftliche* education that I have seen in a man of his age. He speaks with a confidence and clarity, with a command of the material that time and again surprises me."[93] This testimony to the breadth of Hintze's education and knowledge, however, was also a tribute to the university where he had received this training to become a professional historian.

89. Gilbert, "German Historiography during the Second World War," 52–53.

90. Gerhard, "Otto Hintze: His Work and Significance in Historiography," 17–48.

91. This conference, which was held in Berlin from 24–26 April 1980, was called "Otto Hintze und die moderne Geschichtswissenschaft." In 1983 the papers and a summary of the discussion of papers were published in a book edited by Otto Büsch and Michael Erbe called *Otto Hintze und die moderne Geschichtswissenschaft*. For international literature dealing with Otto Hintze from that time, see especially Neugebauer, "Otto Hintze und seine Konzeption der 'Allgemeine Verfassungsgeschichte der neueren Staaten,'" 66–96, and his enlarged edition of this essay in Otto Hintze, *Allgemeine Verfassungs- und Verwaltungsgeschichte der neueren Staaten: Fragmente*, 35–83. With this volume, all—or at least almost all—the material in the Hintze *Nachlass* is now available in print.

92. See, for example, Holborn, *History of Modern Germany, The Reformation*, x.

93. Universitäts-Archiv der Humboldt-Universität Berlin, Habilitationen, Philosoph. Facultät, Littr. H., No. 1, Vol 24, Blatt 104. See also Smith, "Otto Hintze's Comparative Constitutional History of the West," 21.

In fact, it can be argued that Hintze received the best and broadest training that a professional historian *could* receive, for he was trained at the University of Berlin in the early and mid 1880s. Although Ranke was no longer teaching at this time, the seminar method that he had established for training professional historians was now a thoroughly institutionalized system; and in the 1880s, the University of Berlin was the chief model in the field of history of what university presidents today love to call "a world-class university."

One way to substantiate this claim is to look at the training that Otto Hintze received at the University of Berlin in the 1880s. After two years of study at the University of Greifswald (1878–1880), where he was listed as a student of philology, and where he also studied history and philosophy,[94] he moved to Berlin to register for the winter semester (1880) at the University of Berlin. During the early 1880s this university was the greatest center of learning in Germany, and at this time the study of history there was at a peak. Where else, for example, could a student take seminars from scholars such as Mommsen, Waitz, Droysen and Dilthey at the same time?

While Theodor Mommsen (1817–1903) was the most important and influential expert on Roman history after Niebuhr, and a classic example of the professor, researcher, and publisher of document collections during the German Empire, Georg Waitz (1813–1886) had been a member of Ranke's first seminar (1833), was one of his greatest students, was one of many famous medieval historians who was trained in Ranke's seminars, was the author of an eight-volume *German Constitutional History*, and was the editor of the *Monumenta Germaniae Historica*, the oldest of the great state-supported document-publishing enterprises in Germany.

While Johann Gustav Droysen (1808–1884) was best known for his monumental *History of Prussian Policy*, a work that has been called "the most exhaustive survey of the foreign policy of a state ever written,"[95] his lecture course called "Encylopaedia and Methodology of History" was the most sophisticated nineteenth-century lecture course in Germany—and, most likely, in the entire world—on the principles of history. Since this lecture course was first published in the year 1937, only those stu-

---

94. Smith, "Otto Hintze's Comparative Constitutional History of the West," 3.
95. Gooch, *History and Historians in the Nineteenth Century* (1958), 130.

dents who actually attended this course could receive the full benefit of Droysen's vast knowledge and systematic mind.

Droysen began this famous lecture by pointing out that history and nature were two basic ways that the human mind makes sense of the world, that time and space were the basic categories of the human mind for doing this, and that the word *history* (*Geschichte*) was the word we use for the sum of everything that happens in the course of time. For history, therefore, time was the main organizing principle, just as space was the main organizing principle that we use for comprehending nature.[96]

Droysen's starting point for understanding historical methodology, however, was that "our science" is not *die Geschichte* but rather the Greek word for history (ἰστορία): "the research."[97] Therefore the method of history was "forschend zu verstehen" (researching to understand),[98] and the chief practical problem was "how to make history out of the transactions."[99] Thus on the one hand there was the cognitive mind and the life experience of the individual historian or of "the thinking I,"[100] and on the other was the material from the past still existing here and now. More than Ranke, Droysen emphasized the word *understanding*, how history was based on a concept of time, and the original meaning of the word *history*.

It is significant that Droysen chose the word *Historik* for the printed outline of this course,[101] for the course was based on the Greek meaning of the word *history* and on the view that history is basically research, inquiry, investigation, and establishing the truth. The message of this systematic thinker to his students and to the positivists of his day was the necessity of discovering laws of historical cognition rather than laws of history.[102]

In his book titled *Einleitung in die Geisteswissenschaften*, which was published in 1883, or a year before Droysen's death, Wilhelm Dilthey attempted to provide a theory of knowledge not only for history but also for those sciences that were concerned with "historical-social reality." As

96. Droysen, *Historik*, 6, 11.
97. Ibid., 21.
98. Ibid., 22, 26.
99. "Wie wird nun aus den Geschäften Geschichte?" (ibid., 28).
100. Ibid., 10.
101. "Grundriss der Historik" (ibid., 317–66). This outline was translated by E. Benjamin Andrews under the title *Outline of the Principles of History*.
102. Droysen, *Historik*, 424, 428; Stern, *Varieties of History*, 144.

the subtitle of this work proclaimed, it was "An Attempt to Establish a Foundation for the Study of Society and History."[103]

In this *Introduction to the Human Sciences*, Dilthey discussed the development of "the historical school" and a historical consciousness in Germany at the time of the French Revolution and Napoleon. The basic difference between "the historical school" and the other school, which he sometimes called "the abstract school," was a difference between a historical approach to the totality of life and an approach based on abstract theories. The historical school, he said, "considered spiritual life as historical through and through," and from this school a stream of new ideas spread through countless channels into all the particular disciplines.[104]

Although Dilthey associated the development of the historical school with a deeper appreciation of life, of historical reality, and of the idea of development, he was also convinced that biography was the most pure form of historical writing since it was the description of the individual "psychophysical life-unit [*Lebenseinheit*]."[105] Here the will of a human being was grasped in its dignity as a purpose in itself, for biography viewed human beings as "*sub specie aeterni*."[106] For Dilthey, only the historian who conceived of history in terms of such "life-units," and who connected the course of life through the concept of generations could grasp the reality of a historical whole in contrast to lifeless abstractions.[107]

For Dilthey, the historian was like an artist in that each perceived and presented the general in the particular rather than separating them through abstraction.[108] Whereas Dilthey believed that historians naturally loved the extraordinary,[109] he also warned that the connection between the singular and the general that existed in the genial perception of the historian could be torn apart by analysis, or when a single part of a whole

---

103. Dilthey, *Einleitung in die Geisteswissenschaften: Versuch einer Grundlegung für die Studium der Gesellschaft und der Geschichte*. This is volume 1 of *Wilhelm Dilthey Gesammelte Schriften*. Unfortunately, this subtitle does not appear on the title page of the English edition of Dilthey's *Introduction to the Human Sciences*, volume 1 of *Selected Works*, edited by Rudolf A. Makkreel and Frithjof Rodi.

104. Dilthey, *Introduction*, 48; *Einleitung*, xvi.

105. Dilthey, *Introduction*, 85; *Einleitung*, 33.

106. Ibid.

107. Dilthey, *Introduction*, 85; *Einleitung*, 34.

108. Dilthey, *Introduction*, 91; *Einleitung*, 40.

109. Dilthey, *Introduction*, 140; *Einleitung*, 91.

was subordinated to theoretical consideration. For Dilthey, it was pure superstition when sociologists regarded historical presentations merely as raw material for their abstractions; for any thinker who wanted to understand the historical world could not avoid the difficult work of the historian by dealing directly with its raw materials.[110]

Now each of these great scholars had taught at other universities before they were called to the University of Berlin: Mommsen in 1858, Droysen in 1859, Waitz in 1875, and Dilthey in 1882. Because Dilthey became a professor at Berlin just two years before Droysen died, the only time and place that a student could have been trained by two of the greatest minds of the nineteenth century for understanding the nature and method of history as a human science was during the years from 1882 to 1884 at the University of Berlin.

Like most of the great historians in Germany during the nineteenth century, Otto Hintze was trained in philology, history, and philosophy. Most of all, however, he was drawn to the study of history and to the historian Johann Gustav Droysen. Hintze was a member of the inner circle of students surrounding Droysen, and he served as the librarian of Droysen's "Historical Society," the forerunner of the Historical Seminar at the University of Berlin.[111]

His doctoral dissertation, however, was done under the direction of Julius Weizsäcker, a prominent Ranke student and medievalist, who had joined the Berlin faculty in the year 1881. When Hintze was examined on January 10, 1884, the examination committee was composed of two professional historians (Weizsäcker and Droysen), a philosopher (Dilthey), and a well-known German philologist (Wilhelm Scherer). While both Droysen and Weizsäcker praised Hintze's knowledge and his calm understanding and judgement, Droysen concluded his statement with the tribute, "In every respect flawless [*tadellos*]." While Scherer simply stated that Hintze had answered his questions correctly, Dilthey praised his "right satisfactory philosophical training."[112] The result of all this was that Hintze passed the examination magna cum laude.

Like Mommsen, Waitz, Droysen, Dilthey, and many of the great German historians of the nineteenth century, Hintze came from a pi-

---

110. Dilthey, *Introduction*, 141; *Einleitung*, 91–92.
111. Hartung, "Otto Hintze," 497.
112. Smith, "Otto Hintze's Comparative Constitutional History of the West," 5.

ous Protestant family.¹¹³ Unlike the fathers of Mommsen, Dilthey, and Droysen, however, Hintze's father was not a pastor;¹¹⁴ for he was a Prussian official (a county secretary) who could read Hebrew.¹¹⁵

Unlike most nineteenth- and early twentieth-century German historians, however, little is known about Hintze's religious and family background. What we do know is that he left few written statements about his personal and religious life, that he identified himself—when he needed to—as *"Evangelisch,"* and that one of the few times that he made a personal religious remark was not about himself but rather about his favorite professor.

Toward the beginning of his wonderful tribute to Droysen in the year 1904, Hintze related some of Droysen's favorite memories of his army-chaplain father; and toward the end of this essay he testified to Droysen's strong religious faith by saying that for this great and energetic scholar, death "was a gateway to a higher life."¹¹⁶ While Hintze and Meinecke did not have the unwavering faith of Ranke or a Droysen, it was certainly something that they could understand and respect.¹¹⁷

Although the kind of education and training that Hintze had received prior to 1885 certainly was excellent, he was not satisfied with his scholarly background and training. From the fall of 1885 through the summer of 1888 he was registered as a student of law at the University of Berlin, and during these years he studied both civil and public law and especially political economy (the law professors with whom he studied at this time were Ruodolf von Gneist, Ingolf Pernice, Heinrich Brunner, and Paul Hinschius; and the political economists were Gustav Schmoller and

---

113. In *Die Hieroglyphe Gottes: Grosse Historiker der bürgerlichen Epoche von Ranke bis Meinecke*, Karl Kupisch has chapters on Ranke, Burckhardt, Treitschke, Mommsen, Harnack, Dilthey, and Meinecke.

114. According to Felix Gilbert, Droysen's strong religious faith—that was formed in the Protestant parsonage of his father—provided a firm foundation for all his thought and action. There is no evidence, Gilbert also asserts, of any great spiritual crisis in his life (Gilbert, *Johann Gustav Droysen und die Preussisch-Deutche Frage*, 27).

115. Smith, "Otto Hintze's Comparative Constitutional History of the West," 3. Otto Hintze's mother, however, was a pastor's daughter.

116. Hintze, "Johann Gustav Droysen," 498. For some of Droysen's own strong religious statements and emphasis on "the Word," see his *Historik: Vorlesungen über Enzyklopädie und Methodologie der Geschichte*, 220–21, 358.

117. For Meinecke's religious views, see Meinecke, *Autobiographische Schriften*, 17, 44–45, 78.

Adolf Wagner).[118] Since training in law and economics was not customary or traditional for historians at this time, why was it that Hintze decided to turn to these areas?

In his "Inaugural Speech" to the Royal Prussian Academy in 1914, Hintze stated that from the beginning the real goal that he had in mind was "a general comparative constitutional and administrative history of the modern world of states [*neueren Staatenwelt*], especially [*namentlich*] of the Latin and Germanic nations."[119] It was especially in this direction, he thought, that "the great lifework" of Leopold von Ranke "could and needed to be supplemented." Here, also, he thanked Georg Waitz for making him aware of the importance of systematic legal and *staatswissenschaftlicher* studies for such a goal.[120]

In the curriculum vitae that he wrote in Latin for the University of Berlin in 1895 in connection with his *Habilitation*, Hintze indicated another reason for the decision to study jurisprudence, for more and more he had become convinced that the foundation of history lay no less in the knowledge of civil and public life than in the knowledge of human thought.[121] Although it was Waitz who called Hintze's attention to the importance of these studies for the goal of writing a comparative constitutional history of the Western states, it was Gustav Schmoller who influenced him the most once he had taken this step.

When Schmoller became a professor at the University of Berlin in 1882, this university became the leading university in Germany and the world as a center for training scholars in what was known both then and now as the historical school of economics. Hintze's training and long apprenticeship under Gustav Schmoller shaped the whole direction of his life, his career, and his scholarly work, but here it is only possible to mention a few aspects of Schmoller's work that were of basic significance for Hintze.

After Schmoller became a member of the faculty of the University of Halle in 1864, he began a systematic study of Prussian administrative

---

118. Smith, "Otto Hintze's Comparative Constitutional History of the West," 11.

119. Hintze, "Antrittsrede in der Preussischen Akademie der Wissenschaften," *Staat und Verfassung*, 564. This key document for understanding Hintze's work as a whole, was added as an appendix in the third edition of this volume (vol. 1) of Hintze's *Gesammelte Abhandlungen*.

120. Ibid.

121. Smith, "Otto Hintze's Comparative Constitutional History of the West," 11–12.

and economic history. Increasingly he became interested in a comparative approach to the study of institutions, bureaucracy, and administrative history. The way he combined economic, administrative, and institutional history with a comparative approach was a model both for Hintze and for the development of social history in Germany; for today Schmoller and Hintze are regarded as pioneers for the development of social history both at the University of Berlin and in Germany as a whole.[122] Today Hintze can and should be regarded as Schmoller's greatest heir in the twentieth century for a comparative-historical approach to the study of Prussian and Western bureaucracy and institutional development.

In 1887 Schmoller became the head, heart, and soul of a new document-publication enterprise sponsored by the Royal Prussian Academy and known as the *Acta Borussica*; and in 1888 he secured the services of Hintze to work on the history of the silk industry in Prussia during the eighteenth century. In 1892 the results of four years of labor for this publication enterprise appeared in print with two volumes of documents and a third volume that was a written account of the history of this industry in the eighteenth century.[123]

In the year 1901, one of Hintze's greatest achievements in the field of Prussian history appeared when the *Acta Borussica* published his large introductory presentation of the governmental organization and general administration of Brandenburg-Prussia around the year 1740.[124] This volume, which showed how Prussia was changing from a territorial state to a great state based on the idea of power, was the key one for the entire *Acta Borussica* and is still one of the most impressive works on the institutional history of the eighteenth century.

The high point of Hintze's work in the field of Prussian history, however, was *Die Hohenzollern und Ihr Werk*,[125] a large work that received

---

122. See especially Oestreich, "Die Fachhistorie und die Anfänge der sozialgeschichtlichen Forschung in Deutschland," 320–63.

123. Hintze, *Die preussische Seidenindustrie im 18. Jahrhundert*.

124. Hintze, *Einleitende Darstellung der Behördenorganisation und allgemeinen Verwaltung in Preussen beim Regierungsantritt Friedrich II*. Acta Borussica: Denkmäler der Preussischen Staatsverwaltung im 18. Jahrhundert. Behördenorganisation und allgemeine Staatsverwaltung 6:1. Volume 6, part 2 of Acta Borussica: Denkmäler der Preussischen Staatsverwaltung im 18. Jahrhundert. Behördenorganisation und allgemeine Staatsverwaltung was called *Akten vom 31. Mai 1740 bis Ende 1745* and was edited with Gustav Schmoller.

125. Hintze, *Die Hohenzollern und ihr Werk*.

broad circulation because it was part of the five-hundred-year celebration of the Hohenzollern dynasty in Brandenburg in 1915. Despite the facts that this work was an official history, that its subtitle was "Five Hundred Years of Fatherland History," and that it was published (but not written) during World War I, it demonstrated a depth of knowledge, a breadth of view, and a striving for truth that characterized all of Hintze's work and that enabled it to maintain its position through the twentieth century.

This work, however, did not mark the end of Hintze's contributions to the field of Prussian studies; for in 1917 he became Schmoller's successor as director of the *Acta Borussica*. Because of these and many other contributions in the field of Prussian history, Hintze is recognized with Ranke and Droysen as one of the three greatest historians of the Prussian state.

Hintze's Prussian studies and his comparative studies, however, were intimately connected, for as he said to the Academy in 1914, "The history of Prussia became for me a paradigm for the institutions and transformations of a modern state in general."[126] While "from the beginning" his highest goal was to write a comparative constitutional and administrative history of the modern world of states, at this time Hintze also called attention to another field of study and to another life goal.

As a professor of history at the University of Berlin, Hintze held a special chair that was created for him, for it included not only the fields of constitutional, administrative, and economic history but also that Aristotelian and nineteenth-century discipline called *Politik*. By working "in the spirit of Aristotle's methods" and by studying constitutions in a comparative historical way, Hintze hoped to obtain "a typical picture of the modern state in its common features, its tendencies of development, and its individual arrangements." At the same time he also wanted "to search for the causes which underlie the deviations from the particular types or individualities."[127]

Thus at the same time that Hintze was undertaking the most thorough and impressive study of the institutional structure of the Prussian state by a twentieth-century historian, he was also undertaking probably the most thorough comparative-historical study of the modern Western states. Between 1901 and the outbreak of World War I in 1914, he

---

126. Hintze, "Antrittsrede in der Preussischen Akademie," 564.
127. Ibid., 566.

published a number of comparative essays in which he traced the governmental, military, and social/economic institutions of the West since the early Middle Ages. Since World War II, this new kind of historical presentation—which Hintze called "comparative constitutional history" or "comparative constitutional and administrative history"—has been called comparative, institutional, structural, or social history. Whatever it is called, it is clear that by 1914 Hintze was already (1) a master of the comparative method, (2) the chief pioneer for the development of a new, analytical, comparative, and inclusive kind of historical presentation that was quite different from the political histories of his day, and (3) a historian with unsurpassed knowledge of the institutional or structural development of the modern Western states.

As the fortunes of war turned against the great German military machine in the summer of 1918, however, the health of this very Prussian historian collapsed. In 1920, after some attempts to return to the classroom, he permanently gave up his teaching career. Although his sight was too weak for further archival research, gradually he was able to return to his comparative studies and to follow with great interest the new historical, political, sociological, and methodological studies being published inside and outside Germany. From 1926 to 1932 he published a number of brilliant comparative essays and review articles, including the first historical "ideal types" or "models," as they would be called today.

The year 1933 was also a turning point in the life and work of Otto Hintze. At this time, his closest students believed, the manuscript of the comparative constitutional history of the West was ready to be published.[128] After Hitler came to power, however, the manuscript could not be published, and his articles and reviews ceased. Also in 1933 his wife, Hedwig Hintze (a former student and one of the pioneer female historians in Germany), was dismissed from her position as a history lecturer at the University of Berlin because her parents were Jewish. In 1939, just before World War II began, she fled to the Netherlands.

Otto Hintze died a lonely and obscure death in Berlin in 1940, and Hedwig Hintze died a lonely and even more obscure death in Utrecht in 1942 during the Nazi occupation of the Netherlands.[129] By the end of

---

128. This statement is based on interviews with Fritz Hartung and Otto Meisner in 1964. See Smith, "Hintze's Comparative Constitutional History of the West," 86–87, 516–17.

129. For Hedwig Hintze's life and career, see Brigitta Oestreich, "Hedwig and Otto

World War II most of Otto Hintze's manuscripts (including the central part of his comparative constitutional history of the West, which he had worked on most of his adult life) were lost or destroyed.

Shortly after Otto Hintze's death, Fritz Hartung (a Hintze student) gathered and published many of his scattered articles, but because of the severe wartime conditions (1941–1943),[130] the three volumes of this first edition received extremely limited circulation. Thus his articles were not readily available even in Germany until Gerhard Oestreich (a student of Hartung) published a second and greatly enlarged edition of Hintze's *Gesammelte Abhandlungen* between 1962 and 1967.[131] In 1975 some of Hintze's essays were made available in English in a single-volume edition and translation by Felix Gilbert.[132] Thus increasingly since his death, Hintze's work has become more widely available. Availability, however, does not ensure a hearing in a market flooded with many books in a discipline divided into many fields of specialization. The important question is: Why is Hintze's work important for the discipline as a whole?

Both as an active professor at the University of Berlin and as a retired professor in the capital of the Weimar Republic, Hintze never lost sight of the main goal of his life: to supplement the work of Leopold von Ranke through a comparative constitutional and administrative history of the modern world of states. Was he successful in this effort?

Hintze: Eine biographische Skizze," 397–419, and the collection of documents that she prepared and introduced: Otto Hintze and Hedwig Hintze, "*Verzage nicht und lass nicht ab zu kämpfen . . .*": *Die Korrespondenz 1925–1940*. In 1978, I was able to ascertain the date of Hedwig Hintze's death (July 19, 1942) in Utrecht and see the only surviving record from her stay at the Akademisch Ziekenhuis Utrecht (a card with her name and place of birth and the handwritten words "Endogene Depression"). This information was provided to Brigitta Oestreich and was first published in her essay in 1985 and later in the collection of documents cited above. Today we know much more about the last years of Hedwig Hintze especially through the research of Peter Th. Walther and the essay that he kindly mailed to me: "Werkstattbericht: Hedwig Hintze in den Niederlanden 1939–1942," 415–33.

130. Hintze, *Gesammelte Abhandlungen*.

131. The second edition of volume 1 (*Staat und Verfassung*) was published in 1962. The second edition of volume 2 (*Soziologie und Geschichte*) was published in 1964. The second edition of volume 3 (*Regierung und Verwaltung*) was published in 1967. The third edition of volume 1 includes the "Antrittsrede des Hrn Hintze" (563–66) cited above, and some additional book-review references.

132. Gilbert, *Historical Essays of Otto Hintze*.

Even though his comparative constitutional history of the West was never published, the answer to this question must be a strong yes. First of all, Hintze successfully supplemented and broadened Ranke's view of the Latin and Germanic nations as a historical individuality, for the main historical individuality on which he focused was Ranke's "most analogous concept, the concept of Latin Christianity." As Dietrich Gerhard has pointed out, as far as Gerhard himself knew, Hintze was the only researcher who throughout his entire life was occupied with the distinctiveness of the constitutional structure of the occidental European states.[133]

Second, just as from the beginning Ranke was interested in showing how the Latin and Germanic nations were distinctive in the context of universal history, so from the beginning all Hintze's work aimed to show how Latin Christendom or the West was distinctive in comparison with other civilizations. Just as one can see how a young Ranke viewed the Latin and Germanic nations as a distinctive historical individuality especially in the preface and the introduction to *Histories of the Latin and Germanic Nations from 1494–1514*, so especially in Hintze's programmatic essay in 1897 called "Roschers politische Entwicklungstheorie" (Roscher's Theory of Political Development")[134] one can see how from the beginning he pictured the unique constitutional development of the community of nations that grew out of the Latin or Western church in contrast with other civilizations.

Third, from the beginning Hintze sought to supplement Ranke's work not by showing "primarily in the narrative of foreign undertakings" how the Latin and Germanic nations "developed in unity and common enterprise," but rather by showing how the Occidental nations developed in the unity and diversity of their internal constitutions, institutions, and structures.

Fourth, like Ranke, Hintze emphasized how the nature of a state, its constitution, its military structure, and its basic tendency of development were inseparably related to its external situation. While these were basic themes in Ranke's famous essay called "A Dialogue on Politics" (1836),

---

133. Gerhard, "Otto Hintze: Persönlichkeit und Werk," 13.

134. Hintze, *Soziologie und Geschichte*, 1–45. For a summary in English of this important essay, see Smith, "Otto Hintze's Comparative Constitutional History of the West," 36–40.

Hintze developed them in a more systematic way, especially in two of his early essays.[135]

Fifth, like Luther and Ranke, Hintze's basic way of thinking, writing, and viewing life and history can be called an "at-the-same-time" way. Like Luther and Ranke, he constantly used paired opposing concepts as tools of analysis for understanding a particular subject.[136] From the beginning, both Ranke and Hintze liked to contrast the general and the particular; but Hintze's favorite polar but connected concepts were the *herrschaftlich*, or the authoritative principle of organization, and the *genossenschaftlich*, or the associative principle of organization. In adopting these two concepts for analyzing the internal structures of political, social, and economic organizations, he was influenced both by the way Otto von Gierke used these terms in *Das deutsche Genossenschaftsrecht* and by Herbert Spencer's famous "militant" and "industrial" types of society.[137] Throughout his life, Hintze used these polar principles of organization in a masterful, functional-structural, and nonjudgmental way to analyze Western institutions, societies, and states as he sought to supplement the great lifework of Leopold von Ranke.

One of Ranke's most famous "at-the-same-time" uses of polar concepts that Hintze supplemented and demystified was what Ranke called *Das Real-Geistige*, in his essay called "A Dialogue on Politics."[138] For Ranke, a state was a historical, active, and *real-geistige* individuality that was based neither on power alone nor on its "idea" alone. The "formation and the character of every institution," he said, was determined by the "idea that inspires and dominates the whole, the prevailing tendency of

---

135. Two classic examples of this are Hintze's essay of the year 1902, called "Staatenbildung und Verfassungsentwicklung," 34–51; and his essay of the year 1906 titled "Staatsverfassung und Heeresverfassung," 52–85. The former essay was translated in *Historical Essays of Otto Hintze* under the title "The Formation of States and Constitutional Development. A Study in History and Politics" (157–77) and the latter essay as "Military Organization and the Organization of the State" (178–215).

136. For a brief discussion of the importance of the contrast between "the model of evolutionary development" and "the dialectical model whose essence is represented in Nicholas of Cusa's *coincidentia oppositorium*" in relation to Ranke's "materialist and intellectual tendencies of the centuries," see Hintze, "Troeltsch and the Problems of Historicism," 396–98.

137. For brief summaries of Spencer's two functional-structural types of societies and the way Gierke used these two basic concepts, see Smith, "Hintze's Comparative Constitutional History of the West," 109–12, 190–92.

138. Ranke, "Politisches Gespräch," in *Sämmtliche Werke*, 49/50:325.

the minds, and conditions in general."[139] For Ranke, the state was "a living thing, an individual, an unique self,"[140] and all states that counted in the world were "motivated by special tendencies of their own." These tendencies were of a spiritual nature, and everything depended "on the supreme idea." That was meaning, he said, "when we say that states, too, derive their origin from God. For the idea is of divine origin. Each independent state has its own original life, which may have different stages and may perish like all living matter."[141] Thus for Ranke, states were "spiritual substances" and "earthly-spiritual communities called forth by genius and moral energy, growing towards the ideal, each in its own way!"[142]

When Otto Hintze adopted the views of Max Weber that "the state" was not only an *Anstalt* (institution) but also a *Betrieb* (enterprise),[143] Ranke's view of the state as a spiritual entity was completely secularized and demystified. Nowhere is this more apparent than in the essay in which Hintze presented his ideal type of the modern Western state from 1789 to 1914 and his analysis of the European states or "enterprises" during the years of crisis from 1914 to 1931.[144]

Like Ranke, both Weber and Hintze believed that "idealism" and "self-interest" were basic motivating forces in life and history. More than Weber, however, Hintze was able to articulate a useful "at-the-same-time" image that not only characterized the way they approached the study of religion and society but that also supplemented and demystified Ranke's idealistic view of the state as a *real-geistige*, or as an "earthly-spiritual community."

---

139. Ranke, "Dialogue on Politics," 159–60.

140. Ibid., 162.

141. Ibid., 168–69.

142. Ibid., 180.

143. Hintze, "Kelsens Staatslehre," 238.

144. Hintze, "Wesen und Wandlung des modernen Staats," 470–96. At the international conference on Hintze's work in 1980, Dietrich Gerhard and Felix Gilbert reported how they and other young historians at the University of Berlin were "astounded" by the depth and breadth of Hintze's essays that appeared in the last years of the Weimar Republic. They were especially astounded by the three great essays that appeared in the *Historische Zeitschrift* at this time: "Wesen und Verbreitung des Feudalismus" (1929), "Typologie der ständischen Verfassung des Abendlandes" (1930), and "Weltgeschichtliche Bedingungen der Repräsentativverfassung" (1931). See Busch, et al., *Otto Hintze und die moderne Geschichtswissenschaft*, 20.

As Reinhard Bendix noted, nowhere in Weber's work did he clearly articulate a view of "the relative independence and intricate interdependence of ideas and economic interests" that guided his work.[145] Fortunately, Bendix said, such a formulation could be found in the work of Otto Hintze:

> All human action arises from a common source, in political as well as in religious life. Everywhere the first impulse to social action is given as a rule by real interests, i.e., by political and economic interests. But ideal interests lend wings to these real interests, give them a spiritual meaning, and serve to justify them. Man does not live by bread alone. He wants to have a good conscience as he pursues his life-interests. And in pursuing them he develops his capacities to the highest extent only if he believes that in so doing he serves a higher rather than a purely egoistic purpose. Interests without such "spiritual wings" are lame; but on the other hand, ideas can win out in history only if and insofar as they are associated with real interests.[146]

For Hintze, the Marxian image of substructure and superstructure did not give "adequate expression to this peculiar connection of interests and ideas," for in this image "ideologies" quickly lose all reality. Moreover, the Marxian model also had "the flaw that it is static despite the fact that it seeks to portray a dynamic transformation [of society]. Where a substructure is transformed, the superstructure does not follow suit by transforming itself in corresponding fashion; rather the superstructure disintegrates along with the whole of society."[147]

At this point Hintze presented his "at-the-same-time" image that supplemented not only the life work of Leopold von Ranke but also the work of Max Weber, Hintze's greatest contemporary and kindred spirit for understanding Western social-historical thought. "I think," Hintze said,

> a more appropriate image is that of a polar coordination of interests and ideas. In the long run, neither of the two can survive without the other, historically speaking; each requires the other as supplementation. *Wherever interests are vigorously pursued, an*

---

145. Bendix, *Max Weber*, 68.

146. Ibid., 69. Here and in the following quotations, I have used Bendix's translation from Hintze's essay, "Kalvinismus und Staatsräson in Brandenburg zu Beginn des 17. Jahrhunderts," 258. Cf. "Calvinism and Raison d'Etat in Early Seventeenth-Century Brandenburg," 94–95.

147. Bendix, *Max Weber*, 69.

> ideology tends to be developed also to give meaning, re-enforcement and justification to these interests. And this ideology is as "real" as the real interests themselves, for ideology is an indispensable part of the life-process which is expressed in action. And conversely: wherever ideas are to conquer the world, they require the leverage of real interests, although frequently ideas will more or less detract these interests from their original aims.[148]

In these words, Hintze provided his generation and generations of scholars and teachers since his time with an "at-the-same-time" and unsurpassed image to augment the powerful Marxist and materialist substructure/superstructure image.

Just as Hintze's "at-the-same-time" image was a needed supplement to both Ranke's and Weber's ways of seeing and presenting the intricate relationships between ideas and economic interests, so also his definition of *historicism* was a needed supplement to Ernst Troeltsch's earlier (and Meinecke's later) definition of *historicism*. One of the reasons that the decades-long debate between Hintze and Meinecke concerning the nature of history and modern historical thought is so significant for the idea of history is that from beginning to end it focused on two basic concepts of modern historical thought: the concepts of individuality and development. While the concept of individuality was always the basic one for Meinecke, the concept of *Entwicklung*, or development, was the basic one for Hintze.

Their debate, which began in 1888,[149] first became a matter of significance in 1893 when Heinrich von Sybel entrusted Meinecke with the actual direction of the *Historische Zeitschrift*,[150] and when Georg von Below launched an attack on the first three volumes of Karl Lamprecht's *German History* in this journal. One of the reasons that the "Lamprecht controversy" was of major importance for historians was that in part it was also a struggle for control of the *Historische Zeitschrift*,[151] the model and most important historical journal in the world at that time. When Sybel died in 1895 and then when Heinrich von Treitschke died in the

---

148. Ibid. (emphasis added by Bendix)

149. For a good description of Hintze at this time and of the beginning of this friendship, see Meinecke, *Werke*, 8:90–97.

150. Ibid., 8:110–11, 117–20.

151. Ibid.

following year, Meinecke became the sole editor of this journal, a powerful position that he held until 1935.

Two of the first things that Meinecke did as sole editor were to make Hintze a "co-worker" for this journal and to ask him to express his views about "individualist" and "collective" approaches to history in connection with the controversy raging over Lamprecht and his work. In an essay called "The Individual and the Collective Approach to History" (1897),"[152] Hintze took a middle position between Lamprecht and his many critics when he insisted that history could not be identified with a one-sided emphasis on an individual or a collective approach. One of the reasons this essay was important for modern historical thought is that it was, as Meinecke first pointed out, the best that emerged out of this whole controversy,[153] a controversy that is commonly regarded as the classic one within the guild of professional historians.[154]

A second major reason that Hintze's and Meinecke's decades-long debate was significant for the idea of history in the twentieth century is that they were pioneer historians for the development of two major poles of twentieth-century Western historiography. Just as Hintze was the chief pioneer in the early twentieth century for what he called "comparative constitutional and administrative history," Meinecke authored a study, *Weltbürgertum und Nationalstaat* (1908), which was "the first major essay" in what he called "*Geistesgeschichte*."[155] In this and other studies, Meinecke developed a way of writing history that began with a problem or an idea and that traced its development within the thought of one individual, from one individual to another, from one generation to another, and from age to age. As the chief pioneer among professional historians for the writing and development of this new kind of history, Meinecke greatly influenced the writing of history in the twentieth century.

    152. Hintze, "Über individualistische und kollectische Geschichtsauffassung," 315–22; "Individual and Collective Approach to History," 357–67.

    153. Meinecke, *Autobiographische Schriften*, 123. For the significance of Hintze's essay for Lamprecht and for the controversy as a whole, see Chickering, *Karl Lamprecht*, 230–34.

    154. Olábarri, "Controversy in Historical Writing," in *Global Encyclopedia of Historical Writing*, 1:202. The main part of the controversy, however, took place during the last years of the nineteenth century, for as Roger Chickering points out, for "all practical purposes" the controversy was over in 1899 (Chickering, *Karl Lamprecht*, 245).

    155. Hughes, *Consciousness and Society*, 234. As Hughes also states, this work "started historical writing on an extremely fruitful course."

As a professor of history at the University of Berlin (beginning in 1914), Meinecke attracted and trained many excellent students. Some of them became leaders in the profession not only in Germany but also in the English-speaking world, for some of his best students left Germany in or around 1933 to teach in the United States (Hans Baron, Dietrich Gerhard, Felix Gilbert, Hajo Holborn, Gerhard Masur, and Hans Rothfels).[156]

In his "Inaugural Speech" before the Royal Prussian Academy of Sciences in Berlin in 1915, Meinecke reported how increasingly his interest had shifted from personalities to ideas and on two major tasks. The first, he said, was "to understand the transformations in the nature and spirit of power politics since the days of the Renaissance," and the other was "to investigate the rise of our modern concept of history [*Geschichtsauffassung*]."[157] The timing of these two statements is significant, for they were made in the same year that Ernst Troeltsch began his career as a professor of philosophy at the University of Berlin with a special interest in philosophy of history and modern historical thought.

Throughout his life, the writings of Troeltsch were infused by a strenuous effort to overcome "the tension between the absolute and the relative."[158] This tension was especially striking in the conclusion to the large and significant work that he published in 1911 and that was translated into English under the title *The Social Teachings of the Christian Churches*. If, as this study had shown, one could find no absolute and unchanging Christian ethic in the social teachings of the Christian churches, could not this lead to a harmful sense of relativism, skepticism, and doubt? This was a huge problem for Troeltsch, and in 1913 he clearly associated the word *Historismus* with this problem.[159]

When Troeltsch became a professor at the University of Berlin, he also became a colleague and friend of Meinecke and Hintze, and an active participant in their discussions concerning the nature of history

---

156. Eckart Kehr also came to the United States in 1933 but died that same year. For the careers and publications of each of these historians, see especially Epstein, *Past Renewed*.

157. "Antrittsrede des Herrn Meinecke," 496–98. See also Meinecke, *Zur Geschichte der Geschichtsschreibung*, 2.

158. Tillich, *Begegnungen. Paul Tillich über sich selbst und andere*, 166. Cited in Yasukata, *Ernst Troeltsch*, x. In this volume of Tillich's *Gesammelte Werke*, see his helpful review of Troeltsch's *Der Historismus und seine Probleme* in the year 1924, 204–11.

159. See especially Troeltsch, "Das neunzehnte Jahrhundert," 628.

and modern historical thought. Thus in 1915, their longstanding debate became a three-way dialogue. Although at Berlin Troeltsch strenuously sought to make the term *Historismus* a positive one by disconnecting it from its negative connotations, they continued to be a huge problem for him to the end of his life.

At Berlin, Troeltsch wrestled with the problem of historical relativism by studying the development of modern historical thought since the eighteenth century and by focusing especially on the two concepts that his friends had been arguing and joking about—privately but not publicly—since the beginning of their friendship: the concepts of individuality and development. In the year 1922 Troeltsch combined his various essays concerning these and other concepts of modern historical thought into one large volume called *Der Historismus und seine Probleme*.[160] Neither of these two basic concepts, however, was included in Troeltsch's famous definition of *Historismus*: "It is the problem of the *significance and the nature of Historismus itself*, whereby this word is to be completely disconnected from its bad secondary meaning and is to be understood in the sense of the basic historizing of all our thought about man, his culture, and his values."[161]

After the death of Troeltsch in 1923, the public debate between Meinecke and Hintze concerning the nature of historicism began. In that year Meinecke affirmed his position by emphasizing the primacy of "the idea of individuality" over the idea of development both for the rise of historicism in Germany and for Troeltsch.[162] In the following year the term *Historismus* was a basic one in Meinecke's *Die Idee der Staatsräson*, for here he emphasized how around the beginning of the nineteenth century

160. While for Troeltsch the fundamental categories or concepts for historical thinking were the categories of individuality and development, he "devoted more space in *Historicism and Its Problems* to an explication of the meaning of historical development than to the other ten categories combined" (Rubanowice, *Crisis in Consciousness*, 86). For a good summary of each of the eleven categories discussed by Troeltsch, see ibid., 80–89.

161. Troeltsch, *Der Historismus und seine Probleme*, 102 (emphasis in original). For a study that (1) is primarily concerned with Troeltsch's understanding of historicism (called "crisis historicism"), that (2) discusses the relationship between theology and history in the nineteenth century in terms of a "secularizing and historicizing" of a "biblical-theological culture," and that (3) contains very useful bibliographical information for understanding the connection between German religious and historical thought since the late eighteenth century, see Howard, *Religion and the Rise of Historicism*.

162. Meinecke, "Ernst Troeltsch und das Problem des Historismus," 373–74, 378.

an intellectual revolution took place in Germany, a revolution that to him was "perhaps the greatest revolution in thought experienced by the West" and that he associated with the terms "idealism" and "*Historismus*."[163]

In 1927 Hintze presented his understanding and definition of historicism in an essay that Meinecke published in the *Historische Zeitschrift* and that was called "Ernst Troeltsch and the Problems of Historicism: Critical Studies." After Hintze noted how Troeltsch belonged to the tradition of German idealism "that began with Leibniz and reached fruition with Ranke and Hegel,"[164] he discussed some of the problems with Troeltsch's understanding of historicism.

One of the problems, Hintze said, was that it "leads again and again down the path of skepticism and relativism that Troeltsch hoped to close off." "Time after time," Hintze said, "the ghost of 'bad historicism' appears and must be exorcised by a good and true historicism, that is, a historicism imbued with and dominated by ethics."[165] In the latter part of this essay, Hintze stated that Troeltsch's fear of relativity was "a little exaggerated," for "[w]e can openly admit the relativity of all historical phenomena without succumbing to 'relativism.'"[166]

Another problem for Hintze was that Troeltsch had not made a sharp distinction between historicism as a methodology and as a *Weltanschauung*. For Troeltsch, Hintze argued, the general philosophical function of historicism—which was to provide the materials for both a cultural synthesis and the historical process—took precedence over the purely epistemological function. In "interests of a clear methodology," Hintze said, he preferred to see historicism as "nothing more than another mode of thought, another set of methodological categories."[167]

---

163. Meinecke, *Machiavellism*, 362. In 1924 a young scholar named Karl Mannheim published his definition of "Historismus" in an essay with that title in the *Archiv für Sozialwissenschaft und Sozialpolitik* 52 (1924) 1–60. In 1952 this essay was translated into English titled "Historicism" in Karl Mannheim's *Essays on the Sociology of Knowledge*, 84–133. For Troeltsch, Meinecke, Mannheim, and Hintze, the term *Historismus* far transcended professional historiography, for it was of fundamental importance for all the human or cultural sciences.

164. "Hintze, "Troeltsch and the Problems of Historicism," 370 (*Soziologie und Geschichte*, 323).

165. Ibid., 373.

166. Ibid., 413.

167. Ibid., 373. In an essay called "Two Meanings of Historicism in the Writings of Dilthey, Troeltsch, and Meinecke," Calvin D. Rand uses Hintze's distinction between his-

A third major problem for Hintze was that as yet there was "no precise demarcation of the area covered by the concept of historicism. In regard to this problem, Hintze made the significant point that Troeltsch's and Meinecke's emphasis on the differences between German historical thought and the thought of the West European peoples was exaggerated much more than it would have been without wartime propaganda. For Hintze, an exclusively German and idealistic interpretation of historicism was too restricted, for he believed that this concept should be broadened to include Marxism and positivism.[168]

While Hintze also criticized Troeltsch "for having no interest whatsoever in psychological methods," he credited him for discussing "the two concepts fundamental to specifically historical thought: the concept of individuality and that of development."[169] Before Hintze explained how these two concepts were based on two simple analogies that historians use in constituting historical objects, however, he said that in his view the only decisive criterion for determining an object of historical study is "its comprehensibility as a life-unit [*Lebenseinheit*]."[170]

Now Troeltsch had used the term *Lebenseinheit* and had discussed the significance of "individual totalities" in the *Der Historismus* volume, but the way Hintze explained these terms and connected them with his definition of historicism was distinctive: "What we call historicism is a new, unique, categorical-structure of the mind [*des Geistes*] that began to arise in the West in the eighteenth century and achieved authoritative currency in the nineteenth, particularly in Germany, though not in Germany alone. It is characterized by the categories of individuality and develop-

---

toricism as a *Weltanschauung* and as a methodology in discussing the writings of these three scholars. Like Hintze, Rand concludes that "it appears best to regard historicism more formally and only as a methodology," for "if it is judged relevant by historians and philosophers, it will more likely be done so on the basis of its methodological value" (518).

168. Hintze, "Troeltsch and the Problems of Historicism," 376.

169. Ibid., 380.

170. Hintze, "Troeltsch und die Probleme des Historismus," 337. This significant statement follows Hintze's important distinction between possible objects of history and actual objects of history that is translated as the third introductory quotation to chapter 1. See note 3 for chapter 1, and the reference to this passage in English: "Troeltsch and the Problems of Historicism," 384–85.

ment, which postulate a view of historical reality based on the analogy of the life-unit [*Lebenseinheit*] and the life-process [*Lebensprozess*]."[171]

Both chronologically and logically this was a brilliant statement, for here Hintze combined a picture of the rise and full development of historicism with the formal philosophy of Kant, with Dilthey's emphasis on psychology, and with Droysen's emphasis on history as a *Wissenschaft* and as a method of inquiry and understanding based on the concept of time. When Hintze stated that the concepts of individuality and development should be regarded "formally" as "categorical structures of the human mind," he was supplementing Kant's (and Droysen's) two basic forms of "*innere Anschauung*," for to Hintze "space and time were the constituent elements of all historical phenomena." When Hintze argued that historical thinking was basically analogical and that historicism was based on the two basic analogies that historians use to understand and constitute historical objects, he was both supplementing Dilthey's terminology and demonstrating his teacher's views concerning the importance of psychology and psychological understanding for all of the human sciences. When Hintze emphasized that "history could have at its possible object everything dealing with human culture based on a perception of time," and when he defined historicism as a method of inquiry and understanding, he was also supplementing Droysen's basic methodological principles. And when Hintze insisted that historicism should be defined in a "purely epistemological" way and that it was only another mode of thought or another set of methodological categories, he was articulating and supplementing the German understanding of history since the time of Chladenius—the idea of a *Geschichtswissenschaft*.

More than any other historian, Ranke combined all three types of Western historiography in his work: the classical-humanist, the Christian, and modern professional historiography. Certainly there was an epic quality in Ranke's humanistic, rational, and artistic narratives; certainly Ranke's work was based on a Christian view of history; and certainly he personifies the four major characteristics of modern professional historiography.

In Hintze's writings, however, there is no trace of wonder and mystery. Reading Hintze, as Felix Gilbert pointed out, requires "*Verstandsar-

---

171. Hintze, "Troeltsch und die Probleme des Historismus," 342. This is a more literal translation than Gilbert's in *Historical Essays of Otto Hintze* ("Troeltsch and the Problems of Historicism," 390).

beit," or understanding and work, for there is "no appeal to emotion or aesthetic feelings" and "no trace of rhetoric."[172] For Hintze, as Gilbert also emphasized, "history is *Wissenschaft*" and "nothing but *Wissenschaft*."[173] Thus for Hintze, history was a *Wissenschaft* alone, for it was only an organized body of knowledge with its own appropriate methodology.

Now the part of Hintze's *Historismus* definition that influenced Meinecke the most when he published *Die Entstehung des Historismus* in 1936, however, was the chronological part; for in his preliminary remarks he explained how historicism was "nothing else but the application to the historical world of the new life-governing principles achieved by the great German movement from Leibniz to the death of Goethe."[174] In contrast to Hintze, however, Meinecke insisted that historicism was more than just a method of the human sciences, for life and the world appeared differently when one had become accustomed to viewing things in this new way. For Meinecke, "the essence of historism is the substitution of a process of *individualising* observation for a *generalising* view of human forces in history."[175] This did not mean "that the historical method excludes altogether any attempt to find general laws in human life," he said, but it had "to make use of this approach and blend it with a feeling for the individual." For Meinecke the sense of individuality was something new that historicism created.[176]

Although Meinecke admitted not only that some persons might believe that historicism was on the way "to becoming an unrestrained relativism and might paralyse the creative powers of mankind" but also that "historism only finds a hearing with the few and did not appeal to the multitude,"[177] this was followed by a statement of hope and faith that certainly contains a religious element: "But we can discern in it [historism] the highest stage so far reached in the understanding of human affairs, and are confident that it will be able to develop sufficiently to tackle problems of human history that will confront us. We believe that it has the power to heal the wounds it has caused by the relativising of all

---

172. Gilbert, "Otto Hintze und die moderne Geschichtswissenschaft," 206.
173. Ibid.
174. Meinecke, *Historism*, lv.
175. Ibid. (emphasis in original)
176. Ibid.
177. Ibid., lvii.

values, provided that it can find men to convert this 'ism' into the terms of authentic life."[178] How different this "Neo-Idealist" statement of faith is from Hintze's earlier and completely secular definition of historicism!

Although the next few years Meinecke wrote several essays that were supplements to his third great intellectual history, for all practical purposes the publication of this work in 1936 can be seen as the end of the debate between Hintze and Meinecke concerning the nature of historicism. Since World War II, the *Historismus* dialogue between Troeltsch, Hintze, and Meinecke has blossomed into a large and apparently endless one for historians in Germany[179] while many history students and teachers in the United States are blissfully unaware of a dialogue that can be regarded (though in retrospect) as the most significant one in the twentieth century concerning the nature of modern historical thought.

One of the reasons that the *Historismus* debate was of major significance for the idea of history in the twentieth century is its significance for what H. Stuart Hughes called "the reconstruction" or the "reorienta-

178. Ibid.

179. Since the literature on this subject is so vast, here it is only possible to mention a few representative studies. For excellent (1) critical but sympathetic analysis of Meinecke's *Die Entstehung des Historismus*, (2) coverage of literature to 1963 concerning the origin of—and reception to—this book, and (3) understanding of the significance of Hintze's analysis of historicism for Meinecke's third great intellectual history, see Schulin, "Das Problem der Individualität," 102–33. For a thoughtful and critical analysis of the ways the term *Historismus* was used in the 1970s, see Nipperdey, "Historismus und Historismuskritik heute," 59–73. Note both his definition of the term (59), and how many of his suggestions to improve the use of the term at this time (this essay was first published in 1975) are similar to what Hintze sought to accomplish in the Troeltsch essay. For a good summary and analysis of the way the term *Historismus* was used in 1986, see Oexle, "'Historismus'. Überlegungen zur Geschichte des Phänomens und des Begriffs," 119–55. This debate heated up considerably in the early 1990s with the publication of the first (1992) and the second (1994) editions of a book by Annette Wittkau-Horgby called *Historismus: Zur Geschichte des Begriffs und des Problems*. This book heated the debate partly because it sided with Hintze's understanding of the term and used him to attack Meinecke's views. For a brief introduction to this whole subject, see Iggers, *Historiography in the Twentieth Century*. For a broad, helpful, and international discussion of the terms *New Historicism*, *Storicismo*, and *Historismus* at the end of the twentieth century, see Scholtz, *Historismus am Ende des 20. Jahrhunderts*. In the essay "Die Legitimität des Historismus," Volker Steenblock claims not only that Meinecke's life mirrored the entire drama of German historiography from the end of the nineteenth century to the end of the twentieth, but also that he was certainly right in his view that historicism was "one of the greatest revolutions that has ever taken place in Western thought" (ibid., 181). This quotation is from the closing sentence of the first paragraph of Meinecke's *Die Entstehung des Historismus*.

tion" of European social thought, in his book *Consciousness and Society: The Reconstruction of European Social Thought 1890–1930* (1958). Here Hughes claimed that "it was Germans and Austrians and French and Italians—rather than Englishmen or Americans or Russians—who in general provided the fund of ideas that has come to seem characteristic of our time."[180] For Hughes, Sigmund Freud was the towering figure of the generation of the 1890s. Just behind him came Max Weber, and considerably below him came such figures as Benedetto Croce, Emile Durkheim, Vilfredo Pareto, Henri Bergson, Georges Sorel, Carl Jung, Friedrich Meinecke, and Ernst Troeltsch.[181]

In his study Hughes showed how the leading social thinkers of this generation came to grips with Marxism; but most of all he showed how the great intellectual conflict within the *Geisteswissenschaften*—or within those disciplines concerned with what Dilthey called "historical-social reality"—was between the idealist and the positivist traditions. According to Hughes, the decade of the 1890s was a "revolt against positivism," or against "the whole tendency to discuss human behavior in terms of analogies drawn from natural science."[182]

Although Hughes saw Freud and Weber as the two towering figures for European social thought from 1890 to 1930, Weber was the central figure in this intellectual history, for he was the only scholar of this generation who transcended positivism and idealism and who "was able to bridge the chasm" between them.[183]

Despite the facts (1) that here Hughes was more concerned with European sociologists and social thought than with historians and historical thought, (2) that Meinecke was the only professional historian to receive considerable attention in Hughes's study, and (3) that Hintze was not mentioned, nevertheless this excellent intellectual history provides a helpful framework for understanding the significance of Meinecke's and Hintze's work for Western social-historical thought.

---

180. Hughes, *Consciousness and Society*, 13.
181. Ibid., 19–20.
182. Ibid., 37.
183. While the title of the chapter on Max Weber (ibid., 278) is called "Max Weber and the Transcending of Positivism and Idealism," the main point of the concluding paragraph of that chapter (ibid., 335) was that "Alone of his contemporaries, Weber was able to bridge the chasm between positivism and idealism."

For Hughes, Wilhelm Dilthey was "a great precursor" of this generation of the 1890s, for his work represented "the first thorough-going and sophisticated confrontation of history with positivism and natural science";[184] and here he showed how Croce, Troeltsch, and Meinecke were important heirs of Dilthey. What separated Croce and Meinecke, as Hughes succinctly pointed out, was a divergent interpretation of Dilthey's intellectual legacy. Both of them, he argued,

> had narrowed their common inheritance: neither had grasped the full importance of Dilthey's analysis of the interrelationships among the different branches of human study, nor had resumed the attempt to bring history into dynamic accord with social science; each was too exclusively absorbed in preserving the newly won autonomy of historical study. Finally both had failed to see that the relativist implications of Dilthey's thought might not necessarily threaten the whole notion of *Historismus*: it did not occur to them to revise the idealist theory of values within a frankly relativist framework. These were the great tasks that still remained if the intellectual revolution of the 1890s was to be pushed to its furthest limits.[185]

Each of these things that Croce and Meinecke failed to accomplish, however, were accomplished by Hintze, especially in the article "Troeltsch and the Problems of Historicism" in 1927.

Today it is clear that Max Weber was not the only great scholar of the generation of the 1890s who brought history into dynamic accord with social science, who transcended the idealist and the positivist traditions, and who bridged the gap between the social and historical worlds. In the year 1960, Reinhard Bendix testified to the comparability of Hintze's and Meinecke's work when he wrote, "A continuation of Weber's work as he may have intended it, namely a further application and development of his concepts through comparative analysis, is contained in the work of Otto Hintze."[186] It is no accident, however, that a well-known sociologist and Weber scholar would make such a statement and to seek to have Hintze's work known among social scientists, for Hintze was practically

---

184. Ibid., 194.

185. Ibid., 247–48.

186. Bendix, *Max Weber*, 379 n. 53. See also *The International Encyclopedia of the Social Sciences* (1968) for Bendix's excellent articles on Hintze (6:366–68) and Weber (16:493–502).

the only historian of his time in whom one can find a direct influence of the historical sociology of Max Weber and his theory of ideal types.[187]

Although in some respects Hintze's later studies can be seen as a continuation of Weber's work, it is more helpful to see Weber and Hintze as "supplementary antipoles" of Western social-historical thought from the 1890s until the year 1933. Such a view is helpful first of all because in his studies of modern bureaucracy, which reached a culmination in the essays "The Commissary and His Significance in General Administrative History: A Comparative Study" (1910)[188] and "Der Beamtenstand" (1911),[189] Hintze worked out the characteristics that Weber later "joined together, and universalized" in his famous ideal type called "bureaucracy."[190]

This is also a helpful view because this is the way Hintze hoped that his work could and would be viewed. In the year 1922 Hintze wrote a review of Weber's collected writings in the sociology of religion;[191] in 1926 he published a review (titled "Max Weber's Sociology") of the second edition of Weber's *Economy and Society*;[192] and in 1927 he wrote a review of Marianne Weber's biography of her husband.[193] While on the one hand Hintze called Weber's *Economy and Society* an epoch-making work both for sociological and historical research,[194] on the other hand he insisted that "this sociology cries out for a constitutional-historical supplement."[195] Thus in the year 1926, Hintze suggested that the lifework he had set out

187. Schieder, "Der Typus in der Geschichtswissenschaft," 177.

188. "Commissary and His Significance in General Administrative History," 267–301. See also Hintze, *Staat und Verfassung*, 242–74.

189. Hintze, "Der Beamtenstand," 66–125.

190. Kocka, "Otto Hintze, Max Weber, und das Problem der Bürokratie," 153. This essay also appeared in the *Historische Zeitschrift* 233 (1981) 65–105. See also his essay "Otto Hintze and Max Weber: Attempts at a Comparison," 284–95. In his "Introduction" to this collection of essays (*Max Weber and His Contemporaries*), Wolfgang Mommsen stated: "In fact, the strongest connection, relatively speaking, between Max Weber's interpretive sociology and contemporary historiography could be found not in the field of social history, but in comparative institutional and constitutional history. A master in this field was Otto Hintze, one of the few historians whose breadth of perspective and universal-historical orientation did not fall short of Weber's" (11).

191. Hintze, "Max Webers Religionssoziologie," 126–34.

192. Hintze, "Max Webers Soziologie," 135–47.

193. Hintze, "Max Weber, ein Lebensbild," 148–54.

194. Hintze, "Max Webers Soziologie," 147.

195. Ibid., 144.

to accomplish, as a needed supplement to the lifework of Leopold von Ranke, could also serve as a needed supplement to the life work of his great contemporary, Max Weber.

In the year 1929 Hintze published an essay focused on the sociological and historical views of the state and on the sociology of Franz Oppenheimer.[196] Today this long and inclusive essay can be seen as the high point of Hintze's encounter with sociology—the first sophisticated and masterful encounter of history with modern sociology.

In the same year Hintze published two essays dealing with the historical development of modern capitalism in connection with the second, revised, and enlarged edition of Werner Sombart's *Modern Capitalism* (1916-1927).[197] Together these two essays can be regarded as a very helpful historical supplement to Weber's and Sombart's work concerning the development of modern capitalism.

Among Hintze's greatest contributions to social-historical thought in the twentieth century were the three historical ideal types published in essay form from 1929 to 1931. In 1929 he published an ideal type of feudalism, wherein he compared Western feudalism with feudal structures in other parts of the world in the course of world history.[198] The next year he published a typology of Western representative institutions based on corporate estates, or an "estates structure,"[199] an essay in which he was the first historian to speak of "typology" as a historical task.[200] In 1931 he published his most fully developed historical model, an ideal

---

196. Hintze, "Soziologische und geschichtliche Staatsauffassung," 239–305. See also Schulze, "Otto Hintze und die deutsche Geschichtswissenschaft um 1900," 323–39.

197. Hintze, "Der moderne Kapitalismus als historische Individuum," 374–426; and "Wirtschaft und Politik im Zeitalter des modernen Kapitalismus," 427–52. Felix Gilbert translated the latter essay in *Historical Essays of Otto Hintze* under the title "Economics and Politics in the Age of Modern Capitalism," 422–52.

198. Hintze, "Wesen und Verbreitung des Feudalismus," 84–119. Frederick L. Cheyette translated the first part of this essay in a book that he edited called *Lordship and Community in Medieval Europe*, 22–61. See also the following essay in this book, where Otto Brunner stated, "A great merit of Otto Hintze's study on the *Wesen und Verbreitung des Feudalismus* is that it is only one part of a comprehensive constitutional history of Europe in which he deals equally with the bureaucratic organization of the modern state and with "representative governments" (Brunner, "Feudalism: The History of a Concept," 54).

199. Hintze, "Typolgie der ständische Verfassungen des Abendlandes," 120–39.

200. Schieder, "Der Typus," 176.

type of the modern Western state.²⁰¹ Together these three ideal types form a complete and unsurpassed historical typology of Western institutional development. These essays, together with the other Hintze essays from 1927 through the year 1932, mark one of the high points in the twentieth century for the study of the West as a "historical-social reality." Each of these articles, as Dietrich Gerhard emphasized, "stands in lieu of a book," and together "they represent a corpus on which every scholar ought to draw who is concerned with the inner springs of Western civilization."²⁰²

One of the ways Hintze's work is significant for Western social and historical thought is the way he and Max Weber completely rationalized and secularized the Protestant religions traditions in which they were born and raised. While Friedrich Meinecke struggled to preserve a sense of the mystery of life, which he saw and felt in the work of Herder, Goethe, and Ranke, and which he depicted through his new way of writing history, Otto Hintze and Max Weber developed new methodologies for the study of social-historical reality which completely rationalized and secularized a religious tradition that can be called "a Lutheran ethos" or a Lutheran way of viewing life. While Meinecke showed how the rise of historicism was associated with Herder's religious way of viewing life and history (a way that culminated in the work of Leopold von Ranke), Hintze defined *historicism* in a completely secular way so that today it can be used simply as a method for teaching students how to think historically and how to write history.

That does not mean, however, that Troeltsch and Meinecke were wrong in their understanding of the nature of historicism or that one has to take sides when one looks at their views and Hintze's on this subject. Certainly Troeltsch was right in emphasizing the revolutionary nature of the basic historizing or "historization of our thought about man, his culture, and his values."²⁰³ Certainly Troeltsch, Hintze, and Meinecke were correct in linking this revolutionary process with the concepts of individuality and development. Certainly Meinecke was right when he associated the *rise* of historicism with a way of viewing life, for at least to some degree the *origins* of historicism were connected with a distinctly

201. Hintze, "Wesen und Wandlung des modernen Staats," 470–96.

202. "Each of these articles stands in lieu of a book; after the reader has finally mastered any of them he will indeed feel as though he had read a book" (Gerhard, "Otto Hintze," 30).

203. Troeltsch, *Der Historismus und seine Probleme*, 102.

religious way of viewing life. Certainly Hintze was right when he defined historicism as a mode of thought and as another set of methodological categories, for now this term became what it still is today—a useful tool for teaching students how to think historically and how to do history in a pluralistic, culturally diverse, and secular age. And certainly Troeltsch, Hintze, and Meinecke were right in claiming that this new and powerful way of viewing or perceiving life was a basic component of the modern Western world since the end of the eighteenth century and the beginning of the nineteenth; for as Otto Gerhard Oexle points out, "Since the end of the eighteenth and the beginning of the nineteenth century this way of viewing life [*Betrachtungsweise*] was definitely achieved. Historicism is one of those great fundamental forces that are constitutive for modernity; it should take its place with the Enlightenment, with the political revolution, with the Industrial Revolution, and with the adoption of modern natural science and its consequences."[204]

But since the term *historicism* and this basic view have never been fully accepted either within the guild of professional historians in the United States or within the academic community as a whole, it is time for more scholars and teachers to utilize the great insights of Troeltsch, Hintze, and Meinecke and build on them in new ways. *If* the concepts of individuality and development can be seen not only as basic ones for a distinctly modern kind of historical consciousness but also as basic characteristics of a distinctly modern type of Western historiography, would not this be helpful for history teachers everywhere? *If* the rise of historicism or the "historizing" of Western thought can be seen within the context of a "Cultural Revolution in Germany," would not this be helpful for humanities teachers throughout the English-speaking world? *If* the religious views of Luther, Leibniz, Hamann, Herder, and Ranke

---

204. Oexle, "Die Geschichtswissenschaft im Zeichen des Historismus," 18. Here, however, Oexle links his views on this subject with Troeltsch and Mannheim, rather than with Meinecke. This essay, the essay "'Historismus'. Überlegungen zur Geschichte des Phänomens und des Begriffs," and another important essay called "Meinecke's Historismus. Über Kontext und Folgen einer Definition" can be found in a collection of Oexle's essays called *Geschichtswissenschaft im Zeichen des Historismus: Studien zu Problemgeschichten der Moderne*. These thoughtful essays certainly demonstrate both the tremendous influence and some of the unfortunate results of Meinecke's *definition* of historicism for German historiography in the twentieth century. It is important to note, however, that these unfortunate results were the results of *choices* made by Western scholars since the time of Hintze and Meinecke.

were important for and conducive to the rise of a distinctly modern kind of historical consciousness and this aspect of modern Western thought, would not this be helpful for all teachers of religion to know?

Finally, *if* Max Weber and Otto Hintze can be seen as the scholars of their generation who best bridged the chasm between the idealist and positivist traditions, who best demonstrated and articulated an "at-the-same-time" alternative image to augment the Marxist substructure/superstructure image, and who in these and other ways best secularized the particular religious traditions in which they were raised, would not this be helpful knowledge for anyone interested in the history of Western social and historical thought?

conclusion

He [Ranke] was beyond comparison the greatest historical writer of modern times. ... It was he who made German scholarship supreme in Europe; and no one has ever approximated so closely the ideal historian.[1]

—G. P. Gooch (1913)

Taking quality and quantity together, Germany retains her place, which she won a century ago with Ranke and Böckh, at the top of the list in the field of historical studies.[2]

—G. P. Gooch (1931)

IN THE DISCOVERY OF HISTORY, which has added a new dimension to Western thought, the Germany of the first half of the nineteenth century made its most original intellectual contribution to the modern word.[3]

—Hajo Holborn (1964)

In his brilliant, provocative, and controversial study, *The Protestant Ethic and the Spirit of Capitalism,* Max Weber made the striking claim that "[i]t was the power of religious influence, not alone, but more than anything else, which created the [national] differences of which we are conscious today."[4] While the main purpose of this famous study was to suggest how a Calvinist ethic was especially conducive to the development of a capitalist spirit in the Western world, the main purpose behind the present study

---

1. Gooch, *History and Historians in the Nineteenth Century* (1913), 102.

2. Gooch, "German Historical Studies Since the War," 268. This essay was originally written for the German number of the *Times Literary Supplement* of April 18, 1929, and was brought up to date for the publication of this book in 1931 (see page v of the preface).

3. Holborn, *History of Modern Germany, 1648–1940,* 527 (emphasis in original). This quotation is cited by Theodore Ziolkowski in the first paragraph of his preface to *Clio: The Romantic Muse,* ix.

4. Weber, *Protestant Ethic,* 88–89.

is to investigate the significance of religion for the rise of a distinctly modern kind of historical consciousness and type of Western historiography.

Since the time of Ernst Troeltsch, Otto Hintze, and Friedrich Meinecke, scholars have used the terms *Historismus,* or *historicism,* to capture and portray a distinctly modern kind of historical consciousness. As these three scholars agreed, (1) this new kind of historical thought arose first in Germany during the last decades of the eighteenth century and the beginning of the nineteenth; (2) it was based especially on the concepts of individuality and development; and (3) it reached full maturity in the work of Leopold von Ranke. To understand the rise of a distinctly modern kind of historical consciousness, however, it is helpful for readers to have some understanding of "the idea of history" in the West as a whole.

The present study is an innovative work first of all because it provides a sketch of Western historical thought through an historical typology based on the ideal-type or model-building methodology of Otto Hintze. When one looks at Western historiography as a historical individuality, one can see three main periods and three main types of historical thought. Chapter 1, "A Typology of Classical and Christian Historiography," presented a sketch of the idea of history from Herodotus to Voltaire through two ideal types: (1) a model of classical historiography of Greece and Rome, and (2) a model of Christian historiography from St. Augustine to Voltaire.

As an ideal type or model, Greek and Roman historiography was epic, humanistic, rational, and didactic. The model of Christian historiography used in this chapter was based on R. G. Collingwood's significant statement: "Any history written on Christian principles will of necessity be universal, providential, apocalyptic and periodized."[5] Whereas the characteristics of classical historiography were discussed mainly in relation to the histories of Herodotus, Thucydides, Polybius, Plutarch, and to the views of Cicero, the main characteristics of Christian historiography were presented primarily through a discussion of the two most important works for understanding and teaching a distinctly Christian type of Western historical thought: the *Confessions* and the *City of God* of St. Augustine.

---

5. Collingwood, *Idea of History,* 49.

While the *Confessions* was a time-based and exemplary model for life-writing until the time of the *Confessions* of Rousseau, the *City of God* was the most influential work for the development of a Christian view of universal or world history until the traditional Christian way of writing this kind of history was overturned by Voltaire. Although Renaissance historiography is sometimes seen as the beginning of modern historical thought, it is pictured here as a revival and broadening of the classical type of Western historiography within a primarily Christian epoch.

While the first great transition in Western historical thought took place at the time of St. Augustine and when the Roman Empire was becoming Christian, the Enlightenment was the second great time of transition for Western historical thought. The Enlightenment was of decisive importance for the idea of history because this was the time (1) when the classical-humanist type of historiography written by prominent men of letters reached a high point within this Christian era, (2) when the Christian view of universal history was overturned by Voltaire, and (3) when in Germany a distinctly modern kind of historical consciousness (commonly called historicism) and type of Western historiography gradually arose.

Since the rise of historicism and of a distinctly modern type of Western historiography occurred first and mainly in Protestant Germany, was the Lutheran tradition especially conducive for the rise of these particular aspects of our modern world? In order to explore this question, it was necessary first to explore the nature of Martin Luther's thought, the educational foundations of the Lutheran ethos, and Luther's and Melanchthon's contributions to the Lutheran concept of calling. These are the main aspects of chapter 2, a chapter titled "Martin Luther and the Foundations of a Lutheran Ethos," and the place where the second major idea of this inquiry is presented and explored.

The second basic way this study is an innovative work is that it is the first to suggest that in addition to his well-known paradoxical, *simul*, or "at-the-same-time" way of thinking and viewing life, Martin Luther also had a deeply incarnational and dynamic, mystical and holistic, individualizing and historical way of thinking and viewing life that can be called an "in-with-and-under" way. While the paradoxical richness of Luther's *simul* way of thinking and viewing life, and the ideas known as "justification by faith" and *simul justus et peccator* were derived mainly from the writings of Paul, the dialectical richness of Luther's "in-with-and-under" way of thinking, teaching, preaching, writing, and viewing life was based mainly on the Gospel of John and its great Prologue that proclaims, "In the beginning was the Word" (1:1), that "the Word became flesh" (1:14), and how God is acting, creating and redeeming.

Within the Lutheran tradition, the connected prepositions *in*, *with*, and *under* have always been associated with Luther's and Melanchthon's ways of presenting the nature of the Lord's Supper; for while Luther usually used the preposition *under* or the words "in and under" to answer the question of how the bread and the wine could be the body and blood of Christ at the same time, Melanchthon usually used the preposition *with*. Since the time of the Formula of Concord in 1577, Lutheran pastors have usually used the connected prepositions *in*, *with*, and *under* to answer this question and to teach the doctrine of the real presence.

Just as Luther insisted on the presence of Christ in the divine mystery called the Lord's Supper, so also he insisted that God was somehow present in all his creation. It is significant that two of Luther's strongest statements concerning the omnipresence of God and God's hidden presence in all of his creation can be found in two of his books concerning the Lord's Supper. In these and other statements, Luther used virtually every kind of preposition to explain his deeply held views that God created all things, was present in all things, and was the active and preserving force in all things. These views are basic ones not only behind the *Monadology* of Leibniz, the founder of the philosophic tradition known as German idealism and also the chief forerunner for the new kind of historical consciousness called historicism, but also behind the work of Hamann and Herder, and thus behind that great intellectual and spiritual revolution in Germany from the 1760s until 1810.

A distinctly Lutheran ethos, however, was based not only on Luther's two ways of thinking and viewing life but also on the kind of educational and religious experience that young Lutherans received through their pastors from the time of Luther through the first half of the twentieth century. The one common experience of all Lutherans—whether orthodox, pietist, or rationalist—was the confirmation experience based on three main elements: (1) memorizing or attempting to memorize Luther's Small Catechism, (2) being examined (often publicly by the pastor before the congregation during the confirmation service) over Luther's powerful and individualizing explanations of the essentials of the Christian faith, and (3) experiencing the First Communion whereby young Lutherans first received (in, with, and under the bread and wine) the body and blood of Christ at the table of the Lord.

Especially in the Small Catechism one can see how Luther was able to communicate his deepest religious beliefs not only in an "at-the-same-time" way and in a dynamic "in, with, and under" way but also in an individualizing way. Luther was the greatest individualizing writer in German history; for in his preaching, teaching, and writing he was able to present general ideas and/or the universal in, with, and under the particular, and to convince young Christians that "God has created me and all that exists," that Jesus Christ "has redeemed me, a lost and condemned creature," and that "the Holy Spirit has called me through the Gospel, enlightened me with his gifts, and sanctified and preserved me in the one true faith."[6]

In the *Protestant Ethic and the Spirit of Capitalism*, Max Weber emphasized the importance of Luther's concept of a *Beruf* or a "calling" (which was the English translation of this Lutheran word) for the development of the modern Western world. Two callings that have been closely connected within the Lutheran tradition since the time of Luther and Melanchthon were the callings to preach and to teach. Because the Lutheran church in Germany was a pastors' church and Lutheran pastors were university-educated scholars who had been trained in the study of languages and the liberal arts in Melanchthon's Latin schools (before 1810) or in the *Gymnasium* (after 1810) before they were trained in theology, the training to be a pastor and the training to be a historian were closely related. Thus it is no accident that so many historians and history teachers in Germany were either pastors' sons, or decided to become historians after they had first considered the calling to become a pastor. Like Thomas Nipperdey, I believe not only that rationalization and modernization came through the religious views of men like Luther, but also that "the modernizing potential" of Lutheranism was actualized in "a second phase of Protestantism" since the late eighteenth century.[7]

A third major way the present study is an innovative work is that it proposes a new way of seeing, dating, and naming the formative stage for modern German thought, culture, and education: "The Age of the Cultural Revolution in Germany, 1760–1810." Although this is a useful designation for capturing and teaching the formative stage in the devel-

---

6. BC-T, 345.
7. Nipperdey, "Luther and die modernen Welt," 35.

opment of a distinctly modern type of German culture, education, literature, philosophy, and historical and religious thought, the main emphasis in this study is the significance of Luther and of a Lutheran ethos for Hamann, Herder, and Ranke; and for the rise of a distinctly modern kind of historical consciousness and type of Western historiography. Before their work is explored, however, chapter 3 focuses on "Two Forerunners of the Cultural Revolution in Germany and Modern Historical Thought: Leibniz and Chladenius."

During the five decades from 1760 to 1810, a new type of Western historiography gradually arose in Protestant Germany. As an ideal type or model, modern historiography is professional (a *Beruf*), scientific (a *Wissenschaft*), and based on the concepts of individuality (*Individualität*) and development (*Enwicklung*). The formative stage for this new kind of professional historiography comprised the five decades from 1760 to the founding of the University of Berlin in 1810; the full or mature stage of this new type was from Niebuhr and Ranke to Hintze and Meinecke; and the late stage is the years since 1933, when primacy within this professionalized discipline moved from Germany to the United States and also to France. As the introductory quotations to this conclusion point out, Germany was still regarded as top of the list in the field of historical studies both in 1913 and in 1931. To understand the rise of each of these characteristics of Western historiography during the years from 1760 to 1810, it is helpful to examine the thought and work of two important forerunners of the Cultural Revolution in Germany.

The main connecting link between Luther and Melanchthon, on the one hand, and the great scholars, thinkers, and writers in Germany from 1760 to 1810, on the other, was the writings of Leibniz. First of all, Leibniz created a new *simul*, dynamic, and spiritual way (God's acting in, with, and through soul-like substances called monads) of viewing the universe—a view that haunted the minds of those mainly Protestant and mainly Lutheran *Aufklärers*, or scholars of the German Enlightenment.

Second, Leibniz was most responsible for the creation of the modern German conception of *Wissenschaft* or "science," for in Germany any scholarly pursuit could be called a *Wissenschaft* or science if it proceeded on the basis of a method appropriate to the particular subject. Therefore in Germany it was easier for scholars to regard and treat as a science the Greek, Roman, Christian, or humanist art and branch of rhetoric or literature called history.

During the 1750s German scholars began using the word *Geschichte* instead of *historie*; they began to combine the word *Geschichte* with the term *Wissenschaft*; and they began the process of creating a *Geschichtswissenschaft*, or historical science. It is both interesting and significant that the first sophisticated hermeneutics for history as a *Geschichtswissenschaft* was published in 1752 by a "Doctor of Holy Scripture, Professor of Rhetoric and Poetry, and also Pastor of the University Church of Erlangen" who called himself Chladenius. It is also both interesting and significant that at about the same time, the word *Beruf* came to mean a "profession" rather than a calling.

Chapter 4 presents a picture of "The Cultural Revolution in Germany and the Rise of a New Historical Consciousness, 1760–1810," primarily through an examination of just three great and personally connected scholars whose work was of formative significance for this age: Johann Georg Hamann, Johann Gottfried Herder, and Immanuel Kant. Although Göttingen University was the intellectual center in Germany for the gradual rise of history as a science and a profession during the five decades from 1760 to 1810, Königsberg is a good place to begin the story of this Cultural Revolution. It is a good place not only because it was the city of Hamann and Kant, the great "supplementary antipoles" of this spiritual and intellectual revolution, but also because it was here that Johann Herder received the training that made it possible for him to become the person who most personifies this age as a cultural revolution *and* the rise of historicism during this age.

Hamann's work was, first of all, a counterrevolution against the dominance of the French language, thought, and culture in Germany, to the worship of reason, and to the anti-Christian views of Voltaire. At the same time, however, it was also the beginning of a great spiritual revolution based on a revival of Luther and an influential demonstration of the relevance of Luther's language, thought, and ideas for this age. It is also important that Herder wrote *Yet Another Philosophy of History of the Education of Humanity* (1774), a work that Meinecke regarded as epoch making for the rise of historicism, when Herder was a court pastor in Bückeburg (1771–1776); for this is the time when Herder first became intensely interested in Luther's writings. While both Hamann and Herder were greatly influenced by Luther, his language, and his thought, Kant's philosophy developed partly out of a Lutheran tradition and can be called an "at-the-same-time" philosophy.

The institutional culmination of "The Cultural Revolution in Germany" came in the year 1810 with the founding of the University of Berlin (the first modern and modernizing university) and with the new kind of secondary school known as the *Gymnasium*. This university first became the center for the new type of Western historiography, however, primarily through the work of Leopold von Ranke.

Chapter 5, "From a Holy Hieroglyph to a *Wissenschaft* Alone: History as a Calling and a Profession from Ranke to Hintze" explored the early life of Ranke—the greatest and most influential of all modern historians—and shows how his is the best example in Western literature of a calling becoming a profession and how Luther's writings could inspire a historian to develop an "at-the-same-time" way and an "in-with-and-under" way of thinking that was very helpful for viewing and writing history. As Ranke said when he defended the epoch-making book titled *Histories of the Latin and Germanic Nations*, a work that earned him a teaching position at the University of Berlin, his way or method was "to present the general directly through the particular," and "In and with the event ... to portray its course and spirit and ... to ascertain its characteristic traits."[8] For Ranke, history was both a calling and a profession, both an art and a science. Through his many great histories, through his famous seminar for training professional historians, through the many ways he personified the rise of history as a professionalized *Wissenschaft* or science, and through the work of many of his students and colleagues, the University of Berlin became the most famous center in Germany and the world for training professional historians in the theory and practice of history.

Although Ranke was no longer teaching in the early 1880s when Otto Hintze became a student there, Hintze received the best and broadest training a historian could receive; for he was trained in history, philology, philosophy, law, and economics by a number of great scholars, including Johann Gustav Droysen, Wilhelm Dilthey, and Gustav Schmoller. For Hintze, for his friend Friedrich Meinecke, and for many other historians of their generation, however, Ranke was their great model and master. While Hintze's chief life goal was to supplement "the great lifework of Leopold von Ranke" through a "general comparative constitutional history of the modern world of states, especially the Latin and Germanic nations,"[9] Meinecke became the pioneer historian in the twentieth century

---

8. Ranke, "Erwiderung auf Heinrich Leo's Angriff," 664–65.
9. Hintze, "Antrittsrede in der Preussischen Akademie der Wissenschaften," 564.

among professional historians for a new kind of historical presentation that he called *Geistesgeschichte* and what the English-speaking world calls intellectual history or the history of ideas. Whereas Hintze was always looking for what Ranke called "tendencies of development," Meinecke loved the concept of "individuality" and chose to focus on what Ranke called "ideas" in history.

Through his comparative studies, his ideal types, and his review essays, Hintze supplemented not only Ranke's views concerning the Latin and Germanic nations and his "at-the-same-time" way of viewing and writing history but also the views of his teachers Droysen and Dilthey concerning the nature of history and modern historical thought. This is especially apparent in Hintze's debate with Meinecke and Ernst Troeltsch concerning the nature of historicism.

Although these three friends and great scholars agreed that this distinctly modern kind of historical consciousness was based on the concepts of individuality and development, they defined the term *historicism* in very different ways. One of the ways that Hintze completely secularized, rationalized, and demystified Ranke's religious way of viewing history, was the way he defined historicism. For Hintze, history was only a *Wissenschaft*, or method of inquiry with its own appropriate methodology, and historicism was just another mode of thought, another set of methodological categories.

Another major way that Hintze supplemented the Rankean view of history was in the way he and Max Weber demystified what Ranke called *Das Real-Geistige* and the state as a *real-geistige*, or as an "earthly-spiritual community." Like Weber's, Hintze's work was always concerned with interests and ideas at the same time and with their intricate interdependence. More than Weber, however, Hintze was able to articulate an "at-the-same-time" image that not only captured the way they approached the study of religion and society but also provided future generations with an unsurpassed image to express this relationship, and to augment the powerful Marxist and materialist substructure/superstructure image. In these and other ways, Hintze and Weber rationalized and demystified the Rankean view of history, "bridged the chasm" between the idealist and the positivist traditions, and completely secularized the Protestant religious traditions in which they were raised.

bibliography

Ahlstrom, Sydney E. *A Religious History of the American People*. New Haven: Yale University Press, 1972.

———. "What's Lutheran about Higher Education—A Critique." In *What's Lutheran about Higher Education? Papers and Proceedings of the 60th Annual Convention, Lutheran Educational Conference of North America, Chase-Park Plaza Hotel, St. Louis, Missouri, January 11-12, 1974*, 8-16. Washington DC: Lutheran Educational Conference of North America, 1974.

Alexander, W. M. *Johann Georg Hamann: Philosophy and Faith*. The Hague: Nijhoff, 1966.

Althaus, Paul, *The Theology of Martin Luther*. Translated by Robert C. Schultz. Philadelphia: Fortress, 1966.

Andrews, E. Benjamin. *Outline of the Principles of History*. Boston: Ginn, 1897.

An Universal History, from the Earliest Account of Time. Compiled from Original Authors; and Illustrated with Maps, Cuts, Notes, &c. With a General Index to the Whole. 65 vols. London: Osborne, 1747–1768.

Augustine. *The City of God*. Translated by Marcus Dods, with an introduction by Thomas Merton. Modern Library Giants 74. New York: Modern Library, 1950.

———. *Confessions*. Translated with an introduction by R. S. Pine-Coffin. Penguin Classics. Harmondsworth, UK: Penguin, 1961.

Austin, Norman, editor. *The Greek Historians: Herodotus, Thucydides, Polybius, Plutarch; Introduction and Selected Readings*. New York: Van Nostrand-Reinhold, 1969.

Baethgen, Friedrich. "Zur geistigen Entwicklungsgeschichte Rankes in seiner Frühzeit." In *Deutschland und Europa: Historische Studien zur Völker- und Staatenordnung des Abendlandes*, edited by Werner Conze, 337–53. Düsseldorf: Droste, 1951.

Baillet, Adrien. *La Vie de Monsieur Des-Cartes*. Paris: Horthemels, 1691.

Bainton, Roland. *Here I Stand: A Life of Martin Luther*. Nashville: Abingdon-Cokesbury, 1950.

Baudler, Georg. *Im Worte Sehen: Das Sprachdenken Johann Georg Hamann*. Münchener philosophische Forschungen 2. Bonn: Bouvier, 1970.

Baur, Siegfried. *Versuch über die Historik des jungen Ranke*. Historische Forschungen 62. Berlin: Duncker & Humblot, 1998.

Bayer, Oswald. "Johann Georg Hamann." In *Die Aufklärung*, edited by Martin Greschat, 347–61. Gestalten der Kirchengeschichte 8. Stuttgart: Kohlhammer, 1983.

———. *Martin Luthers Theologie: Eine Vergegenwärtigung*. Tübingen: Mohr/Siebeck, 2003.

———. *Zeitgenosse im Widerspruch: Johann Georg Hamann als radikaler Aufklärer*. Serie Piper 918. Munich: Piper, 1988.

Beiser, Frederick C., editor. *The Cambridge Companion to Hegel*. Cambridge: Cambridge University Press, 1993.

———. *Enlightenment, Revolution, and Romanticism: The Genesis of Modern German Political Thought, 1790-1800*. Cambridge: Harvard University Press, 1992.
———. *The Fate of Reason: German Philosophy from Kant to Fichte*. Cambridge: Harvard University Press, 1987.
———. "Hegel's Historicism." In *The Cambridge Companion to Hegel*, edited by Frederick C. Beiser, 240-99. Cambridge: Cambridge University Press, 1993.
Benario, Herbert W. *An Introduction to Tacitus*. Athens: University of Georgia Press, 1975.
Bendix, Reinhard. "Hintze, Otto." In *The International Encyclopedia of the Social Sciences*, edited by David L. Sills, 6: 366-68. 19 vols. New York: Macmillan, 1968-1991.
———. *Max Weber: An Intellectual Portrait*. New York: Doubleday, 1960.
———. "Weber, Max." In *The International Encyclopedia of the Social Sciences*, edited by David L. Sills, 16: 493-502. 19 vols. New York: Macmillan, 1968-1991.
Benz, Ernst. "Johann Gottfried Herder 1744-1803." In *Die Grossen Deutschen: Deutsche Biographie*, edited by Hermann Heimpel et al., 2:210-28. 5 vols. Gütersloh: Prisma, 1978.
Berlin, Isaiah. "The Magus of the North." *New York Review of Books* 40 (1993) 64-71.
———. *The Magus of the North: J. G. Hamann and the Origins of Modern Irrationalism*. Edited by Henry Hardy. New York: Farrar, Straus and Giroux, 1993.
———. *Vico and Herder: Two Studies in the History of Ideas*. New York: Viking, 1976.
Bernheim, Ernst. *Lehrbuch der historischen Methode und Geschichtsphilosophie*. 4th edition. Leipzig: Duncker & Humblot, 1903.
Beutel, Albrecht. *In dem Anfang war das Wort: Studium zu Luthers Sprachverständnis*. Hermeneutische Unterschungten zur Theologie 27. Tübingen: Mohr/Siebeck, 1991.
Beye, Charles Rowan. *Ancient Greek Literature and Society*. Garden City, NY: Anchor, 1975.
Blanke, Fritz. "Hamann als Theologie." In *Hamann-Studien*, 11-42. Studien zur Dogmengeschichte und systematischen Theologie 10. Zurich: Zwingli, 1956.
———. "Hamann und Luther." In *Hamann-Studien*, 43-68.
Bluhm, Heniz. "Herders Stellung zu Luther." In *Studies in Luther—Luther Studien*, 179-201. Bern: Lang, 1987.
———. *Studies in Luther—Luther Studien*. Bern: Lang, 1987.
Blum, Mark E. "German Historical Thought, 1500 to Present: Philosophical Thought and Writing about History by German-Speaking Authors." In *A Global Encyclopedia of Historical Writing*, edited by D. R. Woolf et al., 1:358-64. 2 vols. New York: Garland, 1998.
Bollacher, Martin, editor. *Johann Gottfried Herder: Geschichte und Kultur*. Würzburg: Königshausen & Neumann, 1994.
Bornkamm, Heinrich. *Luther im Spiegel der deutschen Geistesgeschichte*. 2nd edition. Göttingen: Vandenhoeck & Ruprecht, 1970.
———. *Luther in Mid-Career 1521-1530*. Edited with a foreword by Karin Bornkamm. Translated by E. Theodore Bachmann. Philadelphia: Fortress, 1983.
Bossuet, Jacques-Benigne. *Discourse on Universal History*. Translated by Elborg Forster. Edited and with an introduction by Orest Ranum. Classic European Historians. Chicago: University of Chicago Press, 1976.
Brady, Thomas A. Jr. "Confessionalization: The Career of a Concept." In *Confessionalization in Europe 1555-1700: Essays in Honor and Memory of Bodo Nischan*, edited by John M. Headley et al., 1-20. Aldershot, UK: Ashgate, 2004.

———. *The Protestant Reformation in German History*. Occasional Paper 22. Annual Lecture 1997. Washington, DC: German Historical Institute, 1998.
Brecht, Martin. *Shaping and Defining the Reformation 1521–1532*. Translated by James L Schaaf. Martin Luther 1. Minneapolis: Fortress, 1990.
Breisach, Ernst. *Historiography: Ancient, Medieval & Modern*. Chicago: University of Chicago Press, 1983.
Brown, Peter. *Augustine of Hippo: A Biography*. Berkeley: University of California Press, 1967.
Brunner, Otto. "Feudalism: The History of a Concept." In *Lordship and Community in Medieval Europe*, edited by Frederick L. Cheyette, 32–61. New York: Holt, Rinehart, and Winston, 1968.
Brunner, Otto, et al., editors. *Geschichtliche Grundbegriffe: Historisches Lexikon zur politisch-soziale Sprache in Deutschland*. 8 vols. Stuttgart: Klett, 1972–1997.
Bultmann, Christoph. *Die biblische Urgeschichte in der Aufklärung: Johann Gottfried Herders Interpretation der Genesis als Antwort auf die Religionskritik David Humes*. Beiträige zur historischen Theologie. Tübingen: Mohr/Siebeck, 1999.
Bunge, Marcia J. "Herder's Historical View of Religion and the Study of Religion in the Nineteenth Century and Today." In *Johann Gottfried Herder: Academic Disciplines and the Pursuit of Knowledge*, edited by Wulf Koepke, 232–44. Columbia, SC: Camden, 1996.
———. "Human Language of the Divine: Herder on Ways of Speaking about God." In *Herder Today: Contributions from the International Herder Conference Nov. 5–8, 1987, Stanford, California*, edited by Kurt Mueller-Vollmer, 304–18. Berlin: de Gruyter, 1990.
———. "Introduction." In *Against Pure Reason: Writings on Religion, Language, and History*, by Johann Gottfried Herder, 1–37. Edited and translated by Marcia J. Bunge. Fortress Texts in Modern Theology. Minneapolis: Fortress, 1993.
———. "Johann Gottfried Herder's Auslegung des Neuen Testaments." In *Historische Kritik und biblisher Kanon in der deutschen Aufklärung*, edited by Henning Graf Reventlow et al., 249–62. Wiesbaden: Harassowitz, 1988.
Burkhardt, Frederick H. "Introduction" In *God, Some Conversations*, by Johann Gottfried Herder, 3–64. Translated with a critical introduction and notes by Frederick H. Burkhardt. Indianapolis: Bobbs-Merrill, 1940.
Bury, J. G. "Gibbon, Edward." In *Encyclopaedia Britannica*, 10:330–32. 24 vols. Chicago: Encyclopaedia Britannica, 1954.
Büsch, Otto, and Michael Erbe, editors. *Otto Hintze und die moderne Geschichtswissenschaft: Ein Tagungsbericht*. Einzelveröffentlichungen der historischen Kommission zu Berlin 38. Berlin: Colloquium, 1983.
Butterfield, Herbert. *Man on His Past: The Study of the History of Historical Scholarship*. The Wiles Lectures 1954. London: Cambridge University Press, 1969.
Carr, William. *The Origins of the Wars of German Unification*. Origins of Modern Wars. London: Longman, 1991.
Cary, Philip. *Augustine's Invention of the Inner Self: The Legacy of a Christian Platonist*. Oxford: Oxford University Press, 2000.
Cassirer, Ernst. *Leibniz' System in seinen wissenschaftlichen Grundlagen*. Marburg: Elwert, 1902.
———. *The Philosophy of the Enlightenment*. Translated by Fritz C. A. Koelln and James P. Pettegrove. Humanitas: Toward A New Study of Man. Boston: Beacon, 1955.

Cheyette, Frederick L., editor. *Lordship and Community in Medieval Europe: Selected Readings*. New York: Holt, Rinehart, and Wintson, 1968.

Chickering, Roger. *Karl Lamprecht: A German Academic Life, 1856–1915*. Studies in German Histories. Atlantic Highlands, NJ: Humanities, 1993.

Chladenius, Johann Martin. *Allgemeine Geschichtswissenschaft, worinnen der Grund zu einen neuen Einsicht in allen Arten der Gelahrheit gelegt wird*. Leipzig: Erben, 1752.

———. *Einleitung zur richtigen Auslegung vernünftiger Reden und Schriften*. Düsseldorf: Janssen, 1969.

Cicero. *Cicero on Oratory and Orators*. Translated and edited by J. S. Watson. Landmarks in Rhetoric and Public Address. Carbondale: Southern Illinois University Press, 1970.

Cillien, Ursala. *Johann Gottfried Herder: Christlicher Humanismus*. Ratingen: Henn, 1972.

Clark, William. *Academic Charisma and the Origins of the Research University*. Chicago: University of Chicago Press, 2006.

Cochrane, Charles Norris. *Christianity and Classical Culture: A Study of Thought and Action from Augustus to Augustine*. London: Oxford University Press, 1977.

Cochrane, Eric W. *Historians and Historiography in the Italian Renaissance*. Chicago: University of Chicago Press, 1981.

Cole, John R. *The Olympian Dreams and Youthful Rebellion of René Descartes*. Urbana: University of Illinois Press, 1992.

Collingwood, R. G. *The Idea of History*. London: Oxford University Press, 1970.

Collinson, Patrick. *The Reformation: A History*. Modern Library Chronicles 19. New York: Modern Library, 2004.

Conkin, Paul K., and Roland N. Stromberg. *Heritage and Challenge: The History and Theory of History*. Arlington Heights, IL: Forum, 1989.

Conze, Werner. "Beruf." In *Geschichtliche Grundbegriffe: Historisches Lexikon zur politisch-soziale Sprache in Deutschland*, edited by Otto Brunner et al., 1:490–507. 8 vols. Munich: Klett, 1972–1997.

Cottingham, John. "Introduction." In *The Cambridge Companion to Descartes*, edited by John Cottingham, 1–20. Cambridge: Cambridge University Press, 1992.

Crossen, Frederick J. "Book Five: The Disclosure of Hidden Providence." In *A Reader's Companion to Augustine's "Confessions,"* edited by Kim Paffenroth and Robert P. Kennedy, 71–88. Louisville: Westminster John Knox, 2003

Dann, Otto. "Herder und die Deutsche Bewegung." In *Johann Gottfried Herder 1744–1803*, edited by Gerhard Sauder, 308–40. Studien zum achtzehnten Jahrhundert 9. Hamburg: Meiner, 1987.

———. *Nation und Nationalismus in Deutschland, 1770–1990*. Beck'sche Reihe 494. Munich: Beck, 1993.

Dannenfeldt, Karl H. "The Italian Renaissance." In *The Development of Historiography*, edited by Matthew A. Fitzsimmons et al., 91–103. Harrisburg, PA: Stackpole, 1954.

Dawson Christopher. *The Making of Europe: An Introduction to the History of European Unity*. New York: Sheed and Ward, 1952.

Descartes, René. *Discourse on Method*. Translated with an introduction by Laurence J. Lafleur. 2nd revised edition. Indianapolis: Bobbs-Merill, 1960.

———. *"Discourse on Method" and "Meditations."* Translated with an introduction by Laurence J. Lafleur. The Library of Liberal Arts. Indianapolis: Bobbs-Merrill, 1960.

———. *The Philosophical Writings of Descartes*. Translated by John Cottingham et al. 3 vols. Cambridge: Cambridge University Press, 1984–1991.
Despland, Michel. *Kant on History and Religion with a Translation of Kant's "On the Failure of All Attempted Philosophical Theodicies."* Montreal: McGill-Queen's University Press, 1973.
Dickens, A. G., and John Tonkin. *The Reformation in Historical Thought*. Oxford: Blackwell, 1985.
Dickey, Laurence. "Hegel on Religion and Philosophy." In *The Cambridge Companion to Hegel*, edited by Frederick C. Beiser, 301–47 Cambridge: Cambridge University Press, 1993.
Dilthey, Wilhelm. *Einleitung in die Geisteswissenschaften: Versuch einer Grundlegung für das Studium der Gesellschaft und der Geschichte*. Wilhelm Dilthey Gesammelte Schriften 1. Leipzig: Teubner, 1922.
———. *Introduction to the Human Sciences*. Edited by Rudolf A. Makkreel and Frithjof Rodi. Selected Works, Wilhelm Dilthey 1. Princeton: Princeton University Press, 1989.
Dobbek, Wilhelm. *J. G. Herders Weltbild. Versuch einer Deutung*. Cologne: Böhlau, 1969.
———. *Johann Gottfried Herder*. Weimar: Thüringer, 1950.
Dorn, Max. "Melanchthons Antrittsrede von 1518, ein Bekenntnis und ein Appell zum Fortschritt." In *450 Jahre Martin-Luther-Universität Halle-Wittenberg*, 1:141–48. 3 vols. Halle: Martin-Luther-Universität Halle-Wittenberg, 1952/1953.
Dove, Alfred Wilhelm. "Ranke's Leben im Umriss." In *Ausgewählte Schriftchen, vornehmlich historische Inhalts*, 150–86. Leipzig: Duncker & Humblot, 1888.
Droysen, Johann Gustav. *Historik: Vorlesungen über Enzyklopädie und Methodologie der Geschichte*. Edited by Rudolf Hübner. 8th edition. Munich: Oldenbourg, 1977.
Dryden, John. "The Life of Plutarch." In *Plutarch's Lives: In Five Volumes*, 1: n.p. London: 1716.
Ebeling, Gerhard. *Luther: An Introduction to His Thought*. Translated by R. A. Wilson. Philadelphia: Fortress, 1980.
Eiben, Jürgen. *Von Luther zu Kant: Der deutsche Sonderweg in die Moderne*. Wiesbaden: Deutscher Universitäts, 1989.
Elert, Werner. *The Christian Ethos*. Translated by Carl J. Schindler. Philadelphia: Mühlenberg, 1957.
———. *Morphologie des Luthertums*. 2 vols. Munich: Beck, 1931.
———. *The Structure of Lutheranism*. Translated by Walter A. Hansen. St. Louis: Concordia, 1962.
———. *The Theology and Philosophy of Lutheranism Especially in the Sixteenth and Seventeenth Centuries*. Translated by Walter A. Hansen. St. Louis: Concordia, 1962.
Embach, Michael. *Das Lutherbild Johann Gottfried Herders*. Trierer Studien zur Literatur 14. Frankfurt: Lang, 1987.
Epstein, Catherine. *A Past Renewed: A Catalogue of German-Speaking Refugee Historians in the United States after 1933*. Publications of the German Historical Institute. Cambridge: Cambridge University Press, 1993.
Erikson, Erik H. *Young Man Luther: A Study in Psychoanalysis and History*. Austen Riggs Monograph 4. New York: Norton, 1958.

Bibliography

Ermarth, Michael. "Hermeneutics and History: The Fork in Hermes' Path through the 18th Century." In *Aufklärung und Geschichte: Studien zur deutschen Geschichtswissenschaft im 18. Jahrhundert*, edited by Hans Erich Bödeker et al., 193–221. Veröffentlichungen des Max-Planck-Instituts für Geschichte 81 Göttingen: Vandenhoeck & Ruprecht, 1986.

Ferguson, Wallace K. *The Renaissance in Historical Thought: Five Centuries of Interpretation.* Boston: Houghton Mifflin, 1948.

Findlay, J. N. "Foreword" In *Phenomonology of Spirit*, by G. F. W. Hegel, v–xxx. Translated by A. V. Miller. Oxford: Oxford University Press, 1977.

Fisch, Jörg. "Zivilisation, Kultur." In *Geschichtliche Grundbegriffe: Historisches Lexikon zur politisch-soziale Sprache in Deutschland*, edited by Otto Brunner et al., 7:679–774. 8 vols. Stuttgart: Klett, 1972–1997.

Fischer, J. D. C. *Christian Initiation, The Reformation Period; Some Early Reformed Rites of Baptism and Confirmation and Other Contemporary Documents.* Alcuin Club Collections 51. London: SPCK, 1970.

Förster, Wolfgang. "Johann Gottfried Herder: Weltgeschichte und Humanität," In *Aufklärung und Geschichte: Studien zur deutschen Geschichtswissenschaft im 18. Jahrhundert*, edited by Hans Erich Bödeker et al., 363–87. Veröffentlichungen des Max-Planck-Instituts für Geschichte 81. Göttingen: Vandenhoeck & Ruprecht, 1986.

Fouke, Daniel C. "Metaphysics and the Eucharist in the Early Leibniz." *Studia Leibnitiana* 24 (1992) 145–59.

Friedrich, Christoph. *Sprache und Geschichte: Untersuchungen zur Hermeneutik von Johann Martin Chladenius.* Studien zur Wissenschaftstheorie 13. Meisenheim: Hain, 1978.

Fuchs, Walther Peter. "Einleitung" to Leopold von Ranke. In *Das Briefwerk*, edited by Walther Peter Fuchs xvi–lvi. Hamburg: Hoffmann and Campe, 1949.

———. "Vorwort." In *Frühe Schriften*, by Leopold von Ranke. Edited by Walther Peter Fuchs, 9–11. Aus Werk und Nachlass 3. Munich: Oldenbourg, 1973.

Fueter, Eduard. *Geschichte der neueren Historiographie.* 3rd edition. Munich: Oldenbourg, 1936.

Gajek, Bernhard, editor. *Johann Georg Hamann: Acta des Internationalen Hamann-Colloquiums in Lüneburg 1976.* Frankfurt: Klostermann, 1979.

Gay, Peter. *The Rise of Modern Paganism.* The Enlightenment: An Interpretation 1. New York: Knopf, 1966.

Gebhardt, Jürgen, editor. *Die Revolution des Geistes; Politisches Denken in Deutschland 1770–1830: Goethe, Kant, Fichte, Hegel, Humboldt.* List Hochschulreihe 1503. Geschichte des politischen Denkens. Munich: List, 1968.

———. "Zur Physiognomie einer Epoche." In *Die Revolution des Geistes; Politisches Denken in Deutschland 1770–1830: Goethe, Kant, Fichte, Hegel, Humboldt*, 7–16. List Hochschulreihe 1503. Geschichte des politischen Denkens. Munich: List, 1968.

"Geist." In *Historisches Wörterbuch der Philosophie* 3 G–H: 154–204. 13 vols. Edited by Joachim Ritter et al. Basel: Schwabe, 1971–2007.

Gellner, Ernst. *Encounters with Nationalism.* Oxford: Blackwell, 1994.

Gerhard, Dietrich. "Development and Structure of Continental European and American Universities—A Comparison." In *Gesammelte Aufsätze*, 154–74. Göttingen: Vandenhoeck & Ruprecht, 1977.

———. *Old Europe: A Study of Continuity, 1000–1800*. Studies in Social Discontinuity. New York: Academic, 1981.

———. "Otto Hintze: Persönlichkeit und Werk." In *Otto Hintze und die moderne Geschichtswissenschaft: Ein Tagungsbericht*, edited by Otto Büsch and Michael Erbe, 3–18. Einzelveröffentlichungen der historischen Kommission zu Berlin 38. Berlin: Colloquium, 1983.

———. "Otto Hintze: His Work and Significance in Historiography." *Central European History* 3 (1970) 17–48.

———. "Periodization in European History." *American Historical Review* 61 (1956) 900–913.

Gierke, Otto Friedrich von. *Das deutsche Genossenschaftsrecht*. 4 vols. Graz: Akademische Druck, 1954.

Gilbert, Felix. "European and American Historiography." In *History: The Development of Historical Studies*, by John Higham; with Leonard Krieger and Felix Gilbert, 315–87. Englewood Cliffs, NJ: Prentice Hall, 1965.

———. "German Historiography during the Second World War: A Bibliographical Survey." *AHR* 53 (1947) 50–58.

———, editor. *The Historical Essays of Otto Hintze*. With an introduction by Felix Gilbert, with the assistance of Robert M. Berdahl. New York: Oxford University Press, 1975.

———. *History: Politics or Culture? Reflections on Ranke and Burckhardt*. Princeton: Princeton University Press, 1990.

———. *Machiavelli and Guicciardini: Politics and History in Sixteenth-Century Florence*. Princeton: Princeton University Press, 1965.

———. "Machiavelli's *Istorie Fiorentine*: An Essay in Interpretation." In *History: Choice and Commitment*, 135–53. Cambridge, MA: Belknap, 1977.

———. *Johann Gustav Droysen und die Preussisch-Deutche Frage*. Historischen Zeitschrift 20. Munich: Oldenbourg, 1931.

———. "Otto Hintze und die moderne Geschichtswissenschaft." In *Otto Hintze und die moderne Geschichtswissenschaft: Ein Tagungsbericht*, edited by Otto Büsch and Michael Erbe, 195–208. Einzelveröffentlichungen der historischen Kommission zu Berlin 38. Berlin: Colloquium, 1983.

Gilbert, W. Kent, editor, with the Joint Lutheran Commission on the Theology and Practice of Confirmation. *Confirmation and Education*. Yearbooks in Christian Education 1. Philadelphia: Fortress, 1969.

Goethe, Johann Wolfgang von. *Autobiographische Schriften*. Vol. 1, *Aus meinem Leben: Dichtung und Warhrheit*. 6th edition. Goethe Werke 9. Hamburg: Wegner, 1967.

Gooch, G. P. "German Historical Studies Since the War." In *Studies in Modern History*, 268–88. Freeport, NY: Books for Libraries Press, 1931

———. *History and Historians in the Nineteenth Century*. 1913. Revised with a new introduction. Boston: Beacon, 1958.

Green, William M. *Augustine on the Teaching of History*. University of California Publications in Classical Philology 12.18. Berkeley: University of California Press, 1944.

Greschat, Martin, editor. *Die Aufklärung*. Gestalten der Kirchengeschichte 8. Stuttgart: Kohlhammer, 1983.

Greiffenhagen, Martin, editor. *Das evangelische Pfarrhaus: Eine Kultur- und Sozialgeschichte*. Stuttgart: Kreuz, 1984.

Gritsch, Eric W. *A History of Lutheranism*. Minneapolis: Fortress, 2002.

———. "Luther on Humor." *Lutheran Quarterly* 18 (2004) 373–86.
———. *Martin, God's Court Jester: Luther in Retrospect*. Ramsey, NJ: Sigler, 1990.
Gründer, Karlfried. *Die Hamann-Forschung: Geschichte der Deutungen*. Hamanns Hauptschriften erklärt 1. Gütersloh: Bertelsmann, 1956.
Gutek, Gerald L. *A History of Western Educational Experience*. New York: Random House, 1972.
Gwynn, Aubrey. *Roman Education from Cicero to Quintilian*. New York: Teachers College Press, 1926.
Haile, H. G. *Luther: An Experiment in Biography*. Garden City, NY: Doubleday, 1980.
Hamann, Johann Georg. *Briefwechsel*. Edited by Walther Ziesemer and Arthur Henkel. 7 vols. Wiesbaden: Insel, 1955–1979.
———. *Sämtliche Werke*. Edited by Joseph Nadler. 6 vols. Historical-Critical Edition. Vienna: Herder, 1949–1957.
Hansen, Reimer. "Die wissenschaftsgeschichtlichen Zusammenhänge der Entstehung und der Anfänge der modernen Geschichtswissenschaft." In *Geschichtswissenschaft in Berlin im 19. und 20. Jahrhundert*, edited by Reimer Hansen and Wolfgang Ribbe. Veröffentlichungen der Historischen Kommission zu Berlin 82. Berlin: de Gruyter, 1992.
Hansen, Reimer, and Wolfgang Ribbe, editors. *Geschichtswissenschaft in Berlin im 19. und 20. Jahrhundert*. Veröffentlichungen der Historischen Kommission zu Berlin 82. Berlin: de Gruyter, 1992.
Hartle, Ann. *The Modern Self in Rousseau's "Confessions": A Reply to St. Augustine*. Revisions 4. Notre Dame: University of Notre Dame Press, 1983.
Hartung, Fritz. "Otto Hintze." In *Staatsbildende Kräfte der Neuzeit: Gesammelte Aufsätze*, 497–520. Berlin: Duncker & Humblot, 1961.
Harris, H. S. "Hegel's Intellectual Development to 1807." In *The Cambridge Companion to Hegel*, 25–51. Cambridge: Cambridge University Press, 1993.
Haskins, Charles Homer. *The Renaissance of the Twelfth Century*. New York: Meridian, 1968.
Haym, Rudolf. *Herder nach seinem Leben und seinen Werken*. 2 vols. Berlin: Weidmannsche, 1880.
Hazard, Paul. *The European Mind, 1680–1715*. Translated by J. Lewis May. Cleveland: World, 1969.
Headley, John M. *Luther's View of Church History*. Yale Publications in Religion 6. New Haven, CT: Yale University Press, 1963.
Hegel, G. F. W. *Phenomenology of Spirit*. Translated by A. V. Miller. Oxford: Oxford University Press, 1977.
Heimpel, Hermann, et al., editors. *Die Grossen Deutschen: Deutsche Biographie*. 5 vols. Gütersloh: Prisma, 1978.
Hempelmann, Heinzpeter. *"Gott ein Schriftsteller!" Johann Georg Hamann über die End-Äusserung Gottes ins Wort der Heiligen Schrift und ihre hermeneutischen Konsequenzen*. Monographien und Studienbücher. Wuppertal: Brockhaus, 1988.
Henz, Günter Johannes. *Leopold Ranke: Leben, Denken, Wort, 1795–1814*. Cologne: 1968.
Herder, Johann Gottfried. *On World History: An Anthology*. Edited by Hans Adler and Ernest A. Menze. Translated by Ernest A. Menze with Michael Palma. Sources and Studies in World History. Armonk, NY: Sharpe, 1997.

———. *Reflections on the Philosophy of the History of Mankind*. Abridged with an introduction by Frank E. Manuel. Classic European Historians. Chicago: University of Chicago Press, 1968.

———. *Sämmtliche Werke*. Edited by Bernhard Suphan. 33 vols. Berlin, Weidmann, 1877–1913.

———. *Werke in zehn Bänden*. Vol. 1, *Frühe Schriften, 1764–1772*. Edited by Martin Bollacher et al. Bibliothek deutscher Klassiker 1. Frankfurt: Deutscher Klassiker, 1985.

Herodotus. *The History of Herodotus*. Translated by George Rawlinson. Edited by Manuel Komroff. New York: Tudor, 1946.

Hexter, J. H. *More's "Utopia": The Biography of an Idea*. New York: Harper & Row, 1965.

Hildebrandt, Kurt. *Leibniz und das Reich der Gnade*. The Hague: Nijhoff, 1953.

Hillerbrand, Hans. J. *Men and Ideas in the Sixteenth Century*. 1969; Prospect Heights, IL: Waveland, 1984.

Hinrichs, Carl. "Leopold von Ranke." In *Die Grossen Deutschen: Deutsche Biographie*, edited by Hermann Heimpel et al., 3:293–312. 5 vols. Berlin: Propyläen, 1956.

———. "Rankes Lutherfragment von 1817 und der Ursprung seiner Universalhistorischen Anschauung." In *Festschrift für Gerhard Ritter zu seinem 60. Geburtstag*, edited by Richard Nürnberger, 299–321. Tübingen: Mohr/Siebeck, 1950.

———. *Ranke und die Geschichtstheologie der Goethezeit*. Göttinger Bausteine zur Geschichtswissenschaft 19. Göttingen: Musterschmidt, 1954.

Hintze, Otto. *Allgemeine Verfassungs—und Verwaltungsgeschichte der neueren Staaten: Fragmente*. Edited by Guiseppe Di Constanzo et al. Palomar Athenaeum 17. Bari: Palomar, 1998.

———. "Antrittsrede in der Preussischen Akademie der Wissenschaften." In *Staat und Verfassung*, 563–66.

———. "Der Beamtenstand." In *Soziologie und Geschichte; Gesammelte Abhandlungen zur Soziologie, Politik und Theorie der Geschichte*, 66–125.

———. "Calvinism and Raison d'Etat in Early Seventeenth-Century Brandenburg." In *The Historical Essays of Otto Hintze*, 86–154.

———. "The Commissary and His Significance in General Administrative History: A Comparative Study." In *The Historical Essays of Otto Hintze*, 269–301.

———. "Economics and Politics in the Age of Modern Capitalism." In *The Historical Essays of Otto Hintze*, 422–52.

———. *Einleitende Darstellung der Behördenorganisation und allgemeinen Verwaltung in Preussen beim Regierungsantritt Friedrichs II*. Acta Borussica: Denkmaler der Preussischen Staatsverwaltung im 18. Jahrhundert Behördenorganisation und allgemeine Staatsverwaltung 6:1. Berlin: Parey, 1901.

———. "Die Epochen des evangelischen Kirchenregiments in Preussen." In *Regierung und Verwaltung*, 56–96.

———. "The Formation of States and Constitutional Development: A Study in History and Politics." In *The Historical Essays of Otto Hintze*, 157–77.

———. *Gesammelte Abhandlungen*. Edited by Fritz Hartung. 3 vols. Leipzig: Koehler & Amelang, 1941–1943.

———. *Die Hohenzollern und ihr Werk: Fünfhundert Jahre vaterländischer Geschichte*. 5th edition. Berlin: Parey, 1915.

———. "The Individual and the Collective Approach to History." In *The Historical Essays of Otto Hintze*, 357–67.

———. "Johann Gustav Droysen." In *Soziologie und Geschichte: Gesammelte Abhandlungen zur Soziologie, Politik und Theorie der Geschichte*, 453–99.

———. "Kalvinismus und Staatsräson in Brandenburg zu Beginn des 17. Jahrhundert." In *Regierung und Verwaltung*, 255–312.

———. "Kelsen's Staatslehre." In *Soziologie und Geschichte: Gesammelte Abhandlungen zur Soziologie, Politik und Theorie der Geschichte*, 223–38.

———. "Max Weber, ein Lebensbild." In *Soziologie und Geschichte; Gesammelte Abhandlungen zur Soziologie, Politik und Theorie der Geschichte*, 148–54.

———. "Max Webers Religionssoziologie." In *Soziologie und Geschichte: Gesammelte Abhandlungen zur Soziologie, Politik und Theorie der Geschicthe*, 126–34.

———. "Max Webers Soziologie." In *Soziologie und Geschichte: Gesammelte Abhandlungen zur Soziologie, Politik und Theorie der Geschicthe*, 135–47.

———. "Military Organization and the Organization of the State." In *The Historical Essays of Otto Hintze*, 178–215.

———. "Der moderne Kapitalismus als historische Individuum. Ein kritischer Bericht über Sombarts Werk." In *Soziologie und Geschichte: Gesammelte Abhandlungen zur Soziologie, Politik und Theorie der Geschicthe*, 374–426.

———. "The Nature of Feudalism." In *Lordship and Community in Medieval Europe: Selected Readings*, edited by Fredrick L. Cheyette, 22–31. New York: Holt, Rinehart, and Winston, 1968.

———. "Preconditions of Representative Government in the Context of World History." In *The Historical Essays of Otto Hintze*, edited with an introduction by Felix Gilbert, with the assistance of Robert M. Berdahl, 302–53. New York: Oxford University Press, 1975.

———. *Die preussische Seidenindustrie im 18. Jahrhundert und ihre Begründung durch Friedrich den Grossen*. 3 vols. Acta Borussica. Seidenindustrie: Berlin, 1892.

———. Review of *Einleitende Darstellung der Behördenorganisation und allgemeinen Verwaltung in Preussen beim Regierungsantritt Friedrichs II*. Acta Borussica: Denkmaler der Preussischen Staatsverwaltung im 18. Jahrhundert Behördenorganisation und allgemeine Staatsverwaltung 6: vols. 1–2. In *Forschungen zur brandenburgischen und preussicschen Geschichte* 15 (1902) 271–72.

———. Review of *Die Probleme der Geschichtsphilosophie: Eine erkenntnistheoretische Studie* (2nd edition, 1905) by Georg Simmel. *Schmollers Jahrbuch* 30 (1906) 809–14.

———. "Roschers politische Entwicklungstheorie." In *Soziologie und Geschichte: Gesammelte Abhandlungen zur Soziologie, Politik und Theorie der Geschicthe*, 1–45.

———. *Regierung und Verwaltung: Gesammelte Abhandlungen zur Staats-, Rechts- und Sozialgeschichte Preussens*. Edited by Gerhard Oestreich. 2nd edition. Gesammelte Abhandlungen 3. Göttingen: Vandenhoeck & Ruprecht, 1967.

———. *Soziologie und Geschichte: Gesammelte Abhandlungen zur Soziologie, Politik und Theorie der Geschicthe*. Edited by Gerhard Oestreich. 2nd edition. Gesammelte Abhandlungen 2. Göttingen: Vandenhoeck & Ruprecht, 1964.

———. "Soziologische und geschichtliche Staatsauffassung: Zu Franz Oppenheimers System der Soziologie." In *Soziologie und Geschichte: Gesammelte Abhandlungen zur Soziologie, Politik und Theorie der Geschicthe*, 239–305.

———. *Staat und Verfassung: Gesammelte Abhandlungen zur allgemeinen Verfassungsgeschichte*. Edited by Gerhard Oestreich. 3rd edition. Gesammelte Abhandlungen 1. Göttingen: Vandenhoeck & Ruprecht, 1970.

———. "Staatenbildung und Verfassungsentwicklung." In *Staat und Verfassung*, 34–51.

———. "Staatsverfassung und Heeresverfassung." In *Staat und Verfassung*, 52–85.
———. "Troeltsch and the Problems of Historicism: Critical Studies." In *The Historical Essays of Otto Hintze*, 368–421.
———. "Troeltsch und die Probleme des Historismus." In *Soziologie und Geschichte: Gesammelte Abhandlungen zur Soziologie, Politik und Theorie der Geschicthe*, 323–73. 2nd edition. Gesammelte Abhhandlungen 2. Göttingen: Vandenhoeck & Ruprecht, 1964.
———. "Typologie der ständischen Verfassungen des Abenlandes." In *Staat und Verfassung*, 120–39.
———. "Über individualistische und kollectische Geschichtsauffassung." In *Soziologie und Geschichte: Gesammelte Abhandlungen zur Soziologie, Politik und Theorie der Geschicthe*, 315–22.
———. "Weltgeschichtliche Bedingungen der Repräsentativverfassung." In *Staat und Verfassung*, 140–85.
———. "Wesen und Verbreitung des Feudalismus." In *Staat und Verfassung*, 84–119.
———. "Wesen und Wandlung des modernen Staats." In *Staat und Verfassung*, 470–96.
———. "Wirtschaft und Politik im Zeitalter des modernen Kapitalismus." In *Soziologie und Geschichte: Gesammelte Abhandlungen zur Soziologie, Politik und Theorie der Geschicthe*, 427–52.
Hintze, Otto, and Hedwig Hintze. *"Verzage nicht und lass nicht ab zu kämpfen . . .": Otto Hintze und Hedwig Hintze; Die Korrespondenz 1925–1940*. Edited by Robert Jütte and Gerhard Hirschfeld. Schriften der Bibliothek für Zeitgeschichte 17. Essen: Klartext, 2004.
Hintze, Otto, and Gustav Schmoller, editors. *Akten vom 31. Mai 1740 bis Ende 1745*. Acta Borussica: Denkmaler der Preussischen Staatsverwaltung im 18. Jahrhundert Behördenorganisation und allgemeine Staatsverwaltung 6: vol. 2. Berlin: Parey.
Hintzenstern, Herbert von. "Johann Gustav Herder." In *Die Aufklärung*, edited by Martin Greschat, 363–81. Gestalten der Kirchengeschichte 8. Stuttgart: Kohlhammer, 1983.
Holborn, Hajo. *A History of Modern Germany, 1648–1840*. New York: Knopf, 1968.
———. *A History of Modern Germany, The Reformation*. New York: Knopf, 1959.
Holl, Karl. *The Cultural Significance of the Reformation*, with an introduction by Wilhelm Pauck. Translated by Karl and Barbara Hertz. Cleveland: World, 1959.
———. "Die Geschichte des Wortes Beruf." In *Der Westen*, 189–219. Gesammelte Aufsätze zur Kirchengeschichte 3. Darmstadt: Wissenschaftliche Buchgesellschaft, 1965.
Holy Bible. New Revised Standard Version. New York: Oxford University Press, 1989.
Hornig, Gottfried. "Hermeneutik und Bibelkritik bei Johann Salamo Semler." In *Historische Kritik und biblischer Kanon in der deutschen Aufklärung*, edited by Henning Graf Reventlow et al., 219–36. Wolfenbütteler Forschungen 41. Wiesbaden: Harrassowitz, 1988.
Horst, Walter Blanke, and Dirk Fleischer, editors. *Theoretiker der deutschen Aufklärungshistorie*. Vol. 2, *Elemente der Aufklärungshistorik*. Stuttgart: Frommann-Holzboog, 1990.
Howard, Thomas A. *Protestant Theology and the Making of the Modern German University*. Oxford: Oxford University Press, 2006.
———. *Religion and the Rise of Historicism: W. M. L de Wette, Jacob Burckhardt, and the Theological Origins of Nineteenth-Century Historical Consciousness*. Cambridge: Cambridge University Press, 2000.

Hughes, H. Stewart. *Consciousness and Society: The Reorientation of European Thought, 1890–1930*. New York: Vintage, 1961.

———. *The Sea Change: The Migration of Social Thought, 1930–1965*. New York: Harper and Row, 1975

Iggers, Georg G. *Historiography in the Twentieth Century: From Scientific Objectivity to the Postmodern Challenge*. Hanover, NH: Wesleyan University Press, 1997.

Israel, Jonathan I. *Radical Enlightenment: Philosophy and the Making of Modernity, 1650–1750*. New York: Oxford University Press, 2001.

Janz, Denis. *Three Reformation Catechisms: Catholic, Anabaptist, Lutheran*. Texts and Studies in Religion 13. New York: Mellen, 1982.

Jarausch, Konrad H. "The Institutionalization of History in 18th-Century Germany." In *Aufklärung und Geschichte: Studien zur deutschen Geschichtswissenschaft im 18. Jahrhundert*, edited by Hans Erich Bödeker et al., 25–49. Veröffentlichungen des Max-Planck-Instituts für Geschichte 81. Göttingen: Vandenhoeck & Ruprecht, 1986.

Kaiser, Gerhard. "Pietismus und Geschichte." In *Pietismus und Patriotismus im literarischen Deutschland: Eine Beitrag zum Problem der Säkularisation*, 160–79. 2nd edition. Wissenschaftliche Paperbacks. Literaturwissenschaft. Frankfurt: Athenäum, 1973.

———. *Pietismus und Patriotismus im literarischen Deutschland: Eine Beitrag zum Problem der Säkularisation*. 2nd edition. Wissenschaftliche Paperbacks. Literaturwissenschaft. Frankfurt: Athenäum, 1973.

Kant, Immanuel. *Immanuel Kant's "Critique of Pure Reason."* Translated by Norman Kemp Smith. London: Macmillan, 1929. Reprinted 1961.

———. *Kritik der praktischen Vernunft*. Edited by Benzion Kellermann. Immanuel Kants Werke 5. Berlin: Cassirer, 1914.

———. *Prolegomena to Any Future Metaphysics*. Edited by Lewis White Beck. The Library of Liberal Arts 27. Indianapolis: Bobbs-Merrill, 1950.

Kelley, Donald R. *Faces of History: Historical Inquiry from Herodotus to Herder*. New Haven, CT: Yale University Press, 1998.

———. *Fortunes of History: Historical Inquiry from Herder to Huizinga*. New Haven, CT: Yale University Press, 2003.

———. "Mythistory in the Age of Ranke." In *Leopold von Ranke and the Shaping of the Historical Discipline*, edited by Georg G. Iggers and James M. Powell, 3–20. Syracuse, NY: Syracuse University Press, 1990.

———. *Renaissance Humanism*. Twayne's Studies in Intellectual and Cultural History 2. Boston: Twayne, 1991.

———, editor. *Versions of History from Antiquity to the Enlightenment*. New Haven, CT: Yale University Press, 1991.

Kittelson, James L. *Luther the Reformer: The Story of the Man and His Career*. Minneapolis: Augsburg, 1986.

Klempt, Adalbert. *Die Säkularisierung der universalhistorischen Auffassung: Zum Wandel des Geschichtsdenkens im 16. und 17. Jahrhundert*. Göttinger Bausteine zur Geschichtswissenschaft 31. Göttingen: Musterschmidt, 1960.

Klos, Frank W. *Confirmation and First Communion: A Study Book*. Minneapolis: Augsburg, 1968.

Knoll, Renate. "Herder als Promotor Hamanns: Zu Herders früher Literaturkritik." In *Herder Today: Contributions from the International Herder Conference Nov. 5-8, 1987, Stanford, California*, edited by Kurt Mueller-Vollmer, 207-27. Berlin: de Gruyter, 1990.

Kocka, Jürgen. "Otto Hintze and Max Weber: Attempts at a Comparison." In *Max Weber and His Contemporaries*, edited by Wolfgang J. Mommsen and Jürgen Osterhammel, 284-95. London: Allen & Unwin, 1987.

———. "Otto Hintze, Max Weber, und das Problem der Bürokratie." In *Otto Hintze und die moderne Geschichtswissenschaft: Ein Tagungsbericht*, edited by Otto Büsch and Michael Erbe, 150-88. Einzelveröffentlichungen der historischen Kommission zu Berlin 38. Berlin: Colloquium, 1983. Also in *Historische Zeitschrift* 231 (1981) 65-105.

Kolb, Robert, and Timothy J. Wengert, editors. Translated by Charles Arand et al. *The Book of Concord: The Confessions of the Evangelical Lutheran Church*. Minneapolis: Fortress, 2000.

König, Helmut. *Geist und Revolution: Studien zu Kant, Hegel und Marx*. Geschichte und Theorie der Politik. Unterreihe B, Theorie 6. Stuttgart: Klett-Cotta, 1981.

Koselleck, Reinhart. "Geschichte V. Die Herausbildung des modernen Geschichtsbegriffs." In *Geschichtliche Grundbegriffe: Historisches Lexikon zur politisch-soziale Sprache in Deutschland*, edited by Otto Brunner et al., 2:647-91. 8 vols. Stuttgart: Klett, 1972-1997.

Kraminick, Isaac. "Introduction." In *The Portable Enlightenment Reader*, ix-xxiv. The Portable Library. New York: Penguin, 1995.

———, editor. *The Portable Enlightenment Reader*. The Portable Library. New York: Penguin, 1995.

Krieger, Leonard. "The Philosophical Bases of German Historicism." In *Aufklärung und Geschichte: Studien zur deutschen Geschichtswissenschaft im 18. Jahrhundert*, edited by Hans Erich Bödeker et al., 246-63. Veröffentlichungen des Max-Planck-Instituts für Geschichte 81. Göttingen: Vandenhoeck & Ruprecht, 1986.

———. *Ranke: The Meaning of History*. Chicago: University of Chicago Press, 1977.

Kupisch, Karl. *Die Hieroglyphe Gottes: Grosse Historiker der bürgerlichen Epoche von Ranke bis Meinecke*. Munich: Kaiser, 1967.

Lacroix, Benoit. "Early Medieval Historiography." In *The Development of Historiography*, edited by Matthew A. Fitzsimmons et al., 15-25. Harrisburg, PA: Stackpole, 1954.

Lafleur, Laurence. "Introduction: Descartes' Place In History." In *"Discourse on Method" and "Meditations"* by René Descartes. Translated with an introduction by Laurence J. Lafleur. The Library of Liberal Arts. Indianapolis: Bobbs-Merrill, 1960.

La Vopa, Anthony J. *Grace, Talent, and Merit: Poor Students, Clerical Careers, and Professional Ideology in Eighteenth-Century Germany*. Cambridge: Cambridge University Press, 1988.

Lazareth, William H. "Introduction to the Christian in Society." In *The Christian in Society I*, edited by Helmut T. Lehmann, xi-xvi. Luther's Works 44. Philadelphia: Fortress, 1966.

Lehmann, Hartmut. "Pietism and Nationalism: The Relationship between Protestant Revivalism and National Renewal in Nineteenth-Century Germany." In *Religion und Religiosität in der Neuzeit: Historische Beitrage*, edited by Hartmut Lehmann et al., 233-47. Göttingen: Vandenhoeck & Ruprecht, 1996.

Lehmann, Hartmut, and Guenther Roth, editors. *Weber's "Protestant Ethic": Origins, Evidence, Contexts*. Publication of the German Historical Institute. Washington, DC. Cambridge: Cambridge University Press, 1995.

Leibniz, G. W. *Discourse on Metaphysics and Other Essays*. Edited and translated by Daniel Garber and Roger Ariew. Indianapolis: Hackett, 1991.

———. *New Essays on Human Understanding*. Translated and edited by Peter Remnant and Jonathan Bennett. Cambridge: Cambridge University Press, 1981.

———. *Philosophical Essays*. Edited and translated by Roger Ariew and Daniel Garber. Indianapolis: Hackett, 1989.

———. "Principles of Nature and Grace, Based on Reason." In *Philosophical Essays*, edited and translated by Roger Ariew and Daniel Garber, 206–13. Indianapolis: Hackett, 1989.

———. *Vernunftprinzipien der Natur und der Gnade, Monadologie: Französich-Deutsch*. Hamburg: Meiner, 1956.

Lewis, Thomas T. "Biography." In *A Global Encyclopedia of Historical Writing*, edited by D. R. Woolf et al., 1:90–92. 2 vols. New York: Garland, 1998.

Liebel-Weckowicz, Helen. "Herder, J. G." In *Encyclopedia of Historians and Historical Writing*, edited by Kelly Boyd, 1:527–28. 2 vols. London: Fitzroy Dearborn, 1999.

Lindberg, Luther. "Lutheran Confirmation Ministry in Historical Perspective." In *Confirmation: Engaging Lutheran Foundations and Practices*, by Robert L. Conrad et al., 41–84. Minneapolis: Fortress, 1999.

Livingston, James C. *Modern Christian Thought from the Enlightenment to Vatican II*. New York: Macmillan, 1971.

Loewenich, Walther von. *Die Eigenart von Luthers Auslegung des Johannes-프rologes*. Sitzungsberichte der bayerischen Akademie der Wissenschaften. Philosophisch-Historische Klasse. Munich: Heft, 1960.

Lohse, Bernhard. *Martin Luther: An Introduction to His Life and Work*. Translated by Robert C. Schultz. Philadelphia: Fortress, 1986.

———. *Martin Luther's Theology: Its Historical and Systematic Development*. Translated and edited by Roy A. Harrisville. Minneapolis: Fortress, 1999.

Lønning, Inge. *"Kanon im Kanon": Zum dogmatischen Grundlagenproblem des neutestamentlichen Kanons*. Forschungen zur Geschichte und Lehre des Protestantismus. 10 Reihe: 43. Oslo: Oslo Universitets Forlaget, 1972.

Löwenbrück, Anna-Ruth. "Johann David Michaelis' Verdienst und die philologisch-historische Bibelkritik." In *Historische Kritik und biblischer Kanon in der deutschen Aufklärung*, edited by Henning Graf Reventlow et al., 157–70. Wolfenbütteler Forschungen 41. Wiesbaden: Harrassowitz, 1988.

Lull, Timothy F., editor. *Martin Luther's Basic Theological Writings*. Minneapolis: Fortress, 1989.

Luther, Martin. "Enchiridion, The Small Catechism of Dr. Martin Luther for Ordinary Pastors and Preachers." In *The Book of Concord: The Confessions of the Evangelical Lutheran Church*, translated and edited by Theodore G. Tappert, in collaboration with Jaroslav Pelikan et al., 337–56. Philadelphia: Mühlenburg, 1959.

———. *Luthers Werke: Kritische Gesamtausgabe, Briefwechsel*. 18 vols. Weimar: Böhlau, 1930–1985.

———. *Luthers Werke: Kritische Gesamtausgabe [Schriften]*. 65 vols. Weimar: Böhlau, 1883–1993.

———. *Luther's Works*. American edition. Vols. 1–30, edited by Jaroslav Pelikan. St. Louis: Concordia, 1955–1967. Vols. 31–55, edited by Helmut T. Lehmann. Philadelphia: Fortress, 1955–1986.

———. "Preface to the New Testament (1522, revised 1546)." In *Martin Luther's Basic Theological Writings*, edited by Timothy F. Lull, 116–17. Minneapolis: Fortress, 1989.

———. *Works of Martin Luther, with Introductions and Notes*. Edited by Adolph Spaeth and Henry Jacob Eyster. 6 vols. Philadelphia: Holman, 1915–1932.

Mali, Joseph. *Mythistory: The Making of Modern Historiography*. Chicago: University of Chicago Press, 2003.

Mannheim, Karl. *Essays on the Sociology of Knowledge*. Edited by Paul Kecskemeti. The International Library of Sociology and Social Reconstruction. London: Routledge & Kegan Paul, 1952.

———. "Historismus." *Archiv für Sozialwissenschaft und Sozialpolitik* 52 (1924) 1–60.

Manuel, Frank E. "Editor's Introduction." In *Reflections on the Philosophy of the History of Mankind* by Johann Gottfried Herder, abridged with an introduction by Frank E. Manuel, ix–xxv. Classic European Historians. Chicago: University of Chicago Press, 1968.

Maritain, Jacques. *The Dream of Descartes Together with Some Other Essays*. Translated by Mabelle L. Andison. New York: Philosophical Library, 1944.

Marius, Richard. *Martin Luther: The Christian between God and Death*. Cambridge, MA: Belknap, 1999.

Markus, R. A. *Saeculum: History and Society in the Theology of St. Augustine*. Cambridge: Cambridge University Press, 1970.

Marty, Martin E. "*Simul*: A Lutheran Reclamation Project in the Humanities." *The Cresset* 45 (1981) 7–14.

Maurer, Michael. "Die Geschichtsphilosophie des jungen Herder in ihrem Verhältnis zur Aufklärung." In *Johann Gottfried Herder 1744–1803*, edited by Gerhard Sauder, 142–45. Hamburg: Meiner, 1987.

Mayer, Thomas F., and D. R. Woolf, editors. *The Rhetorics of Life-Writing in Early Modern Europe: Forms of Biography from Cassandra Fedele to Louis XIV*. Studies in Medieval and Early Modern Civilization. Ann Arbor: University of Michigan Press, 1995.

Mazlish, Bruce. *The Riddle of History: The Great Speculators from Vico to Freud*. New York: Minerva, 1968.

McClelland, Charles E. *State, Society, and University in Germany, 1700–1914*. Cambridge: Cambridge University Press, 1980.

———. "The Wise Man's Burden: The Role of Academicians in Imperial German Culture." In *Essays on Culture and Society in Modern Germany*, by David B. King et al., edited by Gary D. Stark and Bede Karl Lackner, 45–69. The Walter Prescott Webb Memorial Lectures 15. Arlington: Texas A&M University Press, 1982.

McGrath, Alister E. *Luther's Theology of the Cross: Martin Luther's Theological Breakthrough*. Oxford: Blackwell, 1985.

McMahon, Robert. "Book Thirteen: The Creation of the Church as the Paradigm for the *Confessions*." In *A Reader's Companion to Augustine's "Confessions*," edited by Kim Paffenroth and Robert P. Kennedy, 207–24. Louisville: Westminster John Knox, 2003.

Meinecke, Friedrich. "Antrittsrede des Herrn Meinecke." In Der Preussischen Akademie der Wissenschaften, Sitzungsberichte der Königl. Prussian Academy of the Sciences, Philosophical and Historical Sections, 1915, 496–98.

———. "Antrittsrede des Herrn Meinecke." In *Zur Geschichte der Geschichtsschreibung*, edited by Eberhard Kessel, 1–3. Meinecke Werke 7. Munich: Oldenbourg, 1968.

———. *Autobiographische Schriften*. Edited by Eberhard Kessel. Meinecke Werke 8. Stuttgart: Koehler, 1969.

———. *Die Entstehung des Historismus*. Edited by Carl Hinrichs. Friedrich Meinecke Werke 3. Munich: Oldenbourg, 1965.

———. "Ernst Troeltsch und das Problem des Historismus." In *Zur Theorie und Philosophie der Geschichte*, edited by Eberhard Kessel, 364–78. Meinecke Werke 4. Stuttgart: Koehler, 1959.

———. *Historism: The Rise of a New Historical Outlook*. Translated by J. E. Anderson, with a foreword by Sir Isaiah Berlin. London: Routledge, 1972.

———. *Machiavellism: The Doctrine of Raison d État and Its Place in Modern History*. Translated by Douglas Scott with an introduction by W. Stark. Rare Masterpieces of Philosophy and Science. New Haven, CT: Yale University Press, 1957.

———. "Supplement: Leopold von Ranke." In *Historism: The Rise of a New Historical Outlook*, 496–511. Translated by J. E. Anderson, with a foreword by Sir Isaiah Berlin. London: Routledge, 1972.

Meinhold, Peter. "Hamanns Theologie der Sprache." In *Johann Georg Hamann: Acta des Internationalen Hamann-Colloquiums in Lüneburg 1976*, edited by Bernhard Gajek, 53–65. Frankfurt: Klostermann, 1979.

———. *Luther Heute: Wirken und Theologie Martin Luthers, des Reformators der Kirche, in ihrer Bedeutung für die Gegenwart*. Berlin: Lutherisches, 1967.

———. *Luthers Sprachphilosophie*. Berlin: Lutherisches, 1958.

Menn, Stephen. *Descartes and Augustine*. Cambridge: Cambridge University Press, 1998.

Merk, Otto. "Anfänge neutestamentlicher Wissenschaft im 18. Jahrhundert." In *Historische Kritik in der Theologie: Beiträge zu ihrer Geschichte*, edited by Georg Schwaiger, 37–59. Göttingen: Vandenhoeck & Ruprecht, 1980.

Meuser, Fred E. "Luther as a Preacher of the Word of God." In *The Cambridge Companion to Martin Luther*, edited by Donald K. McKim, 136–48. Cambridge Companions to Religion. Cambridge: Cambridge University Press, 2003.

Momigliano, Arnaldo. *The Classical Foundations of Modern Historiography*. Sather Classical Lectures. Berkeley: University of California Press, 1990.

———. *The Development of Greek Biography: Four Lectures*. Cambridge: Harvard University Press, 1971.

———. "Greek Historiography." *History and Theory* 17 (1978) 1–28.

Mommsen, Theodore E. "Petrarch's Conception of the 'Dark Ages.'" *Speculum* 17 (1942) 226–42.

Mommsen, Wolfgang J. "Introduction." In *Max Weber and His Contemporaries*, edited by Wolfgang J. Mommsen and Jügen Osterhammel, 1–21. London: Allen & Unwin, 1987.

Moser, Friedrich Carl von. *Von dem deutschen Nationalgeist*. Selb: Notos, 1976.

Muhlack, Ulrich. "Historie und Philologie." In *Aufklärung und Geschichte: Studien zur deutschen Geschichtswissenschaft im 18. Jahrhundert*, edited by Hans Erich Bödeker et al., 69–74. Veröffentlichungen des Max-Planck-Instituts für Geschichte 81. Göttingen: Vandenhoeck & Ruprecht, 1986.

———. *Geschichtswissenschaft im Humanismus und in der Aufklärung: Die Vorgeschichte des Historismus*. Munich: Beck, 1991.

Muir, William. *Our Grand Old Bible; Being the Story of the Authorized Version of the Bible, Told for the Tercentenary Celebration*. 2nd edition. New York: Revell, 1911.

Nadler, Joseph. *Johann Georg Hamann 1730-1788: Der Zeuge des Corpus mysticum*. Salzburg: Müller, 1949.

Neugebauer, Wolfgang. "Das Bildungswesen in Preussen seit der Mitte des 17. Jahrhunderts." In *Handbuch der Preussischen Geschichte*, edited by Otto Büsch, 2:605-798. 3 vols. Berlin: de Gruyter, 1992.

———. "Otto Hintze und seine Konzeption der 'Allgemeine Verfassungsgeschichte der neueren Staaten.'" *Zeitschrift für historische Forschung* 20 (1993) 66-96.

———. "Otto Hintze und seine Konzeption der 'Allgemeine Verfassungsgeschichte der neueren Staaten.'" In *Allgemeine Verfassungs- und Verwaltungsgeschichte der neueren Staaten: Fragmente*, by Otto Hintze, 35-83. Edited by Guiseppe Di Constanzo et al. Palomar Athenaeum 17. Bari: Palomar, 1998 35-83.

Neuser, Wilhelm H. "Luther und Melanchthon—Ein Herr, verschiedene Gaben." In *Luthers Wirkung: Festschrift für Martin Brecht zum 60. Geburtstage*, edited by Wolf-Dieter Hauschild et al., 47-61. Stuttgart: Calwer, 1992.

Nipperdey, Thomas. "Auf der Suche nach der Identität: Romantischer Nationalismus." In *Nachdenken über die Geschichte: Essays*, 110-25. Munich: Beck, 1986.

———. *Deutsche Geschichte 1800-1866: Bürgerwelt und starker Staat*. Munich: Beck, 1983.

———. "Historismus und Historismuskritik heute: Bemerkungen zur Diskussion." In *Gesellschaft, Kultur, Theorie: Gesammelte Aufsätze zur neueren Geschichte*, 59-73. Kritische Studien zur Geschichtswissenschaft 18. Göttingen: Vandenhoeck & Ruprecht, 1976.

———. "Luther und die Bildung des Deutschen." In *Luther und die Folgen: Beiträge des sozialgeschichtliche Bedeutung der lutherischen Reformation*, edited by Hartmut Löwe and Claus-Jürgen Roepke, 13-27. Munich: Kaiser, 1983.

———. "Luther und die modernen Welt." In *Nachdenken über die deutsche Geschichte: Essays*, by Thomas Nipperdey, 31-43. 2nd edition. Munich: Beck, 1986.

———. "Preussen und die Universität." *Nachdenken über die deutsche Geschichte: Essays*, by Thomas Nipperdey, 140-55. 2nd edition. Munich: Beck, 1986.

Numbers, Ronald L. "'The Most Important Biblical Discovery of Our Time': William Henry Green and the Demise of Ussher's Chronology." *Church History* 69 (2000) 257-76.

Oberman, Heiko A. *The Dawn of the Reformation: Essays in Late Medieval and Early Reformation Thought*. Edinburgh: T. & T. Clark, 1986.

———. *The Impact of the Reformation*. Grand Rapids: Eerdmans, 1994.

———. *Luther: Man between God and the Devil*. Translated by Eileen Walliser-Schwarzbart. New York: Image, 1992.

———. *The Reformation: Roots and Ramifications*. Translated by Andrew Colin Gow. Grand Rapids: Eerdmans, 1994.

O'Donnell, James J. *Augustine: A New Biography*. New York: HarperCollins, 2005.

Oestreich, Brigitta. "Hedwig and Otto Hintze: Eine biographische Skizze." *Geschichte und Gesellschaft: Zeitschrift für Historische und Sozialwissenschaft* 11 (1985) 397-419.

Oestreich, Gerhard. "Die Fachhistorie und die Anfänge der sozialgeschichtlichen Forschung in Deutschland." *Historische Zeitschrift* 208 (1969) 320-63.

Oexle, Otto Gerhard. "Die Geschichtswissenschaft im Zeichen des Historismus: Bemerkungen zum Standort des Geschichtsforschung." *Historische Zeitschrift* 238 (1984) 17–55.

———. "Die Geschichtswissenschaft im Zeichen des Historismus: Bemerkungen zum Standort des Geschichtsforschung." In *Die Geschichtswissenschaft im Zeichen des Historismus: Studien zu Problemgeschichten der Moderne*, 17–40. Kritische Studien zur Geschichtswissenschaft 116. Göttingen: Vandenhoeck & Ruprecht, 1996.

———. *Die Geschichtswissenschaft im Zeichen des Historismus: Studien zu Problemgeschichten der Moderne*. Kritische Studien zur Geschichtswissenschaft 116. Göttingen: Vandenhoeck & Ruprecht, 1996.

———. "'Historismus'. Überlegungen zur Geschichte des Phänomens und des Begriffs." *Jahrbuch Braunschweigische wissenschaftliche Gesellschaft* (1986) 119–55.

———. "'Historismus'. Überlegungen zur Geschichte des Phänomens und des Begriffs." In *Die Geschichtswissenschaft im Zeichen des Historismus: Studien zu Problemgeschichten der Moderne*, 41–72. Kritische Studien zur Geschichtswissenschaft 116. Göttingen: Vandenhoeck & Ruprecht, 1996.

———. "Meinecke's Historismus. Über Kontext und Folgen einer Definition." In *Die Geschichtswissenschaft im Zeichen des Historismus: Studien zu Problemgeschichten der Moderne*, 95–136. Kritische Studien zur Geschichtswissenschaft 116. Göttingen: Vandenhoeck & Ruprecht, 1996.

O'Flaherty, James C. *Hamann's Socratic Memorabilia: A Translation and Commentary*. Baltimore: John Hopkins University Press, 1967.

———. *Johann Georg Hamann*. Twayne's World Author's Series. Boston: Twayne, 1979.

Olábarri, Ignacio. "Controversy in Historical Writing." In *A Global Encyclopedia of Historical Writing*, edited by D. R. Woolf, 2:201–2. 2 vols. Garland Reference Library of the Humanities 1809. New York: Garland, 1998.

O'Meara, John. *Charter of Christendom: The Significance of the "City of God."* The Saint Augustine Lecture Series: Augustine and the Augustinian Tradition. New York: Macmillan, 1961.

Oncken, Hermann. *Aus Rankes Frühzeit*. Gotha: Perthes, 1922.

Ozment, Steven E. *The Age of Reform (1250–1550): An Intellectual and Religious History of Late Medieval and Reformation Europe*. New Haven, CT: Yale University Press, 1980.

———. *A Mighty Fortress: A New History of the German People*. New York: Harper Perennial, 2004.

———. *Protestants: The Birth of a Revolution*. New York: Doubleday, 1993.

———. *The Reformation in the Cities: The Appeal of Protestantism to Sixteenth-Century Germany and Switzerland*. New Haven, CT: Yale University Press, 1975.

Palmer, R. R. *The Age of the Democratic Revolution: A Political History of Europe and America, 1760–1800*. Volume 2, *The Struggle*. Princeton: Princeton University Press, 1964.

Paulsen, Friedrich. *German Education Past and Present*. Translated by T. Lorenz. New York: Scribner's, 1908.

———. *Geschichte des gelehrten Unterrichts auf den deutschen Schulen und Universitäten vom Ausgang bis zur Gegenwart*. Edited by Rudolf Lehmann. 2 vols. 3rd edition. Berlin: de Gruyter, 1921.

———. *Immanuel Kant: His Life and Doctrine*. Translated by J. E. Creighton and Albert Lefevre. New York: Scribner, 1902.

Pearl, Leon. *Descartes*. Twayne's World Leaders Series: TWLS 63. Boston: Twayne, 1977.
Pelikan, Jaroslav. *The Christian Tradition: A History of the Development of Doctrine*. Vol. 5, *Christian Doctrine and Modern Culture (Since 1700)*. Chicago: University of Chicago Press, 1989.
———. *The Christian Tradition: A History of the Development of Doctrine*. Vol. 4 *Reformation of Church and Dogma (1300-1700)*. Chicago: University of Chicago Press, 1984.
———. *From Luther to Kierkegaard: A Study in the History of Theology*. St. Louis: Concordia, 1950.
———. *The Mystery of Continuity: Time, History, Memory and Eternity in the Thought of Saint Augustine*. The Richard Lectures for 1984-85, University of Virginia. Charlottesville: University Press of Virginia, 1986.
———. "Leopold von Ranke as Historian of the Reformation: What Ranke Did for the Reformation—What the Reformation Did for Ranke." In *Leopold von Ranke and the Shaping of the Historical Discipline*, edited by Georg Iggers and James M. Powell, 89-98. Syracuse: Syracuse University Press, 1990.
Perkins, Mary Anne. *Nation and Word, 1770-1850: Religion and Metaphysical Language in European National Consciousness*. Aldershot, UK: Ashgate, 1999.
Pine-Coffin, R. S. "Introduction." In *Confessions*, by Augustine, 11-18. Penguin Classics. Hammondsworth, UK: Penguin, 1961.
Pinson, Koppel S. *Pietism as a Factor in the Rise of German Nationalism*. New York: Columbia University Press, 1934.
Plutarch. *The Lives of the Noble Grecians and Romans*. Translated by John Dryden and revised by Arthur Hugh Clough. Modern Library. New York: Modern Library, 1932.
Polybius. *The Histories of Polybius*. Translated from the text of F. Hultsch by Evelyn S. Shuckburgh. 2 vols. Indiana University Greek and Latin Classics. Bloomington: Indiana University Press, 1962.
Powell, James M. "Introduction." In *Leopold von Ranke and the Shaping of the Historical Discipline*, edited by Georg Iggers and James M. Powell, xiii-xxii. Syracuse, NY: Syracuse University Press, 1990.
Prenter, Regin. "Luther on Word and Sacrament." In *More About Luther* by Jaroslav Pelikan et al., 65-124. Martin Luther Lectures 2. Decorah, IA: Luther College Press, 1958.
———. *Spiritus Creator*. Translated by John M. Jensen. Philadelphia: Mühlenberg, 1953.
Price Zimmerman, T. C. "Paolo Giovio and the Rhetoric of Individuality." In *The Rhetorics of Life-Writing in Early Modern Europe*, edited by Thomas F. Mayer and D. R. Woolf, 39-62. Studies in Medieval and Early Modern Civilization. Ann Arbor: University of Michigan Press, 1995.
Raabe, Paul, and Wilhelm Schmidt-Biggemann. *Enlightenment in Germany*. Bonn: Hohwacht, 1979.
Rambeau, Eugen. "Über die Geschichtswissenschaft an der Universität Wittenberg." In *450 Jahre Martin-Luther-Universität Halle Wittenberg*, 1:255-70. 3 vols. Halle: Martin-Luther-Universität Halle-Wittenberg, 1952.
Rand, Calvin D. "Two Meanings of Historicism in the Writings of Dilthey, Troeltsch, and Meinecke." *Journal of the History of Ideas* 25 (1964) 503-18.
Randall, John Herman Jr. *The Career of Philosophy*. Vol. 1, *From the Middle Ages to the Enlightenment*. New York: Columbia University Press, 1962.
———. *The Career of Philosophy*. Vol. 2, *From the German Enlightenment to the Age of Darwin*. New York: Columbia University Press, 1965.

Ranke, Leopold. "A Dialogue on Politics." In *Leopold Ranke: The Formative Years*, translated by Theodore Von Laue, 152–80. Princeton Studies in History 4. Princeton: Princeton University Press, 1950.

———. "Dictat vom October 1863." In *Sämmtliche Werke* 53/54:3–32. 54 vols. Leipzig, Duncker & Humblot, 1868–1890.

Ranke, Leopold von. "Autobiographical Dictation (November 1885)." In *The Secret of World History: Selected Writings on the Art and Science of History*, edited with translations, by Roger Wines, 33–52. New York: Fordham University Press, 1981.

———. *Das Briefwerk*. Edited by Walther Peter Fuchs. Hamburg: Hoffmann & Campe, 1949.

———. "The Epochs of Modern History." In *The Secret of World History: Selected Writings on the Art and Science of History*, edited with translations by Roger Wines, 156–64. New York: Fordham University Press, 1981.

———. "Erwiderung auf Heinrich Leo's Angriff." In *Sämmtliche Werke*, 53/54:659–66. 54 vols. Leipzig, Duncker & Humblot, 1868–1890.

———. "Die Entstehungsgeschichte des Fragments," edited by Elisabeth Schweitzer. In *Deutsche Geschicthe im Zeitalter der Reformation*, edited by Paul Joachimsen, 6:378–88. 6 vols. Gesamt-Ausgabe der Deutschen Akademie, Reihe 1, Werk 7. Munich: Drei Masken, 1925–1930.

———."Fragment über Luther. 1817." In *Frühe Schriften*, edited by Walther Peter Fuchs, 329–466. Aus Werk und Nachlass 3. Munich: Oldenbourg, 1973.

———. "Das Luther-Fragment von 1817," edited by Elisabeth Schweitzer. In *Deutsche Geschichte im Zeitalter der Reformation*, edited by Paul Joachimsen, 6:311–99. 6 vols. Gesamt-Ausgabe der Deutschen Akademie, Reihe 1, Werk 7. Munich: Drei Masken, 1925–1930.

———. "Preface to *Histories of the Latin and Germanic Nations from 1494–1514*." In *The Varieties of History, from Voltaire to the Present*, edited, selected, and introduced by Fritz Stern, 54–62. New York: Vintage, 1973.

———. "Politisches Gespräch." In *Sämmtliche Werke* 49/50: 314–39. 54 vols. Leipzig: Duncker & Humblot, 1868–1890.

———. *Sämmtliche Werke*. 54 vols. Leipzig: Duncker & Humblot, 1868–1890.

———. *The Secret of World History: Selected Writings on the Art and Science of History*. Edited, with translations, by Roger Wines. New York: Fordham University Press, 1981.

———. *The Theory and Practice of History*. Edited with and introduction by George G. Iggers and Konrad von Moltke, with new translations by Wilma A. Iggers and Konrad von Moltke. The European Historiography Series. Indianapolis: Bobbs-Merrill, 1973.

———. *Weltgeschichte*. 9 vols. Leipzig: Duncker & Humblot, 1898–1902.

Rasmussen, Larry L. *Earth Community, Earth Ethics*. Ecology and Justice. Maryknoll, NY: Orbis, 1996.

Rauch, Leo. *Hegel and the Human Spirit: A Translation of the Jena Lectures on the Philosophy of Spirit (1805–1806) with Commentary*. Detroit: Wayne State University Press, 1983.

Reill, Peter Hans. *The German Enlightenment and the Rise of Historicism*. Berkeley: University of California Press, 1975.

———. "Science and the Science of History in the Spätaufklärung." In *Aufklärung und Geschichte: Studien zur deutschen Geschichtswissenschaft im 18. Jahrhundert*, edited by Hans Erich Bödeker et al., 430–51. Veröffentlichungen des Max-Planck-Instituts für Geschichte 81. Göttingen: Vandenhoeck & Ruprecht, 1986.

Rescher, Nicholas. *Leibniz: An Introduction to His Philosophy*. APQ Library of Philosophy. Totowa, NJ: Rowman & Littlefield, 1979.

Reu, Jonathan Michael. *Catechetics: Or, Theory and Practice of Religious Instruction*. 2nd revised edition. Chicago: Wartburg, 1927.

Reventlow, Henning Graf, et al., editors. *Historische Kritik und biblischer Kanon in der deutschen Aufklärung*. Wolfenbütteler Forschungen 41. Wiesbaden: Harrassowitz, 1988.

Rhein, Stefan. "The Influence of Melanchthon on Sixteenth-Century Europe." *Lutheran Quarterly* 12 (1998) 383–94.

Rodis-Lewis, Geneviève "Descartes' Life and the Development of His Philosophy." In *The Cambridge Companion to Descartes*, edited by John Cottingham, 21–57. Cambridge: Cambridge University Press, 1992.

Rogness, Michael. *Philip Melanchthon: Reformer without Honor*. Minneapolis: Augsburg, 1969.

Rubanowice, Robert J. *The Crisis in Consciousness: The Thought of Ernst Troeltsch*. Tallahassee: University Presses of Florida, 1982.

Rühs, Friedrich. *Entwurf einer Propädeutik des historischen Studiums*. Edited by Hans Scheiler and Dirk Fleisher. Wissen und Kritik 7. Waltrop: Spenner, 1997.

Rutherford, Donald. "Metaphysics: The Late Period." In *The Cambridge Companion to Leibniz*, edited by Nicholas Jolley, 124–75. Cambridge: Cambridge: University Press, 1995.

Sasse, Hermann. *This Is My Body: Luther's Contention for the Real Presence in the Sacrament of the Altar*. Minneapolis: Augsburg, 1959.

Scheible, Heinz. "Mensch in der Geschichte." In *Melanchthon: Eine Biographie*, 251–63. Munich: Beck, 1997.

Schieder, Theodor. "Der Typus in der Geschichtswissenschaft." In *Staat und Gesellschaft im Wandel unserer Zeit*, 172–87. Munich: Oldenbourg, 1958.

Schloemann, Martin. "Wegbereiter wider Willen. Siegmund Jacob Baumgarten und die historish-kritische Bibelforschung." In *Historische Kritik und biblischer Kanon in der deutschen Aufklärung*, edited by Henning Graf Reventlow et al., 219–36. Wolfenbütteler Forschungen 41. Wiesbaden: Harrassowitz, 1988.

Scholder, Klaus. *The Birth of Modern Critical Theology: Origins and Problems of Biblical Criticism in the Seventeenth Century*. Translated by John Bowden. London: SCM, 1990.

———. "Herder und die Anfänge der historischen Theologie." *Evangelische Theologie* 22 (1962) 425–40.

Scholtz, Gunter, editor. *Historismus am Ende des 20. Jahrhunderts: Eine internationale Diskussion*. Berlin: Akademie, 1997.

Schulin, Ernst. "Das Problem der Individualität: Eine kritische Betrachtung des Historismus-Werkes von Friedrich Meinecke." *Historische Zeitschrift* 197 (1963) 102–33.

———. "Universal History and National History, Mainly in the Lectures of Leopold von Ranke." In *Leopold von Ranke and the Shaping of the Historical Discipline*, edited by Georg G. Iggers and James M. Powell, 70–81. Syracuse: University of Syracuse Press, 1990.

———. *Die weltgeschichtliche Erfassung des Orients bei Hegel und Ranke*. Veröffentlichungen des Max-Planck-Instituts für Geschichte 2. Göttingen: Vandenhoeck & Ruprecht, 1958.

Schulze, Hagen. *States, Nations, and Nationalism from the Middle Ages to the Present*. Translated by William E. Yuilli. The Making of Europe. Oxford: Blackwell, 1996.

Schulze, Werner. "Der Einfluss lutherischen Geistes auf Rankes und Droysens Deutung der Geschichte." *Archiv für Reformationsgeschichte* 39 (1942) 108–42.

Schulze, Winfried. "Otto Hintze und die deutsche Geschichtswissenschaft um 1900." In *Deutsche Geschichtswissenschaft um 1900*, edited by Notker Hammerstein, 323–39. Stuttgart: Steiner, 1988.

Schwiebert, E. G. *Luther and His Times: The Reformation from a New Perspective*. St. Louis: Concordia, 1950.

Schweitzer, Elisabeth. "Die Entstehungsgeschichte des Fragments." In *Deutsche Geschicthe im Zeitalter der Reformation*, edited by Paul Joachimsen, 6:378–88. 6 vols. Gesamt-Ausgabe der Deutschen Akademie, Reihe 1, Werk 7. Munich: Drei Masken, 1925–1930.

Sheehan, James J. *German History, 1770–1866*. Oxford History of Modern Europe. Oxford: Clarendon, 1989.

Sheehan, Jonathan. *The Enlightenment Bible: Translation, Scholarship, Culture*. Princeton: Princeton University Press, 2005.

Shimada, Yoichiro Fukuoka. "Individualgeschichte und Universalgeschichte bei Herder: Geschichtlichkeit als konstruktives Prinzip des *Reisejournals*," In *Johann Gottfried Herder: Geschichte und Kultur*, edited by Martin Bollacher, 39–49. Würzburg: Königshausen & Neumann, 1994.

Smith, Leonard S. "Otto Hintze and a Historical Typology of Western Historiography." Paper presented at the 96th meeting of the American Historical Association, Los Angeles, CA, December 28–30, 1981.

———. "Otto Hintze's Comparative Constitutional History of the West." PhD diss., Washington University, St. Louis, 1967.

Smith, Ronald Gregor. *J. G. Hamann 1730–1788: A Study in Christian Existence; with Selections from His Writings*. New York: Harper, 1960.

Sorley, W. R. "Leibnitz or Leibniz, Gottfried Wilhelm." In *Encyclopedia Briticanica* 13:884–88. 24 vols. 14th edition. Chicago: Encyclopedia Britannica, 1954.

Spickard, Paul R., et al. *World History by the World's Historians*. Boston: McGraw-Hill, 1998.

Spitz, Lewis W. "Luther's View of History: A Theological Use of the Past." In *The Reformation: Education and History*, 139–54. Variorum Collected Studies Series. Aldershot, UK: Variorum, 1997.

———. "The Significance of Leibniz for Historiography." *Journal of the History of Ideas* 13 (1952) 333–48.

Srbik, Heinrich Ritter von. *Geist und Geschichte vom deutschen Humanimsu bis zur Gegenwart*. 2 vols. Salzburg: Müller, 1951.

Stadelmann, Rudolf. *Der historische Sinn bei Herder*. Halle: Niemeyer, 1928.

Steenblock, Volker. "Die Legitimität des Historismus." In *Historismus am Ende des 20. Jahrhunderts: Eine internationale Diskussion*, 174–91. Berlin: Akademie, 1997.
Strauss, Gerald. *Luther's House of Learning: Indoctrination of the Young in the German Reformation*. Baltimore: John Hopkins University Press, 1978.
Stroup, John. "Protestant Church Historians in the German Enlightenment." In *Aufklärung und Geschichte: Studien zur deutschen Geschichtswissenschaft im 18. Jahrhundert*, edited by Hans Erich Bödeker et al., 169–91, Veröffentlichungen des Max-Planck-Instituts für Geschichte 81. Göttingen: Vandenhoeck & Ruprecht, 1986.
Tappert, Theodore G., translator and editor, in collaboration with Jaroslav Pelikan et al. *The Book of Concord: The Confessions of the Evangelical Lutheran Church*. Philadelphia: Mühlenburg, 1959.
Tessitore, Fulvio. "Ranke's 'Lutherfragment' und die Idee der Universalgeschichte." In *Leopold von Ranke und die moderne Geschichtswissenschaft*, edited by Wolfgang J. Mommsen, 21–36. Stuttgart: Klett-Cotta, 1988.
Tillich, Paul. *Begegnungen. Paul Tillich über sich selbst und andere*. Edited by Renate Albrecht. 2nd edition. Gessamelte Werke 12. Stuttgart: Evangelisches, 1980.
———. Review of *Der Historismus und seine Probleme*, by Ernst Troeltsch. In *Begegnungen. Paul Tillich über sich selbst und andere*, edited by Renate Albrecht, 204–11. 2nd edition. Gessamelte Werke 12. Stuttgart: Evangelisches, 1980.
Thucydides, *The Peloponnesian War*. Translated by Rex Warner, with notes by M. I. Finley. New York: Penguin, 1972.
Troeltsch, Ernst. *Der Historismus und seine Probleme. Das logische Problem der Geschichtsphilosopie*. Gesammelte Schriften 3. Tübingen: Mohr, 1922.
———. "Das neunzehnte Jahrhundert." In *Aufsätze zur Geistesgeschichte und Religionssoziologie*, 614–49. Gesammelte Schriften 4. Tübingen: Mohr, 1925.
Turner, Paul. *The Meaning and Practice of Confirmation: Perspectives from a Sixteenth-Century Controversy*. American University Studies. Series VII, Theology and Religion 31. New York: Lang, 1987.
Martin-Luther-Universität Halle-Wittenberg. *450 Jahre Martin-Luther-Universität Halle-Wittenberg*. 3 vols. Halle: Martin-Luther-Universität Halle-Wittenberg, 1952.
Vierhaus, Rudolf. "Historiography between Science and Art." In *Leopold von Ranke and the Shaping of the Historical Discipline*, edited by Georg G. Iggers and James M. Powell, 61–69. Syracuse, NY: Syracuse University Press, 1990.
———. *Ranke und die soziale Welt*. Neue münstersche Beiträge zur Geschichtsforschung. Münster Westfallen: Aschendorffsche Verlagsbuchhandlung, 1957.
———. "The Revolutionizing of Consciousness: A German Utopia?" In *The Transformation of Political Culture: England and Germany in the Late Eighteenth Century*, edited by Eckhart Hellmuth, 561–77. Studies in Modern History. Oxford: Oxford University Press, 1990.
———. "Die Universität Göttingen und die Anfänge der modernen Geschichtswissenschaft im 18. Jahrhundert." In *Geschichtswissenschaft in Göttingen: Eine Vorlesungsreihe*, edited by Hartmut Boockmann and Hermann Wellenreuther, 1–29. Göttingen Universitätsschriften, Serie A: Schriften 2. Göttingen: Vandenhoeck & Ruprecht, 1987.
Viëtor, Karl. *Goethe: Dichtung, Wissenschaft, Weltbild*. Bern: Francke, 1949.
Von Laue, Theodore H. *Leopold Ranke: The Formative Years*. Princeton Studies in History 4. Princeton: Princeton University Press, 1950.
Vrooman, Jack Rochford. *René Descartes: A Biography*. New York: Putnam, 1970.

Walther, Peter Th. "Werkstattbericht: Hedwig Hintze in den Niederlanden 1939–1942," In *". . . immer im Forschen bleiben": Rüdiger vom Bruch zum 60. Geburtstag*, edited by Marc Schalenberg and Peter Th. Walther. Stuttgart: Steiner, 2004.

Wandel, Lee Palmer. *The Eucharist in the Reformation: Incarnation and Liturgy*. Cambridge: Cambridge University Press, 2006.

Wardman, Alan. *Plutarch's Lives*. Berkeley: University of California Press, 1974.

Weber, Max. *The Protestant Ethic and the Spirit of Capitalism*. Translated by Talcott Parsons. New York: Scribner, 1958.

Wengert, Timothy J. "Luther and Melanchthon on Consecrated Communion Wine (Eisleben 1542–1543)." *Lutheran Quarterly* 15 (2001) 24–42.

———. "Melanchthon and Luther/Luther and Melanchthon." *Luther Jahrbuch* 66 (1999) 55–88.

Whitehead, Alfred North. *Science and the Modern World*. New York: Free, 1967.

Wieland, Wolfgang. "Entwicklung, Evolution." In *Geschichtliche Grundbegriffe: Historisches Lexikon zur politisch-soziale Sprache in Deutschland*, edited by Otto Brunner et al., 2:199–228. 8 vols., 9 bks. Stuttgart: Klett, 1972–1997.

Wingren, Gustaf. *Luther on Vocation*. Translated by Carl C. Rasmussen. Philadelphia: Muhlenberg, 1957.

Wittkau-Horgby, Annette. *Historismus: Zur Geschichte des Begriffs und des Problems*. Sammlung Vandenhoeck. Göttingen: Vandenhoeck & Ruprecht, 1992. 2nd edition, 1994.

Wood, Allen W. "Rational Theology, Moral Faith, and Religion." In *The Cambridge Companion to Kant*, edited by Paul Guyer, 394–416. Cambridge: Cambridge University Press, 1992.

Woolf, D. R., editor. *A Global Encyclopedia of Historical Writing*. 2 vols. Garland Reference Library of the Humanities 1809. New York: Garland, 1998.

Yasukata, Toshima. *Ernst Troeltsch: Systematic Theologian of Radical Historicality*. American Academy of Religion Academy Series 55. Atlanta: Scholars, 1986.

Zammito, John H. *Kant, Herder, and the Birth of Anthropology*. Chicago: University of Chicago Press, 2002.

Zedelmaier, Helmut. *Der Anfang der Geschichte: Studien zu Ursprungsdebatte im 18. Jahrhundert*. Studien zum achtzehnten Jahrhundert 27. Hamburg: Meiner, 2003.

Ziolkowski, Theodore. *Clio the Romantic Muse: Historicizing the Faculties in Germany*. Ithaca, NY: Cornell University Press, 2004.

name index

Abelard, Peter, 26
Abraham, 23–24
D'Ailly, Pierre, 72
Ahlstrom, Sydney, 75, 95, 128, 153
Alexander, W. M., 136
Alighieri, Dante, 29, 152
Althaus, Paul, 63
Ambrose, Saint, 20
Aquinas, Thomas, 26, 27, 32, 60, 71–72, 75
Aristotle, 2, 8, 15, 26, 32, 34, 71–72, 97, 115, 120, 128–29, 230
Arnold, Gottfried, 109
Augustine, Saint, ix, x, xiv, 4, 16, 18–25, 27–28, 32, 36–40, 47, 50, 59, 62, 69–70, 77–78, 85, 114, 146, 152, 164, 175, 182, 254–55
Augustus, Caesar, 25, 46
Bacon, Francis, 158
Baillet, Adrien, 36–37, 91
Bainton, Roland, 68, 77
Baron, Hans, 239
Baudler, Georg, 148–49,
Baumgarten, Siegmund Jacob, 49, 179
Bayer, Oswald, 148
Bede, (The Venerable), 24–25, 27–28
Beiser, Frederick C., 138, 141–42, 151, 158, 176–77, 194–95
Below, Georg von, 237
Bendix, Reinhard, 236–37
Benz, Ernst, 159, 170
Bergson, Henri, 246
Berlin, Isaiah, 136–38, 149–50, 165
Beye, Charles Rowan, 6
Blanke, Fritz, 146–48
Bluhm, Heinz, 174–75
Blum, Mark E., 96
Boccaccio, Giovanni, 28–29

Böckh, August, 253
Bodin, Jean, 31
Bolingbroke, Henry Saint-John, 141
Bornkamm, Heinich, 148, 172
Bossuet, Bishop, 47, 49–50
Brady, Jr., Thomas A., xiv, 196
Brunner, Heinrich, 228
Burckhardt, Jacob, 29
Burkhardt, Frederick H., 152
Burke, Edmund, 43
Butterfield, Herbert, 125
Caesar, Julius, 24, 46
Calvin, John, 75
Carion, Johannes, 98
Carlyle, Thomas, 146–47
Carr, William, 184
Cassirer, Ernst, 113–14
Cellarius (Christian Keller), 48
Charlemagne, 25–26, 52
Charles V, 31
Chladenius (or Chladenii, Johann Martin), 100, 116–24, 243, 259
Cicero, 11–12, 32, 50, 254
Cochrane, Charles, 18, 20
Collingwood, R. G. ix, 2–3, 10, 13, 15–16, 21, 104–5, 254
Constantine, Emperor, 18
Croce, Benedetto, 246–47
Daniel (Book of), 24
Darwin, Charles Robert, 135
Descartes, René, 26, 32–44, 57, 104–6, 115
David, King, 17, 22, 161
Despland, Michel, 189
Dilthey, Wilhelm, 1, 14, 223–27, 243, 246–47, 260–61
Dobbek, Wilhelm, 161, 164, 170, 172, 181

Name Index

Dove, Alfred, 212
Droysen, Johann Gustav, 223–24, 226–27, 230, 243, 260–61
Dryden, John, 13
Durkheim, Emile, 246
Eck, Johann, of Ingolstadt, 91
Ebeling, Gerhard, 63, 92
Eisenstadt, Shmuel N., 133
Elert, Werner, 111
Embach, Michael, 145, 170–71
Erasmus, Desiderius, 30–31, 175
Erikson, Erik H., 80
Eusebius, 18, 25
Feuter, Eduard, 156
Fichte, Johann Gottlieb, 127, 158, 195–96, 208–9, 211
Findley, J. N., 194
Fouke, Daniel C., 112–13
Freud, Sigmund, 246
Galilei, Galileo, 40
Gatterer, Johann Christoph, 125, 180
Gebhardt, Jűrgen, 183
Gellner, Ernst, 195,
Gerhard, Dietrich, xiv, 26, 34, 203, 222, 233, 239, 250
Gibbon, Edward, 51
Gilbert, Felix, 30–31, 212, 221–22, 232, 239, 243–44
Gierke, Otto von, 234
Gneist, Rudolf von, 228
Goethe, Johann Wolfgang von, 58, 82, 127, 141, 143, 145, 151–52, 160, 167, 169, 175, 177, 184, 208, 244, 250, 253
Gooch, G. P., 253
Gritsch, Eric, xiv, 62, 65
Guicciardini, Francisco, 30–31
Haile, H. G., 80
Hamann, Johann Georg, ix, 74, 109, 122, 127, 131–51, 155, 157–59, 161, 163, 165, 172–73, 175–76, 182, 184, 187, 251, 256, 258–59
Hartung, Fritz, 232
Haym, Rudolf, 160–61
Hazard, Paul, 47
Heeren, Arnold Hermann Ludwig, 125, 180
Hegel, Georg Wilhelm Friedrich, 109, 127, 151, 192–95
Henry IV, 32,
Herder, Johann Gottfried, ix, xii, 58, 74, 81, 85, 104–5, 109, 111, 115, 122, 126–27, 131–33, 136, 141, 143–45, 151–78, 181–84, 187, 193, 204, 250–51, 256, 258–59
Herodotus 2, 4–8, 11–12, 254
Hexter, Jack, xiv, 31
Heyne, Christian Gottlob, 179–80
Hinrichs, Carl, 203, 207–8, 211
Hinschius, Paul, 228
Hintze, Hedwig, 231–32
Hintze, Otto, ix, xi, xiii, 1–4, 10, 55–56, 58, 91, 100–103, 109, 115, 123, 126, 132–33, 136, 156, 172, 200–2, 214, 219–52, 254, 258, 260–61
Holborn, Hajo, 96–97, 109–110, 178, 183, 188–89, 239, 253
Hölderlin, Friedrich, 177
Homer, 5, 12, 140, 167
Hughes, H. Stuart, 184, 202, 245–47
Humboldt, Wilhelm von, 169, 196
Hume, David, 51, 87, 116, 138, 158, 185, 189–90
Isaiah (Book of), 163
Isidore of Seville, 24
Jacobi, Friedrich Heinrich, 141, 176, 214
Janz, Dennis, 79
Jarausch, Konrad, 124
Jerome, St., 24–25, 98
Jesuits, 32–34, 43
Jesus Christ, 17, 18, 22–25, 36, 45–47, 50, 53, 65, 67–75, 84, 113, 143, 148–49, 163, 208, 256, 258–59
John (Gospel of), 58, 62, 66–69, 111, 143–44, 152, 154–55, 163
Jung, Carl, 246, 256
Kant, Immanuel, xiv, 2, 85, 105, 116, 126–27, 129, 131–33, 136–37, 139, 141–42, 151–53, 157–58, 178, 184–93, 243, 259
Kelley, Donald R., 28, 184
Kittelson, James L., 84
Klempt, Adalbert, 45
Kloss, Frank, 89

König, Helmut, 192
Kosellek, Reinhard, 120–22,
Krause, Carl Christian Friedrich, 178
Krieger, Leonard, 203, 209, 218
Kupisch, Karl, 208,
Lamprecht, Karl, 237–38
Leibniz, Gottfried Wilhelm von, ix,
   xi–xii, xiv, 36, 57–58, 74, 85, 100,
   103–16, 118–21, 131, 143, 163,
   172–73, 175, 178, 183, 185, 216–17,
   244, 251, 256, 258
Leo, Heinrich, 214–16, 219
Lessing, Gotthold Ephraim, 145, 148,
   174–75, 184, 204
Livingston, James C., 189–90
Livy, Titus, 10, 29–30
Locke, John, 47, 57, 85, 104–105, 108,
   115–116, 185
Lønning, Inge, 65
Louis XIV, 44
Loyola, Ignatius, 32
Luke, (Gospel of), 68
Luther, Martin, ix, x, xii, xiii, 31, 40, 54,
   55, 58–98, 109–11, 114, 117, 121,
   129, 133–34, 138–39, 143–46, 148,
   153–55, 158–59, 161, 163, 167,
   170–78, 182, 188–91, 193, 205–9,
   211, 216–17, 220, 234, 251, 255–60
Machiavelli, Niccolo, 30
Manuel, Frank E., 182,
Mark, (Gospel of), 68, 71
Marty, Martin E., 62
Marx, Karl, 192, 197, 236–37, 246, 252
Masur, Gerhard, 239
Matthew (Gospel of), 23, 68
Mauer, Michael, 52
McCelland, Charles E., 198
Meinecke, Friedrich, ix–xiv, 51–52, 57–
   58, 103, 109–11, 115, 130–31, 133,
   136, 143–45, 154–56, 163, 167–69,
   181–83, 187–88, 200, 202, 207–8,
   214–15, 221–22, 227, 237–42,
   244–47, 250–51, 254, 259–61
Meinhold, Peter, 64, 146
Melanchthon, Philip, xii, 49, 54, 69–70,
   76, 90–91, 94, 96–90, 111, 117, 196,
   204, 255–57

Mendelsohn, Frederick, 176,
Michaelis, Johann David, 180
Momigliano, Arnaldo, 15–16
Mommsen, Theodore, 223, 227
Montesquieu, Charles de Secondat, 158
More, Sir Thomas, 31
Moses, 67
Moser, Friedrich Carl von, 195
Möser, Justus, 143
Mozart, Wolfgang Amadeus, 184
Müller, J., xi, 216
Nadler, Joseph, 136,
Napoleon I (Bonaparte), 225
Nero, Emperor, 18
Neugebauer, Wolfgang, xiv, 196, 222
Newton, Isaac, 41, 48
Niebuhr, Barthold Georg, 4, 103, 125,
   199, 209–10, 258
Nipperdey, Thomas, 133–34, 197, 209,
   257
Noah, 23–24, 45
Novalis (Friedrich von Hardenburg), 177
Oberman, Heiko A. xiv, 60, 62, 74
Occam, William of, 60, 71–72
Oestreich, Gerhard, 232
Oexle, Otto Gerhard, 251
O'Flaherty, James C., 139–141, 143
O'Mera, John, 21
Oppenheimer, Franz, 249
Orosius, Paulus, 24–25, 47
Otto I, 26
Palmer, R. R., 127, 192
Pareto, Vilfredo, 246
Pascal, Blaise, 191
Paul, Saint, 18, 61, 62, 64–69, 111, 115,
   175, 204, 207, 255
Paulsen, Friedrich, 153, 186–88
Pelican, Jaroslav, 22, 59, 84, 152, 189
Pericles, 12–13
Pernice, Ingolf, 228
Peter, St., 67–68
Petrarch, 13, 28
Pindar, 167
Plato, 115
Plutarch, 13–16, 28–30, 175, 254
Powell, James W., 207
Polybius 8–11, 13–14, 17, 29–30, 254

Name Index

Pythagoras, 37
Quintilian, 12
Randall, John Hermann, Jr., 44, 65–66, 116–17, 135
Ranke, Heinrich, 211, 217–18, 220
Ranke, Leopold von, ix–xiii, 4, 58, 103, 109, 115, 125, 148, 168, 173, 178, 200–221, 223–24, 227–28, 230, 233–37, 243, 250–54, 258, 260–61
Reill, Peter Hanns, xiv, 44, 104, 130–31
Rescher, Nicholas, 110
Roscher, Wilhelm I, 233
Rothfels, Hans, 239
Rousseau, Jean Jacque, 23, 158, 163, 183, 190, 255
Rutherford, Donald, 113
Schelling, Friedrich Wilhelm, 127, 177
Scherer, Wilhelm, 226
Schiller, Friedrich, 151, 184, 204
Schlegel, August Wilhelm von, 182–83
Schlegel, Friedrich, 151, 208
Schleiermacher, Friedrich, 127, 177–78, 196
Schlözer, August Ludwig, 125, 180
Schmoller, Gustav, 222, 228–30, 260
Schweitzer, Elizabeth, 209
Schwiebert, E. G., 69
Scott, Walter, 210
Scotus, Duns, 60
Semler, Johann Salomo, 125, 180
Shaftesbury, Anthony Ashley Cooper, 109, 158, 183
Shakespeare, William, 80, 140, 154, 158, 167
Sheehan, James J., xiv, 159
Sittler, Joseph, 58, 90,
Sleiden, Johannes, 49,
Socrates, 92, 140
Sombart, Werner, 249
Sorel, Georges, 246
Spencer, Herbert, 234
Spinoza, Baruch, 150, 176–77,
Spittler, Ludwig Timotheus, 125, 180,
Spitz, Lewis W., 98
Stern, Fritz, 213
Strauss, Gerald, 79
Suetonius, 13, 28
Sybel, Heinrich von, 237
Tacitus, 16, 28,
Tieck, Ludwig, 151
Tessitore, Fulvio, 206
Thomas Aquinas, *see* Aquinas, Thomas
Thucydides 5–8, 12, 15, 205, 254
Torsellinis, Orazio, 49,
Treitschke, Heinrich von, 237
Troeltsch, Ernst, xi–xiii, 10, 58, 77, 109, 115, 136, 156, 200, 202, 214, 237, 239–43, 246–47, 250–51, 254, 261
Ussher, James, 44, 46–47, 49, 52–53
Vespasian, 46
Vierhaus, Rudolf, xiv, 193, 206
Vico, Giambattista, 109
Voltaire, ix, 4, 16, 23, 25, 44, 51–52, 136, 151, 156, 183, 254–55, 259
Von Laue, Theodore H., 204–205, 217
Wagner, Adolf, 228
Waitz, Georg, 223, 226–28
Weber, Marianne, 248
Weber, Max, xi, 55–57, 61, 72, 76, 85, 89–91, 133, 235–37, 246–53, 257, 261
Weizsäcker, Julius, 226
Wesley, Charles, 135
Wesley, John, 135
Whitehead, Alfred North, 41–42
Wingren, Gustav, 93
Winkelmann, Johann Joachim, 179–80, 183
Wolf, Christian von, 104
Wood, Allen W., 190–91
Zedelmaier, Helmut, 49
Zwingli, Ulrich, 55, 74–75

www.ingramcontent.com/pod-product-compliance
Lightning Source LLC
Chambersburg PA
CBHW021652230426
43668CB00008B/595